The
DALLAS
FORT WORTH
METROPLEX

LONE ★ STAR
TRAVEL ★ GUIDE

The
DALLAS
FORT WORTH
METROPLEX

Revised Edition

ROBERT R. RAFFERTY
AND
LOYS REYNOLDS

Taylor Trade Publishing
Lanham • Boulder • New York • Toronto • Oxford

Published by Taylor Trade Publishing
A Member of The Rowman & Littlefield Publishing Group, Inc.
4501 Forbes Boulevard, Suite 200
Lanham, MD 20706

Distributed by NATIONAL BOOK NETWORK

ISBN 1-58907-005-4 (pbk. : alk. paper)

♾™ The paper used in this publication meets the minimum requirements of American National Standard for Information Sciences—Permanence of Paper for Printed Library Materials, ANSI/NISO Z39.48-1992.

Manufactured in the United States of America.

To our wonderful grandchildren:
Allyson, Amber, Ben, Brice, Daniel, Ian,
Jacob and Jacob, Jason, Nicole, Read, Rob, Sarah, and
Trey (Ernest III) who are in many ways like the
Metroplex—healthy, strong, intelligent, growing, dynamic,
resourceful, and going confidently into the future.

CONTENTS

ACKNOWLEDGMENTS

Details, DETAILS, **DETAILS!**

Because a guidebook is only as good as the completeness and accuracy of its details, we are deeply indebted to many people for their help in gathering and verifying the thousands of details in the listings in this book, and we want to acknowledge them.

In general, we want to thank the executives and staffs of the various convention and visitors bureaus, city tourism authorities, and other tourism organizations for their invaluable professional assistance and enthusiastic help.

In particular, we want to offer an extra-special thank you to the individuals listed below, who went far beyond the call of their duties to ensure that our details were complete and accurate. In a world of public relations representatives glutted with "talkers," these are all DO-ers.

Addison: Diana George, Sales Manager, and Bob Phillips, Director, Visitor Services Department, Town of Addison.

Arlington: Kay Webb, Director of Tourism, and Angela Bailey, Communications Assistant, Arlington Convention & Visitors Bureau.

Dallas: Cheryl Lewis, Vice President, Public Relations, Communications Division; Priscella Ijoma, Communications Division; and Vickie Blakely, Manager, Tourism Services, Dallas Convention & Visitors Bureau.

Farmers Branch: Maureen Gutierrez, Sales and Marketing Division Manager, and Elizabeth Neel, Account Executive, City of Farmers Branch.

Fort Worth: C. Greg Staley, Director of Communications, and Cissy Bertram, Tourism Coordinator, Fort Worth Convention & Visitors Bureau.

Garland: Dorothy White and Diana Green, Convention & Visitors Bureau, Community Relations Department, City of Garland.

Grand Prairie: Cheri Staples, Public Information Officer, Grand Prairie Convention & Visitors Bureau.

Grapevine: Sallie Andrews, Media Relations Manager, and Michael Woody, Director of Communications, Grapevine Convention & Visitors Bureau.

Irving: Mona Gandy, Director of Communications, and Diana Pfaff, Assistant Director of Communications, Irving Convention & Visitors Bureau.

Plano: Mark Thompson, Manager, and Shaun Mefford, Booking Events Coordinator, Plano Convention & Visitors Bureau.

Richardson: Sandy Snyder, Visitors Services, Richardson Convention & Visitors Bureau.

DALLAS/FORT WORTH METROPLEX

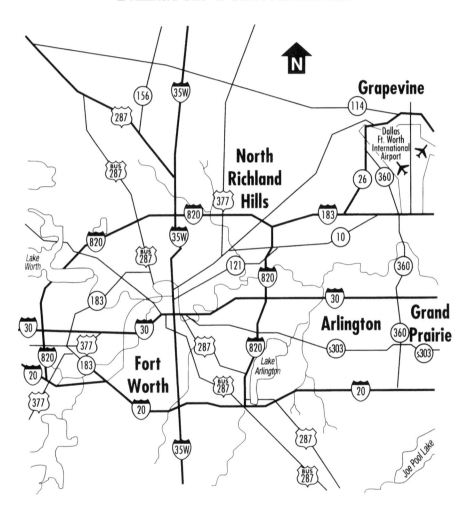

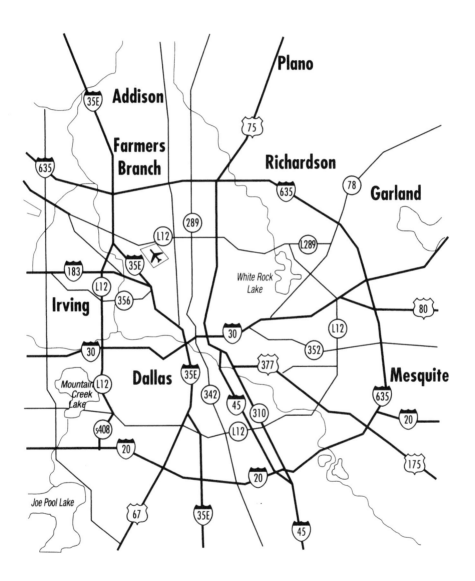

WELCOME TO
THE METROPLEX

For years there was no love lost between Dallas and Fort Worth. In the early days, for example, a Dallas newspaper helped establish the feud by claiming that Fort Worth was so dead a panther had been seen sleeping unmolested in the main street. Fort Worth never forgave that insult, and after that the two cities became bitter rivals in everything. It's said that the feelings were so strong that, rather than eat in a Dallas restaurant, Fort Worth publisher Amon Carter brought his own sack lunch with him when he had to be in Dallas on business.

Over those years the prairies between the two gradually filled with new cities, like Arlington, Irving, and Grand Prairie. More small towns were formed on the outskirts of the two big ones. They all grew and grew until it was hard to distinguish where one ended and the next one started. Most of the towns around and between Dallas and Fort Worth tried to stay neutral in the feud, but if they couldn't they leaned toward the view of the big city nearest to them.

Then, in 1965 Dallas and Fort Worth buried the hatchet, agreeing to build an airport between them that would serve the entire region. The Dallas/Fort Worth International Airport (DFW) proved to be the missing link needed to pull together all the disparate cities in the area and consolidate them into one gigantic Metroplex.

But it wasn't called that just yet. That name didn't come about until several years later, when the North Texas Commission, a sort of regional chamber of commerce, was looking for a catchy advertising slogan that would help lure northern businesses and industry to move to the region once the D/FW airport was opened. After several tries, an ad agency exec dropped a few letters from the words Metropolitan Complex and came up with the magic term "Metroplex." It was catchy and, although some people still don't like it, the name caught on.

Today, it's fairly well established in Texas that if you talk of the Metroplex you're talking about the Dallas/Fort Worth area (although many Texans still don't realize how many other cities there are in the Metroplex besides those two biggies). And don't expect it to be recognized elsewhere. Ask a travel agent to book you a flight to the Metroplex or get you a hotel room in the Metroplex and you'll get a blank stare. However, tell 'em you're going to Dallas or Fort Worth and you'll get a ticket or a reservation.

Be that as it may, once you've decided what you want to do in this part of Texas, you'll usually find it more convenient to ignore the boundaries between the interlocking cities and think of the whole Metroplex instead of its parts. True, you'll need the usual city and street address to get where you're going; just don't think of the city boundaries as walls. It's also true that, to bring some order to this huge whole in this guidebook, we've broken it up into its city parts; however, by using the Metroplex map as your guide, you can cross our paper borders as easily as you can on the ground.

SOME METROPLEX STATISTICS AND FASCINATING FACTS

To most of the rest of the world, the stereotypical Texan is a braggart. Like many other stereotypes, this one is false. Residents of the Metroplex don't brag. It just sounds that way when they tell the truth about their amazing complex of cities. The D/FW area is the number one tourist destination in Texas, and the following facts and statistics give you an idea of why that's so.

The Metroplex
- is the third largest film production center in the United States.
- is the home of the largest wholesale merchandise mart in the world.
- has more shopping centers per capita than any other city in the United States.
- has more restaurants per capita than New York City (more than seven thousand in Dallas alone).
- has teams in all major professional sports: baseball, basketball, football, soccer, and hockey, plus rodeo.
- has major tracks for horse racing and auto racing.
- is home of the largest State Fair in the country.
- has the tallest Ferris wheel in the country.
- has a major amusement theme park and the country's largest water-theme park.
- has the world's largest equestrian sculpture and the world's largest bronze monument.
- is the home of the world's largest honky-tonk.
- is the home of one of the largest permanent flea markets in the country.

- has two major zoos—and the Welcome statue of a giraffe at the Dallas Zoo is the tallest statue in Texas, soaring 67.5 feet.
- has more than thirty museums ranging in theme from modern art to baseball.
- is the home of one of the largest wine festivals in the U.S.
- is the home of one of the largest urban arts districts in the country.
- has more than 50,000 acres of public parkland in Dallas alone and more than 60 lakes within a 100-mile radius.
- offers more live music every night than Nashville, and not just Country and Western but everything from blues to symphony.
- has the only hotel/restaurant rated AAA 5-Diamond and Mobil 5-Star in Texas and as many AAA 4-Diamond hotels as any major city in the nation.

There's lots, lots more, as you'll see as you skim through this book. It adds up to this: There's truly something for everyone in the Metroplex. So use this guidebook to find your something, and *enjoy*!

HINTS TO MAKE YOUR VISIT MORE ENJOYABLE

WHAT TIME IS IT?

The Metroplex is in the Central Standard Time Zone (one hour behind the East Coast and two hours ahead of the West Coast). Daylight savings time is in effect from the first Sunday in April to the last Sunday in October.

WHAT'S THE WEATHER LIKE?

There's an old saying in Texas: If you don't like the weather, wait a few minutes and it'll change. The pleasant weather of spring comes early to the Metroplex, the summer is hot and humid, and fall comes late. Winter—which varies from fairly mild to cold, cold, cold—is usually from about late November or early December to February or early March.

So, if weather is a prime consideration for your trip, spring and fall are the choice seasons.

WHAT TO WEAR WHERE

As in any major cosmopolitan area, dress depends on what you're doing. For business, you can't go wrong with a business suit, at least for your first business visit. If your plans include hitting some of the fancier big-city restaurants with a dress-up policy, or selected events, like a first night, women should have some dressy clothes and men will need a suit, or at least a jacket and tie. Otherwise, casual dress is fine everywhere.

Dress for the season and the weather. Heat is the major factor in deciding what to wear during the late spring, summer, and early fall, and that's when natural fibers, like cotton, serve best—as long as you remember that air conditioning is a way of life here, so even during the hottest days of summer it's comfortable indoors. You'll need some warm clothes for the chilliest winter months—layering works well—otherwise, sweaters and a lightweight coat should get you through most of the cool periods in late fall and early spring.

GETTING TO THE METROPLEX

If you're not driving yourself, you can get there by plane or bus. You might check on trains, but when this went to press passenger trains to the Metroplex were just about as extinct as the dinosaur.

The **Dallas–Fort Worth International Airport** (www.dfwairport.com), or DFW as it's locally known, is located about halfway between the two cities for which it is named. It's the busiest airport in Texas and one of the busiest in the world, averaging about 2,600 passenger flights daily of both domestic and foreign airlines. Many major national and international airlines operate here, but the major player is American Airlines and a secondary one is Delta.

At thirty square miles, it's larger in area than the island of Manhattan. All the passenger facilities at DFW are located along a central north-south highway, called International Parkway. This leads to Highways 114 and 635 on the north and 183 and 360 on the south. All the passenger facilities, including terminals, rental car offices, parking lots, and the airport hotel, are located along this central parkway.

International Parkway is a ten-mile toll road with fees ranging from fifty cents, if you're just passing through, up to a couple of dollars if you enter and stay for several hours. A variety of shuttles and taxis are available to take you to your Metroplex destination at a wide variety of fares. Or, for just a couple of bucks, you can catch a shuttle bus connecting the airport with the Centreport Station of the Trinity Railway Express that runs to both downtown Dallas and downtown Fort Worth.

In addition to being the major airport for flying into or out of the Metroplex, DFW itself is worth a visit as an attraction. For details on what to see and do at the airport, see the listing in the city of GRAPEVINE under OTHER POINTS OF INTEREST (p. 261).

Several commuter airlines operate out of the smaller **Love Field**, but the domestic biggie here is Southwest, which calls this its home base. Love Field, which was the major airport in Dallas until DFW was built, started as a military training base in 1917 and began its first passenger service in 1927. Located within the city limits in the northwest corner of the city of Dallas, it is closer than DFW to Dallas and its neighboring Metroplex cities. You'll still need to plan on a taxi or shuttle to get to where you're going, but the Dallas Area Rapid Transit (DART) Light Rail system is being extended to Love Field and may be there by the time you read this.

DRIVING IN THE METROPLEX

You should know and obey the following Texas driving laws so you don't ruin your visit with a ticket, or worse.

The speed limit on rural interstates (not many of those in the Metroplex) is 70 mph. On freeways it's 60 mph, unless posted lower (rarely higher). The limit on most residential streets is 30 mph. That may go up to 45 mph on major boulevards. The simplest way is to watch the speed limit signs and keep to the limit. And don't think that you won't be the one to get the ticket just because local drivers are speeding past you. The speed limit in school zones is usually 20 mph. These are marked with signs and sometimes also with flashing yellow lights. It's illegal to pass a stopped or stopping school bus.

Drivers and front-seat passengers must wear seat belts, and infant seats are also required by state law.

Controlled-access highway traffic has the right of way and is *not* required to yield to entering traffic. Existing traffic on access roads has the right of way. It's legal to make a right turn on red, after a stop, unless otherwise posted. (Watch for the signs.) It's illegal to consume alcohol while operating a motor vehicle, and an open bottle can also get you into trouble if you're stopped. Texas has a mandatory automobile liability insurance law. If you're stopped for any reason you may be required to show proof of liability coverage. If it's your car, make sure you have proof. If you rent a car, make sure you're given proof to carry in the car.

"Jaywalking" or crossing the street anywhere other than a corner is a ticketable offense in many areas.

GETTING AROUND WITHOUT A CAR

It used to be that a car was essential to get around anywhere in the Metroplex, and overall, a car may still be the best way to go. Now, however, you have some options, especially if you'll be staying in the downtown sections of Dallas or Fort Worth. In those cases, you can take a reasonably priced private shuttle or your hotel's free shuttle to and from the airport (both DFW and Love Field). Many hotels also offer free shuttle service within a three- or five-mile radius of the hotel (See ACCOMMODATIONS), and in the downtowns of those two major cities you can use public transportation to get around.

Public transportation? I never use public transportation!

Well, maybe you should in those two downtowns, where you may find driving a car more of a hassle and parking more expensive than taking advantage of their public systems. This is particularly true where the speedy, clean, and inexpensive DART light rail system has stations (www.DART.org). In Dallas, stations are every few blocks in the downtown area, and the system is pushing steadily out toward points north and south, hooking up with the DART bus system. There are also low-fare special buses that run downtown with routes that are oriented to where visitors want to go (see DALLAS—GETTING AROUND, p. 70). And in Fort Worth, the DART Light Rail and the "T" buses can be combined to get you to all the major tourist areas throughout the city (see FORT WORTH—GETTING AROUND, p. 179).

If you are driving a car and are not familiar with the streets, you can avoid getting into hazardous driving situations, while helping your peace of mind, if you take the time to find your destination on a city map before you start out. To help you find places, we've included a simple map of each city. These aren't as detailed as a city road map, but they do show the main streets. If you're driving without a capable map-reading copilot, it will probably make the trip easier for you if you write the travel directions on a self-stick note and paste it on your dashboard or steering

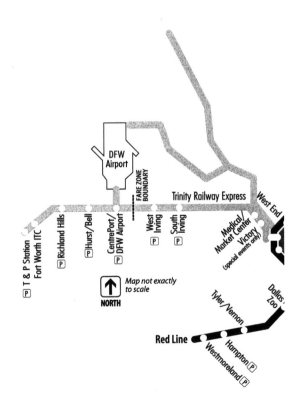

wheel where you can see it easily. Or record the directions on a pocket tape recorder.

ALCOHOLIC BEVERAGE LAWS

The legal drinking age and the legal age to purchase alcoholic beverages in Texas is twenty-one. Under Texas local option laws, the locations where alcoholic beverages (beer, wine, or liquor) may be sold or consumed are decided by the vote of the people within a city or other political division, like a precinct. This means that in the Metroplex you'll find a hodgepodge of designated "wet" areas, where alcoholic beverages can be sold, and "dry" areas, where they can't. The exact rules vary. Sometimes, in a dry area, restaurants and clubs can sell alcoholic drinks, and sometimes you can get an alcoholic drink (no carry-out or package sales) only in a private club. Fortunately, it's not hard to become a club member, since the law allows most restaurants that serve drinks to sell individ-

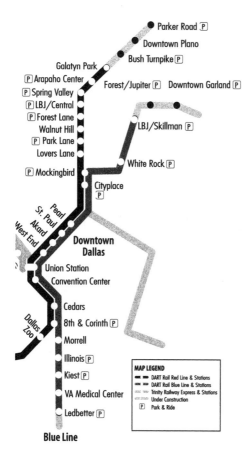

Parker Road P
Downtown Plano
Bush Turnpike P
Galatyn Park
P Arapaho Center   Forest/Jupiter P   Downtown Garland P
P Spring Valley
P LBJ/Central
P Forest Lane
Walnut Hill
P Park Lane   LBJ/Skillman P
Lovers Lane
P Mockingbird   White Rock P
                     Cityplace
                        P
Pearl
St. Paul
Akard
West End
                  Downtown
                    Dallas
Union Station
Convention Center
Cedars
8th & Corinth P
Morrell
Illinois P
Kiest P
VA Medical Center
Ledbetter P

MAP LEGEND
DART Rail Red Line & Stations
DART Rail Blue Line & Stations
Trinity Railway Express & Stations
Under Construction
P Park & Ride

Dallas Zoo

Blue Line

ual annual memberships for a fee of about two dollars. Hotels/motels with a private club in dry areas usually give automatic memberships to guests. The real rub is that, in some places in the Metroplex, because of city or precinct boundaries, you may find a wet area on one side of a street and a dry area on the other. We've tried to include a "wet" or "dry" notation in the introduction to each city in this book. But these can change, so, if the difference between a wet or dry area is important to you, ask before you settle on where you'll stay and go.

SOME FINAL NOTES

All of the Metroplex is on ten-digit dialing, which means you *must* use the appropriate telephone area code before the seven-digit number.

Don't think you're back in the Old West if you see a sign on an entrance door that reads: "State law prohibits carrying a handgun on these premises." Texas is one of many states that now issue permits for citizens to carry concealed handguns. However, it also has laws that prohibit those citizens from carrying a handgun into many places.

Most prices in listings do not include taxes. As a visitor, you can expect to pay at least two types of taxes: sales tax and hotel or bed tax. The sales tax in the various Metroplex cities hovers on one side or the other of 8 percent, and most of the hotel or bed taxes are from about 11 percent to 15 percent.

In an emergency, call 911 for police, fire, or ambulance.

GENERAL WEBSITES

We include websites whenever they are available for each city and many individual listings. In addition, you'll find the following websites are a good source of both general and specific information about the Metroplex. You may have to dig down in some of them to get what you're looking for, but there's a gold mine of information waiting for you.

www.guidelive.com	Dallas and Fort Worth
www.tourtexas.com	Texas cities
www.traveltex.com	Texas cities
www.texashighways.com	*Texas Highways* Magazine
www.texasmonthly.com	*Texas Monthly* Magazine
www.tpwd.state.tx.us	Texas Parks and Wildlife Department
www.artonart.com	Texas Arts and Cultural Events
www.thc.state.tx.us	Texas Historical Commission
www.trinityrailwayexpress.org	For details on how to use the Trinity Railway Express trains to go between Dallas and Fort Worth or to and from the DFW airport

INTRODUCTION

You'll Get the Most for Your Money If You Read This First!

If you are like most guidebook users, you'll be eager to get into the details about your destination, skipping over anything with a mundane title like *Introduction*—or, for that matter, any other sections in the front of the book that might delay getting right to the heart of the matter.

Unfortunately, if you skip this part you'll be missing some crucial information that will help you squeeze the most benefits out of the listings.

You don't have to read it all right now. Just skim through this section so you'll know what's here. Then, if you need the details later on, you'll have a good idea where to look.

HOW IS THIS GUIDE ORGANIZED?

We've tried to organize it to be as user-friendly as possible. The eleven cities we cover in detail are listed alphabetically.

"Eleven cities! I thought this was just a guide for a visitor to Dallas and Fort Worth."

That's partly right! Those two major cities make up the major part of this guidebook. But, as the name implies, the **Dallas/Fort Worth Metroplex** is a conglomerate of many more than a dozen cities tightly bunched together. Dallas and Fort Worth are the largest and anchor the Metroplex on the east and west. But, if you want to go to Six Flags, you'll have to go to Arlington. To see the Cowboys play, you have to go to Irving. To taste Texas wines, you head for Grapevine (where else?). For horse racing, it's Grand Prairie's Lone Star Park and . . . well, you get the idea. It's truly a Metro-complex.

We considered writing this book as just one monstrous city guide, forgetting all about the city boundaries, most of which you may never know you crossed anyway. However, in our visits we found that each of these cities, large and small, has its own distinctive character and flavor. Although they are just minutes apart, for example, the ambience of Grapevine is vastly different from that of Addison. Each also has its own separate convention and visitors bureau, chamber of commerce, or city office to help visitors with specific information for that city.

Admittedly, a few of the smaller Metroplex cities are really just bedroom communities—pleasant places to live, but with little to warrant a special trip. That's why we decided to concentrate on giving you in-depth coverage of those cities that offer the most to you, whether you are a tourist or a business visitor. These are: Addison, Arlington, Dallas, Farmers Branch, Fort Worth, Garland, Grand Prairie, Grapevine, Irving, Plano, and Richardson.

CHANGE IS CONSTANT

It took us a long time to conduct research visits and write, edit, print, and distribute this book. In the meantime, things may have changed. Restaurants, for example, are notorious for changing their names, management, menu, and hours, or—even worse—closing down. Museums change hours or admission fees. Attractions close down and new ones open up. Prices go up or down (rarely down). *In other words, all we can tell you is that the information in this book was as current as we could make it at the time it went to press.*

If you find that a listed restaurant is no longer there, or your hotel doesn't have all the amenities cited, or the museum is closed on Monday when we said it was open, please be understanding. We've included telephone numbers in the listings whenever possible. A call ahead might save you a little irritation, especially if you have to travel any distance. Remember, however, that phone numbers change, too. (While we were researching this guide, for example, the phone company changed a number of area codes.) If you have trouble reaching a listing, check the phone book or call Information or the local visitors bureau.

For the bigger picture, whenever available, we've also included Internet website addresses.

WHAT'S IN THIS GUIDE—AND WHAT'S NOT

It would take a book thicker than a Dallas phonebook to list all the attractions, museums, restaurants, sports venues, hotels, and all the other places of interest to visitors to the cities in this guide. Therefore, our goal is *not* to tell *all*, but to give you a solid *sampling* of the best, to get you started on your visit. Once started, you can get more free information from the listed local tourist information office, the local newspaper or other publications, your hotel concierge or hotel/motel staff, the various websites, or a dozen other local sources. They can update you on what we did list as well as the places and/or events of particular interest to you that space limitations forced us to omit.

HOW TO READ THE LISTINGS

Each city's listings begin with the name of the county in which it is located, the best rounded-off estimate of the city's current population, and its telephone area code(s), and, in some cases, its website. This is followed by a brief history and introduction to the city and a simple city map.

Where a listing gives the days open, a short dash (–) between days means "through," including both days. For example, Monday–Thursday means Monday through Thursday.

To make it easier for you to find the listings that you are particularly interested in, each city's listings are broken down under category headings such as these, as appropriate:

NEIGHBORHOODS

A description of the major neighborhoods of visitor interest in the larger cities.

FREE VISITOR SERVICES

These are convention and visitors bureaus and other organizations that will provide you with free information and answer your questions about their city. Each listing includes the address and phone and website so you can contact them for trip planning as well as when you're in their town. Unless otherwise noted, these offices are usually open regular business hours, Monday–Friday.

HELPFUL LOCAL PUBLICATIONS

These are local newspapers and magazines that regularly include schedules for theaters and current events, restaurant reviews, opening hours for attractions, and other kinds of information about up-to-the-minute details. Some of these you'll have to buy, but several of the weekly publications that highlight local entertainment news are free and widely available.

COMMERCIAL TOUR SERVICES

Tour companies and other organizations offering commercial tours.

INDUSTRY TOURS

Several businesses or industrial plants offer tours of their facilities. Most of these are free, but it's a good idea to call to see if there is a minimum age or other restrictions on who can take the tour.

SELF-GUIDED TOURS

You can take these driving and/or walking tours on your own.

BIRD'S-EYE VIEW

The literal "high point" of your trip might be a panoramic view of the area, so we've listed the best places for that.

HISTORIC PLACES

Whether you are a history buff or just curious about our heritage, there are a number of places that give you a glimpse of what life was like in the Metroplex in the past. Many of the listings are historic homes that are still private residences (please just walk or drive by and not bother the residents). Not included are the many city and state historical markers and plaques attached to walls of historic buildings and set up on roadsides near historic sites. Each of these tells a story of a piece of local history, and most are worth the time it takes to stop and read and think about the lives those who came before us.

MUSEUMS AND PUBLIC ART GALLERIES

The Metroplex has a wealth of museums. Almost every city has at least one. The great ones are comparable to the best in the nation. Others are little gems well worth your time. To get the most from your museum visit, try to avoid weekends and holidays, which are usually crowded, especially if there's a major exhibit going on. Always ask about free tours or lectures. At the least, request a floor plan and/or any free brochures that you can use to guide yourself around. If it's a large museum, don't try to do it all at once. Plan to take a break in some quiet place—perhaps, if there's a café, you can relax over lunch. (If you live in or near the Metroplex and plan to be a regular visitor to a particular museum, consider a membership, which may pay for itself in discounts on admission or other perks.) If you want inexpensive souvenirs, the museum gift shop will probably have postcards with reproductions of the exhibits.

SPECIAL GARDENS

These are city botanical gardens and a few other gardens of special interest.

OUTDOORS

Our listings guide you to selection of city parks, lakes, and other places where you can enjoy the greatness of the outdoors in this metropolitan area.

COLLEGE CAMPUSES OF INTEREST TO VISITORS

College and university campuses are often relatively undiscovered treasure houses for nonstudent visitors. Many offer facilities and events open to the public. These may include art galleries, museums, historic buildings, concerts, plays, film and lecture series, festivals, and major sports events that range from basketball and football to intercollegiate rodeos. Parking is a problem at many schools, so listings include information, when available, on visitor parking.

MUSIC AND PERFORMING ARTS

Theater, dance, and music are not just alive in the Metroplex, they are robust and flourishing. Dallas and Fort Worth, of course, offer the widest possible variety, but many of the smaller cities have a surprising medley of offerings ranging from community theater to symphony orchestras. There are also a number of cultural arts groups that sponsor touring shows and celebrity concerts. Our listings, which barely scratch the surface of what's available, include both specific music and performing arts organizations and the places, like theaters and civic centers that host these events, that you can call to check on their schedule.

FAMILY FUN AND KID STUFF

We have listed a wide variety of special places for kids of all ages.

SPORTS

Listings offer a wide variety of both spectator and individual sports available to visitors. *The Sporting News* has ranked the Metroplex in the Top 5 in sports every year since 1992. In addition to the many professional sports teams, some of the best golf courses in the Southwest are here. Most intercollegiate college sports are open to visitors, and, occasionally, college sports facilities are open on a limited basis for the use of nonstudents. These are listed under each individual school. If your favorite sport or activity isn't listed, or you need more details, contact the local visitors bureau, the local parks and recreation department, or the college or university.

OTHER POINTS OF INTEREST

This is sort of a catch-all category for places that don't fit exactly into any of the categories listed above.

OFFBEAT

And now for something completely different. . . . Listings under this heading don't fit any of the other categories because they are truly unique.

ANNUAL EVENTS

Every community celebrates one or more annual events with a distinctive flavor. Many of these are just one-day affairs that really don't warrant a long trip to attend them. For this reason, we've used three rules to select what to list under this category: (1) it must be well worth attending, (2) it must last at least two days and (3) it must draw visitors from outside the immediate area. Listings don't include specific dates, since these usually change from year to year. For the exact dates and details, call the number in the listing or contact the local visitors bureau.

SHOPPING

According to the Dallas/Fort Worth Area Tourism Council, there's more shopping available in the Metroplex than in New York City. True or hype, several dozen malls and hundreds and hundreds of shops certainly support this claim. The City of Dallas alone has more shopping centers per capita than any other U.S. city; moreover, it is the home of America's oldest shopping center, Highland Park Village.

When Neiman Marcus opened its "exclusive woman's ready-to-wear store" in 1907, it put Dallas on the national fashion map. Since then, many national and international retailers have moved in to offer a variety of fashion alternatives that would impress the most discerning and experienced shopper. As a result, the Metroplex—with Dallas as its heart and hub—is considered one of the nation's top retail and wholesale centers.

A Metroplex shopping spree is not limited to high-end merchandise. In addition to flea markets and trade fairs, in full swing every weekend somewhere in the region, Metroplex shoppers have embraced discount retailing with a passion. From local manufacturer's sample sales to national and regional discount chains offering brand names at off-retail prices, there is a variety to fit the tastes of all shoppers. To rephrase a popular song, "If you can't find it here, you won't find it anywhere."

If you are attracted to flea markets, don't miss Trader's Village in Grand Prairie, and if pursuing discount shopping is your quest, you'll definitely want to check out the Grapevine Mills Mall.

If shopping is your number one priority when you come to the Metroplex and you want to get to it quickly, you might want to try one of the many commercial tour services that offer shopping tours. Contact the

Dallas or other Metroplex city convention and visitors bureaus for lists and recommendations. Even if shopping is not high on your visit agenda, it's nice to know where there is a good mall to satisfy your basic needs, so we've listed a selection of the biggest and/or best. (You can find the others in the Yellow Pages.) In addition, here and there, we've listed a few specialty shops we found that are different from the ordinary stores found in every city. Hours are not given unless they vary from the normal shopping hours in that area.

A SAMPLING OF RESTAURANTS

If you enjoy dining out, the Metroplex is your Garden of Eden. There are thousands of restaurants of every type and every price range, so all we can offer is a sampling in each of the cities. Once you're in town you can check any number of sources to find the restaurants to fit your taste and budget. The alphabetical listings in each city give the details on each of the sample restaurants with notes on the type of cuisine, prices, credit cards accepted, and other basic information that will help you make your selection of where to eat.

Like to try a fine-dining restaurant, but the prices scare you off? Try it for lunch, when prices may be as little as half those at dinner. The lunch entrées probably will not be the most expressive examples of the chef's talents but almost always are a fair sampling of it, and you'll enjoy the same ambience and service and have much less anxiety when the check comes.

The keys to listing a restaurant—plain or fancy—in our sample were simple: cleanliness was a given and ambience was a factor, but most important was that the food was well prepared and enjoyable to eat and that the kitchen lived up to the promises on the menu. It didn't matter if it was a fine-dining, gourmet restaurant or a café or barbecue place, high or low priced; if it delivered in full on its promises and the meal was a pleasure, it made the listing. If it promised and didn't deliver, we didn't list it. *We do not rate restaurants, but the mere fact that it made the listings indicates our recommendation.*

With a few exceptions, major chain restaurants are not listed, since most travelers know of them and can look them up in the phone book. Although not listed, cafeterias are a major part of the eating-out scene here. There are a number of cafeteria chains that do a superior job of providing convenient, well-prepared meals at reasonable prices. One chain we found especially favored and consistently recommended by residents is Luby's. If you want to eat in your room or perhaps have a picnic in a park, other welcome alternatives are takeout places and specialty groceries. We've listed some we feel will give you the best for your money.

Since exact prices are hard to keep current, the following $ symbols are used to indicate the approximate cost of a **typical dinner (or lunch, if dinner is not served) for one person, exclusive of drinks, tax, and**

tip. If two symbols are used, it indicates the price spread of the entrées on the menu.

$	= up to $16
$$	= $16–$30
$$$	= $31–$50
$$$$	= over $50

The symbols for credit cards accepted are:

AE	= American Express
DC	= Diners Club
DIS	= Discover
MC	= Mastercard
V	= VISA
Cr.	= All major credit cards
No cr.	= No credit cards accepted

A SAMPLING OF CLUBS AND BARS

We're more selective about listing clubs and bars than any other category because we don't want to steer you wrong or waste your time. These open and close and change format so frequently that the individual listing may be outdated, at the least, or even dead by the time you want to go there. In an attempt (perhaps foolhardy) to avoid this, we tried to stick to listing only those places that have a history of permanence. If you want more in the way of nightlife, look in the local entertainment newspapers listed under Helpful Local Publications.

A SAMPLING OF ACCOMMODATIONS

When it comes time to pick where you want to spend the night, the Metroplex offers an overwhelming bundle of choices to match just about every lifestyle and budget. The accommodations we selected to list are just a *small* sampling. There are hotels and motels and more hotels and motels, an occasional bed and breakfast inn, and then more hotels and motels. Sometimes you'll find them in clusters to meet the needs of business centers, conventions, or in entertainment areas featuring major attractions. Others are widely scattered throughout the Metroplex. You can go top dollar and luxuriate in all the amenities money can buy, or go budget and get all the basics—frequently, at least in our sampling, with a touch of quality amenities.

When picking accommodations, remember this is a Metro-complex. Let the city borders work for you. If you use a street map, you may find that staying in one city is a better deal, giving you more for your money, even if everything you plan to do is in a another city.

The following $ symbols are used to indicate the approximate rate for a double room or a suite for two persons for one night. If two symbols are used, it indicates the spread between the lowest and highest priced double room or suite. (If they offer suites, most of the high $ signs in the listings are for the suites.) We use what is known in the trade as "rack rates" to make the comparisons. Rack rates are what the accommodation would like to get for the room, but rarely does. Use these symbols only for initial comparison, then always *ask for the best discount you can get!*

$ = Up to $80
$$ = $81–$120
$$$ = $121–$180
$$$$ = $181– $280
$$$$$ = Over $280

In addition to the room rate, some hotels, and especially resorts, add a daily fee to cover a number of miscellaneous extras instead of billing separately for local calls or use of the fitness center or other special facilities. These can range from a dollar up to several dollars per room per day. Ask about this when you make your reservation.

Most accommodations let children stay free in a room with parents. There may be an extra charge if the children require bringing in an extra bed.

And, finally, so you won't be shocked when it comes time to pay, in our listings we also include the **city bed tax percentage** *that they rarely tell you about in advance, but definitely will be automatically added to your bill.*

SIDE TRIPS

Occasionally we'll suggest making a trip to some place of interest outside the cities we cover. The suggested side trips are rarely more than an hour's drive and usually well worth your time and effort.

WHEELCHAIR ACCESSIBILITY SYMBOLS

Under current laws, most public buildings and many businesses are now accessible to the mobility impaired who must use a wheelchair. The following symbols are used in all appropriate listings to indicate wheelchair accessibility.

W   In general this place is accessible to persons in wheelchairs through at least one entrance. However, not all facilities (rest rooms, etc.) are accessible.

W+   This place and *most* of its major facilities, including some restrooms, are accessible.

No symbol indicates this place is either not accessible or accessible only with great difficulty.

THE SECRET OF HOW TO GET
THE BEST RATE

The cost of lodgings is often the biggest part of your travel budget. That means it'll pay you to put in a little extra work to get the lowest rate without sacrificing quality or the amenities you want. You may get this best rate through a travel agent, a hotel/motel price club, a hotel broker or consolidator, or an Internet website. But there's also a good chance that, if you're not shy, you can do as well by yourself.

So, what is the secret of how to get the best rate?

Ask for it!

That's it. If you ask, the odds are you'll get it.

Why? Because the hotel industry works under the law of supply and demand, and each room is a perishable product on a daily basis—every night it's either filled for a profit or empty for a loss. When demand is high (they've booked a huge convention or there's a major event that fills all the rooms) the rates stay high—maybe even go higher. But when demand is low, management must be flexible on its rates to get as many rooms filled each night as possible to avoid a loss. That, in turn, means that, at least up to a point, the rates are negotiable and if you ask for a discount or a special deal there's a good chance you'll get it.

What kind of discounts are there? There are discounts for seniors (AARP members or senior age loosely defined), AAA and other auto clubs and travel organizations, union members, teachers, students, military, clergy, frequent stay and flier programs, government employees; if it's during a slow time, you may even get a discount if you resemble one of the desk clerk's in-laws. In general, the management doesn't care what the discount is called as long as it helps fill that empty room at a reasonable rate.

There are also special package plans that lump a room (or suite) with a number of amenities that, if priced separately, would cost much more. These may range from a golf or tennis package, to a Cowboys football weekend rate to a honeymoon or an anniversary deal. (Honeymoon and anniversary packages are often an especially good deal, and no one is going to ask to see your wedding license to check if you're really celebrating your anniversary on the right day, or even the right month.) Properties located in the business centers of the cities that are filled with business people Monday through Thursday often offer special rates to fill those rooms on weekends. And, here again, the term "weekend" is defined differently by each hotel, depending on its supply and demand; in a slow period they might stretch it for you well into the week. Conversely, resort properties that are packed on weekends may offer a good deal weekdays.

HOW TO ASK FOR THIS BEST RATE

First, from our accommodations listings, or other sources, pick out the properties in your price range that have the location and amenities you want. You'll be dealing with professional sales personnel, so know a range of what you want so you can't be sold into something you don't want. Having several choices to fall back on puts you in a position of strength; if you're really good at negotiating, you might even play one property's offered rate against the others.

It can be one or two steps to find the best rate. Step one: Call direct to each property and negotiate. Step two: Call each chain property's central reservations 800 number first, then call the property direct. The questions are basically the same for each step.

If you call the 800 reservations number first, tell the clerk what you want and ask for the "lowest rate." When you're given the rate, be courteous and friendly, but push without being pushy and ask, "Is that the lowest rate you can give me?" Each time you're given a new rate, ask the same question again. You might come up with a good deal this way, but don't expect it. Central reservation clerks can probably offer you a better rate than the rack rate, but they usually do not have the authority to negotiate anything much below the top rates. Still, it's worth your time to go through the routine of questioning on all the possible discounts and package deals that interest you and any chain-wide promotional rates available.

Now, armed with these possibilities—actually these are your ceiling rates—you're ready for the real negotiations.

Call the property direct. If there's an 800 number direct to the property, fine—just make certain you are talking to someone on-site, not being looped back to central reservations. Even if it's a toll call, it'll probably save you much more than that small phone charge. Call during the day, but not around check-out or check-in time, and you'll have the best chance of getting someone with the authority to negotiate rates.

Once again, say specifically what you're looking for, and ask for the lowest rate. And keep asking and exploring all the options. Be polite, but firm. This is not a conflict; it's just bargaining. The property is selling and wants to get the best price for its product and you're willing to buy, if the price is right. What you're seeking is the price point that makes both of you happy. If they won't lower the price, consider asking for an upgrade of the room or additional amenities for their asking price.

Another tack is to figure how much you're willing to pay and then say "I was looking for something for less than [their figure]." Or even make an offer. If the demand is down, no reasonable offer will be refused.

Once you've reached the best rate you can get (meaning they are about to hang up on you), make your reservation and get a reservation confirmation number.

And enjoy your stay!

ADDISON

Dallas County • 14,200 • Area Code 972 (local calls require area code) • www.ci.addison.tx.us

Although first settled in the mid-1840s, in an area once called Peters Colony, it wasn't until the St. Louis, Arkansas, and Texas Railroad arrived in the 1880s that it grew into a village called Noell Junction. About twenty years later it became known as Addison, named after Addison Robertson, who later became the community's postmaster.

While the main role of many of the smaller cities in the Metroplex is to serve as residential bedroom communities for Dallas and the other major business cities, the 4.3-square-mile Town of Addison can list itself as one of its business centers. While residents number only about 14,000, on workdays the daytime business population jumps to around 100,000. Statistically, that small residential population is a major reason that the town can boast that it has more restaurants (more than 135) per capita than any city west of the Mississippi. Addison's restaurants can seat over 20,000 patrons at one time, close to twice the number of residents. Its "restaurant row," originally developed to service the daily workday influx, has become a large draw for after-work and weekend diners from Dallas and other Metroplex cities.

A major contributor to the expansion of both business and restaurants occurred in 1975 when the residents held an election under the local liquor option laws and voted the town "wet," allowing liquor by the drink. Its growth is also aided by the Dallas North Tollway, which bisects the town, providing a brief trip to and from downtown Dallas. And, while it can't compare to the huge Dallas/Fort Worth International Airport, the Addison Airport can boast that it is the third busiest general aviation airport in the United States, with more than 750 private aircraft based there. It is also the home of several flight academies.

The City of Addison was incorporated in 1953 under the mayor/alderman form of government. In 1982 that was changed to the mayor/city council form, and the place became the Town of Addison. The name change was intended to counter the effects of its impressive growth and encourage the small-town ambience that the residents desired. Retaining

ADDISON

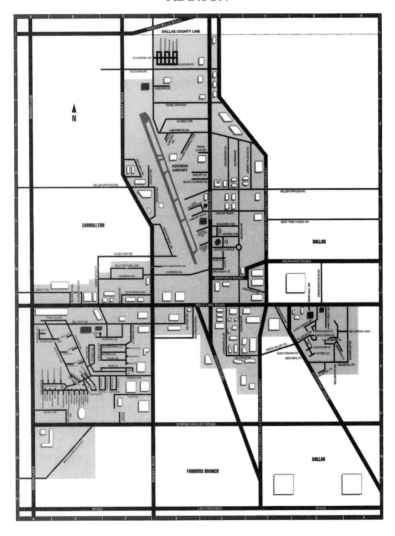

that small-town atmosphere in the midst of the booming Metroplex is not just a name change, though. It's an ongoing policy. For example, the council members and city manager, like all good small-town officials, take it as a duty to know many of the residents by name.

FREE VISITOR SERVICES

TOWN OF ADDISON VISITOR SERVICES DEPARTMENT
15650 Addison Rd. (P.O. Box 9010, 75001-9010) • 972-450-6219 or 800-ADDISON (233-4766) • Monday–Friday, 8–5 • W+ • www.addisontexas.net

This office is located in a building behind the Addison Conference & Theatre Centre. Here you can pick up free brochures, maps, restaurant and hotel information, and theater schedules as well as other information about Addison and the Metroplex. Ample parking in front.

HELPFUL LOCAL PUBLICATIONS

Current information about Addison events, activities, nightlife, theater, movies, and dining is often listed in the *Northwest Morning News* in the local edition of the *Dallas Morning News,* and the *Friday Guide* in that newspaper. The *Fort Worth Star-Telegram* is also a good source, and those two daily papers sponsor a combined website that includes entertainment guides at **www.dfw.com**. Other sources to check are the weekly *Dallas Observer,* which is available free at restaurants and tourist attractions throughout the Dallas area, and the monthly *D Magazine* and *Texas Monthly Magazine,* available on newsstands. Locally, the free *Addison & North Dallas Corridor Guide* is usually available in hotels and other visitor-centered locations around town.

GETTING AROUND

ADDISON'S DART TROLLEY-BUSES
Route and Schedule Information, 214-979-1111 • www.DART.org

The thirty stops on the route of these buses, designed to look like old-fashioned trolleys, will put you within easy walking distance of most of the major accommodations and many of the restaurants in town. They also run to the Galleria, which is technically in Dallas, just across Addison's southern border. Route schedules vary, but generally they run from late morning or early afternoon to late at night Monday through Saturday, and you can ride them all day with a bus pass you can buy from the trolley-bus operator for just $1. No Sunday service. Make sure to check the schedule, since the buses hit each stop only about once an hour.

MUSEUMS AND ART GALLERIES

CAVANAUGH FLIGHT MUSEUM

4572 Claire Chennault (75001) on east side of Addison Airport (follow signs off Addison Rd.) • 972-380-8800 • Monday–Saturday, 9–5; Sunday, 11–5. Closed some major holidays (call first) • Adults, $6; children 6–12, $3; 5 and under free • MC, V, Dis • W+ • www.cavanaughflightmuseum.com

Fifty thousand square feet of display space in four hangars hold this growing collection of fully restored military aircraft flown in wars from World War I to Vietnam. What sets this museum apart from most other aviation museums is that nearly all the historic warbirds, trainers, fighters, jets, and other aircraft on display are air worthy and flown on a regular basis. To keep them flyable, one hangar is devoted to maintenance. Here you can look under the skins of these famous aircraft and talk to the mechanics about them. The more than 30 aircraft in the collection range from the World War I Sopwith Camel to U.S. and Russian jets like the F86E Sabre Jet and the MiG-21. A MiG-17 is set up so you can sit in the restored cockpit. Want firsthand flying experience? Then take a flight in a World War II military trainer. A 30-minute flight in a Stearman open-cockpit primary flight trainer costs about $175 (plus tax). Flying in the AT-6 Texan, a closed cockpit advanced flight trainer, costs about $250 (plus tax.) Warbird passengers must be at least 18 years old, and flights must be booked at least 48 hours in advance. Other facilities include a history of military aviation (memorabilia) gallery, gift shop, snack bar, and outdoor picnic area. Since many of the planes on display are flown in air shows, the best time to see the whole collection is in the winter when the air-show season is over.

OUTDOORS

ADDISON PARKS

Parks and Recreation Department • Addison Service Center, 16801 Westgrove • 972-450-2851

Although only a little over four square miles in area, Addison's parks provide a variety of facilities for recreational activities, including playgrounds and sports courts, as well as quiet areas for relaxing. Several of the parks have lighted walking and jogging trails, the longest being the 2.5-mile jogging and bike trail in **Les Lacs Linear Park** at 3901 Beltway Drive. Call for information.

MUSIC AND PERFORMING ARTS

WATERTOWER THEATRE

Addison Conference & Theatre Centre, 15650 Addison Rd. (75001), under the Addison Water Tower • Conference Center, 972-450-6203; Theater, 972-450-6232 • • W+ • www.watertowertheatre.com

The WaterTower Theatre is actually the resident company that performs in the Theatre Centre. The award-winning state-of-the-art theater is designed so that both the seating and performance area can be transformed for an elaborate stage presentation or a more intimate theater-in-the-round, whichever best fits each production. Under this flexible arrangement, seating can be varied to hold an audience of 250 to 300. The October–August season normally features at least five productions that run the gamut from comedies and musicals to new plays and the classics, plus two holiday specials. Tickets are about $20 for most productions. It also sponsors the annual Out of the Loop Festival, a nine-day event in March featuring a variety of fare performed in the Theatre Centre by other regional theatre companies. Most WaterTower Theatre casts are composed of professionals from the Metroplex area. Each production is presented on Thursday, Friday, and Saturday evenings and Sunday matinees. The **Addison Conference &Theatre Centre** is also used for a wide variety of meetings as well as numerous events to which the public is invited. Call for schedule.

FAMILY FUN AND KID STUFF

FUN FEST

3805 Belt Line (75001), between Midway and Marsh • 972-620-7700 • Sunday–Thursday, 11 a.m.–midnight, Friday–Saturday, 11 a.m.– 2:00 p.m. • W+ • Entrance free; prices depend on activity • Cr. • www.funfest.com

There's something for just about everyone here: adults, kids, and families. This huge game place offers bowling lanes and around 170 state-of-the art video games, as well as some old-time favorite games like foosball, and an area set aside for laser tag. One of the nice things for conscientious parents is the arrangement that makes the adults-only areas, like the full bar with big screen TV, structured so the kids can't get in. Snack bar and gift shop.

SPORTS

ICE SKATING

THE RINK

15100 Midway Rd. (75001) • 972-960-RINK (960-7465) • Open 5 p.m.–midnight • Public skating hours vary • W+ • www.therinkinaddison.com

The two ice rinks here are open for public skating sessions at varying times, days and evenings. Call for schedule. Public sessions, $5. Skate rental, $2. Lessons available. If you like to watch hockey, a number of youth and league teams play here. Admission is free unless you step on the ice. Pro shop.

OTHER POINTS OF INTEREST

BLUEPRINTS AT ADDISON CIRCLE

Addison Circle at Quorum Dr. and Addison Circle Dr.

This massive unique sculpture, dominating the circle, is the result of the town and a local developer wanting to make a statement about Addison's past and their vision of its future. The $2.1 million, vase-like sculpture, with poles that reach out over the street, stands 45 feet high and 140 feet across and weighs 410,000 pounds. The name refers to the five floating art panels that contain detailed elements from the blueprints used to build many of the city's buildings and parks, and it took more than 650 gallons of custom-mixed Sherwin Williams "Sharpie Blue" paint to achieve that blueprint look.

MARY KAY WORLD HEADQUARTERS AND MUSEUM

16251 N. Dallas Pkwy. (P.O. Box 799045, Dallas 75379-9045), on west side of Dallas North Tollway between Keller Springs and Westgrove • 800-MARY KAY (800-627-9529) • 972-687-5720 for tour information recording • Free • W+ • www.marykay.com

Mary Kay herself had said that "With 13 floors and 13 main elevators, this building is perfect for a company that was founded on Friday, September 13th, 1963."

The Mary Kay Museum, which relates the Horatio Alger–type history of Mary Kay and her multibillion-dollar worldwide cosmetics firm, is on the first floor. Attractions at the museum include a 10-minute video of Mary Kay's life and work, products past and present, and a sampling of the rewards she gave her "consultants" (who now number nearly 900,000 in 33 markets worldwide), including the best-known prize, a pink Cadillac. You can see these all on your own on a self-guided tour whenever the building is open (Monday–Friday, 8:30–5). *A hint: The high-quality cafeteria-style restaurant on the first floor is also open to the public for lunch on weekdays.*

Free guided tours are available by appointment only, made at least 48 hours in advance by calling 972-687-5720. In addition to a guided explanation of the museum exhibits, the one-hour conducted tour also takes you to Mary Kay's office on the executive floor. No tours mid-July to mid-August, when the company convention takes over the Dallas Convention Center.

Tours of Mary Kay's manufacturing facility, located at 1330 Regal Row in Dallas, can also be arranged by calling the same tour number at least 48 hours in advance. (See DALLAS—INDUSTRY TOURS, p. 69)

ANNUAL EVENTS

APRIL

NORTH TEXAS JAZZ FESTIVAL • 800-ADDISON (800-233-4766) • www.addisontexas.net • National and local jazz artists perform during this weeklong festival. During the day, the best local bands, combos, and jazz groups from the nation's leading schools and universities perform. At night, top Grammy-nominated artists and other pro headliners take over.

MAY

ANNUAL TASTE OF ADDISON • 800-ADDISON (800-233-4766) • www.addisontexas.net • Sometimes known as the Addison Rhythm and Chews, the main feature of this festival, held next to the Addison Conference & Theatre Centre, is the generous reduced-price tastings from about 50 of the town's restaurants. Continuous entertainment, carnival rides, midway, arts and crafts, children's activities, and a car show round it out.

JUNE

SHAKESPEARE FESTIVAL OF DALLAS IN ADDISON • 800-ADDISON (800-233-4766) • www.addisontexas.net • Three free nights of Shakespeare under the stars in the Addison Arts and Events District. (See DALLAS—ANNUAL EVENTS, p. 124)

JULY

SPIKEFEST • 888-3VOLLEY (888-356-5539) • Volleyball is the second most popular team sport in the United States, second only to basketball, and this is the largest amateur grass court volleyball tournament in the country. Over 500 men's, women's, and coed teams compete in this weekend event at every level from beginners to just a hair below professional. One of the side events is a speed spike contest, with the speed of the strikes measured with a radar gun.

SEPTEMBER

ADDISON'S OKTOBERFEST • 800-ADDISON (800-233-4766) • www.addisontexas.net • Oktoberfest in September? Yes, to coincide with the opening of the world's best known Oktoberfest in Munich, Germany. An authentic recreation of the Munich event, it features four days of family-oriented entertainment. Authentic German food, beer and wine, "oompah" music, folk dancing, and other entertainment follow the official opening ceremony of the tapping of the first keg of Oktoberfest beer. Sing-alongs, yodeling, *schuplatting*, arts and crafts, carnival rides and midway games, and children's activities.

SHOPPING

GALLERIA MALL
(See DALLAS—SHOPPING, p. 129)

DISCOUNT MODEL TRAINS
4641 Ratliff Ln. (75001) off Addison Rd., two blocks north of Keller Springs Rd. • 972-931-8135 or 800-387-2460 • W

With around 60,000 items in stock from more than 600 manufacturers, in scale models from tiny 2-Scale (1/220th size) to G-Scale (1/22nd size), everything you need to begin or expand your personal railroad is available here. In other words, this is a shopping paradise for the model train hobbyist. But, watch out, if you're not a model train buff, dropping into this store is known to give even casual shoppers train fever. All at discount prices.

KITTRELL/RIFFKIND ART GLASS
5100 Belt Line, #820 (75254), in The Village on the Parkway • 972-239-7957 or 888-865-2228 • W+ • www.kittrellriffking.com

The handmade art glass works of more than 300 North American artists are on display and for sale here. This includes items such as jewelry, goblets, delicate perfume bottles, vases, wall pieces, stained glass, and unique sculptures.

THE UNLIMITED LIMITED ANTIQUES MALL

15201 Midway Rd. (75001) • 972-490-4085 • W+ •
www.antiquelandusa/unlimited

More than two hundred dealers are located under one roof in this 40,000 sq. ft. building selling antiques, classic furniture, collectibles, and artwork. The Showcase Gallery consists of about 135 showcases displaying "museum quality" antiques.

SAMPLING OF ADDISON RESTAURANTS

Dinner for one, excluding drinks, tax, and tip: $ = up to $16, $$ = $16–$30, $$$ = $31–$50, $$$$ = over $50. It is strongly suggested that you make a reservation in those restaurants that take them, especially on weekends and holidays.

ADDISON CAFÉ ($$–$$$)

5290 Belt Line #108 (75001), at Montfort, east of Tollway •
972-991-8824 • Lunch, Monday–Friday; dinner, seven days •
Cr. • W+

This café offers French continental cuisine in a romantic bistro setting that belies its place in a strip shopping center. Among the fish entrées available are sea bass, filet of sole, salmon, and a house specialty, roasted lobster. Meat entrées include steaks and sautéed tournedos of beef in bordelaise sauce, plus a variety of classic French versions of lamb, veal, chicken, duck, and rabbit. Reservations suggested. Lounge.

ARTHUR'S ($$–$$$)

15175 Quorum Dr. (75248) • 972-385-0800 • Dinner only, seven days • Cr. • W+

A mainstay in Dallas for years, Arthur's has moved north to a prime location in Addison where the years of the culinary traditions are carried on. One tradition is a house specialty of *tournedos Rossini* in which the beef filet is enhanced with black truffles, *foie gras*, and a bordelaise sauce. Other entrées on the mostly continental menu range from duck to sea bass. In addition to the main dining room, there are several intimate private dining rooms for two or four. Bar.

BLUE MESA GRILL ($–$$)

5100 Belt Line (75240), at Tollway in The Village on the Parkway •
972-934-0165 • Lunch and dinner, seven days • Cr. • W+ •
www.bluemesagrill.com

The Blue Mesa may be located at the southeast junction of the Tollway and Belt Line, but both the decor and the food are contemporary Southwestern. For a taste of this distinctive and innovative Santa Fe cuisine, try some of the sampler appetizers or entrees. The Mesa Sampler appetizer, for example, consists of caramelized onion-basil quesadilla, New Mesa Nachos, and chicken *taquitos*. The *Churrascarita* Sampler includes grilled steak and chicken skewers, Mesa Panna bread, *taquitos*, and smoky black bean Adobe Pie. The Seafood Mixed Grill entrée includes a skewer of jumbo shrimp, grilled red chile salmon, a blue crab *enchilada veracruzano*, and ginger rice. Locally popular Sunday brunch buffet. Signature drink from the bar is the blue margarita, and its Happy Hour has won awards from several local publications as the best in town, including "the best free meal" for the food served at Happy Hour. Other locations in Dallas (7700 W. Northwest Highway), Fort Worth (1600 S. University), and Plano (8200 Dallas Parkway).

CHAMBERLAIN'S FISH MARKET GRILL ($$–$$$)

4525 Belt Line Rd. (75001), at Midway • 972-503-FISH (503-3474) • Lunch, Monday–Friday; dinner, seven days • Cr. • W+ •

Chef Richard Chamberlain decided to expand beyond the steaks and other meat entrées at his highly acclaimed chop house (see below), so he opened this fish house just about a mile down the road. Entrées range from a crispy fried seafood combination, with shrimp, scallops, and redfish, to roasted and grilled fresh fish of the day, and specialties like *cioppino*, a seafood stew with mussels, clams, shrimp, scallops, and fresh fish. There is also a variety of lobster dishes made from Maine lobsters. Bar.

CHAMBERLAIN'S STEAK & CHOP HOUSE ($$–$$$)

5330 Belt Line (75240), east of Tollway between Montfort and Prestonwood • 972-934-2467 • Dinner, seven days • Cr. • W+ • www.chamberlainsrestaurant.com

The decor of warm woods and original 1930s lithographs establish the classic chophouse ambiance, and the menu created by the chef-owner fulfills this image. Naturally, the list of entrées is heavy on beef. Steak options range from a petite filet mignon to a 24-oz. porterhouse. Pork, lamb and veal chops, chicken, and some seafood are also on the menu, plus a mixed wild game grill with prime beef, elk, and pheasant sausage brochette. Bar. Valet parking available.

CHOW THAI ADDISON ($–$$)

5290 Belt Line Rd. (75240), in Prestonwood Place, east of Tollway • 972-960-2999 • Lunch and dinner, seven days • Cr. • W+ • www.chowthai.com

The extensive menu can be overwhelming, especially if you're not familiar with authentic Thai cuisine. If this is the case, a good way to start is with the Thai Sampler appetizer, which includes Thai *sate*, fried shrimp rolls, crab cakes, and both shrimp and vegetable tempura. Among the more popular entrées are *Pad Thai* and the curry dishes. For dessert, any of the mango offerings will make an excellent top-off for your meal. Bar.

DREAM CAFÉ ($–$$)

5100 Belt Line #208 (75240), in The Village on the Parkway, east of Tollway • 972-503-7326 • Breakfast, lunch, and dinner, seven days • Cr. • W+ • www.thedreamcafe.com

In this unpretentious café, the emphasis in the preparation of the food is on organic and natural ingredients. The main entrées on the menu are listed under the simple term "big." And they are BIG. Among the wide variety of choices are Gilroy Chicken and the Garden Stir Fry. Gilroy Chicken is a pan-seared chicken breast smothered with sautéed artichokes, capers, basil tomatoes, and white wine and served with grilled vegetables and garlic mashed potatoes. The Garden Stir Fry gives you the choice of chicken, tofu, or tempeh sautéed with vegetables in a soy-ginger sauce, served with brown rice. Small play area for the kids. Another location in Dallas (2800 Routh St, #170).

FERRARI'S ITALIAN VILLA ($$–$$$)

14831 Midway (75244) • 972-980-9898 • Lunch, Monday–Friday; dinner, seven days • Cr. • W+ • www.ferrarisrestaurant.com

In contrast to the Americanized versions of Italian cuisine served in the chain "Italian" restaurants, traditional Italian recipes are the mainstay in family-owned and operated Ferrari's. In this restaurant, since the Farrari family is from Sardinia, an island in the Mediterranean Sea, the menu features authentic Mediterranean seafood entrées such as Halibut Mediterranean made with capers, basil, garlic, onions, white wine, and sun-dried tomatoes. Classic veal entrées are also on the menu here, ranging from *saltimbocca alla Romana*, with prosciutto, sage, and Italian herbs, and the popular grilled USDA prime veal chop made with Parma ham and mozzarella. Bar.

FOGO DE CHÃO ($$–$$$)

4300 Belt Line (75001), at Midway • 972-503-7300 • Lunch and dinner, seven days • Cr. • W+ • www.fagodechao.com

This is heaven on earth for the serious meat eater. Fogo de Chão (pronounced fo-go dèe shown) carries on the "Churrasco" tradition of the gauchos of Southern Brazil, who pierced large pieces of meat and slowly cooked them over open flamed pits. Be hungry, because it's all you can eat of a variety of rotisserie-cooked beef, lamb, pork, chicken, and sausages, served tableside at your beck and call by gaucho-clad waiters. To round out the meal, there's a buffet of salads, vegetables, and side dishes such as rice and fried bananas. Fixed prices of around $25 for lunch, $39 for dinner.

LOMBARDI MARE ($$–$$$)

5100 Belt Line (75254), at Montfort in The Village on the Parkway •
972-503-1233 • Lunch, Monday–Friday; dinner, Monday–Saturday.
Closed Sunday • Cr. • W+ • www.lombardimare.com

Denizens of the sea dominate the décor here, including bowls of live
goldfish dangling above the bar. And the best of the sea is on the menu,
which features entrées like grilled or sautéed Dover sole, baked Mediterranean turbot, oven-roasted Mediterranean sea bream, and salmon
Wellington. Pasta dishes include sautéed Maine lobster on linguini. Live
music on weekend evenings.

MAY DRAGON ($$–$$$)

4848 Belt Line (75240), west of Tollway at Inwood • 392-9998 •
Lunch and dinner, seven days • Cr. • W • www.maydragon.com

An upscale Chinese restaurant with the reputation of being one of the
best in the Metroplex. The extensive menu offers entrées in a variety of
cuisines from Cantonese to Szechuan, all presented in a tradition of fine
dining. All the Americanized Chinese dishes are available, plus such authentic specialties as Peking-style roast pork and Chinese dumplings.
The May Dragon Combination is a sizzling platter entrée that includes
shrimp, scallops, flank steak, chicken, and roast pork served with Chinese vegetables. If you want to participate, you can "roll your own" appetizer of rolls made from lettuce, Asian pancakes, or rice paper that you fill
with shrimp, chicken, beef, pork, and vegetables. Bar. Piano player Friday–Saturday evenings.

MI PIACI RISTORANTE ITALIANO ($$–$$$)

14854 Montfort (75240), east of Tollway, south of Belt Line •
972-934-8424 • Lunch, Monday–Friday; dinner, Monday–Saturday.
Closed Sunday • Cr. • W+ • www.mipiaci.com

No shortcuts here. They make their own pasta and, since the emphasis
is on Northern Italian cuisine, it's made according to the recipe used at
home by the women of Bologna, a city known for its culinary skills. They
also cure their own meats and use imported pasta and risotto (rice) when
either serves the entrée better. The upscale menu features authentic regional specialties such as *risotto con salsiccia* with Italian rice with roasted
potatoes, homemade Italian sausage, and *rapini*; and *brodetto alla Livornese* of
lobster, shrimp, clams, and mussels in a seafood broth. One restaurant
wall is glass overlooking a small lake. Bar. Valet parking available.

MORTON'S OF CHICAGO ($$$–$$$$)

14831 Midway (75001), between Belt Line and Spring Valley Rd. •
972-233-5858 • Dinner only, seven days • Cr. • W+ •
www.mortons.com

It's part of a chain of steak houses, but a very upscale chain with décor and service that make you feel like you're dining in your private club. There's a written menu, but normally you won't need one, since your server will proclaim the whole list—usually flawlessly and with a dramatic flair—while displaying samples of the various types and sizes of steaks, with some lamb, chicken, lobster (the most popular order after steaks) and seafood choices. The steaks, which are prime cut, can border on the gargantuan and, since the vegetables and everything else are extra, the size of the bill can match them. A great choice for an expense account dinner or a splurge. Bar. Another Metroplex location in Dallas (501 Elm St.)

REMINGTON'S SEAFOOD GRILL ($–$$)

4580 Belt Line (75244), west of Tollway at Inwood • 972-386-0122 • Lunch, Monday–Friday; dinner, seven days • Cr. • W+

Generous serving of consistently good seafood is the reputation this restaurant has built since it first opened in 1978. Specialties include scrod and snapper and soft-shell crabs in season. Among the selection of fried entrées is the pecan-crusted catfish fillet and fried shrimp or oysters. If you prefer your seafood broiled, one choice is the Broiled Seafood Sampler with scrod, sea scallops, and Gulf shrimp. Children's menu. Lounge.

A SAMPLING OF ADDISON CLUBS AND BARS

ADDISON IMPROV COMEDY CLUB

4980 Belt Line # 250 (75240) • 972-404-8501 • Admission • Cr. • W

A comedy club featuring national comedians on the club circuit and live improvisation and sketch comedy. Shows Wednesday–Sunday. Restaurant and bar.

PETE'S DUELING PIANO BAR

4980 Belt Line #200 (75240) • 972-726-7383 • Cr. • W

If you wear out your laugh track listening to the comedians at the Improv, you can wander down a few doors and exercise your vocal cords in this popular bar. Teams of piano players keep the sing-along, clap-along music going nightly Wednesday-Saturday.

SAMBUCCA MEDITERRANEAN JAZZ CAFÉ

15207 Addison Rd. (75248), west of Tollway between Belt Line and Keller Springs Rd. • 972-385-8455 • Cr. • W+ • www.sambuccajazzcafe.com

The name says café, and it is open for lunch, but this is more a supper club where you dine as you enjoy live jazz. The swinging sounds come out at night, every night, with the musicians spanning the many styles of jazz. No cover, but a minimum on food per person at each table, so check out the menu offerings that include everything from lobster-stuffed filet to chicken, seafood, and pasta. Valet parking available. (Another Metroplex location in Dallas (2618 Elm in Deep Ellum).

A SAMPLING OF ADDISON ACCOMMODATIONS

For a double room or suite: $ = up to $80, $$ = $81–$120, $$$ = $121–$180, $$$$ = $181–$280, $$$$$ = over $280. **Room tax 13%.**

Unless otherwise noted: check in at 3:00 p.m.; check out by noon. Unless otherwise noted, all these accommodations have handicapped rooms/facilities and no-smoking rooms. Check on visual alarms and other safety facilities for the hearing impaired when making reservation. Most accommodations permit children to stay free in room with parents. There may be a charge if this requires setting up an extra bed.

COMFORT INN NEAR THE GALLERIA ($–$$ + 13%)
14975 Landmark (75240) • 972-701-0881

There are 85 rooms and one suite on the two floors of this inn. Pets OK. Free local calls. Cable TV with free premium and pay channels. Coffeemaker in room and free coffee in lobby. Dataport in room. Outdoor pool and hot tub. Fitness room. Self-service laundry and one-day dry cleaning. Free continental breakfast. Nearby restaurants will deliver. Business services available. Free outdoor self-parking. Free transportation within a five-mile radius.

COURTYARD BY MARRIOTT ADDISON MIDWAY ($$–$$$$ + 13%)
4165 Proton Drive (75001) • 972-490-7390 • www.courtyard.com

This two-story Courtyard has 145 units, including 14 suites. Cable TV with free premium channel and pay channels. Coffeemaker in room and free coffee in lobby. Dataport in room. Outdoor pool and whirlpool. Fitness room. Gift shop. Self-service laundry and one-day dry cleaning. Coffee shop open for breakfast. Bar. Business services available. Free outdoor self-parking. Free transportation within a three-mile radius. About one mile from Addison's restaurant row.

CROWNE PLAZA NORTH DALLAS ($$$ + 13%)
14315 Midway (75001) • 972-980-8877 • www.crowneplaza.com

There are 411 rooms and 18 suites in this four-story hotel. Concierge floor with extra amenities. Pets OK ($25 fee plus $100 deposit). Cable TV with free premium and pay channels. Coffeemaker in room. Dataport in room. Bell service. Outdoor heated pool and whirlpool. Fitness room. Concierge services available. Gift Shop. Self-service laundry and one-day dry cleaning. Two restaurants, one full-service. Room service. Lounge. Business center. Free outdoor self-parking. Free transportation to nearby shopping. Within walking distance of the Galleria.

HILTON GARDEN INN/ADDISON ($$–$$$ + 13%)

4090 Belt Line Rd. (75001), at Runyon • 972-233-8000 • www.additontx.gardeninn.com

There are 82 rooms and 14 suites in this three-story inn. Cable TV with free premium and pay channels. Coffeemaker in room and free coffee in lobby. Dataport in room. Heated outdoor pool and hot tub. Fitness room. Self-service laundry and one-day dry cleaning. Café serving breakfast. Bar (beer and wine only). Business services available. Free outdoor self-parking. Free transportation within a 4-mile radius. Refrigerator and microwave in each room.

HOLIDAY INN EXPRESS ($$ + 13%)

4103 Belt Line (75001) • 972-991-8888 • www.sixcontinentshotels.com

This two-story inn has 115 rooms. Exterior access to rooms. Free local calls. Cable TV with free premium and pay channels. Coffeemaker in room. Dataport in room. Outdoor pool. Fitness room. Self-service laundry and one-day dry cleaning. Business services available. Free outdoor self-parking. Free transportation within 3-mile radius.

HOTEL INTER-CONTINENTAL DALLAS ($$$$–$$$$$ + 13%)

15201 Dallas Pkwy. (75001) • 972-386-6000 • www.interconti.com

There are 498 rooms and 29 one- and two-bedroom suites on the fifteen floors of this hotel. Concierge section with extra amenities. Cable TV with free premium and pay channels. Coffeemaker in room. Dataport in room. Bell service. Indoor heated pool and outdoor pool. Whirlpool. Sauna. Fitness facilities including sports court, lighted tennis courts and racquetball courts (fee). Guest memberships available for golf (fee). Concierge services available. Barber and beauty shop and shopping arcade. Gift shop. Self-service laundry and one-day dry cleaning. Three restaurants. Room service. Lounge. Convention facilities and business center. Free outdoor self-parking or valet parking (fee). Free transportation within 3-mile radius.

HOMEWOOD SUITES BY HILTON/ADDISON ($–$$$ + 13%)

4451 Belt Line (75001) • 972-788-1342 or 800-225-5466 (reservations) • www.homewood-suites.com

There are 120 one- and two-bedroom suites in this three-story lodging. Pets OK ($75 fee). Inside and outside access to rooms. Cable TV with free premium channels. Coffeemaker in room and free coffee in lobby. Dataport in room. Outdoor heated pool and hot tub. Guest membership available in local fitness club. Gift shop. Self-service laundry and one-day dry cleaning. Free buffet breakfast. Free social hour Monday–Thursday evenings. Several nearby restaurants deliver. Business services available. Free outdoor self-parking. Free transportation within a 5-mile radius. VCR in rooms with video rentals available.

LAQUINTA INN AND SUITES BY THE GALLERIA/ ADDISON ($–$$$ + 13%)

14925 Landmark (75254) • 972-404-0004 or 800-531-5900 (reservations) • www.laquinta.com

This three-story inn has 144 rooms and eight suites. Pets OK (limited). Inside access to all but a few rooms. Free local calls. Cable TV with free premium and pay channels. Coffeemaker in room and free coffee in lobby. Dataport in room. Outdoor pool and hot tub. Self-service laundry and one-day dry cleaning. Free continental breakfast. Business services available. Free outdoor self-parking. Free weekday transportation within a 5-mile radius. Two-room suites include a sleeper sofa.

MARRIOTT QUORUM BY THE GALLERIA ($$–$$$$$ + 13%)

14901 Dallas Pkwy. (75254) • 972-661-2800 or 800-811-8664 (reservations) • www.marriott.com

There are 548 rooms and 10 suites in this 12-story hotel. Concierge section with extra amenities. Cable TV. Coffeemaker in room. Dataport in room. Bell service. Indoor/outdoor heated pool, whirlpool, and sauna. Fitness room and lighted tennis court. Guest membership available in local health club. Concierge services available. Gift shop. Self-service laundry and one-day dry cleaning. Restaurant. Room service. Lounge. Conference facilities and business center. Free outdoor covered self-parking or valet parking (fee). Free transportation within a 2-mile radius.

ARLINGTON

Tarrant County • 333,000 • Area Code 817 (local calls require area code) • www.arlington.org

The first settlers here were the nine tribes of the Caddoan and Wichita Confederation, which included the Cherokee, Delaware, Biloxi, Caddo, and Waco. Over the centuries their agricultural settlements had been visited by several European explorers, including Cabeza de Vaca in 1535 and LaSalle in 1687. But in a 1841 battle they lost their lands to the Texas Rangers. Here, in 1843, Sam Houston, president of the Republic of Texas, signed his new nation's first peace treaty with the Confederation, a treaty that moved them farther west and set up a boundary between them and the new white settlers.

Trading posts soon sprang up along that boundary. One such post was established by Col. Middleton Tate Johnson, who arrived in 1846 to take command of the Texas Rangers at what became known as Johnson Station. He soon bought a large piece of land and built a plantation. His large home became a stage stop for the Overland Stage route that connected Dallas, Fort Worth, and Austin. Johnson founded the site for Fort Worth and donated the land for its courthouse, earning him the historical recognition as the Father of Tarrant County. Johnson County is also named after him.

THE COMING OF THE RAILROAD

By 1876, Dallas and Fort Worth were well enough established to warrant the Texas and Pacific Railway's decision to build a line connecting them. A mid-route depot site was selected on the prairie near Johnson Station, and soon most of the residents of Johnson Station and other small settlements in the area moved to the new depot. The first train came through in July 1876, and that depot grew into the frontier town named Arlington after Robert E. Lee's home town in Virginia.

Arlington was a typical frontier town with false-front buildings, saloons, and gambling. In the 1890s a water well was drilled in the middle of the town, but instead of drinking water, it produced mineral water, which started a local mineral crystal industry that lasted into the 1930s.

ARLINGTON

It was not long before the new town began passing ordinances, such as the prohibition of carrying firearms. In 1902, an alcohol prohibition went into effect. Arlington is still semi-dry today. Beer can be sold in grocery stores and restaurants and bars can serve liquor, but there are no package liquor stores in the city.

GROWTH OF THE ENTERTAINMENT
CAPITAL OF TEXAS

Agriculture was the main industry until the early 1950s, when General Motors opened an auto assembly plant that brought in other industries. Then, in 1961, Six Flags Over Texas opened as the largest amusement park in the state. Still going strong, it now annually draws more than three million visitors.

The choice of Arlington for this theme park was a natural, since it had long been an entertainment center between Dallas and Fort Worth. In the early 1930s people rode the Interurban trains here to bet on the horses at Arlington Downs Race Track and gamble at places like the Top-O-Hill Terrace. Those two early attractions have long since disappeared, but Arlington's reputation as the Midway of the Metroplex continued when the city became home of a major league baseball team in 1971, was enhanced by the 1983 opening of the Wet'N'Wild water park (now called Six Flags Hurricane Harbor) and was solidified by the opening of The Ballpark at Arlington in 1994, the new home of the Texas Rangers and an entertainment complex of itself.

The result is that Arlington now lays claim to being THE Entertainment Capital of Texas.

FREE VISITOR SERVICES

ARLINGTON VISITOR INFORMATION CENTER AND GIFT SHOP

1905 E. Randol Mill (76011) • 817-461-3888 or 800-342-4305 • W+ • www.arlington.org

Free brochures, maps, and information on sightseeing, lodging, dining, and shopping in Arlington and the Metroplex can be obtained here in person or by a mail or phone request (e-mail requests to **visitinfo@acvb.org**). Travel counselors are available Monday through Saturday, 9:00 a.m. to 5:00 p.m., and Sunday from noon to 4:00 p.m. Discount coupons are also available for some attractions. Gift shop.

ARLINGTON CONVENTION AND VISITORS BUREAU

1905 E. Randol Mill (76011) • 817-265-7721 or 800-433-5374 • W+ • www.arlington.org

Upstairs above the Information Center. Although this is more the "big picture" outfit that handles conventions and major events, it also responds to individual mail and phone requests and inquiries from visitors to its website.

THE TROLLEY—ARLINGTON'S ENTERTAINMENT CONNECTION

Schedule and route information 214-668-8280 • W • www.arlingtontrolley.com

If you stay at a participating hotel (and all the major hotels participate), you can get a free trolley pass to get around the city's famous three-square-mile entertainment district. That's not just one trolley but a fleet of air-conditioned red trolley buses that shuttle at frequent intervals between the lodgings and the major attractions, so you won't have to

Arlington Entertainment District

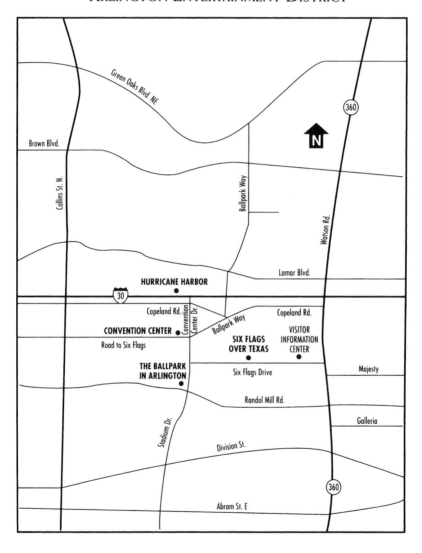

drive or pay for parking. On game days, it also provides service to The Ballpark at Arlington. Check with your hotel's front desk.

HELPFUL LOCAL PUBLICATIONS

Current information about Arlington events, activities, nightlife, theater, movies, and dining are listed in *Star Time*, published every Friday in the *Arlington Star-Telegram*. The *Dallas Morning News* and the *Fort Worth Star-Telegram* are also good sources, and those two daily papers sponsor a combined website at **www.dfw.com** that includes entertainment guides. Other sources to check are the weekly *Dallas Observer*, which is available free at restaurants and tourist attractions throughout the Dallas area; and the monthly *D Magazine* and *Texas Monthly Magazine* available on newsstands.

COMMERCIAL TOURS

THE BALLPARK AT ARLINGTON TOUR
1000 Ballpark Way (76011) • 817-273-5098 • Adults, $5; seniors, $4; youth 4–18, $3 • W variable

The tour visit schedule depends on the Texas Rangers game operations. The 50-minute behind-the-scenes guided tour may include a visit to the clubhouse, the press box, the owner's suite, and the dugout and batting cages. When the team is away, tours are on the hour, 9:00 a.m. to 4:00 p.m. Monday through Friday, 10:00 a.m. to 4:00 p.m. on Saturday, and noon to 4:00 p.m. on Sunday. On nights when home games are scheduled, tours are run on the hour from 9:00 to noon, Monday through Friday, and 10:00 to noon on Saturday. No tours are conducted on days when home games are played during the day or on Sundays. Tickets are available in the lobby of the Legends of the Game Museum. A combination ticket for the tour and a visit to the Legends of the Game Baseball Museum (see MUSEUMS, p. 44) costs about $10 for adults, $8 for seniors, and $6 for youth 4–18.

SELF-GUIDED TOURS

HISTORIC DRIVING TOUR BROCHURE
The Arlington Planning Department offers a map outlining two driving and walking tours of sites and buildings important in Arlington's history.

The map is available free at the Visitor Information Center or from the Planning Department (817-459-6650).

BIRD'S-EYE VIEW

THE OIL DERRICK AT SIX FLAGS

Requires paid admission to **Six Flags Over Texas.** (See FAMILY FUN AND KID STUFF, p. 49)

From the observation deck, on the top of this 300-foot tower, you can orient yourself to the layout of both this park and its water park companion across the highway, as well as enjoy a bird's-eye view of all of Arlington, much of the mid-cities, and the skylines of Dallas and Fort Worth. If you look carefully you may even be able to spot your car in the monster parking lot. Elevator.

HISTORIC PLACES

HISTORIC HOMES

There are a number of well-preserved homes in the city that were built in the late 1800s and early 1900s. The following are a few examples. Many of the houses along West Abram Street, from the 700 to 1600 block, have been renovated to provide a relatively intact street scene from the early 1900s. The **McKinley-Woodard House** at 400 East 1st was built in 1890, and the **Ghormley-Arnold House** at 404 was built in 1906. The **Cooper House** at 211 Willis was built as a Classical Revival residence in 1878 and later moved to this location, where it served as the city library until 1962 and is now the home of the Arlington Women's Club. Also built in the late 1800s was the **Hutchenson-Smith Home** at 312 Oak, which was put up in 1886 as part of the original town site and is listed on the National Register of Historic Places. Most of these homes are private residences not open to the public.

MUSEUMS AND PUBLIC ART GALLERIES

ARLINGTON MUSEUM OF ART

201 W. Main at Pecan (76010) • 817-275-4600 • Wednesday, 10–8; Thursday–Saturday, 10–5 • Free • W • www.arlingtonmuseum.org

Housed in a 1950s art moderne building in downtown Arlington, this small nonprofit museum showcases Texas contemporary art with exhibits of the works of emerging and established Texas artists. It annually features four major exhibitions in the one large downstairs gallery and monthly revolving exhibitions in three smaller galleries on the mezzanine level. Along with traditional media, visitors may encounter digital and video productions and even performance art. Guided tours may be scheduled by calling in advance; self-guided and audio tours are another option. Gift shop.

CENTER FOR RESEARCH AND CONTEMPORARY ART

University of Texas at Arlington, Fine Arts Building, Cooper at Border • 817-272-3143 • Monday–Friday, 10–5; Thursday evening, 5–8; Saturday, 12–5. Closed Sunday • Free • W

This gallery features national artists in all media, ranging from painting to sculpture and performance art. Gallery 171, a student-run gallery, is next door. It is also free, but hours vary. (See COLLEGE CAMPUSES OF INTEREST TO VISITORS, p. 46)

FIELDER HOUSE MUSEUM

1616 W. Abram at Fielder (76013) • 817-460-4001 • Wednesday–Saturday, 10–2; Sunday, 1:30–4:30 or by appointment • Free (donations accepted) • W ground floor only, ramp at side • www.fielderhouse.org (Arlington Historical Society)

When constructed in 1914, this two-story prairie-style home overlooked James Park Fielder's 215-acre farm. One of the first brick homes in the area, it was the first with indoor plumbing. The museum now houses the permanent collection of the Arlington Historical Society, with exhibits that include a replica of a general store, an early 1900s barbershop, a period bedroom, and a basement with an old home laundry and a scale model of a locomotive that used to run between Dallas and Fort Worth. Other exhibits highlight area history, and the museum frequently hosts traveling exhibits. Parking in rear. Picnic tables.

HERITAGE CENTER AT JOHNSON CREEK

512 W. Arkansas • 817-460-4001 • Open by appointment • Donation • W • www.fielderhouse.org (Arlington Historical Society)

Several important Arlington landmarks are at this center, including two log cabins originally built by early settlers and moved to this site. These were used as a one-room schoolhouse and a barn. Two small way stations for the Interurban Trolley, which ran between Dallas and Fort Worth from 1902 to 1936, and the well bowl from the mineral well that once stood in the center of the city are also here. Also at this site are two small cemeteries. In one are buried Col. Middleton Tate Johnson, the Father of Tarrant County, his wife and sons, and a number of prominent early settlers. The other is Arlington's earliest and only African-American cemetery, used until the 1950s.

LEGENDS OF THE GAME BASEBALL MUSEUM AND CHILDREN'S LEARNING CENTER

The Ballpark at Arlington, 1000 Ballpark Way (76011) • 817-273-5099 • Seasonal hours. April–October: Monday–Saturday, 9–6:30; Sunday, noon to 4. Earlier closing rest of year. Call • Adults, $6; seniors, $5; youth 4–18, $4. Combination tickets available for museum admission and ballpark tour • W variable • www.museum.texasrangers.com

The three-story museum covers the history of baseball from an early eighteenth-century version of the game to the present. Exhibits include items from the Texas League, the National Negro League, and the All-American Girls Professional Baseball League, as well as the history of the Texas Rangers, the Ballpark's home team. Among the many exhibits are more than a hundred artifacts on loan from the National Baseball Hall of Fame and Museum in Cooperstown, New York. These change, but typically you might see such baseball treasures as jerseys worn by Ty Cobb and Babe Ruth, bats used by Lou Gehrig and Ted Williams, and Joe DiMaggio's glove. Fans can sit in a booth and create a broadcast of themselves doing a play-by-play for a Rangers game (fee). Upstairs, the Interactive Learning Center is designed to offer children (but it's open to kids of all ages) the opportunity to learn why a curve ball curves and other fascinating facts in the areas of communications, math, science, geography, and history through interactive computer programs and activities related to baseball. This is the first such learning center offered by a major league baseball team. Gift shops. Parking in B Lot is free on non-game days.

RIVER LEGACY LIVING SCIENCE CENTER

703 N.W. Green Oaks (76006), at north end of Cooper St. in River Legacy Parks • 817-860-6752 • Tuesday–Saturday, 9–5; closed Sunday–Monday • Adults, $2; children 2–18, $1; under 2 free • W+ • www.riverlegacy.org

The Center, set in the 1,200-acre River Legacy Parks, is inhabited by more than 400 species of plants and animals. It features ways for children and other visitors to interact with living exhibits of insects, fish, amphibians, reptiles, and other native wildlife. Fitting in perfectly with the preservation-of-nature themes illustrated inside, the building itself is an attraction for the ecology-minded. Designed to resemble the wingspan of a huge bird, it has been described as "a dazzling example of 'sustainable design'—the use of energy-efficient methods and minimal materials in construction." This means that recycling and recycled materials were used in every possible way; even the dark green tiles in the restrooms are made from crushed windshield and bottle glass, and the patio decking is of reclaimed plastic and wastewood. A trail guide brochure is available for a self-guided tour of the Center's Discovery Trail, and every Saturday at 9:30 a.m. (rain or shine) a naturalist leads a nature walk. Saturday morning is also bird-watching time. Call for schedule. Among the many

Center activities is the popular annual fund-raising Cardboard Boat Regatta. Usually held in April, it features around a hundred amateur-built cardboard boats, rowed by crews of up to ten challenging the wave pool at Six Flags Hurricane Harbor. Gift shop.

UNIVERSITY OF TEXAS AT ARLINGTON SPECIAL COLLECTIONS

Central Library, 702 College (76019) • 817-272-3393 • Monday–Friday, 8–5; Saturday, 10–5 • Free • W+

With the exception of the collections at the state capital, this is the largest collection of manuscripts and documents on Texas. It includes a cartography library, Texas writers' manuscripts, and a large collection of manuscripts, newspapers, books, and photographs on Mexican political history. The Texas Labor Archives are also here, but these archives and some of the other collections are restricted to serious researchers. Tours can be arranged for a minimum of ten. (See COLLEGE CAMPUSES OF INTEREST TO VISITORS, p. 46)

OUTDOORS

ARLINGTON PARKS

Parks and Recreation Department • P.O. Box 231 (76004-0231) • 817-459-5474 • W variable • www.ci.arlington.tx.us/park/index/html

A *Guide to Arlington Parks*, available from the Parks and Recreation Department, gives maps and details on the more than seventy parks, six multipurpose centers, and six public swimming pools that offer facilities for hiking, rollerblading, biking, boating, fishing, swimming, picnicking, golf, tennis, and a variety of other sports and activities. Among the major parks are the **River Legacy Parks** (701 N.W. Green Oaks and 1651 N.E. Green Oaks), which combine to form 1,200 acres of natural landscape winding along the Trinity River in the heart of north Arlington. Facilities include more than eight miles of paved trails winding through thick forest and expansive greenbelts. It is also the home of the Living Science Center (See MUSEUMS, p. 44). **Randol Mill Park** (1901 W. Randol Mill) is a 149-acre park with nature trails, tennis courts, and a fishing pond and picnic areas; and **Veterans Park** (3600 W. Arkansas) features a band shell, wildlife areas, playing fields, hiking and equestrian trails, and the water conserving Xeriscape Gardens.

LAKE ARLINGTON

6300 W. Arkansas (76016) • 817-451-6860 • W variable

This 2,250-acre lake on the western edge of the city is popular for boating, sailing, water skiing, and fishing. On its shoreline are Richard Simpson

Park and Bowman Springs Park, which offer boat launching sites and picnic areas. A map, *Guide to Lake Arlington,* is available from the Parks and Recreation Department, P.O. Box 231, 76004-0231 (817-459-5474).

COLLEGE CAMPUSES OF INTEREST TO VISITORS

UNIVERSITY OF TEXAS AT ARLINGTON (UTA)
703 W. Nedderman (76019) • 817-272-2222 • W+ variable

With an enrollment of more than 26,000 students from 80 nations studying in nine academic units, UTA is the second-largest component in the mammoth University of Texas system. The more than 80 buildings on campus trace its history back through a succession of military and vocational schools that occupied the site over the years, to the one wood-frame building of Arlington College, which was founded in 1895 with 75 students. Visitors are welcome at intercollegiate sports events at **Maverick Stadium** and other athletic facilities. In the Fine Arts complex at Cooper and Second are the Music Department's **Irons Recital Hall, Mainstage Theatre, Studio Theatre**, and the university's art galleries (see MUSEUMS, p. 43 and p. 45). **The Planetarium** in the Physics Department (817-272-2467) offers a show every first Friday of the month (admission). Some of the special collections at the **UTA Library** are open to visitors (see MUSEUMS, pp. 43 and 45). There is limited visitor parking near most buildings. Pick up a visitor's pass at the UTA Police Department at 2nd and Davis. Campus tours lasting up to an hour are available with a week's notice. With a week's notice, tours of the UTA Engineering Lab are also available for a minimum of 10 visitors (817-272-2571).

MUSIC AND PERFORMING ARTS

ARLINGTON COMMUNITY BAND
www.geocities.com/arlband

An assortment of professional musicians, music teachers, and others make up this band that performs free concerts featuring lively patriotic music, show tunes, and other band arrangements, at various locations throughout the city. Most concerts are during spring and summer. Check Visitor Information Center or website for dates and locations.

JOHNNIE HIGH'S COUNTRY MUSIC REVUE
Arlington Music Hall, 224 N. Center at Division (76011) • Metro 817-226-4400 or 800-540-5127 • Adults, $14; children 12 and under, $7 • W variable • www.mid-cities.com/cmr

Johnnie High has been putting on this musical revue for around thirty years and it has been voted Best Live Country Music Show of the Year several times by the National Organization of Country Music Associations. His troupe—a seven-member band and 25 singers, dancers, and entertainers—perform hand-clapping country tunes with shows Friday and Saturday nights at 7:30 p.m. Special shows on holidays include the 21 Nights of Christmas shows in December. Free parking. Snack bar and gift shop.

THEATRE ARLINGTON

305 W. Main (76010) • Box office 817-275-7661 or Metro 817-261-9628 • Admission • W • www.theatrearlington.org

This not-for-profit community theater, with a professional director and staff, usually puts on seven mainstage productions and two children's theater productions each year in the intimate 200-seat proscenium theater. In the more than thirty years of continuous operation, the theater has entertained more than 400,000 patrons. Productions range from award-winning plays to musicals. Most shows run four to six weeks with evening performances Thursday–Saturday and a Sunday matinee. Tickets range from $14 to $18 for the seven regular season shows and $8 for the children's theater productions.

UNIVERSITY OF TEXAS AT ARLINGTON CONCERTS AND THEATER

Fine Arts Building • W variable

The Irons Recital Hall is the setting for concerts nearly every night during the fall and spring semesters (817-272-3471). These range from classical to jazz and instrumental to voice. Most concerts by UTA students or faculty are free. A minimum admission is charged for non-university group performances. Student and other theater groups stage a number of productions in the Mainstage and Studio Theatres (817-272-2650). Admission, $2–$5 for most performances. Call for concert and show schedules and reservations.

FAMILY FUN AND KID STUFF

ARLINGTON SKATIUM

5515 S. Cooper (76107) • 817-784-6222 • Open seven days. Call for hours • Open skating, $5–$6 • www.skatium.com

What is reportedly the largest skating center in Texas offers the choice of rollerskating, rollerblading, or speedskating. Rentals available. Spectators welcome at seasonal kids' hockey games on Monday evenings.

THE BALLPARK AFTER DARK SLEEPOVERS

Legends of the Game Baseball Museum, 1000 Ballpark Way (76011)
• 817-273-5087 (Education Curator) • W variable •
www.museum.texasrangers.com

You need a minimum of five children from grades 1 through 5 to do this, but if you can get that group together they'll be treated to an evening and following morning full of baseball activities, tours, and an overnight camp in The Ballpark at Arlington. Cost is $35 per child. One adult (no charge) is required for every five children. (Additional adults $20 each.) Available biweekly on selected Friday nights from November to May. Reservations must be scheduled at least three weeks in advance.

CREATIVE ARTS THEATRE AND SCHOOL (CATS)

1100 W. Randol Mill (76012) • 817-861-2287 or Metro
817-265-8512 • Tickets: $4–$8 (available online) • W+ •
www.creativearts.org

All productions feature young actors and technicians who come from CATS after-school performing arts school for children and youth. There are usually six productions during the school year and three more in its summer series. School-year shows usually run for several weekends with evening performances Friday and Saturday and matinees on Saturday and Sunday. The summer series shows, aimed at smaller children, are usually presented with morning and early afternoon performances. Free theater tours are available Monday–Friday, 10:30 a.m. to 6:00 p.m. Reservations are required for tours which include stops in the costume shop, dance studios and 400-seat theater, where a demonstration of theater lighting is given.

SIX FLAGS HURRICANE HARBOR

1800 E. Lamar (76006), directly across I-30 from Six Flags Over
Texas • 817-265-3356 • Open seven days, mid-May to early
September • Adults, $30; children under 48″ tall and seniors, $20;
children 2 and under free • Parking, $7; preferred parking, $10 •
www.sixflags.com

This 47-acre park offers a wide variety of water activities in 10 entertainment areas for everyone from the thrill-seekers to those who just want to float the day away. Among the dozens of slides of all sizes and heights, the one the daredevils usually go for is the *Black Hole* that starts in a space station atop a tower and zips down through 500 feet of wet black tubes. The *Surf Lagoon's* million-gallon wave pool offers body-surfers waves up to four feet. If you want something gentler you can tube the quarter-mile *Lazy River* at 3 mph or be a little more adventurous and tube the *Raging Rapids*, which takes you through six connected pools to a splash pool ending. Playground and park. Locker rooms, gift shop, tube and raft rentals. Lifeguards.

Note: Admission usually changes every year.

SIX FLAGS OVER TEXAS

2201 Road to Six Flags (76011), I-30 at Hwy. 360 • 817-640-8900 • Open seven days, mid-May to late August; weekends, March to early May and September–October; several weeks in October for Halloween Fright Fest and late November–December for Holiday in the Park (call for schedule) • Adults, $43; children under 48″ tall and seniors (55 and over), $27; under 2 free. Varying admissions Halloween and Holiday in the Park • Parking, $9 • W variable • www.sixflags.com

Open since 1961, this 205-acre theme park now attracts more than three million visitors a year to its more than 100 rides and shows, making it one of the most popular tourist attractions in the state. And it keeps visitors coming back by adding new rides and changing rides and shows every year. Everything is included in the admission price except food, souvenirs, video and concession games, and some of the special concerts.

When the park opened in 1961, it had six themed areas depicting Texas under the flags of Spain, France, Mexico, the Republic of Texas, the Confederate States of America, and the United States. Today, five more themed areas have been added to the original six: *Goodtimes Square* themed for fifties fun, *Looney Tunes USA*™ for younger kids, the Texas oil rush in *Boomtown*, roller coasters in *Gotham City*, and sensational rides like *Roaring Rapids* in the *Tower* area. Perhaps the best known of the park's major thrill rides are: *The Texas Giant*, at 14 stories, one of the world's tallest and fastest wooden roller coasters, hitting speeds over 60 mph; and the *Titan*™, a steel coaster that climbs to heights of 26 stories, towering 100 feet above the *Texas Giant*. These are just two of the dozen roller coasters in the park that compete for heart-pounding thrills. *Mr. Freeze*™, for example, reaches speeds of 70 mph in less than four seconds and after many twists and turns does it all in reverse.

For the less thrill-bent, there are (somewhat) tamer rides like *Space Shuttle America* that offers the excitement of space travel, and *Roaring Rapids*, a white-water rafting adventure. And those who want even softer thrills can ride the old-style narrow-gauge train that circles the park, view the world from the top of the *Oil Derrick* (see BIRD'S-EYE VIEW, p. 42), or attend one of the many shows ranging from stunts to music and animal acts. Concerts by well-known entertainers on selected nights. For smaller children, *Looney Tunes USA*™ has a number of rides and play activities suited to thrill them. Also for little children, and adults with a yen for nostalgia, there's the *Silver Star*, an old-fashioned carousel with 66 prancing hand-carved wooden horses.

Note: Admission usually changes every year.

SPORTS

BASEBALL

THE BALLPARK AT ARLINGTON

1000 Ballpark Way (76011) • 817-273-5222 (Texas Rangers) •
Game day general public parking, $8–$12; valet parking, $20 • W+
more than 475 spaces for wheelchairs spread across all seating levels
• www.texasrangers.com

Seating more than 49,200 on five levels for a ballgame, this red-brick-
and-granite ballpark is the home of the Texas Rangers and an attraction in
itself. On the facade are 35 cast-stone steer heads and 21 cast-stone Lone
Stars, and massive 4' x 19' architectural frieze sculptures depict scenes
from Texas history, including a cattle drive, the Alamo, oil wells, Texas
Rangers (the original ones) calling for volunteers, and baseball scenes. Located outside the 122 luxury bay suites are 67 sepia-toned murals depicting baseball's greatest players. Also in the building are the Legends of the
Game Baseball Museum and Children's Learning Center and the Sports
Legacy—The Gallery of Sports Art. (See MUSEUMS, p. 44) The Ballpark is the centerpiece of a 270-acre complex open all year long that in-
cludes a 12-acre lake with an adjoining park and recreational area and the
Rangers' Walk of Fame, which rings the entire perimeter of The Ballpark.
Among the other facilities in the complex are the Coca-Cola Sports Park,
a fan area with interactive games ranging from Tee-Ball cages to Speed
Pitch; and the Grand Slam and Timeless Treasures Gift Shops. In addition
to the usual food and beverage concessions open during games, Friday's
Front Row Sports Grill is open year round, serving lunch and dinner
daily—not just hamburgers, hot dogs, and sandwiches (in half dozen varieties) but also stone-hearth-baked pizza and *calzones* and dinner entrées
that range from grilled salmon to Kansas City strip steaks.

THE TEXAS RANGERS BASEBALL CLUB

The Ballpark at Arlington, 1000 Ballpark Way (76011) •
817-273-5100 (tickets) • www.texasrangers.com

Before he got deep into the politics that led him to the White House,
George W. Bush was a managing partner of the Texas Rangers. The team
is now a potent force in the American League and contenders against the
Dallas Cowboys for the heart of the Metroplex sports fans. They play
about 80 home games in the season from April until late September.
Tickets range from $5 for grandstand to $75 for VIP infield seats. Or, if
you want to go whole hog and take the (extended) family or entertain a
pack of friends, the plush suite rentals, including food and beverage
packages, start at $1,750 a night.

FISHING AND WATER SPORTS

(See LAKE ARLINGTON in OUTDOORS, p. 45)

GOLF

PUBLIC COURSES

CHESTER W. DITTO GOLF COURSE • 801 Brown (76011) • 817-275-5941 • 18 holes.

LAKE ARLINGTON GOLF COURSE • 1516 Green Oaks (76013) • 817-451-6101 • 18 holes.

MEADOWBROOK GOLF COURSE • 1300 E. Dugan (76010) • 817-275-0221 • 9-hole executive course.

TIERRA VERDE GOLF CLUB • 7005 Golfclub • 817-478-8500 or Metro 817-572-1300 • 18 holes.

ROCK CLIMBING

DYNO-ROCK INDOOR CLIMBING GYM

608 E. Front (76011) • 817-461-3966 • Open seven days except major holidays; hours vary • Day pass, $10 • www.dynorock.com

If you want to get up in the world, this gym offers the chance to go up a climbing wall in a safe, controlled environment. Equipment rentals available. One-hour course in basic techniques of rock climbing ($20) and advanced climbing course available by appointment.

TENNIS

ARLINGTON TENNIS CENTER

500 W. Mayfield (76014) • 817-557-5683 or Metro 817-467-0117

Twenty outdoor lighted courts. Lessons. Pro Shop. Complete locker room facilities. Call for fees.

OTHER CITY PARK TENNIS COURTS

Parks and Recreation Department • 817-459-5474

Tennis courts are available free on a first come basis in eleven city parks. Call for information.

OTHER POINTS OF INTEREST

ARLINGTON CONVENTION CENTER

1200 Ballpark Way (76011), north of The Ballpark at Arlington •
817-459-5000 or Metro 817-265-2602 • W+

In the heart of Arlington's entertainment district. In addition to meetings and conventions, this center hosts a wide variety of shows and annual events open to the public, including the Texas Indian Market, the Texas Guitar Show, Neil Sperry's Garden Show, and the Country Peddler Shows. Admission depends on event. Parking $5.

OFFBEAT

AIR COMBAT SCHOOL

921 Six Flags Drive, # 117, near entrance to Six Flags Over Texas •
817-640-1886 • $43 • www.aircombatschool.com

Here's your chance to try to be a (simulated) Top Gun. The simulation takes about an hour and half, starting with a brief ground-school orientation, vertigo training, and mission briefing and ejection seat training. (Don't worry, the ejection seat lifts only about a foot.) Then you'll suit up in complete flight gear and helmet, get strapped into a fighter cockpit, and spend about a half hour engaged in simulated high-speed air combat that challenges you with enemy targets and SAMS that lock on. The flight simulators are actual jet aircraft cockpits on a hydraulic motionbase that you control. Simulators include an F-16 Fighting Falcon, F-111 Aardvark, A-4 Skyhawk, and F-8 Crusader. Appointment recommended.

ANNUAL EVENTS

FEBRUARY

NEIL SPERRY'S ALL GARDEN SHOW • 817-459-5000 • www.neil sperry.com • Neil Sperry is considered one of Texas's foremost gardening experts, with gardening books and his own gardening magazine and radio show. Usually held at the Convention Center, this show's features include garden displays, demonstrations, a series of lectures by recognized horticultural authorities, dozens of exhibitors, and gardening activities for children.

MARCH

TEXAS INDIAN MARKET AND SOUTHWEST SHOWCASE •
817-459-5000 • www.indianmarket.net • Some 300 artists and craftsmen from 40 states display and sell everything from traditional American Indian jewelry and pottery to paintings and sculpture, at the Convention Center. Entertainment includes Native American and Spanish dancers, singers, and musicians, and special attractions such as Western acts and children's activities.

JUNE

TEXAS SCOTTISH FESTIVAL AND HIGHLAND GAMES • 817-654-2293 • www.texasscottishfestival.com • More than 65 Scottish clans set up colorful clan and family tents (and a large Pub Tent) in Maverick Stadium on the University of Texas campus at Arlington. Lots of kilts and bagpipes provide the authentic Scottish atmosphere for a nonstop flow of events and contests such as Highland bagpipe and drumming competitions, Scottish dance contests, a Caber Toss, and a Kilted Golf Tournament.

OCTOBER

TEXAS GUITAR SHOW • 817-459-5000 • Guitar enthusiasts will find an assortment of rare and expensive guitars displayed side-by-side with the unusual and reasonably priced instruments and accessories, at the Convention Center.

SHOPPING

ANTIQUE SAMPLER MALL
1715 E. Lamar • Metro 817-461-3030 • W variable

More than 250 dealers display antiques and collectibles ranging from crystal, jewelry, and quilts to European and American furniture. Open Monday–Saturday, 10:00 a.m. to 7:00 p.m., Sunday noon to 6 p.m. The Tea Garden Tearoom, a popular lunch spot, is open from 11:30 a.m. to 3:00 p.m. (from noon on Sundays).

ASIAN DISTRICT SHOPS
Strip malls along Pioneer (Spur 303) and Arkansas west of Hwy. 360 • W variable

For a cultural adventure as well as a culinary treat, try shopping the Asian shops and bakeries in this area, which cater to the more than

10,000 residents of Asian descent, mostly Chinese and Vietnamese, who live in the city. Among the more interesting shops is the **Hong Kong Market** at Pioneer and New York. This supermarket is fully stocked with an extensive assortment of fresh and packaged imported oriental foods from the basics to the exotic, plus fresh fish and meats. And if you want to make the presentation of your oriental cuisine look more authentic, they sell everyday china and plastic dishes with colorful patterns. Expect a little trouble getting English-speaking help. There are several restaurants in this market center.

COOPER STREET CRAFTS MALL

1701 S. Cooper (76010) • 817-261-3184

Several hundred artists and crafters exhibit their wares at this small, tightly packed shop. Included in the handmade items available are traditional and country handicrafts, folk art objects, jewelry, silk and dried floral arrangements, woodwork, holiday decorations, and wearable art. Supervised children's play area. Monday, Wednesday, Friday, & Saturday, 10:00 a.m. to 6:00 p.m.; Thursday, 10:00 a.m. to 8:00 p.m.; Sunday, noon to 5:00 p.m.

LINCOLN SQUARE

N. Collins & I-30 • 817-461-7953 (Mall office) • W variable

A major draw for this complex of specialty shops, restaurants, and a movie theater is its location in the Entertainment District, within sight of The Ballpark at Arlington and Six Flags. Merchants here offer everything from apparel and books to jewelry. It also has a large concentration of sit-down restaurants and specialty fast-food eateries.

THE PARKS AT ARLINGTON

3811 S. Cooper (76010) • 817-467-0200 • W+ but not all areas

More than 160 stores and restaurants anchored by Dillard's, Foley's, Mervyn's, JCPenney, and Sears, in a spacious two-story mall on the south side of town.

SPORTS LEGACY—THE GALLERY OF SPORTS ART

The Ballpark at Arlington, 1000 Ballpark Way, Suite 122 (76011) • 817-461-1994 • Open seven days 10-6, during baseball games and for one hour after baseball games • Free • W+

Reputed to be the nation's largest art gallery devoted to sports, it features original art, limited edition lithographs, statues, and autograph memorabilia of all sports.

THE UPSTAIRS GALLERY

1038 W. Abram (76013) • 817-277-6961 • W variable • www.upstairsartgallery.com

Founded in 1968, Arlington's oldest gallery features original one-of-a-kind art in variety of media, including oils, watercolors, prints, drawings, pottery, and sculpture. Many local artists are featured here, some with national recognition. Art classes and workshops also available. Open Tuesday–Thursday, 10:00 a.m. to 5:00 p.m.; Friday–Saturday, 10:00 a.m. to 4:00 p.m.

A SAMPLING OF ARLINGTON RESTAURANTS

Dinner for one, excluding drinks, tip, and tax: $ = up to $16, $$ = $16–$30, $$$ = $31–$50, $$$$ = over $50. Sales tax 7.25%. It is strongly suggested that you make a reservation in those restaurants that take them, especially on weekends and holidays.

ABUELO'S MEXICAN FOOD EMBASSY ($–$$)

1041 I-20W at Matlock (76017) • 817-468-2622 • Lunch and dinner, seven days • Cr. (No checks) • W variable

As soon as you enter, the colorful fountain in the enclosed center courtyard gives a strong clue that this is not your ordinary Mexican restaurant. This is confirmed by the elaborate menu. There are some Tex-Mex dishes, but most are characteristic of interior and coastal Mexico. Upscale entries include mesquite grilled steaks and house specialties such as *alambre de camaron* (mesquite grilled bacon-wrapped shrimp stuffed with jalapeno and jack cheese) and *medallones de pechuga rellena* (medallions of chicken breast, stuffed with *chorizo, poblano,* and cheese). Portions are huge, especially so on the popular Mexican platters and combinations. Bar. Another location in Plano.

CACHAREL ($$$–$$$$)

2221 E. Lamar, Suite 910, northwest of intersection of I-30 and Hwy. 360 • 817-640-9981 • Lunch, Monday–Friday; dinner, Monday–Saturday. Closed Sunday and major holidays • Cr. • W+

Located in the penthouse of the nine-story Brookhollow Two, this entertainment district restaurant offers elegant dining on a Country French–American cuisine. The selections on the small but innovative menu change daily, offering a choice of six or seven different appetizers, entrées, and desserts. For dinner, you may select à la carte or have a no-frills fixed-price three-course dinner for about $40. This dinner menu changes daily, and on a typical evening may offer such selections as an appetizer of sautéed sea scallops with pesto ravioli and roasted bell pepper sauce, an entrée of grilled veal loin steak served with sautéed shrimp and shiitake mushrooms on a tarragon cream sauce, and a dessert of almond tulip with assorted berries and coconut ice cream. Children's menu. Bar. Panoramic skyline view is a plus. No smoking. Semiformal dress for dinner. Reservations suggested. Fixed-price lunch available.

Consistently rated one of the top restaurants in the Metroplex by a variety of travel magazines.

DAVID'S BARBECUE ($)

2224-H W. Park Row (Pantego, 76013), between Bowen & Fiedler • 817-261-9998 • Lunch and dinner, Tuesday–Saturday • V, MC, Dis • W+

The same family has been serving up barbecue here since 1910, and after four generations, they've developed a loyal following of fervent fans for their ribs, beef, turkey, and ham. No smoking. Parking.

PICCOLO MONDO ($–$$)

829 E. Lamar (76011), in strip shopping center, N.W. corner Lamar & Collins • Metro 817-265-9174 • Lunch, Monday–Friday; dinner seven days • Cr. • W • www.piccolomondo.com

This is mostly northern Italian cuisine, which means more cream and less tomato sauces, from a chef trained in an Italian culinary school. For example, a popular combination might be an appetizer of shrimp with mushrooms and cream sauce followed by an entree of medallions of beef tenderloin sautéed with crushed peppercorns, cognac, and cream. The menu offers pasta, veal, beef, seafood, chicken, and vegetarian dishes. Bar. Cozy, intimate setting enhanced by piano music Tuesday through Saturday evenings. Takeout. Shopping center parking.

PORTOFINO RESTAURANT ($$)

226 Lincoln Square (76011), Copeland and Collins • 817-861-8300 or Metro 817-261-3883 • Lunch, Monday–Friday; dinner, Monday–Saturday. Closed Sunday • Cr. • W+

The Continental specialties at this Italian restaurant include three versions of roasted duck (*anitra*), chicken topped with shrimp and mushrooms in light wine, lobster, and a dish of assorted fried seafood. The extensive menu includes classic dishes such as a prosciutto and melon appetizer, tortellini soup, and popular pasta dishes like fettucini Alfredo. Also veal, beef, chicken, and seafood entrees. Romantically lit dining room with chandeliers, flowers, and piano music nightly. Shopping center parking.

TRAIL DUST STEAK HOUSE ($–$$)

2300 E. Lamar (76006) • 817-640-6411 • Lunch: Monday–Friday, 11–2; Sunday, noon to 10; dinner, seven nights • Cr. • W variable • www.traildust.com

The three things the Trail Dust is most noted for are the mesquite grilled steaks, its Old West atmosphere, and its "no neckties policy." There are some seafood and chicken entrées, but the steaks are the main features on the menu—corn-fed beef, naturally aged and hand-cut on the premises. (Steaks and fixings, including mesquite wood chips for grilling, are available in the restaurant butcher shop for take-home or shipping.) The Old West décor is reinforced nightly by the country and western music. And the no-tie policy means that, if a man shows up wearing one, the staff does a ritual tie-clipping ceremony and the tie ends up joining the hundreds already tacked to every wall, pillar, and ceiling beam. Indoor slide for kids of all ages. Bar. Gift shop. Parking lot. Other locations in Dallas, Grapevine, and Mesquite.

A SAMPLING OF ARLINGTON'S CLUBS AND BARS

BOBBY VALENTINE'S SPORTS GALLERY CAFE

4301 S. Bowen (78016), just north of I-20 exit • 817-467-9922 • Cr. • W

A fun sports bar owned by a former manager of the Texas Rangers. A swarm of TVs amidst the memorabilia catch all the sports action. If you can't get tickets to a Rangers game, you can watch it here. Bar. Burgers, sandwiches, and cold brews popular with the fans. Children's menu. Takeout. Parking.

COWBOYS

2540 E. Abram (76011), at Hwy. 360 • 817-265-1535 • Cr. • W

A true Texas honky-tonk in the big city, with dancing to live C&W bands on a Texas-sized 3,500-square-foot dance floor (claimed to be the largest in the state), Wednesday–Sunday evenings starting at 7:00 p.m. If you don't know the Texas two-step or other C&W dances, they offer dance lessons Thursday, 7–8:00 p.m., and Sunday, 4–8:00 p.m. And if you still have energy to spare, they have a mechanical bull. Cover charge varies depending what band is playing.

HUMPERDINKS BAR AND GRILL

700 Six Flags Dr. (76011), between Road to Six Flags and Copeland • 817-640-8553 • Cr. • W

This is also the home of the Big Horn Brewery, Arlington's first microbrewery, and the town's tallest bar. DJ music, karaoke, and 30 TVs, including three big-screen.

J. GILLIGAN'S BAR AND GRILL

400 E. Abram (76010) • 817-274-8561 • Cr. • W

The Grill has been serving lunch and dinner daily since 1979. The bar includes Gillian's Draft House, offering a large selection of brews. Pool, darts, and live entertainment Thursday–Saturday. Every July, Gillian's holds a big block party and street dance.

A SAMPLING OF ARLINGTON'S ACCOMMODATIONS

For a double room or suite: $ = up to $80, $$ = $81–$120, $$$ = $121–$180, $$$$ = $181–$280, $$$$$ = over $280. **Room tax 13%.**

Unless otherwise noted, check in at 3:00 p.m., check out by noon. Unless otherwise noted, all these accommodations have handicapped rooms/facilities and no smoking rooms available. Check on availability of visual alarms and other safety facilities for the hearing impaired when making reservation. Most accommodations permit children to stay free in room with parents. There may be a charge if this requires setting up an extra bed.

COURTYARD BY MARRIOTT ($$–$$$ + 13%)

1500 Nolan Ryan Expressway (76011), south of I-30 • 817-277-2774 or 800-321-2211 (reservations) • www.courtyard.com/dalal

This three-story Courtyard has 147 rooms, 14 suites. Cable TV with free premium channel. Coffeemaker in room and free coffee in lobby. Dataport in room. Outdoor pool. Whirlpool. Fitness facilities. Self-service laundry and one-day dry cleaning. Restaurant for breakfast only. Other restaurants nearby. Lounge. Business services available. Free outdoor self-parking. Many of the rooms have balconies.

HILTON ARLINGTON ($$$ + 13%)

2401 E. Lamar (76006), north of I-30 and just west of Hwy 360 • 817-640-3322 or 800-HILTONS (445-8667) (reservations) • www.arlington.hilton.com

There are 309 rooms and suites in this 16-story Hilton. Concierge section with extra amenities. Cable TV with free premium channel and pay channels. Coffeemaker in room and free coffee available in restaurant. Dataport in room. Bell service. Outdoor pool. Whirlpool and sauna. Fitness facilities. Self-service laundry and one-day dry cleaning. Restaurant. Room service. Bar. Nightclub with weekend entertainment. Gift shop. Business services available. Free outdoor self-parking. Free DFW Airport transportation and free transportation within a 3-mile radius.

HOLIDAY INN ARLINGTON ($$–$$$ + 13%)

1507 N. Watson (76006) • 817-640-7712 • www.hotelatarlington.com

This five-story inn has 237 rooms. Cable TV with free premium channel and pay channels. Coffeemaker in room and free coffee available in lobby in morning. Dataport in room. Bell service. Indoor/outdoor pool (heated indoor) with children's wading pool, whirlpool, exercise room. Self-service laundry and one-day dry cleaning. Restaurant. Room service. Lounge. Business services available. Free outdoor self-parking. Free DFW Airport transportation and free transportation within 5-mile radius. Restaurant in atrium features popular daily lunch buffet.

LAQUINTA CONFERENCE CENTER ($–$$ + 13%)

825 N. Watson (76011), at I-30 and Hwy 360 directly across street from Six Flags • Metro 817-640-4142 or 800-453-7909 • www.laquinta.com

There are 300 rooms and 40 suites in this two-story inn. Some pets OK with refundable deposit. Outside access to rooms. Free local calls. Cable TV with free premium channel and pay channels. Coffeemaker in room and free coffee available in lobby. Dataport in room. Two outdoor heated pools, one with seasonal swim-up bar. Whirlpool. Fitness facilities and small jogging track. Gift shop. Self-service laundry and one-day dry cleaning. Free continental breakfast. Lounge. Convention facilities and business center. Free outdoor self-parking. Free DFW Airport transportation and free transportation within five-mile radius. Several restaurants nearby on N. Watson and Six Flags Drive, including one that provides room service. Checkout 11:00 a.m. Within walking distance of Six Flags.

PARK INN SUITES HOTEL ($–$$ + 13%)

700 Avenue H East (76011) • 817-640-0440 or 800-670-7275 • www.parkhtls.com

There are 185 suites and 18 rooms in this seven-story hotel. Small pets OK (fee). Local calls free. Cable TV with free premium channel and pay channels. Coffeemaker in room and free coffee available in lobby. Dataport in room. Indoor pool, whirlpool, sauna. Fitness facilities. Self-service laundry and one-day dry cleaning. Free cooked-to-order full breakfast. Free cocktails, Monday–Friday. Restaurant serving dinner. Room service when restaurant open. Lounge. Conference facilities. Business center. Free outdoor self-parking. Free DFW Airport transportation and transportation within 5-mile radius. Suites are spacious. Seven-story tropical atrium.

WYNDHAM ARLINGTON–DFW AIRPORT SOUTH ($$$–$$$$$ + 13%)

1500 Convention Center Dr. (76011), adjacent to Arlington Convention Center • 817-261-8200 or 800-996-3426 (reservations) • www.wyndham.com/arlington

This 19-story Wyndham offers 291 rooms and 19 suites. Cable TV with free premium channel and pay channels. Coffeemaker in room. Dataport in room. Bell service. Outdoor pool, whirlpool, and exercise room. Gift shop. Self-service coin laundry and one-day dry cleaning. Restaurant. Room service. Sports bar. Conference facilities. Business center. Concierge services available. Free outdoor and valet parking (fee). Free DFW Airport transportation and free transportation within 10-mile radius. Checkout 11:00 a.m. Large water wall in lobby and lush landscaping and waterfall at pool.

SIDE TRIPS

KOW BELL INDOOR RODEO

1263 N. Main, Mansfield (P.O. Box 292, Mansfield 76063—Hwy.
157 and Mansfield Hwy.). Take Mansfield-157 exit off I-20, then
south about eight miles. • Metro 817-477-3092 • Saturday–Sunday
at 8 p.m. • Admission • W variable

The cowboys compete in all the usual rodeo events every weekend year
round at this old-style rodeo in a weather-worn arena. In fact, it's the only
year-round rodeo in the Metroplex and, having started in 1958, is now reportedly the longest running weekly rodeo in the nation. In addition to the
weekend rodeos, on Monday, Wednesday, and Friday nights, they have
bull-riding practice. Riders vary from semipros to first-timers, and the bulls
are the same.

DALLAS

Dallas County Seat • 1,188,000 • Area Codes 214, 972, 469 (local calls require area code) • www.visitdallas.com

The question that the history of Dallas poses is not how it grew to be the eighth largest city in the United States, but why.

How did what is now the nation's largest inland city overcome its lack of the traditional foundations for the growth of a great city, such as a wealth of natural resources or a port or a navigable natural waterway? Dallasites have a ready answer to that question. They explain the city's growth as the inevitable result of the community's unrelenting can-do attitude, business sense, and an aggressive entrepreneurial spirit, which overcame, and continues to overcome, all obstacles. The citizens have truly learned the fine art of creating advantages where none existed before.

Less imaginative interpreters explain it by the crossing of a north-south railroad and an east-west intercontinental railroad in the 1870s, which tied the city to the extensive rail networks of the Midwest and Northeast. This crucial crossing made Dallas a distribution crossroads that offered cheap rail transport, giving shippers a huge competitive edge over water transport.

But no matter which explanation you favor, Dallas has grown dynamically, and "dynamic" is the word for Dallas.

BRYAN'S TRADING POST

The city had its pioneer beginning in the early 1840s when the Republic of Texas built a military road from Austin across the Trinity River to the Red River. It was on this road on the open prairie near the three forks of the Trinity, that, in 1841, John Neely Bryan, a bachelor and lawyer from Tennessee with a taste for adventure, set up a trading post to sell goods to the Indians. When the Texans forced the Indians to move west, Bryan laid claim to 640 acres and sketched out a town. He soon learned his claim to the land was disputed by both the Peters Colony, which controlled 16,000 square miles of north Texas farmland, and John Grigsby, a hero of the Texas War for Independence. Bryan persisted, however, and, over the years, was able to resolve the claim in his favor.

Bryan's dream was to use the Trinity River to make his town an inland port with steamboats connecting it to the Gulf of Mexico, 400 miles away. But the river didn't cooperate. It remained contrarily unnavigable—sometimes a raging torrent and other times a dry dusty trickle. True, one steamboat did make the treacherous journey, but it took many months to accomplish.

NAMED AFTER "MY FRIEND DALLAS"

Bryan named his new town after "my friend Dallas." To this day, no one is sure who that friend was. Some believe it was the then vice president of the United States, George Mifflin Dallas, who favored the annexation of Texas. As it turned out, in 1846, after the annexation, the Texas Legislature did name the newly established county in honor of the vice president. But there's no proof that he was the friend Bryan meant when he named the city. It might as easily have been some longtime friend back in Tennessee.

With his town mapped out and named, Bryan set out to attract settlers. At first he wasn't too successful. In 1851 the reported population was only 163. But by 1856 that had almost doubled to about 300 residents, who then, perhaps with a sense of future grandeur already in hand, voted to incorporate it. The population just about doubled again a few years later with the arrival of some 350 French, Belgian, and Swiss settlers whose goal was to build a utopian colony they called La Réunion. Many in this group were skilled artisans, writers, scientists, artists, musicians, and naturalists. The colony was a failure, but the nucleus of knowledge, education, and appreciation of art and music in its residents no doubt gave birth to what is today a thriving abundance of cultural activities and strong citizen support of them. Some say it was these new residents who provided the solid bedrock on which was built the modern city's image as the most cosmopolitan city in Texas.

THE CROSSING OF THE RAILROADS

Utopia didn't work, but the can-do attitude of the Dallasites obviously did. In 1872, when the population was about 1,200, the city fathers, by means legal and not so legal, lured the Houston and Texas Central Railroad to divert from its planned route and go through Dallas. Some reports say that Bryan was still living then and was among those who welcomed the first train. A year later, in 1873, the Texas and Pacific line arrived. As their names stated, the Houston and Texas ran from Galveston and Houston north through the center of the state, while the Texas and Pacific started at Texarkana, on the state's eastern border, where it connected with other lines coming from the Midwest and heading to the Pacific. Dallas suddenly became a major trade center as merchants from Chicago and St. Louis rushed to set up warehouses at this crossing.

The railroads provided the economic link that started the city's continuing surge of growth. Dallas became an important shipping point for items like leather and buffalo hides and the area's agricultural products going to the Midwest and East and manufactured products from the Midwest and the East coming to Texas. The population zoomed to around 7,000.

The railroads spurred the first boom and soon that was linked with the agricultural boom, which centered on cotton. Later booms included the oil business. The wells were not even near the city; in fact, attempts to drill for oil within the city all turned up dry holes, but the financial and technical support was in Dallas and the city became the region's business center for the drilling industry. At one point, more than 450 oil companies established headquarters in Dallas. The city also became the home base for many insurance companies, at least one reason being a 1908 Texas law requiring any insurance company doing business in the state to keep a substantial part of its reserves in the state. At various times, banking, real estate, and high tech industries have all brought booms to the city. And for every boom there was usually at least one bust centered around the same business or industry that caused it.

DALLAS BECOMES A FASHION CENTER

In 1907, perhaps drawn by the cosmopolitan ambience of the city, Neiman Marcus opened an "exclusive woman's ready-to-wear store" in downtown. This store put Dallas on the national fashion map and ultimately on the international fashion map. Building on that tradition, in 1957, two young developers, Trammell Crow and John Stemmons, opened their Home Furnishing Mart, inviting manufacturers and wholesalers to come display their products. Over the years this has grown into what is now the Dallas Market Center, the largest wholesale trade complex in the world. Although most of this center is open only to wholesalers, its very presence makes it easier for area shopkeepers to stay in the forefront of the newest trends, especially in fashion.

DALLAS FINALLY BECOMES BRYAN'S DREAM

In 1965 Dallas and Fort Worth agreed to build an airport between them to serve the entire region. This proved to be the link that would pull together all the disparate cities in the area and consolidate it into one gigantic Metroplex. And with the opening of the giant Dallas/Fort Worth International Airport in 1973, John Neely Bryan's dream of Dallas becoming a major inland port was truly realized.

Today, the Dallas Metro area is the No. 1 visitor destination in Texas, annually attracting more than 14 million visitors.

NEIGHBORHOODS

Like any other large city, Dallas is a conglomerate of neighborhoods. Most of these are residential, with just a sprinkling of restaurants and shops. The following neighborhoods are especially worth exploring, since they offer the greatest concentrations of places of special interest to visitors: the Arts District, Deep Ellum, Greenville Avenue, McKinney Avenue, and the West End.

THE ARTS DISTRICT

Northern edge of the downtown business district • (DART Light Rail St. Paul and Pearl Stations) • www.artsdistrict.org

In 1978, as part of its plan to revitalize downtown, the City Council decided to concentrate the building of its new arts facilities in an area just north of the central business district. In 1984, The **Dallas Museum of Art (DMA)** opened as the anchor and centerpiece of this new district, which has since earned a reputation as a world-class arts and cultural center. The district now encompasses 61 acres in 17 blocks. In addition to the DMA, the arts facilities in this district include: **The Annette Strauss Artist Square, Arts District Theatre, Belo Mansion, Booker T. Washington High School for the Performing Arts, Cathedral Santuario de Guadalupe, Dallas Black Dance Theatre, Morton H. Meyerson Symphony Center, Nasher Sculpture Center**, and the privately owned **Trammel Crow Collection of Asian Art**. The final major component to complete the district, presently under development, is the $250 million **Dallas Center for the Performing Arts**. The 2,700 parking spaces in the district include the underground city-owned 1,650 spaces in the Arts District Parking Garage. A free hour-long guided walking tour of the dis-

THE ARTS DISTRICT

St. Paul United Methodist Church

ROUTH STREET

Booker T. Washington High School for the Performing and Visual Arts

Dallas Center for the Performing Arts (Proposed)

FAIRMOUNT STREET

Arts District Theater (temp)

LEONARD STREET

The Annette Strauss Artist Square

Arts District Parking Garage (Underground)

Lone Star Site

Morton H. Meyerson Symphony Center

Symphony Sculpture Garden (Proposed)

CROCKETT STREET

Parking Garage (Underground)

Cathedral Santuario de Guadalupe

PEARL STREET

Olive Loop LP (Proposed)

Arts District Properties 2121 Flora (Proposed)

Belo Mansion Dallas Bar Association

ROSS AVENUE

FLORA STREET

OLIVE STREET

WOODALL RODGERS SERVICE ROAD

Nasher Sculpture Center

Crow Collection of Asian Art

Trammell Crow Center

HARWOOD STREET

Dallas Museum of Art

ST. PAUL STREET

trict, called the **Arts District Stroll**, is conducted on the first Saturday of every month. (See WALKING TOURS, p. 70)

DEEP ELLUM

Just east of downtown. South of the railroad, around Elm Street from Central Expressway (I-75) east to Fair Park

The name originated because locals referred to this area as the deep end of Elm Street—pronounced with a Southern drawl as Deep Ellum. Just east of the 1873 crossing point of the city's first two railroad lines, it was an area of industry, warehouses, and Dallas's earliest black community. Before World War II it was the cultural center, as well as the principal amusement and shopping district, for the city's growing African-American population. During its heyday, Deep Ellum's jazz and blues clubs featured such legendary musicians as Huddie "Leadbelly" Ledbetter and Blind Lemon Jefferson before they became nationally known. After World War II, the people and businesses started moving out and the area declined. But now, Deep Ellum has been revitalized by artists, musicians, actors, and business people opening night clubs, galleries, shops, theaters, and restaurants, and Deep Ellum has once again gained a reputation as an entertainment district. (See: A SAMPLING OF DALLAS CLUBS AND BARS, p. 148)

GREENVILLE AVENUE

Northeast of downtown. From Ross Avenue north to past LBJ Frwy. (I-635) (DART Light Rail Mockingbird Station)

The lengthy Greenville Avenue Strip offers visitors something for both day and night. Although broken up by residential sections, the strip includes clusters of restaurants and nightclubs catering to almost every taste and budget. Also, mainly on the south end are small shops in old storefronts selling everything from antiques to used clothing and resale furniture and specialty food stores that emphasize Mediterranean, Middle Eastern, and health foods. As you go farther north, especially past Mockingbird, you'll find more glitz and glamour in the stores and restaurants, which tend toward the nationally franchised variety.

MCKINNEY AVENUE

North of downtown, just past the Arts District. (DART Light Rail Cityplace Station)

In the late 1800s, the more successful Dallasites began moving their families out of downtown into the more rural areas toward the town of McKinney. Today, most of the old homes along McKinney Avenue have been converted to restaurants, galleries, unique shops, and nightclubs, and the area has been made more popular by the reconstruction of the old McKinney Avenue Trolley, which also connects the area with the Arts District.

THE WEST END HISTORIC DISTRICT

West end of downtown. Centered on west end of Market St. from Commerce to Woodall Rodgers Frwy. • (DART Light Rail West End Station) • West End Association Event Hotline 214-741-7185

Part of the original city laid out by John Neely Bryan, this is where early Dallas had its start. Later, as the downtown moved farther east, this became known as the West End and developed into a factory and warehouse district. Now it is a 20-block historic district that has been transformed into a bustling neighborhood of restaurants, clubs, and shops set in and among the restored buildings. Attractions in this district include "**Old Red**," the 1892 red sandstone courthouse (now the home of the Dallas Tourist Information Center), **West End Marketplace, Bryan Cabin, Kennedy Memorial,** the **Sixth Floor Museum** and its counterpoint, the **Conspiracy Museum. Reunion Arena** and **Reunion Tower** are on the southwest corner of the district.

FREE VISITOR SERVICES

DALLAS CONVENTION & VISITORS BUREAU

325 N. St. Paul, Suite 700 (75201) • (DART Light Rail St. Paul Station) • 214-571-1000 or 800-C-DALLAS (800-232-5527) • W+ • www.visitdallas.com

The Dallas Convention & Visitors Bureau serves all the information needs of visitors to the city. Call or write for an information packet. Free publications include the "Official Visitors Guide" booklet, "50 Free & Fun Things to See & Do in Dallas," and a quarterly calendar of events. Some publications are available in French, German, Japanese, Spanish, and Portuguese. When in Dallas you can pick up brochures on the open racks in the lobby during normal business hours, or at the **Tourist Information Center** listed below. On-street parking only.

TOURIST INFORMATION CENTER

100 S. Houston (75202), in historic "Old Red" Courthouse between Main and Commerce • (DART Light Rail Union Station) • 214-571-1300 or 800-232-5527 • Open seven days, 9–6. Closed Thanksgiving and Christmas • W+ • www.visitdallas.com

You'll find not only just about every brochure, map, and other free publication on Dallas and the Metroplex here, but also knowledgeable counselors who can help you plan the details of your visit. In addition there are high-tech interactive touch-screen computer information kiosks with printing capabilities and a free Internet Café with a number of computers you can use for Internet access and to check your e-mail. Street metered parking.

THE DALLAS AMBASSADORS

The Downtown Improvement District sponsors the Dallas Ambassadors, young men and women who stroll the downtown streets daily (weather permitting) from 11 a.m. to 6:30 p.m. to provide assistance to visitors. Trained in the geography and landmarks of Dallas, they aid visitors with directions and other information. The Ambassadors are easily recognized by their red shirts and blue pants, and in summer they wear straw hats. They are also trained in first aid and CPR.

DALLAS EVENTS HOTLINES

Convention & Visitors Bureau Dallas Events Hotline 213-571-1301

Dallas Morning News Arts and Entertainment Hotline 214-977-8400

West End Association Events Hotline 214-741-7185

Department of Parks and Recreation Hotline 214-670-4100

HELPFUL LOCAL PUBLICATIONS

Current information about Dallas events, activities, nightlife, theater, movies, and dining is published every Friday in the Arts and Entertainment Guide in *The Dallas Morning News;* the weekly *Dallas Observer* and *The Met,* which are available free at restaurants and tourist attractions throughout the Dallas area, and the monthly *D Magazine,* available on newsstands. *Texas Monthly* Magazine, also available on newsstands, highlights reviews of a smaller number of Dallas restaurants and events in its city listings.

TOUR SERVICES

DALLAS HISTORICAL SOCIETY TOURS

3939 Grand, Hall of State at Fair Park (75210) • 214-421-4500 • www.dallashistory.org

Each spring and fall, the Historical Society conducts a variety of city tours. These vary from season to season but usually include a Downtown Dallas Tour, a Fair Park and East Dallas Tour, a JFK Tour, a Cemetery Tour, and a Bonnie & Clyde Tour. All tours depart from the Hall of State in Fair Park at 9:00 a.m. and return about 2:00 p.m. Lunch is included in the ticket price. Most tours are usually around $35 for nonmembers. Call for schedule and reservations.

DFW HELI-TOURS

P.O. Box 985, Midlothian (76065) • 972-623-3000 • www.helicopterrides.com

See the sights of Dallas from the air on helicopter flights that originate at the Dallas Heliport attached to the Dallas Convention Center. Reservations required. Tours range from 10 to 45 minutes' flying time. The 10-minute tour includes views of the Cotton Bowl, Deep Ellum, West End, and the Dallas skyline and costs about $40 per passenger, with a minimum of four passengers. The longest flight includes additional views of Dallas, Lone Star Park at Grand Prairie, and Six Flags and The Ballpark at Arlington. It costs about $185 per passenger, with a minimum of four passengers.

EAGLE/LONGHORN TOURS

1634 E. Irving Blvd., Irving (75060) • 972-721-0545

Daily tours include most of the major sights. Call for schedule and prices.

GRAY LINE TOURS

315 Continental (75027) • 866-767-9849 • www.grayline.com

Several daily scheduled morning and afternoon sightseeing tours are offered, including the Historic Dallas Tour, which lasts about 3½ hours and costs about $30 for adults. Pickups at the major hotels. Reservations required. Call for other tours and prices.

TEXAS STAR CARRIAGE SERVICES

381 E. Greenbriar (75023) • 214-946-9911 • or P.O. Box 1670, Mabank (75156) • 214-616-1694 • www.texasstarcarriage.com

Horse-drawn surreys that can accommodate six to eight passengers operate nightly on Market Street in the West End beginning at about 6:30 p.m., weather permitting. Tours are available to several areas, and prices range from $35 to $150, depending on number of passengers and length of the ride. If you call ahead, arrangements can be made to pick up your party at most downtown locations and restaurants.

INDUSTRY TOURS

MARY KAY COSMETICS MANUFACTURING FACILITY

1339 Regal Row (Mailing address: Mary Kay World Headquarters, 16251 Dallas Pkwy., 75248) • 972-687-5720 for tour information recording • Free • W • www.marykay.com

On Friday, September 13, 1963, Mary Kay opened a small storefront cosmetics store in Dallas. Now, Mary Kay Cosmetics is an international company. Tours of this facility where a variety of Mary Kay products are prepared are conducted Tuesday–Friday at 10:30 a.m. and 2:00 p.m., by appointment only, made at least 48 hours in advance. Mary Kay Museum in the Mary Kay World Headquarters is also open for tours. (See ADDISON—OTHER POINTS OF INTEREST, p. 26)

WALKING TOURS

THE ARTS DISTRICT STROLL

214-953-1977 • www.artsdistrict.org.

A free hour-long guided walking tour of the history and highlights of the architecture of the 17-block Arts District is given on the first Saturday of each month by the Arts District Friends. The tour starts at 10:30 a.m. in front of the Trammell & Margaret Crow Collection of Asian Art at 2010 Flora Street. (Look for the red and white umbrellas.) Since you're in the Arts District, you might want to end the tour with lunch at the café in the Dallas Museum of Art. Group private tours are available, at your convenience, for $7 per person, with a minimum of $50.

SELF-GUIDED DOWNTOWN SCULPTURE TOURS

A "Walking Sculpture" map/brochure is available from the Convention & Visitors Bureau. Created by the Dallas Foundation, a nonprofit organization, it offers six self-guided walking tours of sculptures in more than 30 locations in the downtown area. (See also MUSEUMS AND PUBLIC ART GALLERIES—OUTDOOR PUBLIC ART, p. 93)

GETTING AROUND

DRIVING IN DALLAS

Aside from morning and evening rush hours during the business week, there's probably less traffic congestion in Dallas than in any city of comparable size. However, parking is a problem, especially downtown. There are plenty of commercial garages and parking lots, but they can be expensive. The problem with driving is not so much the traffic as the layout of the city. With a few exceptions, downtown is basically a grid of mostly one-way streets, but spreading out from there, many of the streets seem to run off in all directions like unregulated spokes of a wheel.

If you plan to use only the main highways and streets, a simple map will do. But if you plan any extensive discovery driving we suggest that you invest in a good street map or a streetfinder type of map book, and then plot your route before you set out.

PUBLIC TRANSPORTATION

DALLAS AREA RAPID TRANSIT (DART)

Customer Service 214-979-1111 • www.DART.org

What one word expresses our feelings about a public bus and train system that gets you around Dallas and 12 surrounding cities across a 700-square-mile service area?

Hallelujah!

We don't usually push using public transportation, but this is a valid exception. No matter where you are staying in Dallas, you may be able to eliminate the hassles of driving (and the expense of parking) by using the extensive DART bus, Trolley-bus, trolley, and Light Rail systems, alone or in combination. This is especially true if you stay downtown and use the system to go to many of the popular shopping and entertainment destinations in the city and in a number of surrounding cities. Light Rail, for example, will take you directly from the heart of downtown to see a concert at the Eisemann Center in Richardson, to the West End for dinner, or the Dallas Zoo. Using the Trinity Railway Express, you can even make a quick trip to downtown Fort Worth to see a performance at Bass Hall. (See also WELCOME TO THE METROPLEX—DART LIGHT RAIL SYSTEM MAP, p. 6)

To determine if you can "get there from here," call DART Customer Service at 214-979-111. Tell where you are, where you want to go, and when you want to travel, and the knowledgeable operators will recommend the most convenient route and departure time, quote the fare, and, if you do have to transfer between buses or between a train and bus, advise you where and how to make these transfers.

DART BUSES AND LIGHT RAIL

DART operates about 130 local and express routes throughout the city and a number of neighboring cities. You can ride the M-Line, with real streetcars, or special trolley-buses designed to resemble early 1900s streetcars, offering circular routes in many key areas, including downtown Dallas.

Buses may be the mainstay of the DART system, but DART Light Rail is the jewel. Bus and train schedules are coordinated, so, if it's necessary, it's easy to move from one part of the system to the other without long waits.

DART Light Rail runs safe, clean, air-conditioned electric trains that can whisk you in minutes from one place to another along the lines that run roughly north-south through the center of the city. (See WELCOME TO THE METROPLEX—DART LIGHT RAIL SYSTEM MAP, p. 6) The 44-mile Light Rail system is designed primarily for Dallas commuters, which means it operates every day from early morning to late night, and fares are subsidized by the cities and kept low, making this a real boon to visitors who take the little time necessary to learn the easy steps to using it.

To help you take advantage of this excellent transportation, we've included a note on every Dallas listing that tells if there is a DART Light Rail station within easy walking distance. We've also added a note if you'll need to make a bus or trolley bus connection to reach your destination. And if you're staying outside of downtown and not located near a station, check to see if you can catch a bus to a train station so you can take advantage of this excellent system.

DOWNTOWN DALLAS

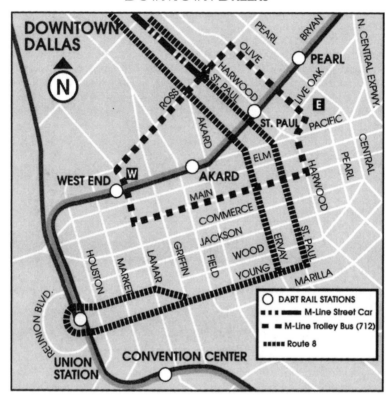

Light Rail route maps and easy-to-follow ticketing instructions are posted at all the stations. For more detailed information on both bus and train routes and schedules, call 214-979-1111.

When you're at a Light Rail station, take a few moments to check the station art and design. Each station has a unique visual identity that tells the story of the area's historic roots, cultural diversity, and architectural heritage.

TRINITY RAILWAY EXPRESS

Downtown Fort Worth is now just about an hour from downtown Dallas on a Trinity Railway Express diesel train. (See WELCOME TO THE METROPLEX—DART LIGHT RAIL SYSTEM MAP, p. 6) The inexpensive 34-mile trip can start at either the Dallas Union Station or the Medical/Market Center Station. And in Fort Worth you can get off at either of the downtown stations, the Intermodal Transportation Center, or the T&P Station. (See FORT WORTH, p. 179) For schedules and fare information, see www.trinityrailwayexpress.org or call 214-979-1111 in Dallas (www.DART.org) or 817-215-8600 in Fort Worth (www.the-T.com).

BIRD'S-EYE VIEW

A good way to get oriented to the city and the Metroplex is to get up high for a bird's-eye view. Three of the skyscraping places open to the public that offer the best panoramic views of the city are the three levels in the 50-story **Reunion Tower** at the **Hyatt Regency Dallas Hotel** (300 Reunion Blvd. 214-651-1234 • DART Light Rail Union Station). The Reunion Tower's geodesic dome has been a landmark in the Dallas skyline since it opened in 1978. View elevators make the trip from ground to observation levels in a little over a minute. The lowest observation floor offers visitors both a 360-degree view of downtown Dallas and a scenic view for many miles in every direction from both indoor and outdoor viewing areas. (Sunday–Thursday, 10–10; Friday–Saturday, until midnight. Adults, $2; seniors and children aged 3–12, $1) On the next level is the hotel's **Antares Restaurant**. Named for the brightest star in the Scorpio constellation, the restaurant offers lunch, dinner, and Sunday brunch, all with a view that changes as the restaurant rotates at the rate of one revolution every 55 minutes. (See A SAMPLING OF DALLAS RESTAURANTS, p. 133) And at the highest level is **The Dome**, the Hyatt's cocktail lounge, which also revolves once every 55 minutes. More than 200 lights on the dome can be programmed to form a huge number of patterns. If you want to test your stamina, there's a 837-step stairway to the top. Parking at the hotel is expensive, but the Tower is within easy walking distance of the DART Light Rail Union Station. Or you might try parking at Reunion Arena.

The view is not 360 degrees, but you can get an enjoyable bird's-eye view of downtown from the following hotel restaurants: the **Chapparral Club** on the 38th floor of the Adams Mark Hotel (400 N. Olive) (DART Light Rail Pearl Station), and the **Nana Grill** on the 27th floor of the tower of the Wyndham Anatole Hotel (2201 Stemmons Frwy.) (See A SAMPLING OF DALLAS RESTAURANTS, p. 135 and p. 143)

HISTORIC PLACES

THE BELO MANSION

2101 Ross Ave. (75201) (DART Light Rail Pearl Station) • 214-220-7487 (Dallas Bar Association) for tours • Free

In the late 1890s, this Neoclassic mansion was constructed for Col. Alfred H. Belo, founder of the *Dallas Morning News*. At the time, Ross Avenue was the first paved street in the city, fashionable, and lined with grand homes. It is reported that the Belo home was the first to have electricity and indoor plumbing. Construction was completed in 1900, a year before Colonel Belo's death. By 1926 Ross Avenue was no longer a fashionable address, and the building became a funeral home, which had its time of fame in 1934 when reports say that 30,000 people stood in line to view the body of Clyde Barrow, of Bonnie and Clyde fame, who lay in state after being killed in an ambush set by Texas Rangers. The Dallas Bar Foundation bought and meticulously restored the mansion in 1977. Today, it is the lone survivor of those early stately homes and is listed on the National Register of Historic Places. Now known as the Dallas Legal Education Center, it houses the offices of the Dallas Bar Association, which offers a once-a-month tour from September to May. Call for details.

BRYAN CABIN

600 Elm, Dallas County Historic Plaza (DART Light Rail West End Station)

When John Neely Bryan settled here in 1841, his first home was a dugout. About a year later, he did build a one-room cabin, but that was later destroyed by a flood. In 1935, the city reconstructed this log cabin as a model of the type of home lived in by Bryan and other early settlers.

DEALEY PLAZA NATIONAL HISTORIC LANDMARK DISTRICT/KENNEDY ASSASSINATION SITE

Downtown in the West End area around the triple underpass of Elm, Commerce, and Houston Streets (DART Light Rail West End Station)

Built over the original townsite, the plaza's art deco garden structures were completed in 1940 and named after George Bannerman Dealey, the publisher of the *Dallas Morning News* and a local civic leader. In November 1963, President John F. Kennedy was assassinated while riding in a motorcade passing through Dealey Plaza. In 1993 the National Park Service declared the plaza and surrounding area a National Historic Landmark District. (See MUSEUMS—The Sixth Floor Museum, p. 91) There are now fountains and a JFK memorial plaque in the plaza's park.

FREEDMAN'S CEMETERY AND FREEDMAN'S MEMORIAL

2470 Five Mile Pkwy. (75223), about a mile north of Downtown, Lemmon and North Central Expressway • (DART Light Rail Cityplace Station and M-Line Streetcar) 214-670-3284 • Free

The first burials here were slaves prior to the Civil War. After that war, it became known as the "Old Colored Cemetery" and then as the Freedman's Cemetery. When it closed in 1927 there were approximately 18,000 graves in the four-acre plot. In 1989, after several intrusions had already been made by roadways and other private developments, Black Dallas Remembered, Inc. and other preservation groups protested a plan to widen a major highway that would desecrate a large portion of the cemetery. After negotiations with the city, the remains of 1,500 of Dallas's earliest citizens, freed slaves who founded Freedman's Town after the Civil War, were reinterred in property adjacent to the original site. The Freedman's Memorial includes a gated granite arch at the entrance, with larger-than-life-size bronze statues by African-American artist David Newton.

HIGHLAND PARK VILLAGE SHOPPING CENTER
(See SHOPPING, p. 130)

"OLD RED" COURTHOUSE
100 S. Houston (75202) • (DART Light Rail Union Station) 214-571-1300 (Tourist Information Center) • Free

Rough-cut Pecos red sandstone and Arkansas blue granite give this Romanesque Revival courthouse its local name. When built in the early 1890s, it was the fifth courthouse to occupy this site, on property donated by John Neely Bryan with the understanding that the land would revert to the family if ever used for anything but a county government building. Listed on the National Register of Historic Places, it is one of the city's oldest remaining buildings. The Tourist Information Center is located on the ground floor (see FREE VISITOR SERVICES, p. 67) and plans are in the works to establish the Museum of Dallas County History here.

PIONEER CEMETERY
1300 Young (75202), downtown near Pioneer Plaza (DART Light Rail Union Station)

As its name states, this is the burial site of early Dallas pioneers. Graves date back to the 1850s and the last burial here was in the 1920s.

OTHER HISTORIC DOWNTOWN BUILDINGS

It wasn't until the mid-1890s that downtown Dallas construction took on any semblance of permanence. And, of course, as in any booming business district, older buildings come down to make way for new and bigger ones that make more efficient use of the precious real estate. As a result, with few exceptions, most downtown buildings of historic importance are not even a century old. The following highlight just a few of the buildings of historic interest to the development of downtown.

The Adolphus Hotel (1912) • 1321 Commerce Street • (Dart Light Rail Akard Station) • 214-742-8200 • The Adolphus is the sole survivor of the several grand downtown hotels from the early twentieth century. St. Louis brewery magnate Adolphus Busch was responsible for the Beaux Arts architecture of his namesake hotel. At the time it was built, it was the highest building in Texas. The high-quality detailing, executed in granite, terra cotta, and bronze, is rare in Texas buildings of that period. It's claimed that the tower on the roof was modeled after a Busch beer stein. (See also A SAMPLING OF DALLAS ACCOMMODATIONS—Adolphus Hotel, p. 150)

Cathedral Santuario de Guadalupe (1902) • 2215 Ross (75201) • (DART Light Rail Pearl Station) • 214-871-1362 • Designed by Nicholas Clayton, the architect whose body of work made a lasting stamp on the city of Galveston, the century-old cathedral is in the process of being restored to its original state and updated so it'll last another hundred years. It is the home church of the Catholic Bishop of Dallas. Among its many architectural features are 101 stained-glass windows. Located on the cathedral altar is an exact replica of the image of Our Lady of Guadalupe that appeared on a peasant's cloak that's now enshrined in a basilica in Mexico City. Many cultural programs are presented here, including exhibits of the works of local and international artists and a wide variety of musical performances. The Brass Quintet, resident at the cathedral, performs music for brass instruments at a variety of churches of various denominations throughout the Metroplex.

Magnolia Petroleum Building (1922) • Commerce and Akard Streets • (DART Light Rail Akard Station) • This 29-story Renaissance Revival skyscraper was thought to be the tallest building south of Washington, D.C., when it was built and retained that title for more than two decades. In 1934 it was crowned with the 30-foot-high, revolving, 15-ton Pegasus, or Flying Red Horse, the symbol for the Magnolia Petroleum Company (later Mobil Oil). Pegasus soon became the symbol for the Dallas skyline and the unofficial mascot of the city. No longer there, Pegasus is still perceived as a beloved sentimental landmark, as evidenced by the program that scattered more than a hundred smaller versions of the winged horse throughout the city in shopping malls, building lobbies, and on street corners. The building is now the Magnolia Hotel.

Majestic Theatre (1922) • 1925 Elm Street • (DART Light Rail St. Paul Station) • 214-880-0137 • The Majestic is all that is left of Dallas's once thriving Theater Row, a Great White Way several blocks long. Originally built as a vaudeville palace, the Majestic was the first to install air-conditioning and began to show talking pictures during the 1920s. Completely restored, the Renaissance Revival–style theater is now a performing arts theater. It is listed on the National Register of Historic Places. (See MUSIC AND PERFORMING ARTS, p. 103)

Municipal Building/Old City Hall (1914) • 2015 Main Street • (DART Light Rail St. Paul or Pearl Station) • The fifth floor of this building was once the city jail. It is still used by the Dallas Police Department and it was in the basement of this building that Lee Harvey Oswald, the alleged assassin of President John F. Kennedy, was shot by Jack Ruby.

Sanger Brothers Department Store/El Centro College (1919) • (DART Light Rail West End Station) • Main and Lamar Streets • The Sanger brothers made marketing history when they opened their first store in Dallas, offering merchandise in departments, a one-price system, retail charge accounts, home delivery, shopping by telephone, and fringe benefits for employees that included an employees' savings and loan association and a free night school at the store. It was also the first store to hire female salespeople and have free rides home for unmarried female employees, with one of the brothers acting as guardian. The Sanger Brothers store made the downtown the place to shop. Most of the original buildings in the Sanger Brothers complex were torn down to make way for the Dallas Community College District's El Centro campus, and the remaining buildings have been completely renovated to house the school. Some of the old millinery items and display counters from the store are now in the Milliner Supply Company, across the street at 911 Elm.

Union Station (1916) • (DART Light Rail Union Station) • 400 S. Houston • 214-653-1101 • During the height of railroad travel, the Union Terminal Company was formed in 1912 to create this one central passenger facility to replace the five depots used by the nine railroads serving the city. At that time, the depot handled as many as 85 trains a day. As train travel declined, so did Union Station. The Beaux Arts–style building was restored in 1974, but the same cannot be said of train travel. Only AMTRAK passenger trains use it now. Listed on the National Register of Historic Places, the station is connected by a one-block tunnel to the DART Light Rail Union Station and to the Hyatt Regency Hotel. A collage of photos decorating the tunnel depict some of the history of Dallas.

SWISS AVENUE HISTORIC DISTRICT

Northeast of downtown, Upper Swiss Avenue

This neighborhood was among the most prestigious in Dallas in the early 1900s. About a mile of the avenue is listed on the National Register of Historic Places because of the restored grand homes. Of particular note are the 2800 and 2900 blocks, which are called the **Wilson Blocks** after Frederick P. Wilson, who built some of the homes in the late 1890s. Most of the historic houses have been restored and are used by nonprofit organizations. Free tours lasting about 45 minutes are available, Tuesday–Saturday, without reservations. For information about tours, contact Preservation Dallas, 2922 Swiss Ave., 214-821-3290. **www.preservationdallas.org.**

FAIR PARK

About 2 miles southeast of downtown, Administrative Office: 1300 Robert B. Cullem (75210); P.O. Box 159090 (75315) • 214-670-8400 • English and Spanish information line, 214-421-9600 • W variable • www.fairparkdallas.com

The design and construction of buildings for most World Fairs assumes a short life, ending when the fair ends. Not so with the building constructed for the Texas Centennial Exposition of 1936, a world's fair in which Texas celebrated its one hundredth anniversary of independence from Mexico. For that event, Fair Park was built on the site used for Texas state fairs since 1886, and it was built solidly to remain after the Centennial as the heart of future state fairs for many years. It was built so solidly, in fact, that the park, now almost 70 years old, is the only intact and unaltered pre-1950 World's Fair site remaining anywhere in the United States. In recognition of its significant collection of art deco buildings from the 1930s, it has been designated a National Historic Landmark— the largest historical landmark in the state.

Fair Park still lives up to its original mission, hosting the annual State Fair of Texas, one of the largest state fairs in the U.S., but that's only for approx-

Fair Park

FAIR PARK
D A L L A S

A CULTURAL AND ENTERTAINMENT CENTER ...

749,000 sq. ft. available for lease for a variety of events, including festivals, parties, exhibitions, concerts, markets, call 214-670-8400.

imately three weeks every fall (see ANNUAL EVENTS, p. 128). The rest of the year, this 277-acre beautifully landscaped city park is an attraction itself as a site rich in museums, historic places, and entertainment and sports venues. Admission is free to the grounds, which are open daily, except for the week before the state fair and during the fair itself. However, individual admissions are charged to most of the major attractions in the park. There are more than 9,000 parking spaces within Fair Park and an additional 3,000 paved spaces adjacent to the park. Parking is free except during the state fair and some special events. More than three million people annually attend the state fair, and another four million visit the entertainment, cultural, and sports attractions in Fair Park during the rest of the year.

HALL OF STATE

3939 Grand • Operated by Dallas Historical Society • P.O. Box 150038 (75315-0038) • 214-421-4500 • Tuesday–Saturday, 9-5; Sunday, 1–5. Closed Monday • Free, except for special exhibits • W+ but not all areas

Built as a centerpiece of the 1936 Texas Centennial, this elegant building is an imposing and outstanding example of art deco architecture. The bronze entry doors, ornamented with symbols of the industrial and agricultural life of Texas, lead into the Hall of Heroes with its bronze, larger-than-life statues of six heroes of the Republic of Texas: Stephen F. Austin, Sam Houston, Mirabeau B. Lamar, Thomas J. Rusk, James Walker Fannin, and William Barret Travis. Five rooms branch off this hall in the shape of a T. Immediately ahead is the four-story Great Hall with its immense gold seal, with symbols representing the six nations of which Texas was a part at one time in its history, and two huge murals depicting major events in the history of the state. To the left and right of the Hall of Heroes are four rooms designated to tell the story of each of the four regions of the state: east, west, north, and south. The Dallas Historical Society, which is the operator and caretaker of the building, sponsors frequent changing exhibits. Gift shop.

THE MUSEUMS OF FAIR PARK

AFRICAN AMERICAN MUSEUM

3536 Grand Avenue; P.O. Box 150153 (75315-0153) • 214-565-9026 • Tuesday–Friday, noon–5; Saturday, 10-5, Sunday, 1–5. Closed Monday • Free except for occasional special events • W+

This museum is the only one in the Southwest devoted to the preservation and display of African-American artistic, cultural, and historical materials. It offers a treasury of art and culture that recognizes the vital presence of black culture in the Metroplex and in the world. Among these treasures is the Billy R. Allen Folk Art Collection, one of the largest collections of

African-American folk art in the nation. In addition, the museum's permanent holdings include a small but rich collection of traditional African art objects, including masks, sculptures, gold, and textiles, and a collection of contemporary works of African-American fine art by local, national, and internationally recognized artists. It houses the Heritage Center, featuring exhibits from its historical collection and archives of materials pertaining to the African-American experience. The museum hosts traveling exhibits as well as a number of lectures and conferences during the year. A popular monthly event is "Jazz under the Dome," usually held every third Friday night (admission). It also sponsors an annual jazz festival and the annual Texas Black Invitational Rodeo, held at Fair Park Coliseum. Gift shop.

AGE OF STEAM RAILROAD MUSEUM

1105 Washington (75315), in northwest corner behind Centennial Hall • 214-428-0101 • Wednesday–Sunday, 10–5. Closed Monday–Tuesday • Adults, $5; children 12 and under, $2.50 • www.dallasrailwaymuseum.com

The significant legacy of the railroads is preserved in this museum. Its outdoor collection displays more than two dozen historic pieces of railroad equipment, including Dallas's oldest surviving depot from 1903, first-class Pullman sleeping cars, lounge cars, and several of the largest and most powerful steam and diesel locomotives in the world. One of them, "Big Boy," the world's largest steam locomotive, weighs over a million pounds. Most of the equipment is from the period 1900–1950. Some of the cars can be boarded. The museum is owned and operated by the Southwest Railroad Historical Society. Guided tours and audio tours are available. Gift shop.

AMERICAN MUSEUM OF MINIATURE ARTS

Sharp Gallery, downstairs in Fair Park Hall of State, 3939 Grand • 214-421-4500 • Office: 2001 N. Lamar, Suite 100 (75202) 214-969-5502 • Tuesday–Saturday, 9–5; Sunday, 1–5. Closed Monday • Free • W+ • www.minimuseum.org

Although the title of "Miniature Arts" is correct, the old name of the Dollhouse Museum was possibly more descriptive, because most of the miniature art forms are historically authentic miniature dollhouses, some five stories high. The exhibits in this three-dimensional tiny world range from General Benedict Arnold's Philadelphia mansion, to rural Texas homesteads, to a sixteenth-century French armory. All are fully furnished with made-to-scale creations by regional professional designers that include clocks that can be wound, scissors that can cut paper, and musical instruments that can be played. There are also displays of room boxes, antique toys, and dolls. Other exhibits from the collection are at the Children's Medical Center, which is where the entire collection is destined to be reestablished in the next couple of years. (See FAMILY FUN AND KID STUFF—Model Train Exhibit, p. 113)

THE DALLAS AQUARIUM

1462 First (75201) (P.O. Box 150113, 75315-0113) •
214-670-8443 • Seven days, 9–4:30. Closed Thanksgiving and
Christmas • Adults, $3; children 3–11, $1.50; under 3 free (usually
lower fee during the Fair) • W+ • www.dallaszoo.com

Fish that live in the desert, fish that wear disguises, four-eyed fish, and
fish that walk are among the weird and wonderful aquatic residents here.
The Aquarium is home to a varied collection of nearly 5,000 examples of
both freshwater and saltwater species of fish, reptiles, amphibians, and
various invertebrates from around the world, on display in 75 exhibit
tanks. Special attractions include the Amazon Flooded Forest Exhibit, a
10,500-gallon tank that showcases approximately 30 species of fish
found in the Amazon River of South America; and the World of Aquatic
Diversity exhibit, featuring 25 displays highlighting the bizarre adapta-
tions of a variety of saltwater and freshwater species. The Breeding Lab's
viewing window provides a behind-the-scenes look at the Aquarium's ongoing projects to preserve rare and endangered species. Among the most
popular feedings to watch are the piranhas on Tuesday, Thursday, and
Saturday, sharks on Wednesday, and alligators on Friday. Most public
feedings take place about 2:30 p.m.

DALLAS MUSEUM OF NATURAL HISTORY

3535 Grand, just inside the Grand Avenue entrance off Cullum;
P.O. Box 150349 (75315) • 214-421-DINO (421-3466) •
Monday–Saturday, 10–5; Sunday, 12–5. Closed Thanksgiving and
Christmas • Adults, $6.50; seniors and students 13–18, $5.50;
children 3 and older, $4; under 3 free • W+ but not all areas •
www.dallasdino.org

"Natural History" in its title means this museum documents the diversity of past and present environments and the changing face of Texas
over millions of years. To do this, it offers extensive displays and dioramas of Texas wildlife, plants, and minerals. Among its features are the
Hall of Prehistoric Texas, which includes a reconstructed dinosaur and
the nation's largest prehistoric sea turtle; a working paleontology lab, and
City Safari, a hands-on science discovery center for children. A program
is under way to revitalize the permanent exhibits by making them more
interactive for visitors. The Museum, which is in association with the
Smithsonian Institution, also usually offers two major national or international traveling exhibits each year. Sleepovers are available for kids 7–12.
(See FAMILY FUN AND KID STUFF, p. 112) Gift shop.

THE SCIENCE PLACE AND TI FOUNDERS
IMAX® THEATER

Main Building: 1318 Second; P.O. Box 151469 (75315) •
Planetarium: 1620 First • 214-428-5555 • Monday–Friday,
9:30-4:30; Saturday, 9:30–5:30; Sunday, 11:30–5:30. Closed

Thanksgiving, Christmas, and New Year's Day and some Mondays in winter • Adults, $7.50; seniors, $6.50; children 3–12, $4; under 3 free. Admission to IMAX Theater: Adults, $7; seniors and children 3–12, $6. Planetarium $3 all ages • Combination tickets at reduced prices • W+ but not all areas • www.scienceplace.org

Science Place bills itself as "an amusement park for the brain." Lift 1,000 pounds with one hand, learn the shocking truth about electricity (and make your hair literally stand up), step inside the body shop to see a real beating heart, or get face-to-face with a (robotic) dinosaur that growls. You can do all these things in a variety of hands-on exhibits among the hundreds exhibits in this popular museum that goes to the limit to let you touch and turn and press buttons to explain science and make it interactive and fun. Imaginature is a special place for children (and adults) to observe bees, beavers, and other critters at work in their habitats. In addition, Kids Place is an ideal place for kids, up to age seven, to work and explore science with their adult companion. And for a real moving movie experience, take in the show at the IMAX Theater, in which each of the 329 seats is scientifically designed to give the viewer such an optimum view of the 79-foot dome screen that it feels like you're in the film. Cafeteria and gift shop. In a separate building, on First Avenue, about a block away, are more examples of science and technology in action including the **Science Place Planetarium**, which features sky shows in the afternoons Tuesday–Sunday.

THE WOMEN'S MUSEUM: AN INSTITUTE FOR THE FUTURE

3800 Parry (75226), northwest corner by the Main Pedestrian Gate, across from the Music Hall • 214-915-0860 or toll-free 877-915-0860 • Tuesday, 10–9 (5–9, free); Wednesday–Saturday, 1–5; Sunday, noon–5 • Adults, $5; seniors and students 12–18, $4; children 5–12, $3; 4 and under free • W+ • www.thewomensmuseum.org

Considering the profound disrepair of the original 1910 building restored to house this museum, it's both fitting and symbolic that the one thing still in fair shape before the revitalization was the 1936 Centennial statue in front of the entrance, depicting a woman rising from a cactus. This comprehensive women's history museum tells the stories and contributions of thousands of American women. It honors the past, and at the same time provides glimpses of the future, all with cutting edge technology like the Electronic Quilt and Mentor phones. The quilt represents the quilts women have pieced together over the years to tell their stories. The electronic version, however, one of the dominant attractions on the main floor, towers more than 30 feet and comprises 35 changing images of photos, quotes, and video showcasing the museum's permanent exhibits. Four celebrity mentors—Ann Richards, Connie Chung, Maria Conchita Alonzo, and Gladys Knight—are the voices on the mentor phones that are available to tell visitors about the exhibits. Among the several permanent exhibits are "Milestones in Women's History," presenting a timeline of important events affecting and affected by women from the sixteenth century to the present; "Unforgettable Women," "Sports and Adventure," "Mothers of Invention," and "Words That Changed Our Lives," featuring women authors and speechmakers who had a major and lasting impact on American society and culture. On the lighter side, there's an exhibit honoring "Funny Women," using clips from stand-up routines, movies, and television to showcase the genius and power of women's wit. In addition to the permanent exhibits, the museum frequently has rotating exhibits, some of which are in association with the Smithsonian Institution. Ample free parking nearby, except during the Fair.

FAIR PARK PERFORMANCE AND SPORTS VENUES

For schedules and ticket information, call English and Spanish information line at 214-421-9600.

BAND SHELL

(214-670-8400)

Musical concerts and plays are performed in this 3,800-seat amphitheater.

COTTON BOWL STADIUM

(214-939-2117)

The original Cotton Bowl had a capacity of 46,200. But thanks to an SMU player named Doak Walker and the tremendous crowds he attracted to see SMU play, in 1948 the stadium was expanded to a capacity of 67,431. Later, "The House that Doak Built" was expanded again to its present capacity of around 72,000. It is the site of a number of sports events, including the Cotton Bowl Football Classic on January 1 (www.swbellcottonbowl.org); the annual football games pitting rivals Grambling and Prairie View A&M each September; University of Texas and University of Oklahoma during the State Fair; SMU and other college football games; and the home soccer matches of the Dallas Burn. It also hosts a variety of concerts and the spectacular Fourth of July fireworks display. (Wheelchair access at stadium sections 4–7.)

COLISEUM

(214-670-8400)

With 7,116 seats, it hosts rodeos, horse shows, and other sporting events.

CREATIVE ARTS BUILDING

(214-670-8496)

This art deco building contains two performance stages, exhibition sites, and a music arena.

MUSIC HALL

(214-565-1116)

The 3,420-seat hall is home for the Dallas Summer Musicals, the opera, ballet, and a variety of concerts. Restaurant.

SMIRNOFF MUSIC CENTRE

(214-421-1111)

This amphitheater is the site of numerous live concerts each year featuring world-renowned entertainers. The 7,500 reserved seats are under a covered performance awning and seating for an additional 12,500 is available on a grassy sloped lawn. Call for information on schedule and ticket prices.

OTHER POINTS OF INTEREST IN FAIR PARK

TEXAS DISCOVERY GARDENS

3601 Martin Luther King • 214-428-7476 • Tuesday–Saturday, 10–5; Sunday, 1–5. Closed Monday. Closed Thanksgiving, Christmas, and New Year's Day. (Grounds open at all times, access through rear gate) • Free • W • www.texasdiscoverygardens.org

There are a number of separate gardens, a conservatory, and a greenhouse on the seven acres. Among these are the **Heirloom Garden**, with plantings of antique and fragrant roses and a selection of perennials; the **Barry J. Simpson Texas Native Plant Collection**, the **Butterfly Garden**, a garden with over 300 varieties of iris, and a xeriscape garden of native and adapted plants that require minimal supplemental water and maintenance. Among the more popular gardens is the **Grand Allee du Meadows**, which is patterned after the classic French landscape garden, with colorful plants outlining a broad promenade that culminates in a 50-foot geyser fountain in the midst of an expansive "Fan of Color." The **Conservatory** houses the Plants of Africa Collection. Admission is charged only for occasional special exhibits held in the Conservatory.

TEXAS STAR FERRIS WHEEL

At a little over 212 feet (about 20 stories high), this is the tallest Ferris wheel in North America. It can carry 264 riders in 44 gondolas on a ride that lasts from 12 to 15 minutes. It provides the best bird's-eye view of Fair Park and, from the top on a clear day, riders can see 40 to

45 miles. Operates only during the State Fair and for selected special events. Admission.

OTHER MAJOR BUILDINGS IN FAIR PARK

The **Automotive Building, Grand Place, Centennial Hall** and other major buildings in the park not only have important roles as exhibit areas during the State Fair, but are also used during the rest of the year for a variety of exhibits and events, including antique and craft shows and flea markets.

MUSEUMS AND PUBLIC ART GALLERIES

For general list: City of Dallas Office of Cultural Affairs 972-504-6658 • *www.dallasculture.org & www.culturefinder.org*

AFRICAN AMERICAN MUSEUM

(See FAIR PARK, p. 79)

AGE OF STEAM RAILROAD MUSEUM

(See FAIR PARK, p. 80)

BATH HOUSE CULTURAL CENTER

521 E. Lawther (75218), on the shore of White Rock Lake (DART Light Rail White Rock Station and bus) • 214-670-8749 • Event hotline, 214-670-8570 • Tuesday–Saturday, 12–6; theater weekends until 10 • W+ • www.bathhousecultural.com

At one time, back in the 1930s and 1940s, the Art Deco building actually was a bathhouse for swimmers at White Rock Lake. Abandoned in the 1950s, it was rescued by the city in 1979 and turned into a neighborhood cultural center. Now it is well known for its wide range of activities that include concerts, children's theater, art and photography exhibitions, dance performances, and classes and workshops in the arts. The three small art galleries annually present 12 to 18 exhibitions featuring the works of both local and international artists in a variety of media. (See also MUSIC AND PERFORMING ARTS, p. 101)

BIBLICAL ARTS CENTER

7500 Park Ln. (75225), at Boedeker next to North Park Shopping Center (DART Light Rail Park Lane Station and North Park Trolley) • 214-691-4661 • Tuesday–Saturday, 10–5 ; Sunday, 1–5; Monday and evenings by appointment. Closed Thanksgiving, Christmas Eve & Day, and New Year's Day • Galleries free (donations accepted). Admission to major exhibits. • W+ • www.biblicalarts.org

Nondenominational art that illustrates the Bible is the theme at this nonprofit center, with several permanent exhibits in the galleries, including a life-size replica of the Garden Tomb of Christ and other exhibits that change every 8 to 12 weeks. The major attractions are the "Miracle of Pentecost" and "Experience Israel." The Miracle is a 30-minute light-and-sound show highlighting the 124' x 20' oil painting by Torger Thompson depicting the day of Pentecost when the Apostles received the Holy Spirit. The mural, which took almost three years to create, contains over 200 Biblical characters, many of them life-size. A unique feature of the light-and-sound show is that it is totally audio narration in darkness for the first several minutes. Shows are usually hourly, starting on the half hour. Admission: Adults, $7; seniors and children 6–18, $6; under 6 free. The "Experience Israel" exhibit, produced in cooperation with the State of Israel, lets visitors see and walk through scenes from Bethlehem, the Sea of Galilee, and the Via Dolorosa. Adults, $4; seniors and children 6–18, $3; under 6 free. Reduced price combination tickets are available. Gift shop.

THE CONSPIRACY MUSEUM

(See OFFBEAT, p. 122)

DALLAS CENTER FOR CONTEMPORARY ART

2801 Swiss (75204), in the Swiss Avenue Historic District • 214-821-2522 • Tuesday–Saturday, 10–5 • Free • www.thecontemporary.net

The name tells it all. Formerly known as the Dallas Visual Arts Center, it changed its name to The Contemporary to make clear that the theme of this small museum is to complement the larger established art institutions with theme-based cutting-edge exhibitions of contemporary art. Its goal is to show avant-garde art by serious professionals with exhibitions showcasing emerging Texas, national, and international contemporary artists. About 15 exhibits are presented annually in the high-ceilinged, naturally lit galleries. Among the many programs offered by The Contemporary that are open to visitors is the Art Movie Night series, which airs documentaries showing contemporary artists at work. These are shown in the evening on the second Tuesday of most months ($5 for nonmembers). Call to confirm. Gift shop.

DALLAS FIREFIGHTERS MUSEUM

3801 Parry (75226), at Commerce, across from Fair Park • 214-821-1500 • Wednesday–Saturday, 10–4, or by appointment • Adults, $1; children $.50 • W downstairs only

This museum is crowded into an historic firehouse that was a working hook-and-ladder company station from 1907 until 1975. Packed tight inside are fire trucks, fire-fighting equipment, photographs, and other memorabilia illustrating the history of the Dallas Fire Department from

1873 to the present. Displays include a 1936 Texas Centennial Exposition Hook and Ladder Truck and the 1884 Ahrens horse-drawn steam pumper called "Old Tige" after the nickname of W. L. Cabell, mayor of Dallas at the time. Upstairs rooms show how the firemen lived at the station in quarters at the top of the brass sliding pole they used to make a quick descent to the truck. Mainly staffed by retired firefighters who will give informal tours. Parking is a problem only during the State Fair. Gift Shop. (See also TEXAS FIRE MUSEUM, p. 93)

DALLAS MEMORIAL CENTER FOR HOLOCAUST STUDIES

7900 Northaven (75230), in the Jewish Community Center • 214-750-4654 • Monday–Friday, 9:30–4:30, and Sunday, noon–4. Closed Jewish and most national holidays • Free (donations accepted) • W (elevator)

Visitors enter this small museum and research library through a boxcar once used to transport people to the concentration camps. Audio tapes are provided for a free self-guided tour that lasts about 45 minutes as it traces, in photos and other artifacts, the horrors of the Holocaust from the first days of the Nazi regime in 1933 through the liberation of the death camps. Films are shown on request. Video documentaries and testimony tapes and other audiovisual materials are available for loan. These are free for teachers; for all others there is a $2 fee and $10 deposit. Bookstore.

DALLAS MUSEUM OF ART

1717 N. Harwood (75201), in the Arts District (DART Light Rail St. Paul Station) • 214-922-1200 • Tuesday–Wednesday, Friday–Sunday, 11–5; Thursday, 11–9. Closed Monday, Thanksgiving, Christmas, and New Year's Day • Adults, $6; seniors and children 12 and older, $4; children under 12 and students with current school ID free. First Tuesday of each month free. • W+ • www.dm-art.org

In 1984, the Arts District was born when this elegant museum opened. The new facilities provided the Dallas Museum of Art (DMA) with a large and impressive home for its significant collections of treasures, which it had been gathering since 1903 from many cultures and disciplines.

In the Art of the Americas collection, there are extensive examples from the lost civilizations of Aztec, Maya, Nasca, and Anasazi, as well as noted twentieth-century artists such as Church, Sargent, Hopper, Benton, O'Keeffe, and Wyeth. Art of Europe includes works by Monet, van Gogh, Gauguin, Degas, Cézanne, and Vuillard. This collection also includes twentieth-century works by Picasso, Giacometti, and Léger. The extensive Arts of Africa collection includes Egyptian, Nubian, and sub-Saharan sculpture and important masterworks by the Ibo, Luba, Yoruba, and Senufo peoples. Arts of Asia and the Pacific feature beautiful examples from Southeast Asia and China and decorative arts from the Japanese Meiji and Edo periods, as well as Indonesian textiles and sculpture.

The pieces in the Contemporary Art collection trace the development from abstract expressionism through pop art to the present. One of the largest collections of post-1945 art in the Southwest, it includes masterpieces by Pollock, Johns, Rothko, Stella, and Warhol. One of the notable components of this collection is the range of works created by Texas artists.

Of special interest is the Reves collection in the Decorative Arts wing. Donated by Mr. and Mrs. Reves, it is presented in a unique setting patterned after their French Riviera villa. It showcases important works by Renoir, Toulouse-Lautrec, Redon, and others, as well as English silver, Chinese porcelain, and original painting and correspondence from Sir Winston Churchill.

The DMA also hosts some of the world's most significant and exclusive traveling exhibitions, usually three each year.

A portion of the DMA's sculpture collection is on exhibit in the Sculpture Garden, which is divided into galleries by a series of water walls. (For more sculpture, take a short walk across the street to the Nasher Sculpture Center.)

A number of tours and talks are given by both docents and staff. Call for times. In the GTE Collections Information Center, visitors can use computer workstations to view images from the DMA, read short essays about artists and their works, and even print out a color image of a DMA masterpiece to take home. Gift shop.

There are two restaurants in the DMA. **Seventeen-Seventeen** is an upscale dining room open for lunch Tuesday through Friday, 11:00 a.m.–2:00 p.m. and occasionally for dinner, even after the museum is closed; Sunday brunch, 11 a.m.–2 p.m. Closed Monday and Saturday. Reservations strongly recommended (214-880-0158). The more casual **Atrium Café** is open for lunch every day the DMA is open and also for dinner on Thursday evening. Parking in the underground garage (fee) with access from either Harwood or St. Paul streets.

DALLAS MUSEUM OF NATURAL HISTORY
(See FAIR PARK, p. 81)

FRONTIERS OF FLIGHT MUSEUM
Love Field at Terminal (75235) until December 2003; thereafter 6811 Lemmon at Love Field • 214-350-1651 • Monday–Saturday, 10–5; Sunday, 1–5 • Adults, $3; children 2–12, $1.50 • www.flightmuseum.com

The exhibits here take the visitor through the history of flight from Greek mythology to man's first balloon flights and on to the Space Shuttle. The collection includes photographs, models, uniforms, and vintage airplane parts. One of the unique displays is the "Lighter Than Air" collection, presenting the history of the mighty dirigibles like the *Hindenburg*, which carried 50 passengers across the Atlantic thirty-seven times before an airliner managed that task. Memorabilia include a radioman's chair that survived the fiery crash of that ill-fated dirigible, structural components from the U.S. Navy airship *Akron*, and the propellers from the USS *Shenandoah* and *Los Angeles*. Tickets from the terminal parking can be validated for a discount.

INTERNATIONAL MUSEUM OF CULTURES

7500 W. Camp Wisdom Rd. (75236), west of Clark Road, on campus of the International Linguistics Center • 972-708-7406 • Tuesday–Friday, 10–5; Saturday–Sunday, 1:30–5. Closed Monday • Free (donations accepted) • W • www.sil.org/imc

The goal of this museum is to increase understanding of cultural diversity. It does it through both life-size and miniature exhibits depicting the lives of culturally diverse people living today throughout the world. For example, in one section progressive exhibits tell the life story of a Peruvian native boy from birth to retirement. Exhibits change about every six months. The museum is affiliated with the **International Linguistics Center** next door. Less than half the world's 5,000-plus languages are in writing, and this is the international headquarters of the Wycliffe Bible Society, which trains linguists to work with remote native populations to establish a written language and teach the people to read and write it. Wycliffe linguists have made more than 450 translations of the Bible. Call for information on tours.

MCKINNEY AVENUE CONTEMPORARY

3120 McKinney (75204) (DART Light Rail Cityplace Station and M-line Streetcar) • 214-953-1MAC (953-1612) • Wednesday–Saturday, 11–10; Sunday, 1–5. Closed Monday–Tuesday • Free • W+ • www.the-mac.org

This gallery provides exhibition space to showcase the latest developments in all disciplines and media as part of its interdisciplinary program of art exhibitions, theater performances, concerts, and lectures. Under one roof, it offers opportunities for experimentation and for the presentation of new art in all disciplines. In addition, it provides a forum for critical dialogue between emerging and established artists and their audiences. Call or check website for schedule. The MAC also has a Cybercafe offering free internet access and classes. Free parking. (See also MUSIC AND PERFORMING ARTS—Kitchen Dog Theater, p. 103)

MEADOWS MUSEUM OF ART

5900 Bishop (75275), on Southern Methodist University campus (DART Light Rail Mockingbird Station and SMU's Mustang Express) • 214-768-2516 • Monday–Tuesday, Friday–Saturday, 10–5; Thursday, 10–8; Sunday, 1–5. Closed Wednesday and most holidays • Free • W+ • www.meadowsmuseum.smu.edu

During trips to Spain in the 1950s, Texas oil financier and philanthropist Algur H. Meadows was so impressed by the spectacular collection of Spanish masterpieces in Madrid's Prado Museum that he began his own collection of Spanish art. In 1962, as part of a $35 million endowment, he donated his collection to SMU. As a result, this museum houses one of the finest and most comprehensive collections of Spanish art outside of Spain. The permanent collection features major works dating from the Middle Ages to the present, including masterpieces by some of Europe's greatest painters: Velázquez, Rivera, Zubarán, Murillo, El Greco, Goya, Miró, and Picasso. Highlights of the collection include Renaissance altarpieces, monumental Baroque canvases, exquisite rococo oil sketches, polychrome wood sculptures, Impressionist landscapes, Modernist abstractions, and a comprehensive collection of the graphic works of Goya. The museum plaza showcases sculptures from the **Elizabeth Meadows Sculpture Collection**, including works by Auguste Rodin, Henry Moore, and David Smith. Free public tours are given every Thursday at 6:00 p.m. and every Saturday and Sunday at 2:00 p.m. Group tours are also available for a fee.

Throughout the year, the Meadows Museum presents a variety of public programs for visitors of all ages, including Family Days, Artful Thursday Evenings, Gallery Talks, and the Music in the Meadows series. Call or check the website for details. Free parking is available in the garage beneath the museum. The **Gates Restaurant** is open Monday–Friday for lunch. In keeping with the museum's theme, it offers a Spanish-inspired menu. Reservations are recommended. Museum gift shop.

The **Pollack Gallery** is located in SMU's Hughes-Trigg Student Center (3140 Dyer). This gallery exhibits contemporary works by regional, national, and international artists and historical works from all cultures. It also showcases works of students of the Meadows School of Arts. The gallery is open Monday–Tuesday and Thursday–Friday, 11–5; Saturday, 1–5. Closed Wednesday and Sunday except by appointment. Admission is free. Parking is available in the lot north of Boaz Hall at Binkley Avenue and Ownby Drive.

NASHER SCULPTURE CENTER

2001 Flora (75201), in the Arts District (DART Light Rail St. Paul Station) • 214-242-5100 • Adults, $10 • W+ • www.nashersculpturecenter.org

Located on 2.4 acres adjacent to the Dallas Museum of Art, the major pieces of sculpture on display in this $60 million center are from the Raymond and Patsy Nasher Collection, considered the foremost privately owned collection of twentieth-century sculpture in the world. Opened in October 2003, it includes masterpieces by Calder, de Kooning, di Suvero, Giacometti, Hepworth, Kelly, Matisse, Miró, Moore, Picasso, Rodin, and Serra.

A glass and travertine marble entrance building houses 10,000 square feet of indoor gallery spaces, plus classrooms, an auditorium, café, and gift shop. Outside, the two-acre sculpture garden displays, on a rotating basis, about twenty-five large-scale outdoor sculptures from the Nasher Collection and from other collections around the world.

OLD CITY PARK—THE HISTORICAL VILLAGE OF DALLAS

1717 Gano (75215), between Harwood and Ervay Sts., just south of I-30 • 214-421-5141 • Tuesday–Saturday, 10–4; Sunday, 12–4. Closed Thanksgiving, Christmas Eve, and Christmas Day, New Year's Eve and New Year's Day. Only open evenings during "Candlelight" event first two weekends in December • Adults, $7; seniors, $5; children 3-12, $4. • W variable • www.oldcitypark.org

Step into the past in Texas as you stroll the red brick streets and visit around three dozen historic structures that illustrate how people lived in North Texas between the 1840s and the early 1900s. All the structures have been moved from their original sites to this 13-acre park and meticulously restored. These include: the 1860s Living Farmstead, 1907 General Store, 1905 Citizen's Bank, an 1847 log cabin, the 1885 Sullivan House, and the Victorian parlors of the 1900 George House and Hotel. Authentically costumed interpreters bring to life the daily work of the blacksmith, printer, potter, and others. The park is operated by the Dallas County Heritage Society, which sponsors a number of special events and festivals during the year, including "Candlelight at Old City Park" on several weekends during the Christmas season. An audio tour is available ($3) for those who want to see the Village at their own pace. Guided one-hour tours are also available late morning and early afternoon. Call for details. Gift shop. The grounds are open daily even on days the Village buildings are closed. Limited parking inside park. Ample free parking across Gano Street. **Brent Place**, a restaurant in an 1876 farmhouse, offers lunch daily. It has its own parking. Reservations, 214-421-3057.

THE SCIENCE PLACE AND TI FOUNDERS IMAX® THEATER

(See FAIR PARK, p. 81)

THE SIXTH FLOOR MUSEUM

411 Elm (75202), at Houston in the West End District (DART Light Rail West End Station) • 214-747-6660 or 888-485-4854 toll-free • Open seven days, 9–6. Closed Thanksgiving and Christmas • Adults, $10; seniors and children 6–18, $9; under 6 free • W+ but call for information on access • www.jfk.org

The original corner window from which Oswald fired the shots that killed President John F. Kennedy is one of the many exhibits in this museum, which examines JFK's life, times, death, and legacy. The Kennedy family did not want this site memorialized, and the people of Dallas surely wanted to put this dark period in the city's history behind them. But every day people came to the assassination site to retrace the motorcade route, explore the grassy knoll, and point to the corner window of "the sixth floor." Finally, it was decided that it was better to provide a clear and even-handed historical presentation than to continue to hope that the memories of the assassination would fade. Today this museum annually hosts close to half a million visitors.

Operated by the Dallas County Historical Foundation, the museum is located on the sixth and seventh floors of the Dallas County Administration Building (formerly the Texas School Book Depository), and includes the sixth-floor location of the so-called sniper's perch. JFK's life and death are illustrated through the use of nearly 400 photographs, 45 minutes of documentary film, and other interpretive artifacts and material. Views from the sixth floor include Dealey Plaza National Historic Landmark, where the assassination took place, and among the exhibits is a large scale model of Dealey Plaza prepared by the FBI for the Warren Commission in 1964. One exhibit includes over a dozen still and movie cameras that were used to record the events taking place on November 22, 1963, including the amateur movie camera used by Abraham Zapruder that was the only camera to record the entire assassination. For additional insight on how people still recall this tragic event many decades later, read (and write in) the Memory Books.

Audio tour tapes are available in English and six foreign languages for an additional $3 (for all ages). There are special tapes for children 6–12 (English only). Gift shop. Pay parking lots to the north and west of the building.

Note: For a differing view of the JFK assassination, see the Conspiracy Museum, in OFFBEAT, p. 122.

SOUTH DALLAS CULTURAL CENTER

3400 S. Fitzhugh (75210) • 214-939-2787 • www.dallasculture.org/sdcc

This multipurpose arts facility serves the African-American community. The 18,000-square-foot facility, located just outside Fair Park, includes a popular visual arts gallery that frequently features the works of African-American artists. It also periodically holds a Marketplace where original works of art are sold. Other facilities at the center are a 100-seat theater and studios for dance and arts and crafts.

TELEPHONE PIONEER MUSEUM OF TEXAS

One Bell Plaza, 208 S. Akard (75222) (DART Light Rail Akard Station) • 214-464-4359 • Monday–Friday, 9:30–2:30 • Free • W (elevator)

Access to the upper floors of this building is restricted to employees; however, there is a special elevator that goes only to this museum. Here you'll find the story of the past, present, and future of telephone technology told in a number of interactive audiovisual displays. Exhibits include a life-sized mannequin of Alexander Graham Bell and dioramas of the people behind the scenes who make your telephone work today. One display allows visitors to dial a number and see how the call is completed. Little kids will enjoy the talking bear and the huge talking telephone. Gift shop.

TEXAS FIRE MUSEUM

2600 Chalk Hill Rd. (75212) • 214-267-1867 • Thursday–Friday, 10–2, and third Saturday of month, 8–5 • Free • www.texasfiremuseum.com

Founded in 1999, this museum is in the process of development in the old City of Dallas Fire Department Maintenance Facility. A number of old fire trucks are on display. The purpose of the museum is to acquire, restore, and preserve old fire apparatus, including assisting with the apparatus located in the Dallas Firefighters Museum and the North Texas Historical Fire Society. (See MUSEUMS AND PUBLIC ART GALLERIES—Dallas Firefighters Museum, p. 86)

TRAMMELL & MARGARET CROW COLLECTION OF ASIAN ART

2010 Flora (75201), in the Arts District (DART Light Rail Pearl Station) • 214-979-6430 • Tuesday–Sunday, 10–5; Thursday, 10–9. Closed Monday • Free • W+ • www.crowcollection.org

A Daoist deity seated in the midst of a splashing fountain welcomes visitors to the three tranquil galleries that display hundreds of rare works of art from one of the most important private collections of Asian art in the United States. The art from Japan, China, India, and Southeast Asia offers visitors a peaceful world of beauty and spirituality. Because many objects now considered "art" were created for religious purposes, many of the pieces in the permanent collection represent deities from various religions, including Buddhism, Confucianism, and Hinduism. Dating from 3500 B.C. to early twentieth century, the works of art include precious jade ornaments from China, delicate Japanese scrolls, and a rarely seen 28' × 12' sandstone façade of an eighteenth-century Indian residence.

Public tours available every Saturday and Sunday at 1:00 p.m. Visitors may also rent an audio tour ($5) and multimedia computer stations are available to help guide you through the huge collection. There are also frequent public lectures and artist talks (fee).

Paid parking is available in the underground garage at the Trammel Crow Center, next door. Access from Harwood or Olive.

(See also OUTDOOR PUBLIC ART—Trammel Crow Center, p. 94)

OUTDOOR PUBLIC ART • WWW.DALLASCULTURE.ORG/PUBLIC.HTML

The City of Dallas Public Arts Program maintains a city-owned collection of more than 115 pieces of artworks exhibited in public spaces. In addition, a number of private collections and pieces are on exhibit through-out the city. A "Walking Sculpture" map/brochure is available from the Convention & Visitors Bureau. Created by the Dallas Foundation, a non-profit organization, it offers six self-guided walking tours of sculptures in more than 30 locations in the downtown area. The following are just a few of these pieces of art you can see on your travels around the city.

Bank of America Plaza (Main and Griffin) • Works by John Kearney, Michael Todd, Alexander Liberman, and William Martin.

Dallas City Hall (1500 Marilla) • Henry Moore's *The Dallas Piece* and Robert Summers *Pioneer Plaza Cattle Drive.*

Lubben Plaza (Young and Market) • Works of Linnea Glatt, George Smith, and Jésus Bautista Moroles.

Myerson Symphony Center (2301 Flora) • Works by Eduardo Chillida, Jacques Lipchitz, and Henri Laurens.

Trammell Crow Center Sculpture Collection (2001 Ross) • The gardens and lobby of this 50-story skyscraper feature more than twenty bronze statues from the French masters, including Auguste Rodin, Aristide Maillol, and Emile Antoine Bourdelle.
Note: Every DART light rail station was designed with input of a Texas artist.

SPECIAL GARDENS

DALLAS ARBORETUM AND BOTANICAL GARDENS

8525 Garland (75218), on eastern shore of White Rock Lake (DART White Rock Station and bus) • 214-327-8263; events hotline 214-327-4901 • Open seven days, 10–5, longer hours in summer. Closed Thanksgiving, Christmas, and New Year's Day • Adults, $6; children 3–12, $3; 2 and under free. Parking $3 • W variable • Trams to major garden areas March–December. (Wheelchairs available at the front gate for loan, free; first come, first served.) • www.dallasarboretum.org and www.dallasplanttrails.org

This 66-acre arboretum, which overlooks the eastern shore of White Rock Lake, offers visitors both a variety of ornamental gardens and acres of natural woodlands, creating an oasis in the heart of one of Dallas's old-est neighborhoods.

The Lay Ornamental Garden, also known as Mimi's Garden, offers two acres of perennials in an English-style garden. It was designed to uti-lize both native Texas plants and others adapted to local conditions. Among the many flowers displayed in the six-acre **Jonsson Color Garden** is one of the nation's largest azalea collections, more than 2,000 varieties, in bloom each spring, and over 15,000 chrysanthemums each fall. **The**

Palmer Fern Dell features shade-loving ferns and rhododendrons that are kept cool with a periodic micro-mist fog. The **Hunt Paseo de Flores** is a quarter-mile linear garden. The 1.8-acre **Woman's Garden** is the most formal of all the gardens in the Arboretum. Its site features a series of terraced walkways and garden spaces aligned to enhance views of the lake.

A major attraction is the **Degolyer House,** one of two historic homes on the grounds that are on the National Register of Historic Places. Completed in 1940, the one-story house encompasses 13 rooms and seven baths in 21,000 square feet. The 4.5-acre **Historic DeGolyer Gardens,** surrounding the house includes a rose garden, fountains, and hundreds of annuals. Tours of the home are given on a regular schedule.

Special events are held every season, the major one being **Dallas Blooms,** held for about a month in the spring when more than 180,000 flowering bulbs color the gardens. In fall there is the colorful **Dallas Blooms Autumn,** and the holiday season, from late November through late December, brings **Christmas at the Arboretum.** About 300,000 visitors tour the Arboretum annually. Gift shop. Picnic area.

TEXAS DISCOVERY GARDENS
(See FAIR PARK, p. 84)

OUTDOORS

DALLAS NATURE CENTER
7171 Mountain Creek Pkwy. (75249), southwest near Joe Pool Lake • 972-296-1955 • Open Tuesday–Sunday, 7 a.m. to sunset. Closed Monday • $3 donation per car • W Visitor Center • www.dallasnaturecenter.org

Part of this 630-acre wilderness preserve sits on the escarpment that runs from north of Dallas south almost to Austin, making it the highest point in Dallas County and offering great views of Joe Pool Lake. It is the habitat for a wide variety of native wildlife and wildflowers and other plants. Facilities include 10 miles of hiking trails, which vary widely in length and difficulty. One of the shortest and most popular is the Butterfly Trail, which takes you through the Mary Alice Bland Butterfly Garden, designed to attract butterflies to its colorful habitat. Guided hikes are available for a small fee. Other facilities include picnic areas, a visitor center, and an observation tower. The Center is a bird-of-prey rescue facility. Dallas County Audubon Society sometimes sponsors free birding field trips here. Gift shop.

DALLAS PARKS
Park and Recreation Department, City Hall, 1500 Marilla (75201) (DART Light Rail Convention Center Station) •

214-670-4100; for activities in Dallas parks, 214-670-7070 •
www.ci.dallas.tx.us

If you want to get away from it all, the Park and Recreation Department
has just the places for you. This department maintains more than 21,000
park acres, including 18 lakes with 4,400 surface acres of water and more
than 61 miles of jogging and bike trails at 25 locations. It provides leisure,
recreational, and cultural activities at 336 neighborhood/community/re-
gional parks: 5 tennis centers and 263 tennis courts, 227 playgrounds, 127
soccer fields, 321 multipurpose fields, 97 softball diamonds and 28 baseball diamonds, 23 community swimming pools, 45 recreation centers, 41
football fields, six 18-hole golf courses, and three golf driving ranges. In
addition, its facilities include the Dallas Aquarium, Dallas Arboretum,
Dallas Zoo, and Fair Park.

Details on the parks and recreation system are in the department
brochure, "The Ultimate Adventure," which is available from the department and at the Visitors Information Center and Dallas Convention and
Visitors Bureau. (See FREE VISITOR SERVICES, p. 67)

Following are a few of its larger parks and the facilities in each. Most
are open from 6:00 a.m. to midnight, and admission is free.

Bachman Lake Park • 2750 Bachman Dr. (75220), near Love Field •
214-670-6266 • Fishing is permitted in 205-acre Bachman Lake, which is
ringed by three miles of paved trails for hiking, jogging, and biking.
Other facilities include picnic tables with grills, multipurpose fields, a
soccer field, and playground. A concession rents paddle boats. In addition to its regular programs, the Recreation Center here offers facilities
and programs designed to meet the needs and interests of persons with
disabilities aged 6 and up. The center is staffed by therapeutic recreation
professionals. Facilities include a 25-meter pool, hot tub, full gymnasium,
weight room, arts and crafts room, and a theater. A fishing pier is located
on the lake adjacent to the building.

L. B. Houston Park and Nature Trail • California Crossing at Wild-
wood • Located along the Dallas side of the Elm Fork of the Trinity
River, south of Northwest Highway, most of this 476-acre wilderness
preserve has remained undisturbed for hundreds of years. As a result it is
a jewel for nature lovers and bird-watchers. Facilities include four miles
of soft-surface and four miles of hard surface trails, and well over 100 picnic tables. It is also the site of the L. B. Houston Tennis Center (11225
Luna • 214-670-6367), which has 16 lighted courts, and the L. B. Houston Golf Course (214-670-6322).

Kiest Park • 3080 S. Hampton Rd. (75224) • 214-670-1918 • Among
the facilities in this 258-acre park are a number of varied sports courts
and fields, more than two miles of hard-surface trail, and picnic areas.
Also located here is Fantasy Landing, Dallas's first public playground designed so that able-bodied children and those with disabilities can play
together. Facilities at the recreation center (2324 W. Kiest Blvd.) include
16 lighted tennis courts.

White Rock Lake Park • 8300 Garland Rd. (75218) (DART Light Rail White Rock Station) • 214-670-8239 • The park's 2,115 acres include the 1,088-acre lake. Facilities include a 9-mile hike and bike trail that follows the water's edge most of the way and connects to the 7-mile trail along White Rock Greenbelt. Variety of sports fields, and more than 200 picnic tables. The Dallas County Audubon Society hosts bird-watching tours every Saturday morning, rain or shine (972-498-8930). The **Bath House Cultural Center**, a meeting, art exhibition, and performance space, is located in the park on the east side. The **Dallas Arboretum and Botanical Gardens** adjoins the park on the east. Fishing is permitted (license required) in the frequently stocked lake. Paddleboats can usually be rented on the west side of the lake. Canoes and sailboats are permitted on the lake. Free parking in the park.

COLLEGE CAMPUSES OF INTEREST TO VISITORS

DALLAS COUNTY COMMUNITY COLLEGE DISTRICT
Headquarters: 701 Elm (75202) (DART Light Rail West End Station) • 214-860-2135 • W • www.dcccd.edu

In 1966, the District's first college, El Centro, began operation in the downtown Central Business District with more than 4,000 students. Today it is a comprehensive two-year system comprising seven campuses throughout the county enrolling nearly 62,000 students in credit courses leading to associate degrees and an additional 27,000 noncredit, continuing education students each semester, making it the largest undergraduate institution in Texas and among the largest community college systems in the nation. Most of the campuses offer visitors student theatre, dance, art, and photographic exhibitions.

El Centro College • 801 Main (75202) (DART Light Rail West End Station) • 214-860-2037 • W+ • This college is located at the gateway to the city's historic West End District. The main building is the completely renovated nine-story historic Sanger Brothers Department Store Building, built in 1919, that was ahead of its time in the days of gaslights and buggies. (See HISTORIC PLACES, p. 76) A two-story student and technology center is being built on the south side of the campus. Visitors are welcome at theater performances and some other campus activities.

Mountain View College • 4849 West Illinois (75211) (DART Light Rail Westmoreland Station and bus) • 214-860-8680 • W+ but not all areas • www.mvc.dcccd.edu • Located on 200 acres in the southwestern section of the city, the campus features stunning scenic landscaping that includes rocky ravines, native plants and trees, and a meandering stream. The college holds the distinction of being the only college campus in the nation with an Urban Wildlife Sanctuary designated by the Humane Society of the United States. Glassed-in pedestrian bridges connect the east and west complexes and provide a spectacular view of the area. Visitors are welcome at theater performances, guest lecture series, and sports events. Student and faculty artwork is also prominently displayed throughout the campus. Designated visitor parking on the east side of the campus.

SOUTHERN METHODIST UNIVERSITY (SMU)

Hillcrest between Mockingbird and Daniel (75275) (DART Light Rail Mockingbird Station and SMU's Mustang Express) • 214-768-2000 • W variable • www.smu.edu

Dallas's oldest and most prestigious university, SMU was founded in 1911 and opened with 706 students in 1915, when it had two buildings and a 35-member faculty. Today its spacious, tree-lined 165-acre campus of red brick buildings has grown up around the neoclassical style of Dallas Hall, one of those original buildings named in appreciation of the city's support. SMU now has more than 500 full-time faculty and serves more than 10,000 students.

SMU is a rich center of cultural activity for Dallas and the North Texas region, with museum offerings, visual and performing arts productions, and lecture series. Intercollegiate sports are also popular with fans of football, basketball, volleyball, and other sports.

The Meadows School of the Arts is a cultural focal point of the university. The major attraction here is the Meadows Museum of Art, which houses one of the finest collections of Spanish art outside of Spain. (See MUSEUMS AND PUBLIC ART GALLERIES, p. 89) The school offers hundreds of public arts events each year including theater, dance, opera, symphony, choral, wind ensemble, organ, and special events productions. Facilities include the Bob Hope Theatre, Greer Garson Theatre, Margo Jones Theatre, Caruth Auditorium, Charles S. Sharp Performing Arts Studio, and the O'Donnel Lecture/Recital Hall. For information, call the Meadows Box Office, 214-768-2787. (See MUSIC AND PERFORMING ARTS, p. 105)

Hundreds of public lectures are given each year in McFarlin Auditorium (Hillcrest and McFarlin), as well as in various colleges within the university. Many lectures feature SMU faculty and local, national, and international leaders and personalities. Some programs are free and others, such as the Willis M. Tate Distinguished Lecture Series, have an admission fee. For information call the SMU Lecture Programs Office, 214-768-8283.

More than 2.9 million volumes are housed in the six general and special libraries on campus. All libraries present occasional special exhibitions and some have limited access arrangement for nonstudents.

Southern Methodist University

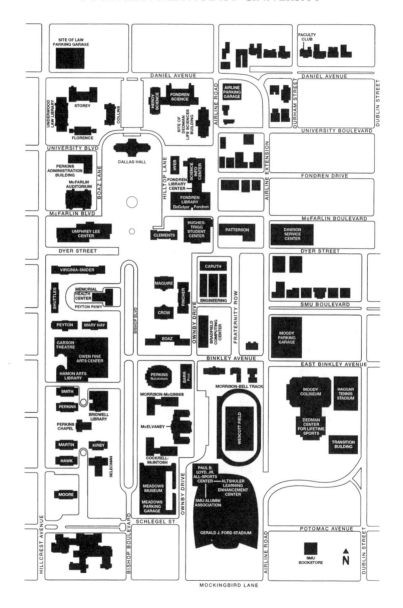

SMU students participate in Division 1-A football, basketball, track, golf, soccer, tennis, volleyball, and rowing. Nationally ranked teams include men's and women's swimming and diving, men's golf, soccer, and tennis. SMU also offers a large program of intramural and club sports. The SMU Mustang football team is part of the 16-member Western Athletic Conference. Home football games are held in the Gerald J. Ford Stadium on campus. Almost all sports events are open to visitors, most are free, and usually only the major intercollegiate sports have admission fees.

For information on any sport or event, call 214-768-2864 or check the athletics website at www.athletics.smu.edu.

Visitors to campus may park in the Moody Parking Garage, SMU Blvd. and Airline; the Airline Parking Garage, 6506 Airline and University; and the lot at the 3100 block of University. Parking fees vary by event. Metered spaces are also available on campus. Occasionally, some lots are designated for special events parking. Call SMU Department of Public Safety for information, 214-768-3388.

SMU is a private, comprehensive university comprising six colleges: Dedman College of Humanities and Sciences, Meadows School of the Arts, School of Engineering, Cox School of Business, Perkins School of Theology, and Dedman School of Law. The university offers degree programs for undergraduate, master's, doctoral, professional, and certificate studies, in addition to continuing education for adults in business, liberal arts, and other disciplines. Students can also participate in international study programs in 12 countries throughout Europe, North America, Australia, and Asia. Founded by what is now the United Methodist Church, SMU is nonsectarian in its teaching and committed to values of academic freedom and open inquiry. Management is vested in the Board of Trustees, which includes civic, business, education, and religious leaders representing various faiths and geographic areas.

MUSIC AND PERFORMING ARTS

The Dallas Morning News Arts and Entertainment Hotline, 214-977-8400; *also* www.guidelive.com • *Dallas Convention & Visitors Bureau Events Hotline*, 214-571-1301; *also www.visitdallas.com* • *City of Dallas Office of Cultural Affairs*, 972-504-6658 • *www. dallasculture.org and www.culturefinder.org*

THEATER GROUPS AND
PERFORMANCE/ENTERTAINMENT VENUES

For a comprehensive list of theater groups, see **www.dallastheatreleague.org**.

AMERICAN AIRLINES CENTER

2500 Victory (75201) • (DART Light Rail Victory Station—usually open only for special events) • 214-222-3687 • Event line,

214-665-4200; Box Office, 214-665-4797 • W+ • Public tours of
the Center Monday, Wednesday, and Friday. Event days, 11–2;
non-event days, 11–4. Adults, $5; seniors and children 3–18, $3.
Reservations required (214-665-4213).
www.americanairlinescenter.com

Best known as the home of the Dallas Mavericks and Dallas Stars (See
SPORTS, pp. 116–17), this huge $420 million center is also a prime en-
tertainment complex. (When planning its use as an entertainment center,
the architects even designed the loading bay ramps at the optimum angle
at which circus elephants can walk uphill.) Set up for a concert or other
major show, it offers 20,000 seats, all with an unobstructed view. Parking
locations and prices vary by event and usually cost $8 to $15. Gift shop.
If you want to go all the way and take your family and/or friends, about
a dozen of the 130 corporate suites are usually available for rent for any
event. Suites hold 18 to 25 people, include parking passes and a catering package, and, depending on the event, cost from $2,000 to $10,000.
The Center is the cornerstone of the ongoing 70-acre Victory Project,
which will eventually include 8 million square feet of entertainment,
shopping, and business facilities connecting the Center and the West
End.

BATH HOUSE CULTURAL CENTER

521 E. Lawther (75218), on the shore of White Rock Lake (DART
Light Rail White Rock Station and bus) • 214-670-8749 • Event
hotline, 214-670-8570 • Tuesday–Saturday, 12–6; theater weekends
until 10 • W+ • www.bathhousecultural.com

The 120-seat theater is used for both professional and community productions by a number of theater companies. The annual summer Festival
of Independent Theaters brings together these diverse theater groups to
present a month-long repertory of new, original, avant-garde, and rarely
seen works. It also hosts concerts ranging from jazz to classical, ethnic
and world music, plus literature and poetry readings, modern and classical dance, and multidisciplinary performances. Admission to theater and
concert performances usually $10–$20. Free parking. (See also MUSE-
UMS AND PUBLIC ART GALLERIES, p. 85)

BLACK ACADEMY OF ARTS AND LETTERS

Dallas Convention Center Theaters, 650 S. Griffin (DART Light Rail
Convention Center Station) • 214-743-2440 • W+ • www.tbaal.org

For almost three decades, this nonprofit organization has presented
theater, music, dance, and visual and literary arts of African-American,
Caribbean, and African culture. Many of the performances are touring
shows and nationally and internationally known celebrities on the national Black Theater Circuit. Performance spaces are in the two Convention Center theaters: the 1,750-seat Naomi Burton Theater and the
225-seat Clarence Muse Café Theater. Gift shop.

BRONCO BOWL ENTERTAINMENT CENTER

2600 Fort Worth (75211) • 214-943-1777 • W+ •
www.broncobowl.com

The 3,000-seat arena with a state-of-the-art sound and lighting system
hosts concerts by top entertainers and Broadway-style shows. A 140,000-
square-foot eclectic entertainment complex, it also offers a nightclub with
dancing, bowling, billiards, and a games arcade.

DALLAS CONVENTION CENTER

650 South Griffin (75202) (DART Light Rail Convention Center
Station) • 214-939-2700 • W+ • www.dallascc.com

Of the approximately four million people who annually attend conventions in Dallas, many attend in this modern facility that contains
more than a million square feet of exhibit space, ballrooms, more than
100 meeting rooms, an arena, two theaters, and a heliport. And when it
isn't being used for conventions, this center's arena and theaters are used
for live theater and concerts by visiting artists and other major entertainment events.

DALLAS THEATER CENTER

DTC Box office 214-522-8499 • www.dallastheatercenter.org and
www.dtcinfo.org

One of the leading regional theaters in the country, DTC has two performance spaces, the Kalita Humphreys Theater and the Arts District
Theater. Both theaters are used for the main season productions. Individual tickets about $20 to $60.

Kalita Humphreys Theater • 3636 Turtle Creek (75219) • 214-526-
8210 • W+ • The Dallas Theater Center's home base is in this theater,
which opened in 1959 and is one of only three existing theaters designed
by Frank Lloyd Wright. Its square boxes and circular core are reminiscent
of Wright's design of the Guggenheim Museum in New York City, which
he did about the same time. Wright's design is based on nature, where
30/60-degree angles prevail, and he stated that there was not a right
angle in the theater. Even the window and door frames are made slightly
off. (Actually there are right angles, but only where the ceiling and floor
meet the walls.) The theater seats about 500 and hosts professional
theater productions ranging from the classics to new works. Behind-the-
scenes tours can be arranged by appointment.

Arts District Theater • 2401 Flora (75201) (DART Light Rail Pearl Station)
• 214-922-0422 • W+ • Located across Artists Square from the Meyerson,
this 700-seat theater in a converted metal warehouse opened in 1985. It is
one of the largest flexible seating and staging performance spaces in the
country, designed to meet the needs of each production in relation to the
interaction between the actors and the audience. Because of its size and
flexibility, it is often used for musicals and other large productions.

EL CENTRO COLLEGE THEATER

(See COLLEGE CAMPUSES OF INTEREST TO VISITORS, p. 97)

FAIR PARK MUSIC HALL

(See FAIR PARK, p. 84)

THE KITCHEN DOG THEATER

3120 McKinney (75204), in the McKinney Avenue Contemporary (The MAC) (DART Light Rail Cityplace Station and M-Line Streetcar) • 214-953-1055 • W+ • www.kitchendogtheater.org

Founded in 1990 by five graduates of Southern Methodist University's MFA Theater Program, the Kitchen Dog is now the resident company at the MAC. The name is from a symbol in Samuel Beckett's play *Waiting for Godot*. Their emphasis is on plays that challenge our moral and social consciences and invite the audience to be provoked, challenged, or amazed. Performances Thursday–Sunday. Tickets are $8–$20 and all Thursday night performances are Pay-What-You-Can (for walk-ups only), as long as there are tickets left to sell. Free parking at the MAC. Overflow parking at the Travis Academy, 3001 McKinney.

MAJESTIC THEATRE

1925 Elm (75201) (DART Light Rail Pearl Station) • 214-880-0137 • W+

A beautifully restored historic theater, it seats 1,649 and hosts local and touring concerts and a Broadway show series as well as dance productions. (See also HISTORIC PLACES, p. 76)

MORTON H. MEYERSON SYMPHONY CENTER

2301 Flora Street (75201), in the Arts District (DART Light Rail Pearl Station) • 214-670-3600 • W+ • www.dallasculture.org/themeyerson/

This musical centerpiece of the Dallas Arts District hosts over 500 events a year. It is home of the Dallas Symphony Orchestra, the Dallas Wind Symphony, and the Turtle Creek Chorale and used extensively by other Dallas-based cultural organizations. Opened in 1989, the 2,062-seat center was named by its principal donor, H. Ross Perot, after one of his top assistants. This is the only symphony center designed by the internationally known architect I. M. Pei. McDermott Concert Hall, the centerpiece of the Meyerson, has won acclaim for its acoustics which include a 42-ton four-piece acoustical canopy, located above the stage and first few rows of the audience chamber, that can be raised, lowered, and tilted to enhance the sound.

Another feature of the center is the hand-built $2 million, 4,535-pipe Lay Family Concert Organ, one of the largest mechanical-action organs ever built for a concert hall. It consists of 84 ranks with 65 stops, a 4 manual keyboard with 61 notes, and a pedal keyboard with 32 notes. Once a month, schedule permitting, there is a 30-minute organ recital followed by a tour of the center. Other public tours of the center are offered on a regular basis several times a week. Call for details.

Both a fine dining and a buffet restaurant are open before the symphony performances. Reservation suggested (214-670-3721).

In addition to street-level parking, there is underground parking in the Arts District Garage. Main entrance on Ross between Crockett and Leonard. Gift shop.

MOUNTAIN VIEW COLLEGE PERFORMING ARTS THEATRE

(See COLLEGE CAMPUSES OF INTEREST TO VISITORS, p. 97)

PEGASUS THEATER

3916 Main Street (75226) • 214- 821-6005 • W+ •
www.pegasustheatre.org

Since its founding in 1985, this small professional theater troupe located in Deep Ellum has specialized in presenting original and offbeat comedies with productions year round. Shows Thursday–Sunday. Tickets about $12–$17. Preview performances, $5. On-street parking.

POCKET SANDWICH THEATER

5400 E. Mockingbird, #119 (75206) (DART Light Rail Mockingbird Station) • 214-821-1860 • W • www.pocketsandwich.com

A neighborhood theater known locally for professional productions of all types of plays, but with a leaning toward comedies and melodramas—the sillier the better. Its Christmas season production of *Scrooge* has earned the status of a city tradition. The sandwich in the name may have come from the sandwiches and other food (and drinks) for sale—also popcorn, which is primarily to throw at the villain in the melodramas. Performances Thursday–Sunday. Tickets $6–$14. Free parking. Theater also used for late-night stand-up comedy and occasional concerts on Wednesday and after the main stage shows.

REUNION ARENA

777 Sport (75207) (DART Light Rail Union Station) • 214-800-3000, Box Office 214-800-3089 • W+ • www.reunionarena.org

Home of the Dallas Sidekicks indoor soccer team. When they are not kicking, Reunion Arena hosts other sports events and is the frequent site of major pop and country concerts, ice shows and competitions, and other performance events. Seats 16,800 for soccer and around 19,000 for concerts. And there isn't a bad seat in the house. More than 6,000 paid parking spaces available in the area with prices ranging from $6 to $10. Connected by walkways and pedestrian tunnels to Union Station and Hyatt Regency Hotel.

SAMMONS CENTER FOR THE ARTS

3630 Harry Hines (75219) • 214-520-7789 • Facility open
Monday–Saturday, 8:30–10:30; Sunday, noon–9 • W •
www.sammonsartcenter.org

The performance spaces here include a hall with performance seating
for up to 260 and recital halls. One popular series given here for nominal
ticket prices is Sammons Jazz, featuring local jazz artists in a relaxed setting. (See MUSIC, p. 110). The facilities are also used for rehearsals and
workshops by dozens of other local music, arts, and cultural organizations.
This multi-use facility is also known as a nonprofit arts incubator providing
an office home for more than a dozen emerging and mid-sized nonprofit
arts organizations. The building is the converted Turtle Creek Pump station, which is the oldest public building in Dallas, completed in 1909, and
the sole source of water for the City of Dallas until 1930. The Center is
sometimes difficult for visitors to find; call for voice directions. About 100
parking spaces. When these are filled, valet parking available (usually free).

SOUTHERN METHODIST UNIVERSITY PERFORMANCE SPACES

(See COLLEGE CAMPUSES OF INTEREST TO VISITORS—SMU,
p. 98)
(DART Light Rail Mockingbird Station and SMU Mustang Express)
• Events Hot Line and Box Office, 214-768-2787 • Lecture Program
Office, 214-768-8283

Bob Hope Theatre: A 390-seat proscenium stage theater that features an
assortment of events including dance, opera, theater productions, and film
screenings.

Caruth Auditorium: A 490-seat concert hall. A variety of music recitals
and concerts are given here.

Greer Garson Theatre: A 392-seat thrust stage theater offering theatrical
performances.

Margo Jones Theatre: A 125-seat black box theater offering theatrical
events.

McFarlin Memorial Auditorium: SMU's largest performance facility hosts
year-round activities including classical music concerts, the Willis M. Tate
Distinguished Lecture Series, dance performances, screenings, and plays.

SMIRNOFF MUSIC CENTRE

(See FAIR PARK, p. 84)

THEATRE THREE AND THEATRE TOO

2800 Routh (75201), in the Quadrangle (DART M-Line Streetcar) •
214-871-3300 • W (Call ahead) • www.theatre3dallas.com

The name refers to the three ingredients of theater: playwrights, production, and audiences. This theater group has been presenting plays and musicals by major playwrights and composers since 1963. The upstairs, Theatre Three, is a theater in the round seating 242. Downstairs, Theatre Too is an intimate black box theater seating 72. Each show runs six weeks. Performances Thursday–Sunday. Tickets $25–$35.

TRINITY RIVER ARTS CENTER

2600 Stemmons (75207) (TRE Medical/Market Center Station) • 214-630-5491 • W

A nonprofit center for local theater groups that presents a variety of productions including children's theater. **Kim Dawson Theater** seats 160. Tickets vary by performance. Box office 214-219-2718. Also small art gallery.

TEATRO DALLAS

1925 Commerce (75201) • 214-741-1135 • W • www.teatrodallas.org

The primary goal of this nonprofit professional theatrical institution is to enrich the community with theatrical works from the Latino cultures with plays by classical and contemporary Latin American and Hispanic American playwrights. Provides Latino playwrights with a place to develop their talents. Also produces Latino works translated and performed in English. Performances in theaters throughout the Metroplex. Hosts annual International Theater Festival showcasing groups from Latin America. Tickets to most performances $10–$18.

UNDERMAIN THEATRE

3200 Main (75226) in Deep Ellum • 214-747-1424; Box Office, 214-747-5515 • W • www.undermain.com

The resident theater group here is an ensemble of sixteen artists committed to providing the community with innovative, thought-provoking professional theater, specializing in regional and national premieres of mostly avant-garde works by nationally known playwrights. It not only produces, but even commissions and publishes, new works. The group has performed in New York and abroad, but most of its productions can still be seen in its basement theater in Deep Ellum. Shows normally Tuesday–Saturday. Tickets $15–$25, except for the one Pay-What-You-Can night each week.

BOOKER T. WASHINGTON HIGH SCHOOL FOR THE PERFORMING AND VISUAL ARTS

2501 Flora (75201), in the Arts District (DART Light Rail Pearl Station) • 972-925-1200 • W •

This is a unique Texas high school where Friday night football doesn't reign supreme. In fact, there is no football in this Arts Magnet school that has about 700 multi-ethnic students from the Dallas community enrolled in a full range of academic studies and intensive training in theater, dance, music, and the visual arts. The theater cluster produces thirty-five performances annually, ranging from classics to new works produced by the playwriting classes, which are performed in the school's two theaters. Call for schedule.

DANCE

For additional information on dance and music, see the Texas International Theatrical Arts Society website at **www.titas.org.**

The Dallas Dance Council • 3630 Harry Hines (75219) • 214-219-2290 • www.thedancecouncil.org . This is the umbrella organization for dance in the Metroplex. Write for a free issue of their quarterly publication *Dance.*

ANITA N. MARTINEZ BALLET FOLKLORICO
4422 Live Oak (75204) • 214-828-0181 • www.anmbf.org

What started in 1975 as a presentation by neighborhood children in a recreation center in west Dallas has grown into one of the leading professional Hispanic dance companies in the Southwest. Each year, the company puts on several performances at the Majestic Theater and throughout the Metroplex at major events and festivals.

DALLAS BLACK DANCE THEATRE
2627 Flora (75221) • 214-871-2376 • www.dbdt.com

Founded in 1976, the professional members of the city's oldest continuously operating dance company perform modern dance by well-known choreographers. Its repertoire also includes jazz, ethnic, spiritual, and ballet dance styles. Local performances are given at the Majestic Theatre and at other performance spaces in the city. The company has performed in Washington, D.C.'s Kennedy Center and other major cities throughout the United States, as well as internationally in Spain, Great Britain, South Africa, and a number of other countries.

FORT WORTH DALLAS BALLET
817-212-4280 • www.fwdballet
(See FORT WORTH, MUSIC AND PERFORMING ARTS, p. 199)
Dallas performances are usually held at the Music Hall in Fair Park.

MUSIC

CHILDREN'S CHORUS OF GREATER DALLAS
1928 Ross (75201) • 214-965-0491 • www.thechildrenschorus.com

This chorus includes boys and girls with unchanged voices in the fourth through eighth grades, selected by auditions. Concerts are held throughout the year in a variety of locations, including the Guadalupe Cathedral, SMU Chapel, other churches, the Dallas Museum of Art, and various malls. Tickets are sold for most performances except in the malls.

DALLAS BACH SOCIETY

P.O. Box 140201 (75214-0201) • 214-320-8700 • www.dallasbach.org

Under the auspices of this society, not just Bach but the full range of Baroque and Classical period music is performed by outstanding professional vocalists and instrumentalists from Dallas, the United States, and abroad. Its season runs from September through April with at least one performance each month, usually on a Saturday or Sunday. Performances are given in the Meyerson Symphony Center, in several Dallas neighborhood churches, and in facilities in nearby Metroplex cities.

DALLAS CHAMBER ORCHESTRA

Sammons Center for the Arts, 3630 Harry Hines Blvd. (75219) (Office) • 520-3121

This group performs classic works from the seventeenth and eighteenth centuries. Concerts are European style—without a conductor. It usually performs eight concerts in its September–May season. Friday evening performances are given at the Episcopal Church of the Transfiguration, Hillcrest and Spring Valley; Sunday matinee and evening performances are at the Caruth Auditorium at Hillcrest and Binkley on the SMU campus. Individual tickets: Adults, $17; seniors, $12; students $10.

DALLAS CLASSIC GUITAR SOCIETY

P.O. Box 190823 (75219) • 528-3733

The greatest classical guitarists in the world have appeared in concert with the Society, including: Andrés Segovia, John Williams, and Julian Bream. The Society's season runs from September through April with at least one concert each month in two series: the International Series, featuring the best in the world, is held at the Morton H. Meyerson Symphony Center; and the Master Series which showcases outstanding but lesser known international guitarists is held at SMU's Caruth Auditorium. It also sponsors a series of concerts by emerging artists at the Dallas Museum of Art.

DALLAS JAZZ ORCHESTRA

Sammons Center for the Arts, 3630 Harry Hines • 972-644-8833 • www.djo.org

A 20-piece big band that plays original and traditional big band jazz. It gives a spring and fall concert at the Meyerson Symphony Center and other performances around the city including free summer concerts in various city parks on Sunday afternoons.

DALLAS OPERA

Campbell Center 1, 8350 N. Central Expressway, Suite 210 (75206)
• 214-443-1000 • www.dallasopera.org

Nationally known, the Dallas Opera company has been staging the classics for more than 40 years. Its November–February season usually features five operas performed at Fair Park Music Hall. Single tickets range from $25 to $104.

DALLAS SYMPHONY ORCHESTRA

Morton H. Meyerson Symphony Center, 2301 Flora (75201), in the Arts District (DART Light Rail Pearl Station) • 214-871-4000 • www.dallassymphony.com

The Dallas Symphony celebrated its 100th anniversary in the year 2000. The Symphony presents a full schedule of programs from late August through May in a variety of series from Classical to SuperPops featuring a number of guest artists and conductors, and they also offer the popular Family Concert Series. The Symphony has played in Carnegie Hall and gained an international reputation on several European tours. It performs during the summer in the parks and at various events including the International Summer Music Festival. It is joined in selected performances by the 250-voice **Dallas Symphony Chorus** (214-871-4084). Tickets $15–$70. Parking at the Arts Center Garage, entrance on Ross between Crockett and Leonard. Valet parking also available. A fine dining and a buffet restaurant in the Meyerson are open on performance nights and matinees. Reservations suggested (214-670-3721).

DALLAS WIND SYMPHONY

Office: c/o TITAS, 3101 Fitzhugh, Suite 301 (75204) • 214-528-5576 • www.dws.org

The 50-piece brass, woodwind, and percussion players make up this group known as "America's Premier Wind Band." The band performs an eclectic blend of musical styles ranging from Bach to Bernstein and Sousa to Strauss. The DWB makes its home at The Meyerson and most of its concerts during its September to April season are given there. Tickets $12–$40.

FINE ARTS CHAMBER PLAYERS

Sammons Center for the Arts, 3630 Harry Hines (75219) • 214-520-2219 • www.fineartschamberplayers.org

Since its founding in 1981, this group has been providing free chamber music concerts to the public. The "players" are professional classical musicians mainly from the Dallas Symphony Orchestra, Dallas Opera, Fort Worth Symphony, and area university faculties. From October–May they present seven free concerts in the Bancroft Family Series each Saturday afternoon at the Dallas Museum of Art. Each Sunday afternoon in

July they perform the Basically Beethoven Festival in the Discovery Gardens in Fair Park.

GREATER DALLAS YOUTH ORCHESTRA

Sammons Center for the Arts, 3630 Harry Hines (75219) • 214-528-7747 • www.gdyo.org

Since its founding in 1972, the Greater Dallas Youth Orchestra (GDYO) has offered musical education for young musicians, aged 6 to 18, who have been selected by competitive auditions. The GDYO performs five concerts a year in the Meyerson Symphony Center, usually including one "Side-by-Side" Concert with the Dallas Symphony. In addition to performing at the Meyerson, the GDYO has toured internationally. Depending on age and training, the students also may participate in one or more of another half dozen or so concerts as members of the Young Performers Orchestra, the Philharmonic, the Wind Symphony, the Sinfonietta, or the Dallas String Ensemble, all of which give concerts at the Meyerson, SMU's Caruth Auditorium, the Majestic Theatre, and other locations in the city. Call for schedule and ticket prices.

SAMMONS JAZZ

Sammons Center for the Arts, 3630 Harry Hines (75219) • Tickets, 520-7789 • www.sammonsartcenter.org

This is the only regular ongoing jazz performance series in the Metroplex featuring local jazz artists playing all forms of jazz from Swing to Bebop, from Dixieland to Fusion. February–May and September–December, the jazz sessions are held in Meadows Hall at the Sammons Center the first Wednesday of each month at 7:00 p.m. Tickets cost $25 but include valet parking and complimentary appetizers and beverages. The group also holds a Jazz Festival in downtown Dallas in October and performs free jazz concerts in conjunction with the Shakespeare Festival of Dallas. (See ANNUAL EVENTS, p. 127)

TURTLE CREEK CHORALE

Sammons Center for the Arts, 3630 Harry Hines (75219), P.O. Box 190137, 75219-0137 • 214-526-3214 or 800-746-4412 • www.turtlecreek.org

Bach to Broadway, sacred and secular, is the range of programs in the concerts offered by this 200-plus-member all-volunteer male chorus. They perform at least five subscription concerts each year at the Meyerson, plus other concerts in the Eisemann Center in Richardson. They have performed in Barcelona, Berlin, and Prague, as well as in Carnegie Hall. They also hold the Guinness Book Record for the World's Longest Choral Concert.

THE WOMEN'S CHORUS OF DALLAS

Sammons Center for the Arts, 3630 Harry Hines (75219) • 214-520-7828 or 888-275-1021 toll-free • www.twcd.org

Formed in 1989 with only 32 members, this chorus is now over 100 strong. Its repertoire ranges through classical, traditional, ballads, folk songs in their native language, spirituals, and contemporary compositions. In addition to its three concert subscription series, the Chorus also performs at many community events. Caruth Auditorium, on the SMU campus, is the primary home of this chorus, but performances are also held at the Meyerson and at other locations in the Metroplex.

FAMILY FUN AND KID STUFF

AMERICAN MUSEUM OF MINIATURE ARTS
(See THE MUSEUMS OF FAIR PARK, p. 80)

DALLAS AQUARIUM
(See THE MUSEUMS OF FAIR PARK, p. 81)

DALLAS CENTRAL LIBRARY-CHILDREN'S CENTER
**1515 Young (75201) (DART Light Rail Akard Station) •
214-670-1671 • W+ • www.dallaslibrary.org**

This center is designed to excite the imagination of children. In addition to the extensive collection of books, magazines, audio and visual materials, there are interesting exhibits and specifically designed areas for storytelling, puppet shows, and other programs to encourage the child's participation in the activities. There's a free family movie most Saturdays and Sundays at 2:00 p.m.

DALLAS CHILDREN'S MUSEUM
308 Valley View Center (75240), in mall on second level next to JCPenney • 972-386-6555 • Monday–Friday, 9–6; Saturday, 11–6; Sunday, noon–6 • Children 2–12, $4, under 2 free; adults, $3; seniors, $2 • www.dallaschildrens.org

This museum is all hands-on play for young children that encourages exploration and learning experiences. With only 6,500 square feet, it's relatively small for a museum, but still it squeezes in play areas that give children the opportunity to work with touch screen computer games, do simple arts and crafts, do their own puppet show, shop in a scaled-down grocery store with working checkout counters, do puzzles, dress up, and learn about health in a play hospital setting. Commercial sponsors' names are a little more prominent than they need be, but the kids will probably ignore them anyway. Occasional programs with storytellers, musicians, dancers, and craft artists. Separate discovery play area for babies and toddlers. Parents and grandparents can participate or just enjoy watching their youngsters in the discovery process. Undoubtedly, some parents will use this merely to drop off their small kids while they go shopping, but if it's babysitting they want, at least it can be babysitting at its best.

DALLAS MUSEUM OF NATURAL HISTORY SLEEPOVERS

3535 Grand, just inside the Grand Ave. entrance off Cullum; P.O. Box 150349 (75315) • For information and registration, 214-421-DINO (421-3466) • www.dallasdino.org

Children 7–12 can attend a sleepover program at the museum. This includes a tour of exhibit halls, science activities throughout the museum, and late-night pizza plus breakfast. Cost is $30 per child. One adult ($10) is recommended for every four children. One big catch for visitors is registration, must be made at least five weeks before the desired date. If your child is interested, call early.

DALLAS WORLD AQUARIUM

1801 North Griffin (75202), in the West End Historic District (DART Light Rail West End Station) • 214-720-2224 • Seven days, 10–5. Closed Thanksgiving and Christmas • Adults, $11; seniors, $8; children 3–12, $6; under 3 free • W+ • www.dwazoo.com

There are more than 85,000 gallons of seawater in the numerous large aquarium tanks here that include a 22,000-gallon walk-through tunnel tank. Each tank represents a different dive destination, ranging from British Columbia to Fiji, and each teems with marine life indigenous to that part of the world. Aquatic exhibits in this privately owned aquarium include bonnet head sharks, stingrays, cuttlefish, seadragons, jellyfish, giant groupers, and a vast assortment of colorful smaller fish that live in the reefs. Also featured is a South American Rainforest Exhibit with lush tropical vegetation, toucans in a free flight aviary, sloths, anacondas, several species of monkeys, and crocodiles. There are feedings at the various exhibits several times a day. Restaurant open for lunch. Gift shop. Pay parking nearby.

DALLAS ZOO

650 South R. L. Thornton Frwy. (I-35E) (75203), about 3 miles south of downtown; from I-35E take Marsalis exit and follow Zoo signs (DART Light Rail Zoo Station) • 214-670-8626 (office), 214-670-5656 (recording) • Seven days, 9–5 (can stay until 6); winter hours close at 4 • Adults, $8; seniors, $4; children 3–11, $5; under 3 free • Parking, $5 • W+ • www.dallaszoo.com

The tallest statue in Texas, a 67½-foot-tall giraffe, marks the entrance to this 95-acre zoo, which is the home for more than 2,000 mammals, reptiles, amphibians, and birds representing 377 species, with many roaming freely in areas designed to closely duplicate their natural habitat. Founded in 1888, today's zoo is divided into two major areas: ZooNorth and the

Wilds of Africa. Follow the walkways of ZooNorth to get a close-up view of rhinos, giraffes, lions, tigers, ocelots, cheetahs, elephants, red pandas, camels, llamas, wallabies, kangaroos, and many of the more than 700 birds in the Zoo's collection. This area also features the Bird and Reptile Building, with its renowned collection of nearly 120 reptile and amphibian species, including Chinese alligators, which are in extreme danger of extinction, and the Rainforest Aviary, where you can watch brightly colored exotic birds fly all around you. Another highlight of ZooNorth is the Lacerte Family Children's Zoo, where children can touch and pet a number of smaller and domestic animals as well as learn how to be responsible pet owners.

The 25-acre Wilds of Africa features the six major habitats of Africa. This is the first zoo exhibit in the world to include every major habitat of the entire continent and has been named the best African zoo exhibit in the country. Within the exhibit, bush, desert, forest, woodland, river, and mountain environments allow some 86 species of birds and mammals to dwell in surroundings that accurately mimic their native habitats. Some of these are mandrill baboons, bongos, zebras, the rare okapi, storks, klipspringers, and lowland gorillas. Much of the exhibit can be seen from the walking trail, but to see it all take the Monorail Safari ($2 for age 3 and up). This specially designed monorail is the only one in the United States that is engineered to climb and turn. The cars are open on the side facing the exhibit, so all have a good view. (Operates seasonally: September 15–December 1 and March 1–June 15.) Live narration is given during the 20-minute ride, which covers one mile.

Zookeeper talks at various exhibits every Saturday and Sunday. Instead of the traditional carousel with horse figures, the Zoo carousel has endangered species figures to ride ($2). Restaurants, picnic areas, and gift shop. Strollers, including doubles, and wheelchairs can be rented.

LE THÉÂTRE DE MARIONETTE

440 NorthPark Center (75225) (DART Light Rail Park Lane Station and NorthPark shuttle) • 214-369-4849 • W+ • www.letheatre.net

Today's kids are used to seeing puppets come alive through the magic of TV and film, but these are the real thing. They seem to almost come alive through the magic of the skilled puppeteers and the intimate setting. Since seeing them up close can be scary to little ones, each show starts with a puppeteer who shows how a wooden puppet "moves" and "acts." Forty-five minute shows in this mall puppet store most Saturdays and Sundays. Adults, $8; children, $7. Gift shop.

MODEL TRAIN EXHIBIT

Children's Medical Center of Dallas, 1935 Motor St. (75235), between Stemmons Frwy. (I35E) and Harry Hines (TRE Medical/Market Center Station) • 214-640-2000 • Open seven days, 5:30 a.m.–10 p.m. • Free (parking fee) • W+

One of the largest permanent model train exhibits in the United States is in the lobby of this children's medical center. As you enter you see a two-story train exhibit in which eight G-scale model trains run simultaneously over more than 1,000 feet of track that winds around models of some of America's most famous landmarks, including Mount Rushmore, the Grand Canyon, and even the Dallas skyline. For a bird's-eye view, go to the second-floor observation area. The exhibit is free, but there's a small fee for parking. The best time to visit is on weekends and holidays when the hospital activities are a little less hectic.

PIONEER PLAZA TRAIL DRIVE MONUMENT

(See OTHER POINTS OF INTEREST, p. 121)

ROSEWOOD CENTER FOR FAMILY ARTS

5938 Skilman (75231) • 214-978-0110 • W+ • www.dct.org

When the Dallas Children's Theatre moved into its new theater it changed it name to the Rosewood Center. This nationally recognized professional company uses both child and adult actors in its annual program of about a dozen productions. Rather than strictly for children, most of these productions offer theatrical excitement, fun, and adventure for the whole family. Some of the plays are based on popular books, like *Amelia Bedelia*, while others deal with serious subjects that present the many issues and ideas that young people and their families face. Tickets for most shows cost about $15 for adults and $12 for children. Tickets for holiday productions and musicals are a few dollars more. The touring company has brought full-scale productions to more than 50 cities around the country. Free parking.

THE SCIENCE PLACE AND TI FOUNDERS IMAX® THEATER

(See THE MUSEUMS IN FAIR PARK, p. 81)

SPEED ZONE

11130 Malibu (75229), at I-35E and Walnut • 972-247-RACE (247-7223) • Open seven days: Sunday–Thursday, 11–11; Friday–Saturday, 11 a.m.–1 a.m. • Admission free, pay by activity with playcard prices starting at $3 for racers • W • www.speedzone.com

If speed and competition give you an adrenaline rush, this is the place for you. You have your choice of four types of racing, from 300 hp dragsters that will take you from 0 to 70 mph in 3.2 seconds, to Turbo Track cars that let you drive through 14 tight corners in competition. These are not for little kids. Outside the cars, there are more than 100 of the latest video simulator and skill games and miniature golf. Café and bar.

SPORTS

MAJOR SPORTS VENUES

AMERICAN AIRLINES CENTER

2500 Victory (75201) (DART Light Rail Victory Station, open for major events only) • Event Hotline, 214-665-4200; Box Office, 214-665-4797 • W+ • www.americanairlinescenter.com

Home of the Dallas Mavericks and Dallas Stars, it holds 19,200 seats for basketball and 18,500 seats for hockey. All available parking at the Center for Mavs and Stars games reserved for season ticket holders. Cash parking available south of Woodall Rogers between Griffin and I-35E. Fan gift shop. (See also MUSIC AND PERFORMING ARTS—American Airlines Center, p. 100)

COTTON BOWL STADIUM

Fair Park • 214-939-2217 • W+

The 72,000-seat stadium is the site for football and a number of other sports events including soccer. (See FAIR PARK, p. 83)

REUNION ARENA

777 Sport (75207) (DART Light Rail Union Station) • Box Office, 214-800-3089 • W+ • www.reunionarena.org

Home of the Dallas Sidekicks, indoor soccer team, it also features other sports events including ice-skating competitions. Seats 16,800 for soccer. Paid parking available in area for $6–$10. (See also MUSIC AND PERFORMING ARTS, p. 104)

MAJOR AND MINOR SPORTS

Arena Football

DALLAS DESPERADOS

One Cowboys Pkwy., Irving (75063) • 972-785-4900 • www.dallas desperados.com

Games played in spring and summer, during the NFL off-season. Most games played at the American Airlines Center.

Professional Auto Racing

(See FORT WORTH—SPORTS—Texas Motor Speedway, p. 206)

Professional Baseball

(See ARLINGTON—The Ballpark in Arlington/Texas Rangers, p. 50, and FORT WORTH—SPORTS—Fort Worth Cats, p. 207)

Professional Basketball

DALLAS MAVERICKS

American Airlines Center, 2500 Victory • 214-747-MAVS (747-6287) • www.nba.com/mavericks

The Mavericks play in the National Basketball Association. (Mavericks Fan Shop on ground floor in AAC has an outside no-ticket-required entrance off the parking lot.)

Bicycling

The City of Dallas maintains more than 500 miles of bike trails all over the city. Bike trail maps are available for sale at most bike shops. Bachman and White Rock Lake areas have the longest trails, and bike shops in those areas have rentals.

College Sports

(See COLLEGE CAMPUSES OF INTEREST TO VISITORS—SMU, p. 98)

Equestrian Sports

(See FORT WORTH—SPORTS—Equestrian, p. 207–8)

Professional Football

(See IRVING-SPORTS—Dallas Cowboys, p. 282)

Golf

Following is a list of the public golf courses in Dallas. The Dallas Convention and Visitors Bureau offers a free DALLAS GOLF MAP detailing nearly 100 private and semi-private courses in the Metroplex. Also check **www.visitdallas.com** *and* **www. golfindallas.net**

Cedar Crest Park Golf Course • 1800 Southerland (75203) • 214-670-7615 • 18 holes.

L. B. Houston Municipal Golf Course • 11223 Luna (75229) • 214-670-6322 • 18 holes.

Grover Keeton Park Golf Course • 2323 Jim Miller • 214-670-8784 • 18 holes.

Stevens Park Golf Course • 1005 N. Montclair (75208) • 214-670-7506 • 18 holes.

Tenison Park Golf Courses • 3501 Samuell (75223) • 214-670-1402 • Two 18-hole courses.

Ice Hockey

DALLAS STARS

American Airlines Center, 2500 Victory • 214-GO-STARS (467-8277) • www.dallasstars.com.

The Stars play in the National Hockey League. (Stars Fan Shop on ground floor in AAC has an outside no-ticket-required entrance off the parking lot.) (See also FORT WORTH—SPORTS—Fort Worth Brahmas, p. 209)

Ice Skating

AMERICA'S ICE GARDEN

Plaza of the Americas, 700 N. Pearl (75201) (DART Light Rail Pearl Station) • 214-720-8080 • www.icesk8aig.com

This rink is located in the atrium of the elegant Plaza of the Americas office tower and hotel complex. The $7 admission fee includes skate rental. Validated parking available across street from rink at Pearl and San Jacinto.

GALLERIA ICE SKATING CENTER

Galleria, 13350 Dallas Pkwy. N. (75240), at LBJ Frwy. (I-635) • 972-702-7100 • www.dallasgalleria.com

The rink is located on the lower level of Galleria mall. Admission, $5; skate rental, $3. Free beginner classes on Saturdays. Free mall parking.

Horse Racing

(See GRAND PRAIRIE—SPORTS—Lone Star Park, p. 246)

Rodeo

(See SIDE TRIPS—MESQUITE CHAMPION RODEO, p. 158, and FORT WORTH—SPORTS—Stockyards Championship Rodeo, p. 209)

Professional Soccer

DALLAS BURN

2602 McKinney #200 (75204) • 214-979-0303 • www.burnsoccer.com

The Cotton Bowl is home field for Dallas's professional (outdoor) soccer team, which competes in the Western Conference.

DALLAS SIDEKICKS

Reunion Arena, 777 Sports St. (75207) (DART Light Rail Union Station) • 214-653-0200 • www.kicksfan.com

This is Dallas's professional indoor soccer team, playing in the Continental Indoor Soccer League.

Tennis

DALLAS PARKS TENNIS CENTERS

Park and Recreation Department, City Hall, 1500 Marilla 6FN (75201) • 214-670-4100

There is a scattering of tennis courts in neighborhood parks all over the city; however, each of the following parks has a tennis center that is city-owned but privately managed. Reservations must be made one day in advance, with fees based on prime time (evenings, weekends, and holidays) and non-prime time (weekdays, 9–5). The tennis centers also offer lessons and ball-machine rentals, and each has a tennis pro shop.

Fair Oaks • 7501 Merriman Pkwy. • 214-670-1495 • 16 lighted courts.

Fretz • 14700 Hillcrest • 214-670-6622 • 15 lighted courts.

Kiest • 2324 W. Kiest • 214-670-7618 • 16 lighted courts.

Samuell-Grand • 6200 E. Grand • 670-1374 • 20 lighted courts.

L. B. Houston • 11225 Luna • 214-670-6367 • 16 lighted courts.

OTHER POINTS OF INTEREST

ANNETTE STRAUSS ARTIST SQUARE

1800 Leopold (75201), in Arts District (DART Light Rail St. Paul or Pearl Stations) • W • www.artsdistrict.org

Nestled in the midst of the Arts District, this open-air plaza is the scene of a diverse selection of arts, music, and dance activities and festivals throughout the year.

DALLAS CITY HALL

1500 Marilla (75201), at Ervay (DART Light Rail Convention Center, Akard, or Union Station) • W+

Famed architect I. M. Pei designed this building to slope outward and upward at a 34-degree angle, with the building held and balanced by a network of U-shaped cables in the floors and walls. A 27-ton bronze cast sculpture by Henry Moore, officially called *The Dallas Piece*, and a reflecting pool adorn the ceremonial plaza in front, which is often used for public events and festivals.

DALLAS CENTRAL PUBLIC LIBRARY

1515 Young Street (75201), downtown (DART Light Rail Akard
Station) • 214-670-1700 • W+

Among the highlights in this eight-story library are its outstanding ge-
nealogy collection, one of the largest children's centers in the country
(See FAMILY FUN AND KID STUFF, p. 111). A permanent exhibit area
on the seventh floor features one of the original printed copies of the De-
claration of Independence from 1776; and the First Folio of *Mr. William
Shakespeare's Comedies, Histories & Tragedies*. This important book, printed in
1623, marks the first printing of Shakespeare's plays. The library offers
frequent performances of dance, theater, music, children's shows, films,
and lectures. Call for schedule of events. Gift shop.

DALLAS MARKET CENTER COMPLEX

2100 N. Stemmons Frwy. (I-35E), just north of downtown (TRE
Medical/Market Center Station) • 214-655-6100 • W+ •
www.dallasmarketcenter.com

This is the world's largest wholesale trade complex, with more than
2,200 permanent showrooms. About 50 merchandise markets are held
here annually attended by more than 200,000 wholesale buyers. Visitors
are not permitted. You must be a registered buyer to attend any of the
marts in five of the six separate marketing facilities: The World Trade Center, Trade Mart, International Apparel Mart, International Floral Design
Center, and 2350 Stemmons, which houses companies dealing with western apparel. The only building within the Center open to the public, and
then only on a limited basis, is Market Hall. The largest privately owned
exhibition hall in the United States, it is the scene of boat shows, car
shows, craft shows, and numerous other events open to the public. The In-
fomart building, which adjoins the complex, is also open to the public.
(See p. 120)

FOUNTAIN PLACE

1445 Ross (75201) • (DART Light Rail Akard Station) •
214-855-7766 • Free

Waterfalls, 172 bubbling fountains, and 360 fountainheads making
dancing waters in a central fountain, all set amid trees and flowing
streams, make this six-acre plaza at the base of a downtown skyscraper a
true downtown oasis. About half-million gallons of water fuel the fabu-
lous fountains. The 60-story blue glass tower was designed by noted architect I. M. Pei.

HIGHLAND PARK PHARMACY

3229 Knox (75205) • 214-521-2126 • W

If you ever get nostalgic for an old-fashioned lunch counter with a
genuine soda fountain, this is the place to go to refresh your memories.

They've been serving fountain sodas and grilled cheese sandwiches to satisfied customers for more than 85 years.

INFOMART

1950 N. Stemmons Frwy. (75207), adjoining the Dallas Market Center (TRE Medical/Market Center Station) • 214-800-8000 • W+ • www.infomartusa.com

Telecommunications and other hi-tech companies of the modern age are among the many tenants in this office building, but the building itself features glass and lacework arch architecture designed to resemble London's Crystal Palace, which was built in 1851 for the first World's Fair and International Technology Exhibition. Great Britain's Parliament has recognized the building as the official successor to the Crystal Palace, which was destroyed by fire in 1936. The 4,200 windows measure 10' x 6'; the exterior arches are made of recycled aluminum. The Crystal Fountain in the atrium is made of 471 pieces of handmade crystal and is an exact replica of the Crystal Palace's original fountain. The building and some of its facilities are open to the public. Free parking.

JOHN F. KENNEDY MEMORIAL

Memorial Plaza, Main and Market Streets, West End Historic District (DART Light Rail West End Station) • W

This memorial to our thirty-fifth president, who was assassinated nearby, was designed as a place for meditation by architect Phillip Johnson, a Kennedy family friend. Stark and simple, it consists of four walls, about 30 feet high, around a 50-foot square, open to the sky, creating the effect of an open tomb enclosing a memorial plaque. Lighted at night.

LATINO CULTURAL CENTER

2600 Live Oak (75240), at Good Latimer • 214-670-3320 • W+ • www.dallasculture.com/latinocc

Opened in the fall of 2003, this center is the focal point of the rich cultural and artistic expressions of the 800,000-strong Latin community in the area. Designed by Mexican architect Ricardo Legorreta, the Center includes a 300-seat theater, gallery, artist workspaces, workshop, and teaching areas and a grand plaza for cultural events and festivals.

LOVE FIELD

8008 Cedar Springs (75235), at Mockingbird • 214-670-6073 • W+ • www.dallas-lovefield.com

Convenient to downtown, this city-owned airport is home base for Southwest Airlines and also serviced by smaller commuter airlines. It is used annually by about seven million passengers. Founded in 1917 as a World War I military training base, it was named after Lt. Moss Lee Love, a pilot killed in an airplane crash a few years earlier. The main place of visitor interest at the airport is the small Aviation Art Gallery in the lobby, and the Frontiers of Flight Museum (See MUSEUMS AND PUBLIC ART GALLERIES, p. 88). Pay parking.

NEIMAN MARCUS ORIGINAL DALLAS STORE

One Marcus Square—1618 Main (75201), at Ervay Street (DART Light Rail St. Paul Station) • 214-741-6911 • W+ •
www.neimanmarcus.com

In Texas, and just about everywhere else in the world, the name Neiman Marcus stands for a long tradition of sophisticated service and good taste, all at a price. It wasn't long after it opened in 1907 that Texans who could afford to shop anywhere in the world started to shop here instead of New York or Paris. Neiman Marcus helped put Dallas on the national and international fashion map. This store was built in 1914 and enlarged over the years. It is now the flagship store of the chain. Among Neiman Marcus's many claims to fame is its annual Christmas catalog, which always includes His and Her gifts that gently spoof its rich customers. Among past His and Her gifts offered were a two-seater submarine, matching hot-air balloons, and a pair of Chinese junks (all of which sold). A permanent exhibit on the fifth floor that tells the history of "The Store" is worth a visit, as is the sixth floor's original legendary **Zodiac Room**, where Dallas socialites have been lunching for decades. Valet parking or fee parking in nearby garage. "The Store" and another downtown tradition, the Adolphus Hotel, jointly sponsor the nation's only holiday parade just for kids, on a Saturday early in December. Called "The Miracle on Commerce Street," it draws corporate sponsorship that benefits the Children's Medical Center of Dallas and is broadcast on TV to more than 100 million households from Alaska to the Bahamas.

PEGASUS PLAZA

1500 Main (75201), at Akard in City Center (DART Light Rail Akard Station) • W

This small park, created by artists, is dedicated to recreating the myth of Pegasus, the symbol of rebirth and the adopted symbol of the city. While most Dallasites may not know the mythology, they are familiar with the symbolic red neon and steel flying horse that once dominated the Dallas skyline from its perch on top of the Magnolia Building.

PIONEER PLAZA CATTLE DRIVE MONUMENT

Young and Griffin Streets, between Dallas Convention Center and City Hall (DART Light Rail Convention Center Station) • Free • W

Forty larger-than-life-size bronze longhorn steers move down a rocky bluff through a flowing stream in this plaza park, driven by three cowboys on horseback; one leading, one watching from the bluff, and one chasing a stray. Sculpted by Robert Summers of Glen Rose, it's not a large herd, as old-time herds went, but it still makes the world's largest bronze monument. The sculpture is wide open, so you can walk through it, and as you do you may get a feeling of the immense power and energy of the longhorns that the riders had to control on those legendary cattle drives when the herds numbered in the thousands. A favorite spot for photos, especially of kids breaking the rules and climbing on the longhorns (except in summer, when the critters can get too hot to touch). The 4.2-acre park is actually located on a site of the historic "Shawnee Trail" that was used for drives like this starting in the mid-1850s. It adjoins Pioneer Cemetery, founded in 1848 and the resting place of some of Dallas's first citizens. Free but limited parking.

THANKS-GIVING SQUARE

Downtown, bordered by Ervay, Bryan, and Pacific (DART Light Rail Akard Station) • Thanks-Giving Square Foundation, P.O. Box 1777, 75221 • 214-969-1977 • Free • W variable

Architect Phillip Johnson, who designed the John F. Kennedy Memorial (see above), designed this three-plus-acre triangular park in praise of the universal spirit of the Thanksgiving tradition found in all the world's religions. An island of serenity amidst the bustle of downtown, it includes a 50-foot bell tower with three large bronze bells, a water wall, a reflecting pool, and the spiraling white marble interfaith Chapel of Thanksgiving. Beneath the chapel, the Hall of Thanksgiving tells of the American Thanksgiving tradition. The Chapel is open weekdays, 9–5, and weekends and most holidays, 1–5. There is an entrance to the park from the underground pedestrian walkway (see OFFBEAT, p. 124).

SARA ELLEN AND SAMUEL WEISFELD CENTER

1508 Cadiz at Browder (75201) • 214-752-8989 • W+ • www.weisfeldcenter.com

Originally the neoclassical First Church of Christ, Scientist, built in 1910, this is now a beautifully restored 800-seat multipurpose facility. Details include arched stained-glass windows, pilasters, and carved moldings, all highlighted in gold leaf. The historic centerpiece is a 2,373-pipe organ dating from 1911 in the upstairs stage area. The center is used for music recitals and by theater and dance groups as well as for weddings and other private functions. Free architectural and historical tours are given by reservation. Free parking.

OFFBEAT

THE CONSPIRACY MUSEUM

110 S. Market (75202), between Main and Commerce, downtown (DART Light Rail West End Station) • 214-741-3040 • Daily, 10–6 • Adults, $7; seniors, $6; children 9–12, $3 • W variable • www.conspiracymuseum.com

This small, privately funded museum came into existence because so many people rejected the Warren Commission Report that Oswald assassinated President Kennedy. The exhibits present a case that it was a conspiracy and that there were powerful forces behind it and someone other than Oswald did it. But the displays aren't just confined to who killed JFK. They offer conspiracy theories on the assassinations and cover-ups of Presidents Lincoln, Garfield, and McKinley, as well as of Bobby Kennedy and Martin Luther King. Gift shop just inside entrance is open without a ticket. Pay parking on nearby lots.

FAMOUS HANDS COLLECTION

Baylor University Medical Center–Truett Hospital Building, 3500 Gaston • 214-820-6684 • Open at all times • Free

Roger Staubach has a misshapen pinkie caused by multiple dislocations during his career as Dallas Cowboy quarterback. You can see this on the bronze casting of his hands in the **Adrian E. Flatt MD Hand Exhibit** in the lobby of the Truett Hospital. Staubach is just one of about 100 well-known people who let hand surgeon Dr. Flatt make molds of their hands, which he later had an artist turn into an antique-bronzed copies so precise they even show fingerprints. Hands in the collection, which Flatt donated to BUMC after his retirement, include famous actors, artists, astronauts, athletes, and international leaders. They range from pianist Van Cliburn and cartoonist Charles Schulz to Katherine Hepburn, Andre the Giant, Presidents Harry Truman and Dwight D. Eisenhower, and Sir Winston Churchill. A short film, narrated by Troy Aikman, explains Dr. Flatt's casting technique, which was fast enough that it helped him persuade all these busy famous people to take the time to plunge their hands into his box of mold-making material.

MEDIEVAL TIMES DINNER AND TOURNAMENT

2021 N. Stemmons Frwy. (I-35E) (75207), at Market Center Blvd. exit • 214-761-1801 or toll-free 888-WE-JOUST (888-935-6878) • Adults, about $42; children 12 and under, about $30 • Reservations strongly suggested • W+ but not all areas

Once you cross the drawbridge, you are in the Middle Ages as a guest in the (air-conditioned) castle of the royal family. For about two hours, as you dine on a dinner in authentic Middle Ages style, without utensils, you'll witness medieval pageantry, horsemanship, swordplay, falconry, sorcery, and a jousting tournament. Show times are seasonal. Call. The "castle" is open for free self-guided tours Monday–Friday, 10–4.

OLDE FAN MUSEUM

1914 Abrams Pkwy. (75214), in Lakewood Shopping Center • 214-826-7700 • W • www.fanmanuse.com

Although the name may seem a little pretentious, since this is in a simple shopping-center store, it's hard to deny that this collection of more than 400 antique, restored, and reproduction electric fans is impressive, especially if you grew up during a time when this type of circulating fan was a blessing in hot weather. The cluttered display area includes fans from the 1890s to the present, with every type from old coin-operated fans to reproductions that cost several thousand dollars. Owner opens and gives tours when visitors come, but you'll probably have to go to the repair shop in the rear of 1907 to find the Fan Man.

UNDERGROUND PEDESTRIANWAYS AND SKYBRIDGES

Downtown • (Nearest entrance from DART Light Rail Akard Station) • Open normal business hours weekdays • Free • W variable (elevators at some entrances)

Except for downtown workers, most Dallasites don't even know that on business days you can get around much of downtown without crossing a street (or getting out in the weather) by using the several miles of underground pedestrianway tunnels. These aren't dark, dank, and spooky tunnels, either. Most of them are bright and lined with shops and restaurants. A few exit on the street, but most exit to the lobbies of major office buildings and hotels. One even gets you right to the heart of Thanks-Giving Square (See above). Unfortunately, this system is in three clusters that aren't interconnected, so, depending on where you want to go, you may occasionally have to come up and actually cross a street or two to get to the next section. This tunnel system is also tied in with a series of pedestrian skybridges. Check with your hotel personnel or a downtown worker to find your way into this secret underground world.

WEST END CATTLE DRIVE

West End Association 214-741-7185 • Free • www.dallaswestend.org

It's nothing like the daily drive of the Fort Worth Herd (See FORT WORTH, p. 203), but one Saturday each October, a small, but real cattle drive takes over Market Street as part of a West End festival with music, entertainment, crafts, and food.

ANNUAL EVENTS

There are one or more festivals or other major events going on in Dallas every month of the year. These just a few of the major ones. All these annual events last at least two days and attract both local residents and visitors. Dates, admission fees, and (sometimes) locations change from year to year, so call or check the Dallas Convention & Visitors Bureau website (www.visitdallas.com) or the event website for details.

JANUARY

KIDFILM FESTIVAL • 214-821-6300 • This is the oldest and largest children's media festival in the nation. It features a diverse lineup of film and videos that appeal primarily to families and children. Events include appearances by acclaimed TV and film makers. Tickets usually about $3 per show.

DALLAS MORNING NEWS SWIMMING AND DIVING CLASSIC • 214-768-2883 • The best men's NCAA college swimming teams in the country compete in this annual event, which is usually held in the SMU Natatorium. Frequently these teams include Olympic champions or contenders.

DALLAS SAFARI CLUB EXPO • 972-980-9800 • Usually held in the huge Market Hall with wildlife displays and informative seminars put on by about 600 sports exhibitors from Alaska to Zimbabwe.

JANUARY–FEBRUARY

DALLAS WINTER BOAT SHOW • 469-549-0673 • www.dallas boatshow.net • Hundreds of boats and boat accessories are to be seen in the more than 210,000 square feet of Market Hall's display space. This show has been presented for more than 40 years and always features new models of all types of boats, from large cruisers to personal watercraft; most at special "Boat Show" prices. Look for discount admission coupons in the local papers. Free parking. (Summer boat show usually held in July.)

FEBRUARY

TRI DELTA CHARITY ANTIQUES SHOW • 214-691-3533 • For more than 20 years, dealers from United States and abroad have been selling fine antiques and art at this popular charity event held every February or early March.

MARCH

DALLAS BLOOMS • Dallas Arboretum and Botanical Gardens • 214-327-4901 • www.dallasarboretum.org • When spring comes to Dallas, then Dallas blooms at the Arboretum with a spectacular display of more than 300,000 plants and colorful flowers. (See SPECIAL GARDENS, p. 94)

DALLAS INTERNATIONAL ORGAN COMPETITION • 214-692-0203 • Participants come from around the world for this competition. Preliminaries are usually at the SMU Caruth Auditorium and finals at the Meyerson Symphony Center.

DALLAS NEW CAR AUTO SHOW • 214-939-2700 • Close to half a million people attend this annual auto show. Usually held at the Dallas Convention Center, it is one of the largest new car shows in the country, with almost all the new models on display, both domestic and foreign.

GREATER SOUTHWEST GUITAR SHOW • 972-260-4201 • This show has been bringing guitar enthusiasts to Dallas for close to twenty-five years. Usually held at Fair Park, it features everything about guitars, as well as nonstop guitar music.

NORTH TEXAS IRISH FESTIVAL • 214-821-4174 • www.ntif.org • This is the largest Celtic festival in the Southwest. During the weekend at Fair Park, it routinely offers music (by 40 to 50 different bands), dance, and other entertainment on more than half dozen stages; cultural displays, and traditional Irish food and drink.

APRIL

USA FILM FESTIVAL • 214-821-6300 • Created in 1971, it is now one of the oldest film festivals in the United States. It brings together professional filmmakers from around the world, noted film critics, celebrities, and film enthusiasts for screenings and discussions. Ticket prices are kept low to ensure maximum accessibility.

DEEP ELLUM ARTS FESTIVAL • 214-855-1881 • This arty street party goes on during a long weekend in the historic blues district. Features lots of music and art, fashion shows, a pet parade, food, and anything else they can create to add to the fun.

DANCE FOR THE PLANET • 214-219-2290 • www.thedance council.org • The goal of this free weekend multicultural festival is to "bring out the dancer in everyone." In other words—everybody dance! More than 120 dance organizations give dance classes and demonstrations in all styles and cultures. Then everyone is encouraged to get out on the lawn at the Annette Strauss Artist Square and shake, rattle, and roll, or do whatever else (legal) that goes with moving to the music.

APRIL–OCTOBER

MESQUITE CHAMPIONSHIP RODEO (See SIDE TRIPS, p. 158)

MAY

ARTFEST • 214-361-2036 • Typically, about 300 artists, representing all mediums, are selected to be in this three-day family festival of arts and entertainment at Fair Park. Activities include live and silent art auctions, continuous musical entertainment, demonstrations by artists, and arts and crafts activities for kids.

DALLAS VIDEO FESTIVAL • 214-428-8700 • This annual event has successfully grown to be known as "The Key American Video Festival." It features more than 250 screenings of local, regional, and internationally produced programs for video professionals and fans.

MAY–SEPTEMBER

DALLAS SUMMER MUSICALS • 214-691-7200 • www.dallassummer musicals.org • For more than sixty years, Fair Park has been the site for the best of the national touring companies' productions of Broadway musical theater. DSM also presents the Broadway Contemporary series of plays in the fall and winter seasons.

JUNE

DALLAS INTERNATIONAL FESTIVAL • 972-458-7007 • More than 200 ethnic communities in North Texas come together in Fair Park at this free festival. Cultural dances and traditions, world music, arts and crafts, and ethnic foods are the main elements of the two-day event.

NBA HOOP-IT-UP • 972-392-5750 • www.dallaswestend.org • What started as a popular street basketball tournament in Dallas in 1986 went national in 1989, got an NBA/NBC relationship in 1992, and is now a huge nationwide charity event. Two days of continuous basketball on 110 street courts in the West End is how Dallas participates for its part of the competitions in 55 U.S. cities. Players are matched by age, skill, and height in the 3-on-3 games. Wheelchair teams included. You can watch for free, and in Dallas many thousands of spectators do that. While the highlight of this weekend is basketball, there's also music and entertainment.

JUNE–JULY

SHAKESPEARE FESTIVAL OF DALLAS • 214-559-2778 • This is the oldest free Shakespeare festival in the Southwest and the second oldest in the nation. Each summer it presents two of the Bard's plays outdoors in Samuell-Grand Park Amphitheatre with a cast of mostly professional actors. (Sigourney Weaver and Morgan Freeman were two of the talents who performed in this festival during its early years.) Bring a blanket or lawn chair—and insect repellent.

JULY

TASTE OF DALLAS • 214-741-7185 • www.dallaswestend.org • The attraction here is the samplings of the diverse cuisine from some of Dallas's finest restaurants. More than 275,000 come to the West End for this three-day food fest. Continuous live entertainment on three stages and a special children's area. Admission and entertainment are free, but to do the tasting you have to buy coupons.

JULY–AUGUST

ANNUAL FESTIVAL OF INDEPENDENT THEATRES • 214-670-8749 • www.bathhousecultural.com • This festival showcases the smaller unique theater companies in Dallas with mostly short plays, performed in a rotating repertory at the Bath House Cultural Center.

AUGUST–SEPTEMBER

DALLAS MORNING NEWS DANCE FESTIVAL • 214-953-1977 • www.thedancecouncil.org • This four-evening extravaganza showcases both the professional and the emerging dance talent in the Metroplex. Held at the Annette Straus Artist Square in the Arts District, it usually includes performances by dance groups that include the Fort Worth Dallas Ballet, the Anita N. Martinez Ballet Folklorico, the Dallas Black Dance Theatre, and the dance students at Booker T. Washington High School.

SEPTEMBER

GREEK FESTIVAL OF DALLAS • 972-991-1166 • www.greekfestival ofdallas.com • A three-day, exuberant celebration of Greek culture at the Holy Trinity Greek Orthodox Church, with traditional costumes, music, dancing, arts and crafts, and, of course, authentic food.

SEPTEMBER–OCTOBER

STATE FAIR OF TEXAS • 214-565-9931 • www.bigtex.com • With annual attendance figures well over three million, this is the largest state fair in the nation. It may also have the largest greeter of any state fair. Big Tex, a 52-foot cowboy wearing 7'7" high boots and a 5-foot-high 75-gallon cowboy hat, greets all his visitors with a booming "Howdy folks!" The first State Fair was held at this location in 1886. As with all state fairs, the livestock competitions (with an average of 10,000 entries), agricultural exhibits, cooking contests, and the arts play a continuing role. But there's more—much, much more. In fact, each year they seem to cram in more exhibits, more musical entertainment, more shows, and more demonstrations. During this time, all the Fair Park museums (see FAIR PARK, pp. 79–83) have extended hours. Other events include a special musical in the Music Hall, major college football games in the Cotton Bowl, loads of events and activities for kids, and a carnival midway with the tallest Ferris wheel in North America, an 80-year old carousel, and about 60 rides. Check the newspapers for admission discount coupons.

OCTOBER

TEXAS STAMPEDE • 214-373-8000 • www.texasstampede.org • This annual charity event, at the American Airlines Center, brings together the powerful combination of one of the largest and richest purse Professional Rodeo Cowboys Association's championship rodeo and country music's biggest stars.

WOMEN'S SWIMMING AND DIVING CLASSIC • 214-768-2883 • SMU's Natatorium hosts the best women's NCAA college swimming teams in the country. Frequently these teams include Olympic champions or contenders.

NOVEMBER

ANNUAL CHI OMEGA CHRISTMAS MARKET • 214-890-8131 • www.chiomegaxmas.org • About 120 carefully selected merchants set up in the Convention Center for this three-day market of holiday merchandise, which has benefited community charities for more than 25 years.

NOVEMBER–DECEMBER

CHRISTMAS AT THE ARBORETUM • 214-327-8263 • www.dallas arboretum.org • One of the highlights of this month-long event is the tour of the historic DeGolyer Home, elaborately decorated for the holidays. (See SPECIAL GARDENS, p. 94)

SHOPPING

In spite of the enthusiasm for the Cowboys, the Rangers, and other major sports teams, many Dallasites agree that the number one sport here is shopping. As one Dallas booster put it: "If it can't be bought in Dallas, it can't be bought anywhere." Statistically, Dallas averages 26.3 square feet of retail space for every man, woman, and child—that's 42 percent above the national norm. The following are just for starters.

GALLERIA

LBJ Frwy. (I-635), at Dallas Pkwy. North (75240) • 972-702-7100 • W+ • www.dallasgalleria.com

One of the best-known shopping centers in Texas, and possibly in the country, it is patterned after and named for the barrel-vaulted glass atrium style of the nineteenth century Galleria Vittorio Emanuele in Milan, Italy. There are more than 200 upscale stores and boutiques in this visually impressive four-level mall, including Macy's, Marshall Field's, Nordstrom, Saks Fifth Avenue, and Tiffany & Company. It also features more than two dozen fast-food and full-service restaurants, an indoor ice rink, cinema, and the attached Westin Hotel. In the holiday season, it boasts that it has the largest indoor Christmas tree in the country, decorated with 100,000 lights. Some covered parking. Valet parking available at the Westin Hotel.

HIGHLAND PARK VILLAGE

Mockingbird at Preston (75205) • 214-559-2740 • W+

One of the first shopping centers in the country when it was built in 1931, the Mediterranean plaza-style Highland Park Village has been designated a National Historic Landmark by the U.S. Department of the Interior and is on the National Register of Historic Places. But being more than 70 years old and historic doesn't mean it's antiquated. It has been continuously updated and refurbished and is now the home of an eclectic collection of about 80 shops and restaurants that include both the ordinary and some prestigious international shops and boutiques that could be equally at home on Los Angeles's Rodeo Drive. Complimentary valet parking.

INWOOD TRADE CENTER

1300 Inwood Rd. (75247), two blocks west of I-35E • 214-421-4777 • W variable

This Center is an example of the many outlet centers in Dallas. Bargain shoppers can find some quality products here at outlet prices. Parking in front of stores.

KNOX-HENDERSON AREA

Just off Central Expressway north of downtown • W

Many Dallasites claim this is the best nonmall shopping area in Dallas, with a number of one-of-a-kind stores lining Knox (often called Furniture Row) to the west of the Central Expressway. The name changes to Henderson as you go east across the Expressway, and Henderson has multiple specialty and antique shops. Also check shops on the side streets, like McKinney, that flow off these two main streets.

LOVE FIELD ANTIQUE MALL

6500 Cedar Springs (75235) at Mockingbird, across from the Mockingbird entrance to Love Field • 214-357-6500 • W

The ads for this mall describe it as the largest antique and classic car mall in the United States. There are a couple of hundred dealer booths and a section of classic cars under one roof in this air-conditioned 70,000-square-foot building. The booth area overflows with antique furniture, art objects, china, silver, crystal, jewelry, and collectibles. Whether you're a classic car buff or not, the collection here is worth a visit. Some of the cars are on consignment for sale, but most of the collection is only for display. Restaurant and tearoom.

MAP STORES

If you want to get around Dallas, the Metroplex, or the world, without getting lost, these stores have everything you need in the way of street guides and maps to get from point A to point B. A smaller selection of area maps and street guides is also available at bookstores and supermarkets and other retail locations in the Metroplex.

Mapsco • 11811 Preston (75230) • 972-960-1414 • W • www.mapsco.com

One Map Place • 3128 Forest Ln. (75230) • 972-241-26809 • W

Rand McNally Map and Travel Store • 211 NorthPark Center • 214-987-9941 • W

SAM MOON TRADING COMPANY
11635 Harry Hines (75229) • 972-484-3084 • W •
www.sammoon.com

If you are interested in getting mega discounts (retail at wholesale prices), this women's accessories and handbags store is for you. But be warned, when it's busy—-which is often, since bargain hunters come here from all over Texas and neighboring states—this can be elbows-out bargain-basement-type shopping. Sam Moon's is now the center of more than a hundred smaller wholesale/retail shops like it on Harry Hines.

NEIMAN MARCUS ORIGINAL DALLAS STORE
(See OTHER POINTS OF INTEREST, p. 121)

NORTHPARK CENTER
Northwest Hwy. (Loop 12), at North Central Expwy. (US75)
(75231) (DART Light Rail Park Lane Station and North Park Trolley)
• 214-361-6345 • W+ • www.northparkcenter.com

What is reportedly the most popular (and profitable) Neiman Marcus in the chain is located in this mall along with Lord & Taylor, Foley's, Dillard's, JCPenney, and more than 150 other specialty stores and restaurants. Opened as the most elegant mall in Dallas in 1965, it has continued to maintain its upscale ambience for shoppers while at the same time attracting nonshoppers to its impressive displays of twentieth-century art, activities, and festivities. It is especially known for its holiday events, including the six-week display of "The Trains at NorthPark" featuring more than 40 type O–gauge trains running in a setting that has detailed reproductions of landmarks from the Empire State Building to the Golden Gate Bridge. (Admission fee for charity.)

WEST END MARKETPLACE
603 Munger Ave. (75202), at Market Street (DART Light Rail West
End Station) • 214-748-4801 • W

Located in what was originally an early 1900s cracker and candy factory in the heart of the West End Historic District, this is a combination shopping and entertainment center. There are four levels in three adjoining buildings filled with unique shops—including the Official Dallas Cowboy

Pro Shop—fast food eateries, restaurants, and a multi-nightclub complex. You can buy everything from souvenirs to cowboy hats, fine Texas wines to art created by local artists and artisans. Pay parking in nearby lots or metered parking on street.

SPORTS FANS SHOPS

OFFICIAL DALLAS COWBOY PRO SHOP • 214-979-0500 (See WEST END MARKETPLACE, p. 131)

DALLAS MAVERICKS AND STARS FAN SHOP (See SPORTS, pp. 116–17)

A SAMPLING OF DALLAS RESTAURANTS

Dinner for one, excluding drinks, tax, and tip: $ = up to $16, $$ = $16–$30, $$$ = $31–$50, $$$$ = over $50. It is strongly suggested that you make a reservation, in those restaurants that take them, especially on weekends and holidays.

On average, Dallas has more than 7,000 restaurants. That's four times as many restaurants per resident as New York City. Restaurants come and restaurants go, but the following list is of restaurants that have stayed by earning accolades from their patrons.

ABACUS ($$$–$$$$)

4511 McKinney (75205) • **214-559-3111** • **Dinner, Monday– Saturday. Closed Sunday** • **Cr** • **W+** • **www.abacus-restaurant.com**

The open kitchen is like a stage and the dining room, with its pleasantly warm colors, is the theater for the presentation of chef/owner Kent Rathburn's eclectic menu that features new American cuisine with a Pacific Rim accent. From the lobster-scallion "shooters" appetizer, made with red chile and coconut sake, to the prime tenderloin filet entrée, with red wine butter on grilled Portobello whipped potatoes, the dishes show his culinary imagination and passion. For about $90 per person, up to a dozen guests can sit at the Chef's Table for a seven-course dinner with Rathburn's personal touch. Lounge. AAA rates it a 4-Diamond and Mobil a 4-Star. Street and valet parking.

ADELMO'S RISTORANTE ($$–$$$)

4537 Cole (75205), at Knox • **214-559-0325** • **Lunch, Monday– Friday; dinner, Monday–Saturday. Closed Sunday and major holidays** • **Cr.** • **W** • **www.adelmos.com**

A quick scan of the dinner menu will show that this bistro is not your everyday Italian restaurant. Adelmo's creative cuisine is inspired by the eastern Mediterranean region, from France to Italy to the Middle East.

Choices for starters, for example, include *escargot,* lobster ravioli, and crab cakes. Among the specialties of the house are a 16-oz. veal chop with truffle brandy sauce, grilled rack of lamb with couscous and rosemary wine sauce, and a mixed seafood linguine with crabmeat and shrimp in a marinara sauce. Also check the blackboard specials. Family owned and operated since 1989, the restaurant is in a charming narrow two-story house with close but cozy seating. Bar.

ANTARES ($$–$$$)

300 Reunion Blvd. (75207), in Reunion Tower (DART Light Rail Union Station) • 214-712-7145 • Lunch and dinner, Monday– Saturday; brunch, Sunday • Cr. • W

At 50 stories above the street, the menu can run second to the view, but a close second. Since the restaurant gently revolves to give you an enchanting 360-degree panorama of the city in a little less than an hour, it might be expected that the menu would slip into typical tourist-trap items. But it doesn't. Instead, it features New American cuisine with global influences. The menu rotates, too, but usually includes a wide choice of beef dishes, like southwestern dry-rubbed sirloin, and seafood entrées that range from grilled swordfish to seafood Zarzuella, which has lobster, scallops, shrimp, seasonal fish, mussels, and clams over black pepper fettuccine in a saffron-fennel broth. Bar. Valet parking (fee).

BEAU NASH ($$–$$$)

2200 Cedar Springs (75201), in Hotel Crescent Court (DART Light Rail Cityplace Station and M-Line Streetcar) • 214-871-3240 • Breakfast, lunch, and dinner, seven days. Closed major holidays • Cr. • W+

This hotel dining room offers casual dining in an elegant setting overlooking serene gardens. The chefs work in an open kitchen on a menu that creatively fuses New American cuisine with a touch of Northern Italian. Frequent menu changes offer a variety of entrées, including grilled Atlantic salmon, pan-seared turbot, Black Angus filet, and tea-smoked pork tenderloin. Three-course *prix fixe* "Taste of Beau Nash" usually available. Professional level of unobtrusive service. Children's menu. Music Thursday–Saturday evenings. Lounge. Valet parking.

BOB'S STEAK AND CHOP HOUSE ($$$–$$$$)

4300 Lemmon (75219), at Wycliff • 214-528-9446 • Dinner, Monday– Saturday. Closed Sunday • Cr. • W+ • www.bobs-steakandchop.com

In a city where there are a number of excellent steak houses, this one consistently comes out among the best in popular rankings, both for the steaks and for the ambience of the refined but clubby dining room, with its warm, dark wood, brass, and white tablecloths. In addition to the no-nonsense steaks, in every size and variety, the menu also offers veal and pork chops, roasted duck, and seafood. Among the side dishes offered are glazed carrots and onion rings that consistently draw raves even from the most confirmed carnivores. Bar. Cigar-friendly. Self-parking or valet. Another location at 5760 Legacy in Plano.

CAFÉ EXPRESSO ($$–$$$)

6135 Luther (75225), at Preston • 214-361-6984 • Lunch, Monday–Friday; dinner, Monday–Saturday. Closed Sunday • Cr. • W+

One of items that make this upscale, high-quality Italian restaurant consistently popular with its patrons is that the owner, Dieter Paul, personally calls his regulars when he has been able to gather and put together the ingredients for one of their favorite dishes. And his personal touch carries over in the small-neighborhood-restaurant type of service he gives even first-time customers. The menu favors classic Southern Italian cuisine, like veal scaloppini, osso buco, and a variety of pastas and sauces you can mix and match. Bar (membership required).

CAFÉ IZMIR ($–$$)

3711 Greenville (75206) (DART Light Rail Mockingbird Station and bus) • 214-826-7788 • Dinner, seven nights • Cr. • W

In one way, it's just like home. No menu. Meals are served family style and, in general, if you want the fixed price dinner you take what Mama cooks, which is authentic upscale Middle Eastern cuisine. You do have a choice of with meat or without. The selection of the day could be entrées such as lemon buttered grilled shrimp, Cornish hen, chicken or tenderloins kabobs, and/or vegetarian dishes like falafel, dolmas, or char-grilled seasonal vegetables. If you must go à la carte, there's a menu of Tapas (starters). At $3–$10 each, you could combine them to make a tasty and economical meal.

CAFÉ PACIFIC ($$–$$$)

24 Highland Park Village (75205), corner of Mockingbird and Preston • 214-526-1170 • Lunch and dinner, Monday–Saturday. Closed Sunday, Thanksgiving, Christmas, and New Year's Day • Cr. • W+

Although there are a variety of entrées for the meat-and-potato lovers on the menu, the house is most famous for its seafood specialties. Among the starters is ceviche, stocked with chunks of lobster, shrimp, and scallops, and New England clam chowder that would make Boston proud. Entrées range from short smoked salmon to such culinary delights as three-onion crusted sea bass or a lobster-tail trio. All served in an intimate, sophisticated, club-like setting—dark wood, glass, and brass. Bar. Shopping center and valet parking.

CAPITAL GRILLE ($$$–$$$$)

500 Crescent Court, Suite 135 (75201), Maple and McKinney (DART Light Rail Cityplace Station and M-Line Streetcar) •

214-303-0500 • Lunch, Monday–Friday; dinner, seven days •
Cr. • W+

The menu offers both a variety of dry-aged beef entrées and fresh seafood. Among the meat entrées available are a 20-oz. prime aged steak *au poivre* with Courvoisier cognac cream sauce, and the Grille's signature veal chop with Roquefort butter sauce. Side dishes, like a one-pound baked potato or roasted seasonal mushrooms, come in generous portions and are all à la carte. Servers are so professional that many of them have a business card. The sophisticated, clubby setting features dark woods, gleaming brass, and linens so snowy white they could be the "after" in a detergent commercial. Bar.

CELEBRATION ($–$$)

4503 W. Lovers Lane (75209), between Inwood and Lemmon •
214-358-0612 • Lunch and dinner, seven days. Closed Thanksgiving, Christmas Eve, and Christmas • Cr. • W+ •
www.celebrationrestaurant.com

From the outside it looks like home (a rustic home), and inside you'll find it's as close as you'll get to down-home cooking in a restaurant. Since 1971 they've been serving meat loaf, pot roast, southern fried or baked chicken, catfish, and other homestead mainstays. The unpretentious, hearty meals are served family style at dinner, with serve-yourself bowls of salads and loads of vegetables—naturally including choices like southern-style black-eyed peas and okra. And just like at home, most meals even include seconds, either of what you ordered or of any other entrée of equal or lesser value. The comfortable setting and cheerful service are just as unpretentious as the food. Bar. And next door (at 4515, across the parking lot) is the Celebration Market, where you can get most of the menu items prepackaged to heat and eat at home (214-351-2456). Parking lot.

CHAPPARAL ($$$–$$$$)

400 N. Olive (75201), in the Adams Mark Hotel (DART Light Rail Pearl Station) • 214-777-6539 • Dinner, Tuesday–Saturday. Closed Sunday, Monday • Cr. • W+ • www.adamsmark.com/dallas

The location of this glass-enclosed restaurant, on the thirty-eighth floor of this huge downtown hotel, offers guests a spectacular view with dinner. The Texas and international cuisine includes entrées that include a range of choices from a BBQ Cowboy steak to an antelope chop, tequila gulf shrimp to wasabi-crusted tuna steak. Excellent service and live music entertainment round out this high-in-the-sky dining experience. Bar. Hotel (fee) or valet parking (fee).

CHEZ GERARD ($$–$$$)

4444 McKinney (75205), at Armstrong • 214-522-6865 • Lunch, Monday–Friday; dinner, Monday–Saturday. Closed Sunday and major holidays • Cr. • W+ • www.chezgerardrestaurant.com

Don't let the unpretentious outside fool you. Inside this is the type of small, cozy restaurant you'd expect to find in the French countryside, right down to the hardwood floors, flowery print wall covering, and lace curtains. And the menu of classic French dishes promotes the same feeling of authenticity. Substantial, time-honored Gallic recipes are reinterpreted here with a respect for tradition that combines with a spark of creativity to produce specialties like grilled snapper with rosemary mignonnette and pine nuts served with calamata and sardine caviar, and the house signature dish of tenderloin rubbed with black pepper, served with mushrooms and a cognac cream sauce. Other entrées of seafood, veal, lamb, and beef are both elegantly presented and pleasing to the palate. Children's menu. Outdoor dining area. Bar. Parking.

CITIZEN ($$$–$$$$)

3858 Oak Lawn (75233), in Turtle Creek Village • 214-522-7253 • Lunch, Monday–Friday; dinner, Monday–Saturday. Closed Sunday • Cr. • W+

It's named after the movie "Citizen Kane," which seems a little incongruous since he was the epitome of the American powerbroker while the menu features innovative and stylish Pan-Asian dishes. The Asian influence is evident both in the appetizers, like tempura shrimp stuffed shiitake mushrooms, and the entrées that include spicy pork lo mein with udon noodles, and filet of black cod with blonde miso and spiced ginger root. Definitely upscale, the menu also features Kobe beef and designer sake. Sushi bar. Bar. Parking.

CITY CAFÉ ($$–$$$)

5757 W. Lovers Lane (75209), just west of North Dallas Tollway • 214-351-2233 • Lunch and dinner, seven days. Closed major holidays • Cr. • W+

It started out as a casual neighborhood restaurant that offered variety to its local customers by changing the menu every two weeks. Except for a few customer favorites, like its famed fresh tomato soup, the handpainted menu is still changed every other Wednesday, rotating dishes of seafood, veal, game, beef, pasta, fowl, pork, and lamb. But the biggest change is that the little neighborhood bistro's reputation for culinary creativity has broadened its following throughout the Metroplex. The menu offers both simple and sophisticated choices of regional and New American fare that ranges from California through the Southwest to the Cajun country, with a typical menu including entrées like pan-seared swordfish stuffed with parmesan, roasted free-range chicken, and grilled jerk-rubbed pork tenderloin. Most of the dishes are available for takeout at City Café To Go Bar. Valet parking.

CIUDAD ($$–$$$)

3888 Oak Lawn, Suite 135 (75219), in Turtle Creek Village •
214-219-3141 • Lunch, Tuesday–Friday; dinner, Tuesday–Saturday;
Sunday brunch. Closed Sunday dinner and Monday • Cr. • W+ •
www.ciudaddf.com

You know you are in an authentic Mexican restaurant, a world away
from Tex-Mex, when the menu includes corn tortilla *flautas* filled with
duck and served with ginger pineapple *pico de gallo, cabrito* tacos with
roasted goat and plum-butter apples, and an 8-oz. beef tenderloin *carne
adobo* with black beans and blistered tomato sauce topped with melted
Chihuahua cheese. If you want a sampling of the real regional food from
the Yucatan and central Mexico, prepared from traditional recipes with a
touch of creativity, go on a Tuesday night, when a separate menu of
starters is offered. Called *bocadillos*, little tastes of Mexico, they can be
combined to make a meal of taste treats. Hacienda setting with large patio. Bar. Free parking weekdays, valet parking weekends.

DAKOTA'S ($$–$$$)

600 N. Akard (75201), at San Jacinto (DART Light Rail Akard
Station) • 214-740-4001 • Lunch, Monday–Friday; dinner, seven
days • Cr. • W+ (elevator) • www.dakotasrestaurant.com

This elegant downtown and below-ground restaurant offers subter-
ranean courtyard dining by a five-tier cascading waterfall, with Carrara
marble and the Dakota granite that inspired its name, or inside dining in
a grill-room setting of rich wood paneling. Why below ground? To get
around the deed clause that prohibited selling alcohol "on the former
church grounds"—but not *under* them. Entrées grilled over native hard-
woods highlight the menu of classic American cuisine with a touch of the
Southwest, offering choices that include beef, seafood, lamb, and fowl.
Bar. Valet parking.

FERRE ($$–$$$)

3699 McKinney (75204), at Lemmon (DART Light Rail Cityplace
Station and M-Line Streetcar) • 214-522-3888 • Lunch and dinner,
Monday–Saturday; dinner only, Sunday • Cr. • W+

The menu offers the classic Italian-Tuscan pasta, pizza, and other familiar dishes but with a creative upscale flair. The tomato soup, for example
is listed as *cappuccino al pomodoro*, which translates into a roasted organic
tomato soup, served like a cappucinno in a large cup topped with a light
creamy froth. The crispy gourmet pizzas include *pollo e caprino* made of
rosemary chicken with goat cheese, tear-drop tomatoes, and caramelized
onion. And in the entrée section is *pesce al tegame*, which is shrimp, scallops,
mussels, artichokes, potatoes, and olives baked in a chive crust. Full service Crú Wine Bar.

THE FRENCH ROOM ($$$$)

1321 Commerce (75202) at Akard, in the Adolphus Hotel
(DART Light Rail Akard Station) • 214-742-8200 • Dinner,
Tuesday–Saturday. Closed Sunday, Monday, and major holidays •
Reservations required • Cr. • W+ • www.hoteladolphus.com

Opulent. Posh. Sumptuous. Plush. Elegant. Beautiful. Those are a just
a few of the words frequently used to describe the French Room's setting.
With its French baroque painted domed ceiling festooned with frescos of
cherubs, layered tablecloths, drapes, and hand-blown crystal chandeliers
of seventeenth-century design, the room evokes the sensation of entering a realm in which King Louis XV would feel at home. The service is
just as regal, impeccable, and unobtrusive. The cuisine is Neoclassic, that
is, classic French and continental recipes creatively adapted to contemporary American tastes. If you want gourmet dining in an ultra-romantic
setting, at a reasonable price, order one of the multi-course *prix fixe* dinners that offer several choices for each course ($60–$80). Semiformal
dress. Bar. Hotel (fee) and valet parking (fee). Rated 5-Diamond by AAA
and 4-Star by Mobil.

THE GRAPE ($$–$$$)

2808 Greenville (75206) (DART Light Rail Mockingbird Station and
bus) • 214-828-1981 • Lunch, Monday–Friday; dinner, seven days •
Cr. • W

Over the years, what began as a simple wine bar in 1972 has grown
into a popular restaurant. Since it's still in its original location, it now lays
claim to being the oldest wine bistro in Dallas—still dark, cozy, and romantic. Now, however, as many patrons come here for the eclectic menu
as for the wine. That menu changes frequently, featuring regional specialties from Europe and Asia as well as New American cuisine, but always includes a cream of mushroom soup starter that even jaded food
critics say is among the best in the world. No reservations.

THE GREEN ROOM ($$–$$$)

2715 Elm (75226), in Deep Ellum • 214-748-7666 • Dinner, seven
days. Closed Thanksgiving, Christmas, and New Year's Day • Cr. •
W+ • www.thegreenroom.com

The décor is offbeat funky, with angel sculptures and electric guitars on
the wall, and Chef Marc Cassell's culinary fusion creations are often called
"Collision Cuisine." So if you're looking for deliciously creative and innovative dishes, this brash restaurant is the place to go. For starters, how
about pan-roasted black mussels with shiitakes, champagne, and ginger,
or lemon braised pork pot roast? Regular menu entrées include grilled
lamb loin, seared gulf shrimp, and Rhode Island stripped bass, and daily
market specials may include grilled Texas quail. An intriguing deal is the
prix fixe "Feed Me" special, which offers four courses of the chef's choice
special (his surprise) selections for a little over $40, or about $65 with the

accompanying "Wine Me" selections. Live music most nights. Bar. Valet parking.

GUTHRIE'S HISTORICAL AMERICAN FOOD ($$–$$$)

400 S. Ervay (75201), near the Central Library and City Hall (DART Light Rail Union Station and bus) • 214-760-7900 • Lunch, Monday–Friday; dinner, Wednesday–Saturday. Closed Sunday • MC, V • W+

With a few exceptions, the name says it all. Most of chef/owner William Guthrie's menu highlights up-to-date versions of classic American comfort food, like roasted chicken, roast pork loin, and baked salmon. One of the exceptions is his signature dish of all-you-can-eat beer battered fish and chips (maybe that can be labeled "historical colonial"). Regulars also claim his soft-centered chocolate cake is the ultimate dessert.

HOFSTETTER'S SPARGEL CAFÉ ($$–$$$)

4326 Lovers Ln. (75225), at Douglas • 214-368-3002 • Lunch, Monday–Friday; dinner, Monday–Saturday; Sunday brunch • Cr. • W+

The menu features a number of creatively contemporary versions of Euro-Continental classics, but the emphasis is on Austrian dishes like the platter-sized Wiener schnitzel and *jager* schnitzel (fillet of veal sautéed in brandy cream sauce with mushrooms). In keeping with the name, most dishes come with a side of grilled asparagus (*spargel*). For the true fan of Austro-German food, there is the Butcher Platter, which has wurst, grilled pork loin, and smoked pork chop piled on a bed of mellow sauerkraut. Seafood entrées include grilled salmon, perch, and sea scallops in tarragon champagne cream. Don't expect an "oompah" setting. The subtle green interior actually has been characterized as "serene." Bar. Parking.

HOTEL ST. GERMAIN RESTAURANT ($$$$)

2516 Maple (75201) • (DART Light Rail Cityplace Station and M-Line Streetcar) • 214-871-2516 • Dinner, Tuesday–Saturday • Cr. • W+ • www.hotelstgermain.com

The setting for dinner in this restored historic hotel is romantic Old World, with candlelight, classical background music, elegant French décor, widely spaced tables, and flawlessly attentive white-gloved waiters serving on antique Limoges china, all while overlooking an ivy-covered New Orleans–style garden courtyard. The seven-course gourmet dinner is *prix fixe* (about $85). Selections change with the seasons. When you make your reservation (required) you are offered choices of several appetizers, entrées, and desserts. Jackets required, ties optional. Champagne bar. Hotel and valet parking. AAA gives it a 4-Diamond rating.

INDIA PALACE ($$)

12817 Preston Road , Suite 105 (75230), in Preston Valley
Shopping Center • 972-392-0190 • Lunch, Monday–Saturday;
dinner, seven days • Cr. • W • www.indiapalacedallas.com

The extensive menu of traditional Northern Indian cuisine gives you a
wide choice of exotic tastes to try. The intense dry heat of the traditional
tandoor ovens generates the flavor while retaining the moistness of many
of the dishes; such as tandoori chicken and lamb kebab. There are also
many grilled items using beef, chicken, lamb, and seafood, in addition to
numerous vegetarian dishes, all imbued with delicate spices. And, of
course, there are curries and curried dishes; you can call the shots on how
spicy hot you want yours. Children's menu. Bountiful lunch buffet. Consistently rated one of best Indian restaurants in the city. Jacket suggested
in evening. Bar. Parking.

JAVIER'S ($$$)

4912 Cole (75205) • 214-521-4211 • Dinner, seven days • Cr. • W+

They've been serving authentic Mexican food here for more than
twenty years. The decor is cozy old colonial Mexico, studded with antiques, but the cuisine leans more to modern, sophisticated Mexico City
style. No Tex-Mex here. Instead there are traditional dishes like *barra de
navidad*, in which shrimp is sautéed in a diablo sauce of orange juice, coffee, and tomato; *filete Cantinflas* (named after the famous Mexican comic)
of thin sliced tenderloin beef stuffed with Chihuahua cheese, or *mole
poblano* of broiled chicken with authentic mole sauce. Cigar room. Bar.
Valet parking.

LA CALLE DOCE ($-$$)

415 W. 12th (75208) (DART Light Rail Zoo Station and bus) •
214-941-4304 • Lunch and dinner, seven days • Cr. • W+ •
www.lacalledoce.com

Seafood Mexican style, like its signature dish of grilled peppery catfish, is the specialty of the house. Dine on the patio or in one of the cozy
rooms in the old house that is the setting for this family-run restaurant
that has been around since 1982. Patrons especially boast about the oc-
topus cocktail and the ceviche, but the shrimp *veracruzana*, paella, chile
relleno *de mariscos*, and other entrees can match them. Children's menu.
Another location at 1925 Skillman (213-824-9900). Lounge. Parking.

LANDMARK CAFÉ ($$$-$$$$)

3015 Oak Lawn (75219), in Melrose Hotel • 214-522-5151 •
Breakfast, seven days; lunch, Monday–Friday; Sunday brunch; dinner,
Monday–Saturday. Closed Saturday lunch, Sunday dinner. • Cr. • W+

The attractively serene dining room, done in mirrors and marble with
muted lighting, is the setting for an eclectic menu that changes monthly.

Among the creative choices for a typical first course is pan-seared jumbo sea scallops over a celery root purée with sturgeon caviar. Second course selections include Portobello mushroom "eggroll" over roasted tomatoes. And for the entrée, among the lamb, beef, and seafood choices is grilled venison loin with *spaetzle*, fava beans, *mousserons*, sweet tomatoes, and wild huckleberry sauce. Jackets at dinner. Bar. Valet parking.

LA TRATTORIA LOMBARDI ($$–$$$)

2916 N. Hall (75204), near McKinney Avenue (DART Light Rail Cityplace Station and M-Line Streetcar) • 214-954-0803 • Lunch, Monday–Friday; dinner, seven days. Closed major holidays • Cr. • W

For more than two decades, consistently good old-style Italian offerings have been the heart of the menu at this comfortable neighborhood trattoria-style restaurant with polished old style service. Pasta dishes include fettucine *del pescatore* with shrimp, scallops, and green lip mussels in garlic olive oil and herb sauce, and penne *alla piriano* served with Italian sausage in a tomato sauce with onions, peppers, and mushrooms. Among the meat choices is a veal chop marinated with special herbs, grilled and served with Marsala wine sauce; fish specialties include crab cannelloni and cioppino. Outdoor dining available. Lounge. Valet parking.

LAVENDOU ($$$)

19009 Preston, Suite 200 (75252), at Lloyd • 972-248-1911 • Lunch, Monday–Friday; dinner, Monday–Saturday. Closed Sunday • Cr. • W+ • www.lavendou.com

This charming outpost of Southern France in North Dallas is named after a region in France where lavender is grown. The warm décor is cozy blue and yellow with screened Pierre Deux fabics. The dinner menu offers entrées such as *la sole de Douvres*, Dover sole sautéed in lemon butter, and *tournedos felix faure*, tenderloin with cracked black pepper, mushrooms, cognac and cream sauce. Does own baking. And, of course, you can savor authentic *pommes frites* (French fries) and French onion soup. "French high tea," Monday–Friday afternoons (about $15). Retail section sells pottery, linens, and tea. Bar. Parking.

LIBERTY NOODLES ($$–$$$)

5600 Lovers Ln. (75225) (DART Light Rail Mockingbird Station and bus) • 214-350-1133 • Lunch, Tuesday–Saturday; dinner, Tuesday–Sunday. Closed Monday • Cr. • W+

The name implies it's just a "noodle shop," but the imaginative and ambitious menu quickly shows it's lots, lots more than that. Annie Wong, who is credited with making Thai food almost an art form in her other Dallas restaurants, goes all out here with a crossover pan-Asian menu that brings together Thai, Vietnamese, Japanese, Korean, Chinese, Indian, and even some Southwestern specialties. Here you'll find Thai tacos, Vietnamese spring rolls, Japanese beef, Saigon soup, Shanghai noodles, Korean grill, curry, and just about anything else that Annie Wong can concoct from some basic recipes and her imagination. Chef's *prix fixe* multi-course dinner about $40, $60 with wine. Sake and wine. Valet parking.

THE MANSION ON TURTLE CREEK ($$$$)

2821 Turtle Creek Blvd. (75219), in The Mansion on Turtle Creek Hotel • 214-559-2100 • Lunch, Monday–Saturday; dinner, seven days; Sunday brunch • Cr. • W+ • www.themansiononturtlecreek.com

This nationally known restaurant is appropriately sited in a wing of a 1920s-era cattle baron's Italian Renaissance mansion converted to an award-winning hotel. While opulent, the restaurant's rooms easily create a warm, residential ambience since they occupy what was originally the living room (with an intricately carved ceiling and fireplace at each end), the library (which retains its original oak paneling), and the glass-walled veranda (with a view of the landscaped courtyard). The cuisine is basically Southwestern with a Texas flair, created by the award-winning longtime executive chef Dean Fearing. It is also delightfully varied and creative, making superlative use of seasonal regional ingredients, including Hill Country game. Now classic Mansion choices range from starters of tortilla soup and warm lobster taco, to sugarcane glazed salmon and pan-seared ostrich filet. Four-course *prix fixe* dinner available. Impeccable service. Bar. Music nightly. Jackets for dinner and Sunday brunch. Hotel and valet parking. The restaurant consistently earns a rating of 5 diamonds from AAA and at least 4 stars from Mobil.

THE MERCURY GRILL ($$$–$$$$)

11909 Preston (75230) • 972-960-7774 • Lunch, Monday–Friday; dinner, Monday– Saturday. Closed Sunday • Cr. • W+

Don't let the unpretentious setting in a strip mall put you off; there are imaginative versions of good comfort food inside. A popular starter is duck confit. Among the entrées are Cracklin' chicken, pork chops with rosemary risotto, tenderloin and grilled asparagus, lamb shank with a red-onion tart, and crusted halibut set on a potato cake. Sleek, modern décor. Tends to have a high noise level. Bar. Valet parking.

MIA'S TEX-MEX ($–$$)

4322 Lemmon (75219) • 214-526-1020 • Lunch and dinner, Monday–Saturday. Closed Sunday, Christmas, and New Year's Day • Cr. • W+

This small, family-owned, no-frills neighborhood restaurant has been taking Tex-Mex to new heights for more than twenty years. All the classics are here: chimichangas, fajitas, flautas, enchiladas, chalupas, and homemade salsa; it's just that they are all of the high quality that Mama would serve to her own family. Mia's ever popular chiles rellenos, stuffed with beef, raisins, and almonds, are usually only available—and a sell-out—on

Tuesdays. Children's menu. Beer and margaritas. Large portions—some of the appetizers could make a meal—and family-friendly service. Parking.

NANA ($$$$)

2201 Stemmons Frwy. (75207), in the Wyndham Anatole Hotel across from the Market Center • 214-761-7479 • Lunch, Monday–Friday; dinner, seven days; Sunday brunch • Cr. • W+

This 27th-floor restaurant offers a winning combination: a stunning view of the city from every table and sumptuous dining in an elegant dining room, decorated with crystal chandeliers and museum-quality pieces of Asian art from the Trammell and Margaret Crow collection. Not to forget the painting of Nana, the Rubenesque nude after whom the restaurant is named. The fine dining, which is the reason for it all, features a new menu each night. A typical menu may start with appetizers such as grilled filled Texas quail or Tsar Imperial Caviars ($60–$110). Entrées range from grilled prime filet to the more exotic wild Texas antelope chop, plus a variety of succulent seafood choices. Seven-course tasting menu available. Semiformal dress at dinner. Bar with music and dancing Wednesday–Saturday. Rated 4-Star by Mobil and 4-Diamond by AAA. Hotel and valet parking.

NUEVO LEON ($–$$)

2013 Greenville (75206) (DART Light Rail Mockingbird Station and bus) • 214-887-8148 • Lunch and dinner, seven days • Cr. • W+

They say they are Mex-Mex, and the variety of authentic dishes on the menu based on the cuisine of south central and northeastern Mexico bears this out. Examples among the many specials include: *Mancha manteles* of beef tips sautéed in a mole sauce, *cabrito al horno* of slow-cooked marinated young goat wrapped in banana leaves, and *pescado San Jose*, a pan-seared fish fillet topped with shrimp and scallops. Most Tex-Mex favorites also available. Other locations in Dallas and Farmers Branch. Bar.

THE OLD WARSAW ($$–$$$)

2610 Maple (75201) (DART Light Rail Cityplace Station and M-Line Streetcar) • 214-528-0032 • Dinner only, seven days • Cr. • W+ • www.theoldwarsaw.com

The "old" in the name has a double meaning. It has been serving satisfied patrons for more than half a century, making it one of the oldest Continental restaurants in Dallas, and it is an apt description of the Old World elegance, style, and service. The "Warsaw" was the name given by its original owner, who was Polish, but otherwise it can be misleading because the cuisine is definitely French, not Polish. Sticking to the tried and true, they serve superb renditions of traditional French and other European fare like roast rack of lamb, milk-fed veal, sweetbreads, chateaubriand for two, braised pheasant, fish, and duckling. The darkly rich atmosphere of the mirrored room, tuxedoed waiters performing exemplary tableside service, and musicians playing the classics all add to the romantic setting. AAA rates it 4-Diamond. Semiformal dress. Lounge. Valet parking.

THE PALM ($$$–$$$$)

701 Ross (75202), at Market in the West End Historic District (DART Light Rail West End Station) • 214-698-0470 • Lunch, Monday–Friday; dinner, seven days. • Cr. • W+ • www.thepalm.com

It's best known for its huge steaks (a house specialty is a 36-oz. New York strip for two), but if you want a BIG lobster, say at least three pounds, they can also satisfy that hunger, too. They claim that some of the lobsters they jet in are big enough to pilot the plane. This Palm is the local branch of a family-owned chain of white-tablecloth restaurants spread coast to coast. Like all the others in the chain, a major part of décor is the colorful cartoon caricatures of local and other celebs on the wall. This is a chain tradition that reportedly started when the original owners let local newsmen draw a cartoon in exchange for a plate of spaghetti. Besides beef and lobster, the menu also offers chops, seafood, poultry, and, never forgetting its Italian family origin, bountiful pasta dishes. Semiformal dress for dinner. Bar. Valet parking.

PEGGY SUE BBQ ($)

6600 Snider Plaza (75205), at Hillcrest and Lovers Ln. near SMU (DART Light Rail Mockingbird Station and bus) • 214-987-9188 • Lunch and dinner, seven days. Closed major holidays • MC, V • W

Its reputation for great smoked ribs and brisket is the reason most customers choose Peggy Sue's over the many other barbecue places in town. What's a little unusual here is that you get an extra reward in the steamed vegetable sides, which are just as tasty and almost as famous. Some Tex-Mex crossovers include smoked chicken quesadillas and brisket fajitas. It also has a claim to fame in its homemade fried pies, which customers say are the best in town. Children's menu. The decor pleasantly harks back to its start in the 1950s. No reservations taken. Bar (with membership). Street parking.

THE PYRAMID GRILL ($$$–$$$$)

1717 N. Akard (75201), at Ross in Fairmont Hotel (DART Light Rail Akard Station) • 214-720-2020 • Breakfast, lunch, and dinner, seven days • Cr. • W+ • www.fairmont.com

If one item could sum up and embody the refined cosmopolitan ambience of this hotel's flagship restaurant, it would be the between-course champagne sorbet served in lighted ice-sculpted cygnets. From the comfortable oversized armchairs, set at tables covered with brilliant linens, to the glistening silver, the whole setting speaks of opulence and elegance. The New American menu features an intriguing variety of well-prepared and presented grill choices in beef, veal, lamb, fowl, and seafood entrées. The mixed grill entrée features duck breast, a lamb chop, and shrimp.

Prix fixe dinner is an excellent value. Children's menu. Semiformal dress. Lounge. Hotel and Valet parking. AAA rates it 4-Diamond.

THE RIVIERA ($$$–$$$$)

7709 Inwood Road (75209), just south of Lovers Ln. (DART Light Rail Lovers Lane Station and bus) • 214-351-0094 • Dinner, seven days. Closed major holidays • Cr. • W+ • www.rivieradallas.com

Geographically, Southern France and Northern Italy share the real Riviera on the Mediterranean, and the innovative cuisine at this petite restaurant is inspired by the classic dishes of both those sunny regions and the bounty of the sea. The setting is simple but elegant Country French. While some of the offerings are classic French or classic Italian in origin, most are a joyful blending of the two, like herbed potato gnocchi with crab claws. Other seafood entrées include dover sole in a meunière sauce, sea scallops with tomato gratin, and golden trout. Meat dishes include rack of lamb, grilled veal chops with saffron risotto, and duck *maigret* with Roquefort soufflé. Appetizers include caviar with champagne ($60–$95). Consistently cited as one of the top restaurants in Dallas for food, service, and unhurried dining, it is rated 4-Star by Mobil and 4-Diamond by AAA. Semiformal dress. Bar. Lot and Valet parking.

RUTH'S CHRIS STEAK HOUSE ($$$–$$$$)

5922 Cedar Springs (75235), between Inwood and Mockingbird • 214-902-8080 • Dinner, seven days • Closed Thanksgiving and Christmas Day • Cr. • W+ • www.ruthschris.com

When Ruth Fertel took over the Chris Restaurant in New Orleans in 1965, she added her name as a possessive in front and started a nation-wide chain of upscale steak houses that now has two locations in Dallas. The steaks are all aged, never-frozen, corn-fed prime beef. Except for the petite filet, steak portions are large. All are cooked in specially built broilers at 1700 to 1800 degrees, to lock in the juices, and served sizzling in melted butter. In addition to beef, the menu offers seafood, including lobster and crab, lamb and veal chops, and chicken. A la carte side dishes include seven types of potatoes. Cigar-friendly bar. Valet parking. Second location at 17840 N. Dallas Pkwy., between Trinity Mills and Frankford (972-250-2244).

S & D OYSTER COMPANY ($–$$)

2701 McKinney (75204) (DART Light Rail Cityplace Station M-Line Streetcar) • 214-880-0111 • Lunch and dinner, Monday–Saturday. Closed Sunday and major holidays • MC, V • W

S & D has been serving New Orleans–style seafood in this neighborhood store setting since 1984. Gumbo, oysters on the half shell, oyster loaf, barbecued shrimp, and a variety of other fresh Gulf seafood dishes are on the menu. All are simply prepared, and you can have most of them broiled, boiled, or fried to your liking. Children's menu. Beer and wine only. Street parking.

SONNY BRYAN'S SMOKEHOUSE ($)

2202 Inwood (75235) • 214-357-7120 • Lunch only, seven days. Closed major holidays • No Cr. • W • www.sonnybryansbbq.com

With walls tinted by years of pit smoke and an all-pervading aroma of meat and spicy barbecue sauce, this shack is considered by many to be a piece of Dallas history. First opened in 1958, it still offers seating in one-armed school desks or outside on picnic tables. More important, it still serves up sandwiches, po' boys, and plates of tender smokehouse brisket, ribs, turkey, ham, pulled pork, chicken, and sausage that have pleased customers all these years. Always crowded, but service is fast. Beer only. This is the original, but there are more than a dozen other locations in the Metroplex. No reservations. Street parking.

STAR CANYON ($$$–$$$$)

3102 Oak Lawn, Suite 144 (75219), at Cedar Springs • 214-520-STAR (214-520-7827) • Lunch, Monday–Friday; dinner, seven days. Closed major holidays • Cr. • W+ • www.starcanyon.com

This popular restaurant offers both sophisticated Texas ranch house ambience and upscale Texas cuisine that tastes as good as it looks. Among the signature dishes is bone-in cowboy ribeye on a bed of pinto beans with red chile onion rings. Other inventive Texan entrées include hickory-smoked pork tenderloin with green-chile polenta, rainbow trout in cilantro cream sauce, and grilled coriander-cured venison. Even the sides include a palate-pleasing twist, like black-bean roast banana mash or grits laced with bits of littleneck clams. Chef's tasting menu available for about $40. Bar. Valet parking.

YORK STREET ($$$)

6047 Lewis (75206), at Skillman • 214-826-0968 • Dinner, Tuesday–Saturday. Closed Sunday–Monday • AE, MC, V • W+

While reservations are strongly suggested at all restaurants, they are almost essential here since this tiny jewel only has about a dozen tables. Talented owner/chef Sharon Hage bases her daily menu changes on the best and freshest ingredients, preferably organic, that she can find that day. Her cooking is simple and ingredient-driven. Once she has found the best ingredients, she uses them to develop the daily recipes and then skillfully prepares everything from appetizers to entrées. There are a few standards, but no signature dish here. Instead you may be offered entrées ranging from beef filet to fallow-deer venison, or rack of lamb Provençal to grilled sea bass with crabmeat. Beer and wine. Street parking.

ZIZIKI'S ($$–$$$)

4514 Travis (75205), south of Knox • 214-521-2233 • Lunch and dinner, seven days • Cr. • W+ • www.zizikis.com

Both classic and contemporary Greek and Italian specialties are prepared in the exhibition kitchen in this upscale bistro. Ziziki's is named for a Greek sauce made from yogurt and cucumbers that's used in many of the menu items. In addition to the à la carte menu items, they offer three tasting menus. You could make a meal out of the appetizer platter (about $22) that lets you select three from a list that includes choices like calamari, *dolmades*, and *spanakopita*. The chef's platter (about $23) gives you a sampling of *dolmades*, leg of lamb, *spanakopita*, *pastichio*, and new potatoes. And if you want the ultimate in a tasting menu, there's the Greek God's Platter (about $32 each, with a two-person minimum). This includes ziziki bread, Greek salad, Greek island chicken, spinach pie, rack of lamb, and *pastichio*, all served family style. Outdoor dining available. Bar. Parking. Another Dallas location at 15707 Coit (972-991-4433).

GOURMET TAKEOUTS

If you don't want to brave waiting lines, call to find out if the restaurant that interests you offers takeout. Surprisingly, many of them, even the most upscale, do. Or, you can try one of the following to-go places that have a reputation for outstanding takeout. Most are open all day and well into the evening.

City Café to Go • 5757 Lovers Ln. • 214-351-3366

City Harvest • 939 N. Edgefield • 214-943-2650

Celebration Market • 4515 Lovers Ln. • 214-352-0031

Eatzi's • 3403 Oak Lawn • 214-526-1515

H-E-B Central Market • See SPECIAL FOOD MARKETS, p. 148.

Izmir Market and Deli • 3607 Greenville • 214-824-8484

Whole Foods Market • See SPECIAL FOOD MARKETS, p. 148.

SPECIAL FOOD MARKETS FOR DO-IT-YOURSELF

If you prefer to prepare your own meals or make a picnic basket as a change from dining out, you might want to visit one of the markets below, where fresh, high-quality food is the standard.

DALLAS FARMERS MARKET

1010 S. Pearl (75201) • 214-939-2808 • Open seven days, dawn to dusk • W • www.dallasfarmersmarket.org

After more than six decades still operating on its original site on 12 downtown acres, this is one of the few remaining true farmers' markets in the country. It is also one of the largest, with many hundreds of farmers here daily selling their fresh fruits, vegetables, herbs, plants, and flowers in open sheds spread over four city blocks, annually attracting more than five million shoppers. During the year, several special holiday festivals and events are offered. Parking.

H-E-B CENTRAL MARKET

Lovers Ln. at Greenville (75206) (DART Light Rail Lovers Lane Station) • 214-234-7000 • Open seven days, 8 a.m.–10 p.m. • W+ but not all areas • www.centralmarket.com

H-E-B is one of the major grocery chains in Texas, and this Central Market is one of their several upscale groceries in the state. You'll find most of the usual grocery items here, but this huge store also routinely stocks about 700 varieties of fresh (really fresh!) produce, 600 varieties of cheese, 80 varieties of fish and meats, including bison and emu, and deli and bakery items. Its Café on the Run provides a wide variety of meals to go. Other Metroplex locations in Plano and Fort Worth.

WHOLE FOODS MARKET

2218 Greenville (75206) • 214-824-1744 • Open seven days, 8 a.m.–10 p.m. • W+ but not all areas • www.wholefoodsmarket.com

There are a number of stores in the Metroplex that carry natural foods, but this is one of just three in Dallas and six in the Metroplex that are part of the country's largest chain of natural and organic foods supermarkets. It carries what is probably the largest selection in the area of organically grown vegetables and fruits, plus seafood and meats without growth hormones or other additives. Deli/restaurant in the store. Other Dallas locations: 11661 Preston (214-361-8887) and 4100 Lomo Alto (214-520-7993). Other Metroplex locations in Arlington, Plano, and Richardson.

A SAMPLING OF DALLAS CLUBS AND BARS

From real dives to the most sophisticated clubs, Dallas has it all. But clubs and bars change almost as often as the phases of the moon, so it's hard to keep up with what's open, what's closed, what's in, what's out. For current information about Dallas nightlife, see the **Arts and Entertainment Guide** in the Friday edition of *The Dallas Morning News*; and the weekly *Dallas Observer* and *The Met*, which are available free at restaurants, clubs, and tourist attractions throughout the area. The following is just a small sampling of a few of the clubs and bars that have stood the test of time and were open and popular at the time this book was published. Some are bars in restaurants. Some are pure bars, while others offer music/entertainment to go with the drinks. Call for times, admission, cover, and other details.

The Balcony Club • 1525 Abrams • 214-826-8104 • A mostly jazz club on top of the Lakewood Theater.

The Bone • 2724 Elm • 214-744-BONE (214-744-2663) • Blues, jazz, swing, and a mix of other music in a New Orleans–style bar.

The Cavern • 1914 Greenville • 214-841-9091 • Mostly live 1960s music.

Club Clearview • 2803 Main • 214-939-0077 • www.clubclearview.com. • The oldest club in Deep Ellum. Variety of swing, disco, and other music in four-clubs-in-one.

Cowboys • 10310 Technology • 214-352-1796 • Live country music and a Texas-sized dance floor.

Cuba Libre Café • 2822 N. Henderson • 214-827-2820 • Libre Lounge upstairs over restaurant features South American sounds.

Dallas Alley • 2019 N. Lamar • 214-720-0170 • Bourbon Street setting for several bars under one roof, offering a variety of dance and listening music.

Flying Saucer Draught Emporium • 1520 Greenville • 214-824-7468 • A beer drinker's delight, with probably the most extensive list of draft and bottled beers in the city.

Gypsy Tea Room • 2546 Elm • 214-744-9779 • Features top country, rock, and swing groups.

Liberty Bar in Melrose Hotel • 3015 Oak Lawn • 214-521-5151 • A comfortable, pleasant, live music standout among the many Dallas hotel bars.

Martini Ranch • 2816 Fairmont • 214-220-2116 • Martini aficionados will appreciate the extensive martini menu.

Samba Room • 4514 Travis • 214-522-4137 • Basically a restaurant, but *Playboy* magazine says it has one of the best bars in the country.

Sambucca Jazz Café • 2618 Elm • 214-744-0820 • Jazz every night in this restaurant/nightclub.

Sons of Hermann Hall • 3414 Elm • 214-747-4422 • www.sonsof hermann.com • Upstairs in this fraternal organization hall is a vintage Texas dance hall featuring both country and swing music.

Times Square • 5640 Arapaho • 972-701-9751 • Five club settings under one roof.

Trees • 2709 Elm • 214-747-9663 • Mostly live rock concerts.

XPO Lounge • 408 Exposition • 214-823-2329 • A funky place with a DJ.

A SAMPLING OF DALLAS ACCOMMODATIONS

*For a double room or suite: $ = up to $80, $$ = $81–$120, $$$ = $121–$180, $$$$
= $181–280, $$$$$ = over $280.* **Room tax 15%.**

*Unless otherwise noted, check in at 3:00 p.m., check out by noon. Unless other wise
noted, all the major accommodations have handicapped rooms/facilities and no-smoking
rooms. The hearing impaired should check on visual alarms and other safety facilities
when making reservations. Most accommodations permit children to stay free in room
with parents. There may be a charge if this requires setting up an extra bed.*

Dallas has more than 60,000 hotel rooms, ranging from basic places to
sleep to some of the world's top-rated (and highest-priced). The follow-
ing is just a sampling of the many Dallas accommodations with outstand-
ing reputations.

ADAM'S MARK HOTEL DALLAS ($$–$$$$ + 15%)

**400 N. Olive (75201) (DART Light Rail Pearl Station) •
214-922-8000 or 800-444-ADAM (800-444-2326) (reservations) •
www.adamsmark.com**

There are 1,840 rooms and 211 suites in this huge 38-story downtown
hotel. Concierge section with extra amenities. Cable TV with free premium channel and pay channels. Coffeemaker in room. Dataport in
room. Bell service. Heated indoor and outdoor pools. Large fitness center. Concierge services available. Gift shop. Self-service laundry and one-
day dry cleaning. Five restaurants, including full service and fine dining.
Room service. Lounge with entertainment/dancing. Convention facilities. Business service center. Garage (fee) with self or valet parking.
Largest hotel in Texas. Panoramic view from 38th floor Chapparal Club.
(See CHAPPARAL, p. 135)

THE ADOLPHUS ($$$$–$$$$$ + 15%)

**1321 Commerce (75202) (DART Light Rail Akard Station) •
214-742-8200 or 800-221-9083 • www.hoteladolphus.com**

The 21 floors in this hotel have 404 rooms and 23 suites. Concierge
section with extra amenities. Pets OK ($250 deposit). Cable/satellite TV
with free premium and pay channels. Coffeemaker in room. Dataport in
room. Bell service. Fitness facilities and guest membership available in local health club. Concierge services available. Gift shop. Barber and
beauty shops. One-day dry cleaning. Four restaurants include one fine
dining (See THE FRENCH ROOM, p. 138). Room service. Lounge with
entertainment and dancing. Convention facilities. Business services available. Self (fee) and valet parking (fee). AAA rates it 4-Diamond, Mobil
rates it 4-Star. Hotel has won dozens of architectural, design, and hospi-
tality awards. Afternoon tea in Grand Lobby (reservations suggested).
Built in 1912 by beer baron Adolphus Busch, it still retains Old World
opulence.

ARISTOCRAT HOTEL
(See HOLIDAY INN ARISTOCRAT, p. 153)

BEST WESTERN MARKET CENTER ($$ + 15%)
2023 Market Center Blvd. (75207), at I-35E (Stemmons Frwy.) (TRE Medical/Market Center Station and bus) • 214-741-9000 or 800-275-7419 (reservations) • www.bestwestern.com

There are 98 rooms in this three-story inn. Inside and outside access to rooms. Cable TV with free premium channel and pay channels. Coffeemaker in room. Dataport in room. Bell service. Outdoor pool and hot tub. Fitness facility. Business services available. Self-service laundry and one-day dry cleaning. Free continental breakfast. Restaurant. Bar. Free self-parking. Close to the Market Center.

COMFORT INN SOUTH ($$ + 15%)
8541 S. Hampton (75232) • 972-572-1030 • www.comfortinn.com

This two-story inn has 50 rooms. Exterior access to rooms. Cable TV. Dataport in room. Outdoor pool and hot tub. Self-service laundry. Free continental breakfast. Business services available. Free outdoor self-parking. Rooms with microwave and refrigerator and whirlpool mini-suites available.

COURTYARD BY MARRIOTT-LBJ @ JOSEY ($$–$$$ + 15%)
2930 Forest Ln. (75234) • 972-620-8000 • www.courtyard.com

The 146 units in this three-story Courtyard include 12 suites. Cable TV with free premium and pay channels. Coffeemaker in room. Free coffee in lobby. Dataport in room. Outdoor pool and hot tub. Fitness facilities. Self-service laundry and one-day dry cleaning. Restaurant (breakfast only). Delivery service available from nearby restaurants. Lounge. Business services available. Free outdoor self-parking.

CROWNE PLAZA SUITES DALLAS ($$–$$$ + 15%)
7800 Alpha (75240) • 972-233-7600 or 800-922-2222 (reservations) • www.crowneplaza.com

There are 291 suites and 4 standard rooms in this 10-story atrium-style hotel. Pets OK (fee plus partially refundable deposit). Cable TV with free premium channel and pay channels. Coffeemaker in room. Dataport in room. Indoor/outdoor pool and hot tub. Fitness facilities. Concierge services available. Gift shop. Free full breakfast. Restaurant. Room service. Bar. Business center. Convention facilities. Free outdoor self-parking. Every suite has kitchenette with microwave, refrigerator, and wet bar.

DOUBLETREE HOTEL AT LINCOLN CENTRE ($$–$$$ + 15%)
5410 LBJ Frwy. (I-635) (75240), at N. Dallas Tollway • 972-934-8400 or 800-222-8733 (reservations) • www.doubletree.com

This 20-story hotel has 500 units that include 18 suites. Concierge section with extra amenities. Cable TV with free premium and pay channels. Dataport in room. Bell service. Room service. Outdoor pool and hot tub. Children's pool. Sauna. Fitness facilities. Guest memberships available in health club. Concierge services available. Gift shop. One-day dry cleaning. Three restaurants include one for fine dining. Bar. Conference facilities. Free outdoor self-parking, garage self-parking and valet parking (fee). Free transportation to nearby Galleria Mall and within 3-mile radius. Rated 4 diamonds by AAA. Grounds feature a four-acre lake with a jogging trail around it.

EMBASSY SUITES DALLAS MARKET CENTER ($$$–$$$$ + 15%)

2727 Stemmons Frwy. (I-35E)(75207) (TRE Medical/MarketCenter Station and bus) • 214-630-5332 or 800-EMBASSY (800-362-2779) (reservations) • www.embassysuites.com

There are 244 one- and two-bedroom suites in this nine-story atrium style hotel. Pets OK (fee). Cable TV with free premium and pay channels. Coffeemaker in room. Dataport in rooms. Indoor heated pool, hot tub, dry and wet sauna. Fitness facilities. Gift shop. Self-service laundry and one-day dry cleaning. Free full breakfast. Free evening cocktails. Restaurant. Lounge. Business services available. Free outdoor self-parking. Free airport transportation to Love Field and within 3-mile radius. Suites have microwave, refrigerator, wet bar, two TVs.

THE FAIRMONT HOTEL ($$$$–$$$$$ + 15%)

1717 N. Akard (75201), at Ross in the Arts District (DART Light Rail Akard Station) • 214-720-2020 or 800-527-4727 (reservations) • www.fairmont.com

The 550 units in this 18-story hotel include 51 one- and two-bedroom suites. Concierge section with extra amenities. Small pets OK. Cable TV with pay channels. Coffeemaker in room. Dataport in room. Bell service. Room service. Outdoor heated Olympic-size pool. Hot tub. Guest memberships available for golf, tennis, and health club. Concierge services available. Barber, beauty, retail, and gift shops. One-day dry cleaning. Restaurants including one for fine dining (see PYRAMID GRILL, p. 144). Room service. Lounge with entertainment and dancing. Convention facilities. Business center. Valet parking (fee). Connected to underground pedestrian walkways that go under much of downtown (see OFFBEAT, p. 124). AAA rates 4-Diamond.

HILTON DALLAS PARK CITIES ($$–$$$$$ + 15%)

5954 Luther (75225) (DART Light Rail Lovers Lane Station and bus) • 214-368-0400 • www.hilton.com

This 11-story boutique-style hotel offers 224 rooms. Concierge section with extra amenities. Local calls free. Cable TV with free premium and pay channels. Coffeemaker in room. Dataport in room. Outdoor rooftop pool. Hot tub. Fitness facilities. Concierge services available. Gift shop and retail stores. One-day dry cleaning. Restaurant. Room service. Lounge. Business services available. Self (fee) and valet parking (fee). Free transportation within 5-mile radius. Walking distance to restaurants and upscale shopping. Skyline view from rooftop pool.

HOLIDAY INN ARISTOCRAT HOTEL ($$$–$$$$ + 15%)

1933 Main (75201) at Harwood, downtown (DART Light Rail St. Paul Station) • 214-741-7700 or 800-231-4235 (reservations) • www.hotel-dallas.com

This 14-story hotel has 172 units, including 72 suites. Cable TV with free premium and pay channels. Coffeemaker in room. Dataport in room. Bell service. Limited fitness room. Guest memberships available in Health Club. Concierge services available. Self-service laundry and one-day dry cleaning. Bar. Self (fee) and valet parking (fee). Originally built in 1925 by Conrad Hilton and the first to carry his name. Building listed on the National Register of Historic Places. Faithfully restored and renovated. Connected to underground tunnels and pedestrian walkways that go under much of downtown (see OFFBEAT, p. 124).

HOLIDAY INN SELECT—LOVE FIELD ($$–$$$ + 15%)

3300 W. Mockingbird (75235) • 214-357-8500 or 800-231-4235 (reservations) • www.holiday-inn.com

The 244 units in this eight-story inn include 14 suites. Concierge section with extra amenities. Cable TV with free premium and pay channels. Coffeemaker in room. Dataport in room. Bell service. Outdoor pool and hot tub. Limited fitness facilities. Gift shop. One-day dry cleaning. Free beverages Monday–Friday evenings. Restaurant. Room service. Bar. Business center. Free outdoor self-parking. Free transportation to Love Field. Closest full-service inn to Love Field.

HOTEL CRESCENT COURT ($$$$–$$$$$ + 15%)

400 Crescent Court (75201), in the Crescent Complex (DART Light Rail Cityplace Station and M-Line Streetcar) • 214-871-3200 or toll-free 888-667-3966 (reservations) • www.crescentcourt.com

This seven-story European-style hotel offers 220 units, including some two-story suites. Pets OK (limited). Cable TV with free premium and pay channels. Coffeemaker in room. Dataport in room. Bell service. Outdoor pool and hot tub. Sauna. Fitness facilities. Spa. Concierge services available. Gift shop and retail stores. One-day dry cleaning. Fine dining restaurant (See BEAU NASH, p. 133) Room service. Bar. Business services available. Valet parking (fee). Guests can use the Crescent Club in office complex. Afternoon tea. Spa rated one of best hotel spas in the country. Mobil rates hotel 4-Star.

HOTEL ST. GERMAIN ($$$$$ + 15%)

2516 Maple (75201) (DART Light Rail Cityplace Station and M-Line Streetcar) • 214-871-2516 • www.hotelstgermain.com

There are only seven suites on the three floors of this European-style boutique hotel. Check-in 4:00 p.m. Cable TV with free premium channels. Dataports in rooms. Bell service. Room service. Guest memberships available for health club. Concierge services and butler service available 24 hours. One-day dry cleaning. Free deluxe continental breakfast. Fine dining restaurant (see HOTEL ST. GERMAIN RESTAURANT, p. 139). Room service. Champagne bar. Business services available. Valet parking. Elegant Victorian home built in 1906. Each suite decorated in antiques reminiscent of a French chateau. Rated 4-Diamond by AAA and 4-Star by Mobil.

HYATT REGENCY DALLAS ($$$–$$$$$ +15%)

300 Reunion (75207), downtown (DART Light Rail Union Station) • 214-651-1234 or 800-233-1234 (reservations) • www.hyatt.com

This downtown landmark hotel has 1,122 units on its 28 floors that include 55 suites. Concierge section with extra amenities. Cable TV with free premium and pay channels. Coffeemaker in room. Dataport in room. Bell service. Small outdoor pool, hot tub, sauna, fitness facilities. Tennis. Guest memberships available in health club. Concierge services available. Gift shop. One-day dry cleaning. Restaurants include one fine dining (See ANTARES, p. 133). Room service. Lounge with dancing. Convention facilities. Business center. Self and valet parking (fee). Excellent view of city from upper-floor rooms. Fifty-story Reunion Tower adjoining. (See BIRD'S-EYE VIEW, p. 73) Rated 4-Diamond by AAA.

LE MERIDIEN DALLAS ($$$–$$$$ + 15%)

650 N. Pearl (75201), in Plaza of the Americas Complex (DART Light Rail Pearl Station) • 214-979-9000 or 800-543-4300 (reservations) • www.lemeridien-dallas.com

The 407 units in this 14-story atrium-style hotel include two suites. Concierge section with extra amenities. Pets OK. Cable TV with free premium and pay channels. Dataport in room. Bell service. Hot tub. Sauna. Fitness facilities. Concierge services available. Gift shop and retail shops. One-day dry cleaning. Restaurant. Room service. Lounge. Business center. Self and valet parking (fee).

MANSION ON TURTLE CREEK ($$$$$ + 15%)

2821 Turtle Creek (75219) • 214-559-2100 or toll-free 888-767-3966 (reservations) • www.mansiononturtlecreek.com

Once the mansion of a cattle baron, now it is the only hotel in Texas to provide a standard of luxury and service to earn the highest 5-Diamond rating by AAA and 5-Star rating by Mobil. It is also cited as one of best hotels in the United States in *Conde Nast Traveler's* magazine Readers Choice Awards. The nine-story hotel has 143 units that include 16 suites. Small pets OK ($100 fee). Cable TV with free premium channel and pay channels. Dataport in room. Bell service. Outdoor heated pool, sauna, fitness facilities. Guest memberships available for tennis and golf. Barber, beauty, and gift shops. One-day dry cleaning. Two restaurants, one fine dining (see MANSION ON TURTLE CREEK, p. 142). Room service. Lounge with entertainment and dancing. Business center. Self and valet parking (fee). Free sedan transportation within 5-mile radius.

MELROSE HOTEL ($$$–$$$$$ + 15%)

3015 Oak Lawn (75219), at Cedar Springs • 214-521-5151 or 800-635-7673 (reservations) • www.melrosehotel.com

There are 22 suites among the 184 units in this eight-story European-style hotel. Cable TV with free premium and pay channels. Dataport in room. Bell service. Outdoor pool. Limited fitness facilities. Guest memberships available in nearby health club. Concierge services available. Gift shop. One-day dry cleaning. Fine dining restaurant (see THE LANDMARK, p. 140). Room service. Lounge with entertainment. Business services available. Valet parking (fee). Free transportation within 5-mile radius. Restored 1924 hotel designated a Dallas Historic Landmark. No two rooms are alike.

RADISSON HOTEL AND SUITES ($$$–$$$$ + 15%)

2330 W. Northwest Hwy. (75220), at I-35E • 214-351-4477 or 800-333-3333 (reservations) • www.radisson.com

This eight-story hotel has 199 units, including 23 suites. Concierge section with extra amenities. Pets OK (limited, with deposit) • Cable TV with free premium and pay channels. Coffeemaker in room. Dataport in room. Bell service. Outdoor heated pool and hot tub. Fitness facilities. Guest memberships available in health club. Concierge services available. Gift shop and retail shops. Self-service laundry and one-day dry cleaning. Free continental breakfast. Restaurant. Room service. Bar. Conference facilities. Business services available. Free outdoor self-parking. Free airport transportation to both DFW and Love Field. Free transportation within a 3-mile radius. Microwave and refrigerator in most rooms.

RENAISSANCE DALLAS HOTEL ($$$$–$$$$$ + 15%)

2222 N. Stemmons Frwy. (I-35E)(75207), near the Market Center • 214-631-2222 or 800-811-8893 (reservations) • www.renaissancehotels.com

There are 27 suites among the 540 units in this 30-story hotel. Concierge section with extra amenities. Pets OK (limited). Cable TV with free premium and pay channels. Coffeemaker in room. Dataport in room. Rooftop outdoor heated pool, hot tub, fitness facilities. Concierge services available. One-day dry cleaning. Two restaurants. Room service.

Lounge with entertainment. Convention facilities. Business center. Self and valet parking (fee). Walking distance to the Market Center. The pink granite, elliptically shaped hotel is home of what is reportedly "the world's longest chandelier," with 7,500 Italian crystals following the winding marble and brass staircase up four floors. Excellent view from upper-floor rooms.

SHERATON SUITES MARKET CENTER ($$$–$$$$ + 15%)

2101 Stemmons Frwy. (I-35E) (75207) (TRE Medical/Market Center Station and bus) • 214-747-3000 or 800-325-3535 (reservations) • www.sheraton.com

There are 251 suites in this 11-story all-suites hotel. Concierge section with extra amenities. Pets OK (limited, with deposit). Cable TV with free premium and pay channels. Coffeemaker in room. Dataport in room. Indoor/outdoor heated pool, hot tub. Fitness facilites. Concierge services available. Gift shop. One-day dry cleaning. Restaurant. Room service. Bar. Business center. Self and valet parking (fee).

STONELEIGH HOTEL ($$$$ + 15%)

2927 Maple (75201) • 214-871-7111 or 800-255-9299 (reservations) • www.stoneleighhotel.com

This small European-style 11-story hotel has 153 units of which seven are suites. Cable TV with free premium and pay channels. Coffeemaker in room. Dataport in room. Pool. Fitness facilities. Concierge services available. Beauty shop. Fine dining restaurant (dinner only) and Sushi Bar. Room service. Bar. Business services available. Self or valet parking (fee). Free transportation within a 5-mile radius. Restored 1920s hotel. Member of Historic Hotels of America. Within walking distance of upscale shops and restaurants.

WESTIN GALLERIA DALLAS ($$$$–$$$$$ +15%)

13340 N. Dallas Pkwy. (75240), just north of I-635 in the Galleria Mall • 972-934-9494 or 800-228-3000 • www.westin.com

This 21-story hotel has 431 units that include 13 suites. Concierge section with extra amenities. Small pets OK (limited). Cable TV with free premium and pay channels. Coffeemaker in room. Dataport in room. Rooftop outdoor heated pool and jogging track. Sauna. Guest membership available in health club. Concierge services available. Barber, beauty, and gift shop. One-day dry cleaning. Restaurants. Room service. Lounge with entertainment. Convention facilities. Business center. Free self outdoor and covered mall parking, valet parking (fee). Part of the Galleria Mall complex, which has more than 200 shops, restaurants, a movie theater, and an ice skating rink. Westin Kids club and playground. Rated 4-Diamond by AAA.

WYNDHAM ANATOLE HOTEL ($$$–$$$$$ +15%)

2201 Stemmons Frwy.. (I-35E) (75207), across I-35E from the Market Center • 214-748-1200 or 800-WYNDHAM (800-996-3426) • www.wyndham.com

The complex of wings and towers that range from 10 to 27 floors of this hotel include 1,620 units, of which 129 are suites. Concierge section with extra amenities. Cable TV with free premium and pay channels. Coffeemaker in room. Dataport in room. Bell service. Extensive fitness and health facilities including one outdoor and two indoor pools, hot tubs, sauna, basketball gym, six lighted tennis courts, racquetball and squash courts, boxing gym. Spa. Concierge services available. Barber, beauty, retail, and gift shop. One-day dry cleaning. Three restaurants, including one fine dining (See NANA, p. 143). Room service. Bars and lounge with entertainment. Convention facilities. Business center. Self outdoor parking or valet parking (fee). One of largest convention hotels in the Southwest. Spread over 45 acres, it calls itself a village within the city. Excellent view from upper floors. (See BIRD'S EYE VIEW, p. 73) Self-guided tour brochure for museum-quality art collection, scattered throughout hotel, that includes the world's largest piece of Wedgwood china and one of the largest private jade collections in the country.

BED AND BREAKFAST INNS

AMELIA'S PLACE ($$ + 15%)

1775 Young (75201) (DART Light Rail Union Station and bus) • 214-651-1775 or toll-free 888-651-1775 (reservations) • www.inntravels.com/usa/tx

Of the six rooms in this converted downtown warehouse, the four upstairs each have a private bath and the two downstairs share a bath. No children or pets. Full breakfast. Free parking. The rooms are named for Dallas women who have made outstanding contributions to the city. A block from City Hall and two blocks from the Convention Center.

AMERICAN DREAM ($–$$ + 15%)

I-635 at Marsh Road (P.O. Box 670275, 75220) • 214-357-6536 or 800-373-2690 • www.inntravels.com/usa/tx

The three rooms available in this northwest Dallas B&B include a bedroom/sitting room suite with bath and a master suite with whirlpool tub. No pets. Children over 10 with approval. Full breakfast. Free parking. Multilingual hosts. Garden filled with native plants designated a Texas Wildscape by Texas Parks and Wildlife Department.

COURTYARD ON THE TRAIL ($$–$$$ + 15%)

8045 Forest Trail (75238) • 214-553-9700 • www.bbonline.com/tx/courtyard

Each of the two rooms and one suite available has a private bath. No pets. Pool. Full breakfast. Catered meals available. Free parking. A gated Spanish-style home with a garden in a country setting, in the woods of White Rock Lake.

THE SOUTHERN HOUSE ($$–$$$ + 15%)

2625 Thomas (75204) (DART Light Rail Cityplace Station and M-Line streetcar) • 214-720-0845 • www.southernhouse.com

The three rooms with bath available include one with a separate sitting area. No children or pets. Full breakfast. Free parking. Home built in 1997 to conform to Historical District's exterior code. Antique front door salvaged from State Capitol of Texas. Within walking distance of Dallas Museum of Art and Meyerson Symphony Hall.

SIDE TRIPS

MESQUITE CHAMPIONSHIP RODEO

Resistol Arena, 1818 Rodeo Dr. (75149), exit Military Pkwy. (Exit 4) off I-635 (approximately 15 minutes from Downtown Dallas) • 972-285-8777 or 800-833-9339. Tickets 972-222-BULL (972-222-2855) • Friday and Saturday evenings from first weekend in April through first weekend in October. Reserved tickets $5–$30 • www.mesquiterodeo.com

Most rodeos on the Professional Rodeo Cowboy Association circuit last a few days to a week; then the cowboys move on to the next one. The Mesquite rodeo goes on and on for a six-month season each year. Since its modest start, in 1958, this rodeo now annually draws about 200,000 spectators and is one of the most widely known rodeos in the nation. A Texas Legislature proclamation named Mesquite as "The Rodeo Capital of Texas."

Every Friday and Saturday night at 8:00, the rodeo kicks off with a colorful Grand Entry of cowboys and cowgirls riding to the tune of "The Eyes of Texas." For the next two hours, the show features all the traditional rodeo competitions, including bull and bronco riding, calf-roping, and steer wrestling. Other events include the cowgirl barrel-racing, a calf-scramble for kids, chuck wagon races, and Cowboy Poker—which might be the most hazardous game of poker in the world. In this event, four rodeo cowboys, each with $100, play poker at a card table set up in the middle of the arena. The hazard starts when a Mexican fighting bull is released into the arena. The last player seated wins the $400.

Don't be concerned if you don't know anything about rodeo. The announcer explains each event before it starts. TV monitors hanging from the ceiling give you close-ups and replays. The air-conditioned area seats

5,500 and has seventy luxury suites on the third floor, some of which are available, with catered food and beverages, for a nightly rental of $800 for 12 people. Paved/lighted parking.

Gates open at 6:30 p.m., and a Sonny Bryan's Smokehouse BBQ is available ($6.50–$9.50). Also pony rides and a petting zoo, and souvenir and gift shop.

FARMERS BRANCH

Dallas County • 27,700 • Area Code 972 (local calls require area code) • www.ci.farmers-branch.tx.us

This city is considered the birthplace of Dallas County since it traces its origin to 1841 when it was part of Peters colony, a large land grant awarded by the Republic of Texas to the Texas Land and Emigration Company in exchange for bringing settlers to this vast unoccupied territory. Thomas and Sarah Keenan were the first to claim the head of family rights to 640 acres in this new tract. They built a house on a creek known as Mustang Branch, most likely named for both the mustang horses that frequented the area and the mustang grapes that grew there. When other settlers moved in they called the area after the creek. But as Keenan and the other settlers began farming the rich black soil of the area, the creek became known as Farmers Branch and the settlement took on that name. Baby John Keenan, the first child born in the new colony, lived only two months and is buried in the cemetery that was originally set apart by the Keenans from their claim. Located in the 2500 block of Valley View Lane, it is one of the oldest cemeteries in Dallas County.

As one of its many "firsts" in Dallas County, Farmers Branch has been credited with the first organized school. In 1846 it made another first by growing cotton, and the first cotton gin in the county was built here in 1849. The first tanning yard was set up around 1845. There was such a demand for leather at the time that the owner didn't allow the hides to cure long enough, so they became extremely hard when dry. Because of this, the stream on which the tanning yard was located soon became known as Rawhide Creek, a name that is still used.

There's not much farming done here anymore. In the city's twelve-and-a-half square miles there are about 3,000 small and mid-sized firms, 85 corporate headquarters, and 35 Fortune 500 companies. While its residential population is approximately 28,000, as a business center, that number jumps to a workday population of 85,000. As a result of this business support of its tax base, the city is unique in that it offers free after-school care to qualified Farmers Branch families and free garbage pick-up to all residents.

The city is dry under the local options laws.

FARMERS BRANCH

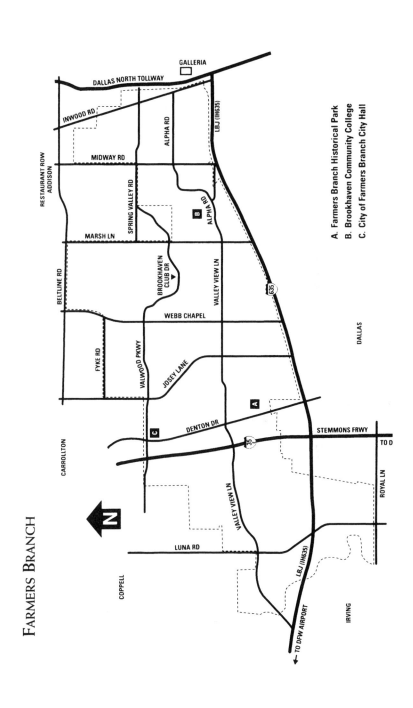

A. Farmers Branch Historical Park
B. Brookhaven Community College
C. City of Farmers Branch City Hall

FREE VISITOR SERVICES

OFFICE OF ECONOMIC DEVELOPMENT AND TOURISM

13000 William Dodson Pkwy., in City Hall (75234) • 972-919-2510
or 800-BRANCH-9 (800-272-6249) • W+ • www.farmersbranch.info

Note that this is an administrative office in City Hall, not a visitor information center. You can pick up brochures and such here during business hours, Monday–Friday, but it's best if you write or call in advance and let them send you the information you want. If you do visit, ask for Tourism Department at the reception desk.

HELPFUL LOCAL PUBLICATIONS

Current information about Farmers Branch events, activities, nightlife, theater, movies, and dining are sometimes listed in the local edition of the *Dallas Morning News*, and the *Friday Guide* in that newspaper. Other sources to check are the local *Branch Review*, the weekly *Dallas Observer*, which is available free at restaurants and tourist attractions throughout the Dallas area; and the monthly *D Magazine* and *Texas Monthly Magazine* available on newsstands.

HISTORIC PLACES

FARMERS BRANCH HISTORICAL PARK

2540 Farmers Branch Ln., at Ford Road (P.O. Box 819010, 753810 • 972-406-0184 • Summer: Monday–Thursday, 8–8; Saturday–Sunday, noon–8. Closed Friday. Closes at 6 in winter • Free (donations accepted) • W variable • www.farmersbranch.info

In this 22-acre tree-shaded park on Farmers Branch Creek are a number of historic buildings that have been restored. Several of these were moved here from their original locations. The **Gilbert House**, considered the cornerstone of this park, is the oldest rock structure in Northeast Texas that's still on its original foundation. It's listed on the National Register of Historic Places and Landmarks. Completed in 1857, it has two-foot-thick limestone walls and chestnut plank floors. The **Depot** was built around 1877 by the Dallas and Wichita Railroad, which was later sold to Jay Gould and the Missouri-Kansas-Texas Railroad. In 1924 it became a stop on the newly electrified Interurban Railway (see PLANO, p. 296). The **Queen Anne Victorian Cottage** was originally built in Gainesville in 1885 during the Victorian period when the architecture tended to be ornate, with crossed gables, turrets and cupolas, wraparound porches and porticos. The **North Texas Methodist Church** was built in the 1890s in Renner, Texas. It's the type of area church built during the end of the nineteenth century, when the churches were commonly referred to as meeting houses because of their multiple use for church services, town meetings, and school and social events. The **Log Culture Area** represents a pioneer homestead in the 1840s. Living history interpreters can often be seen here performing such tasks as blacksmithing, open-hearth cooking, and quilting. Other original buildings include the **School**, built around 1900, and the **Dodson House**, built in 1937. Tours can be arranged by calling at least two weeks in advance.

The park is the site of a number of major events during the year, including arts and crafts and antique car shows, concerts, and holiday festivities. Also, on Saturday afternoons in December, authentic Christmas English High Teas are held in the Dodson House ($20. Reservations, 972-406-0184). Museum gift shop.

OUTDOORS

FARMERS BRANCH PARKS

Parks and Recreation Department • 972-919-2620

The facilities in the city's more than two dozen parks include fields for most team sports, tennis courts, jogging trails, playgrounds, and picnic areas. Call for information.

COLLEGE CAMPUS OF INTEREST TO VISITORS

BROOKHAVEN COLLEGE

**3939 Valley View (75244), between Marsh and Midway •
972-860-4700 • W+ but not all areas • www.brookhavencollege.edu**

One of the seven colleges in the Dallas Community College District, Brookhaven offers two-year academic and technical/occupational programs for approximately 8,000 students in the northern portion of Dallas County. Located on a 200-acre campus, the facilities include a 680-seat performance hall where a variety of cultural and entertainment events are held that are open to the public. Call 972-860-4118 (Monday–Friday afternoons) for information on programs and ticket prices. Also open to the public are the frequent exhibits at the two art galleries, and a two-mile jogging/exercise track.

MUSIC AND PERFORMING ARTS

RICH-TONE CHORUS

2740 Valwood Pkwy., Suite 124 (75083) • 972-234-6065 •
www.richtones.org

This chorus is dedicated to promoting one of America's original art forms: Barbershop harmony. But this is not barbershop as you may think of it. It's 130 women singing four-part harmony a cappella. Several times world champions of the Sweet Adelines' International, their shows include a mixture of pop, rock, blues, jazz, and popular classics, with a little dance thrown in. Farmers Branch is their home base, but their performances are held in the Eisemann Center in Richardson (See RICHARDSON, p. 316) and other performance venues throughout the Metroplex. Call for schedule and ticket prices. Rehearsals that are usually open to the public are held at their headquarters each Tuesday night, starting at 7:30.

ANNUAL EVENTS

DECEMBER

CHRISTMAS TOUR OF LIGHTS

Farmers Branch Historical Park, 2540 Farmers Branch Ln. •
972-919-2631 • Two weeks in middle of month • Free (donations accepted)

More than 400,000 lights and holiday figures are on display on this tour which starts at Valley View Ln. and I-35, visits City Hall, and then goes to the Farmers Branch Historical Park.

A SAMPLING OF FARMERS BRANCH RESTAURANTS

Dinner for one, excluding drinks, tax, and tip: $ = up to $16, $$ = $16–$30, $$$ = $31–$50, $$$$ = over $50. It is strongly suggested that you make a reservation in those restaurants that take them, especially on weekends and holidays.

NORMA'S CAFÉ ($)

3300 Belt Line (75234) • 972-243-8646 • Breakfast, lunch, and dinner, Monday–Saturday; breakfast and lunch only, Sunday • W

This is a classic no-frills restaurant that might make you recall your favorite original hometown restaurant. Nothing fancy, just reasonably priced and solid home cooking, a breakfast menu with every choice you can imagine. The inexpensive blue plate specials include pot roast, country fried catfish, and chicken fried steak. Two other locations in Dallas.

NUEVO LEON ($)

12895 Josey (75234) • 972-488-1984 • Lunch and dinner, Monday–Saturday; Sunday brunch • Cr. • W

This is not your typical shopping-center Tex-Mex restaurant. Sure, they serve some Tex-Mex here, but they don't call themselves a Mex-Mex restaurant for nothing. The main attractions on the menu are traditional Mexican dishes like *puerco en pasilla*, tender chunks of pork and slices of mushrooms in a *pasilla* pepper sauce, and *cabrito al horno*, marinated young goat wrapped in banana leaves. Children's menu. Vegetarian dishes including *fajitas de vegetales*. Bar. Two other locations in Dallas.

A SAMPLING OF FARMERS BRANCH ACCOMMODATIONS

For a double room or suite: $ = up to $80, $$ = $81–$120, $$$ = $121–$180, $$$$ = $181–280, $$$$$ = over $280. **Room tax 13%.**

Unless otherwise noted, check in at 3:00 p.m., check out by noon. Unless other wise noted, all the major accommodations have handicapped rooms/facilities and no-smoking rooms. The hearing impaired should check on visual alarms and other safety facilities when making reservations. Most accommodations permit children to stay free in room with parents. There may be a charge if this requires setting up an extra bed.

Note: Although physically located in Farmers Branch, a number of the following accommodations still use a Dallas address.

BEST WESTERN DALLAS NORTH ($–$$ + 13%)

13333 Stemmons Frwy. (I-35E), Dallas (75234) • 972-241-8521 or 800-308-4593 (reservations) • www.bestwestern.com

This two-story Best Western has 185 rooms, including four suites. Small pets OK (deposit). Outside access to rooms. Local calls free. Cable TV with free premium and pay channels. Coffeemaker in room. Dataport in room. Outdoor pool, hot tub. Sauna. Guest membership available in health club. Self-service laundry. One-day dry cleaning. Free breakfast buffet. Free cocktails weekday evenings. Restaurant. Lounge. Business services available. Free outdoor self-parking. Free transportation to DFW Airport and Love Field. Free transportation within 3-mile radius.

DAYS INN NORTH DALLAS ($ +13%)

13313 Stemmons Frwy. (I-35E)(75234), at Valley View •
972-488-0800 or 800-DAYS-INN (800-329-7466) (reservations) •
www.daysinn.com/farmersbranch07525

Some of the 73 rooms in this two-story inn have whirlpools. Pets OK (deposit). Local calls free. Cable TV with free premium and pay channels. Coffeemaker in room. Dataport in room. Outdoor pool and hot tub. Fitness facilities. Self-service laundry and one-day dry cleaning. Free continental breakfast. In-room food service available. Free outdoor self-parking. Free transportation available to DFW airport and Love Field.

DOUBLETREE CLUB HOTEL ($$$ + 13%)

16111 Luna (75234) • 972-506-0055 or toll-free 888-444-CLUB
(888-444-2582) (reservations) • www.doubletreehotels.com

There are 160 rooms in this six-story hotel. Small pets OK (deposit). Cable TV with free premium and pay channels. Coffeemaker in room. Dataport in room. Outdoor pool. Fitness facilities. Jogging trail. One-day dry cleaning. Restaurant. Bar. Conference facilities. Business center. Free outdoor self-parking. Free transportation within 5-mile radius. Landscaped pool overlooks 120-acre lake. Pool table in bar area.

HOLIDAY INN SELECT NORTH DALLAS ($$$–$$$$$ + 13%)

2645 LBJ Frwy., Dallas (75234) • 972-243-3363 or 800-465-4329
(reservations) • www.hoteldallastexas.com

The 380 units in this six-story inn include three suites. Concierge section with extra amenities. Cable TV with free premium and pay channels. Coffeemaker in room. Dataport in room. Bell service. Indoor/outdoor pool and hot tub. Fitness facilities. Gift shop. Self-service laundry and one-day dry cleaning. Restaurant. Room service. Bar. Conference facilities. Business center. Free outdoor self-parking. Free transportation available to DFW Airport. Free transportation within 5-mile radius.

LAQUINTA INN ($–$$ + 13%)

13325 Stemmons Frwy. (I35E), Dallas (75234) • 972-620-7333 or
800-531-5900 (reservations) • www.laquinta.com

There are 121 rooms in this two-story inn. Small pets OK. Local calls free. Cable TV with free premium and pay channels. Coffeemaker in room. Dataport in room. Outdoor pool. One-day dry cleaning. Free continental breakfast. Business services available. Free outdoor self-parking. In-room microwave and refrigerator available.

OMNI DALLAS PARK WEST ($$$–$$$$$ + 13%)

1590 LBJ Frwy. (I-635) (75234) • 972-869-4300 or 800-528-0444
(reservations). www.omnihotels/dallasparkwest.com

The 337 units in this 12-story hotel include 18 suites. Concierge section with extra amenities. Pets OK (fee). Cable TV with free premium and pay channels. Coffeemaker in room. Dataport in room. Bell service. Outdoor heated pool. Hot tub. Fitness facilities. Tennis courts. Concierge services available. Gift shop. One-day dry cleaning. Two restaurants. Room service. Lounge with entertainment. Conference facilities. Business center. Free outdoor self-parking or valet parking (fee). Free transportation to DFW Airport Sunday–Thursday. Free transportation within 5-mile radius. The complex features a 125-acre lake with marina and jogging trails. Omni Kids Program. AAA rates 4-Diamond.

RENAISSANCE DALLAS NORTH HOTEL
($$–$$$$$ + 13%)

4099 Valley View, Dallas (75244) • 972-385-9000 or 800-468-3571 (reservations) • www.renaissancehotels.com

There are 289 rooms and five suites in this 10-story atrium-style hotel. Concierge section with extra amenities. Cable TV with free premium and pay channels. Coffeemaker in room. Dataport in room. Bell service. Outdoor pool. Fitness facilities. Guest membership available for golf. Tennis courts and jogging track at adjacent Brookhaven College. Concierge services available. Gift shop. Self-service laundry and one-day dry cleaning. Restaurant. Lounge. Convention facilities. Business center. Free outdoor self-parking. Free transportation within a 5-mile radius. Ten-story atrium lobby with garden fountain and waterfall. Free coffee and newspaper delivered after wake-up call.

FORT WORTH

Tarrant County Seat • 535,000 • Area Code 817 (local calls require area code) • www.fortworth.com

In June 1849, with the war between the United States and Mexico over the border of the new state of Texas not long over, Company F, 2nd Dragoons, established a frontier outpost on the bluffs overlooking the Trinity River. Its mission was to protect the scattered settlements, like Lonesome Dove and Dallas, from Indian raids. The post was named in honor of Maj. Gen. William Jenkins Worth, a hero in the conquest of Mexico City, now commander of the U.S. Army in Texas and New Mexico. Worth never got to see the post named after him, dying of cholera in San Antonio about the time the post was being created. (Worth's heroism was also recognized in his home of New York City, with a 50-foot monument at Broadway and Fifth.)

By 1853, the frontier had moved farther west and the soldiers went with it. The settlers immediately moved in and occupied the post buildings, which were far better than the ramshackle cabins and dugouts they were living in.

FORT WORTH "STEALS" THE COUNTY SEAT

By 1856, the population had reached about a hundred. Among its citizens were a number of town boosters who would make any present-day chamber of commerce proud. Dissatisfied that the town of Birdville was the county seat, they promoted an election to move it to Fort Worth. They won, but the people of Birdville cried "foul," saying Fort Worth had stolen the election by bringing in men from outside the county to vote. True or not, another election was ordered, but by the time it could be scheduled, it was 1860, the county government was well entrenched in Fort Worth, and nobody wanted to move it again.

CHISHOLM TRAIL MAKES IT A BOOM TOWN

Soon after the Civil War, Texas cattlemen found out that longhorns selling for $5 a head in Texas would fetch $30 or more in northern markets. Thus started the long drives that saw some 10 million head of Texas cattle driven north—and into the history books and legends—between 1866 and the mid-1880s.

Among the many trails used for the drives was one to the railhead at Abilene, Kansas, set up by Jesse Chisholm. The Chisholm Trail, which ran through Fort Worth, often right down the main street, caused the town to boom. This was the last stop before crossing into the Oklahoma Indian Territory, so the cowboys stocked up on beans and bacon and other supplies here and whooped it up a bit before setting out to push the huge herds through the last 300 miles of dust and mud. On the return trip, with the herd sold and their pay burning in their pockets, this was the first Texas town they hit. And they usually hit it hard. The favorite place to let off steam was known as Hell's Half-Acre, which spanned an area of about 14 city blocks where the modern Fort Worth Convention Center and the Water Gardens now stand. This wide-open section of town, made up almost entirely of saloons, gambling houses, and bordellos, was filled with lowlifes who did everything they could to separate the cowboys from their hard-earned dollars.

The townspeople saw prosperity just over the horizon when the Texas and Pacific Railroad headed their way in 1873. This could make Fort Worth the railhead instead of Abilene. They even incorporated and set up a bank, and the population quickly doubled from about 2,000 to 4,000. But their high hopes were dashed when the financial panic of 1873 struck, the railroad went bankrupt, and construction stopped 26 miles short. Overnight the population dropped to about 1,000 as many people gave up their dream and moved to Dallas.

It was during this time that a Dallas newspaper, feeding the feud that was growing between the two towns, reported that Fort Worth was so dead a panther had been seen sleeping unmolested in the streets. This insult goaded the people of Fort Worth to action. At first it was a simple thumbing of the nose at Dallas: The fire department adopted a panther for a mascot, and many clubs in town added Panther to their names. Then they turned serious. They needed a railroad to survive, and if the railroad wouldn't come to them, they'd go out and drag it in.

DRAGGING IN THE RAILROAD

The people of Fort Worth formed a construction company, reached an agreement with the railroad, and started to lay track. Every business operated with a minimum of help and sent its employees out to work on the right-of-way. The women worked in shifts to feed the men and take care of the mules. As if this wasn't enough of a challenge, they worked under the threat that if the railroad didn't reach Fort Worth before the Texas Legislature adjourned, they would lose the land grant that the state would give the railroad. True or not, it's said that when it got down to the last days, the crews just threw down track on ungraded ground, weighing them down with stones, while, at the same time, the ailing representative from Fort Worth had himself carried into the legislature each day to cast a vote against adjournment. And to clinch the deal, the city council moved the city limits out to meet the tracks.

Their tenacity and Fort Worth spirit paid off. On July 19, 1876, the railroad reached Fort Worth. As they had dreamed, this was the start of something big. Fort Worth became the end of the trail drives instead of the start. The ranchers made it their main shipping point, and the city soon became known as "Cowtown." In time, a number of railroads had terminals here. Fort Worth soon had the second largest stockyards in the country, and in 1902 the big Chicago meat packers, Swift and Armour, built plants here.

BUTCH AND SUNDANCE IN HELL'S HALF ACRE

With the cowboys still driving herds to town, Hell's Half Acre continued to be a magnet for them. It was also a hangout for famous outlaws like Butch Cassidy and the Sundance Kid. Butch and Sundance, whose real names were George Leroy Parker and Harry Longbaugh, often hid out here from the police and Pinkerton's. And it was also here that Sundance met Etta Place, who later went with them on their ill-fated journey to South America. In 1900, while in town celebrating a bank robbery they did in Nevada, Butch, Sundance, and the rest of the Hole in the Wall Gang had their picture taken. According to the legend, Butch sent a copy of the picture to the Nevada bank's president with a note of thanks.

Hell's Half-Acre was pretty well demolished around the time of World War I. It was also around this time that oil was discovered in nearby counties. Hundreds of oil companies set up in the city, and it soon became an oil center. And during and after World War II, the defense industry came to town to stay, and a number of major corporations followed. All of that new industry took up the economic slack of the declining stockyards' business as trucks replaced railroads and as shippers and local feedlots and cattle auctions made obsolete the large centralized stockyards. Although no cattle are processed here now, the unique Fort Worth Stockyards are a tourist attraction that remains an important part of the city's economy.

CULTURE COMES TO COWTOWN

Probably the first sign that culture was coming to Cowtown was in 1892, when some prominent women started the Fort Worth Public Library and Art Gallery. It really took off in the 1930s with a big push from city boosters like millionaires Amon Carter, founder of the *Fort Worth Star-Telegram*, and industrialist Kay Kimbell. Following the example of these philanthropists, other wealthy citizens were equally generous in their support of the arts. Today, in addition to "Cowtown," Fort Worth calls itself "The Museum Capital of the Southwest." Among its numerous museums giving support to that title are such gems as the Amon Carter Museum, the Modern Art Museum of Fort Worth, and the Kimbell Art Museum. The arts also abound with a number of theaters, including the $60 million Nancy Lee & Perry R. Bass Performance Hall, in Sundance Square, the home of the symphony, opera, ballet, as well as local and touring theater companies. The city is also the home of the Van Cliburn International Piano Competition, one of the most prestigious musical competitions in the world, the Cattle Raisers Museum, and the Sid Richardson Collection of Western Art.

Not exactly art, but definitely fun, it is also the home of a zoo that has been acclaimed as one of America's "Top Five."

As a result, although the city still calls itself Cowtown and the town "Where the West Begins," and continually projects that image to pay tribute to its Old West heritage (businessmen in suits wearing 10-gallon hats and cowboy boots are a common sight), it now might more appropriately be thought of as the home of the sophisticated cowboy.

NEIGHBORHOODS

The three neighborhoods of special interest to visitors are the Cultural/Museum District, including nearby parks, gardens, and the zoo; the Sundance Square Downtown Entertainment District; and the Stockyards National Historic District.

CULTURAL/MUSEUM DISTRICT

West of downtown. Museums: South of Camp Bowie Blvd. between University and Montgomery. Parks and Gardens: off University, north and south of I-30

The Cultural District lives up to its name. In a highly concentrated area, within easy walking distance of each other, are the **Amon Carter**

Fort Worth Cultural District

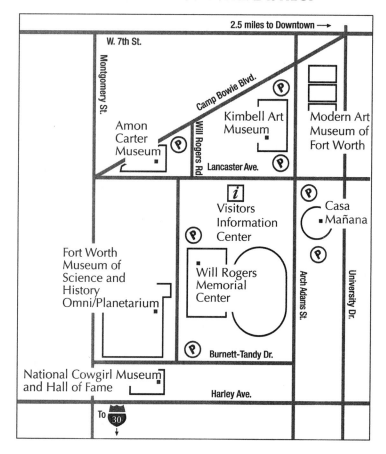

2.5 miles to Downtown →

W. 7th St.

Montgomery St.

Camp Bowie Blvd.

Will Rogers Rd.

Amon Carter Museum

Kimbell Art Museum

Modern Art Museum of Fort Worth

Lancaster Ave.

Visitors Information Center

Casa Mañana

Fort Worth Museum of Science and History Omni/Planetarium

Will Rogers Memorial Center

Arch Adams St.

University Dr.

Burnett-Tandy Dr.

National Cowgirl Museum and Hall of Fame

Harley Ave.

To 30

Museum, **Kimbell Art Museum**, **Modern Art Museum of Fort Worth**, **Scott Theatre**, **National Cowgirl Museum and Hall of Fame**, and **Fort Worth Museum of Science and History**, with its Omni Theater and **Noble Planetarium**. And you don't have to go far to take in the **Will Rogers Memorial Center**, where for more than 200 days a year you'll find equestrian and livestock events, including the **Southwestern Exposition and Livestock Show and Rodeo** (the oldest in America, held annually for more than 100 years) and the **Casa Mañana Theatre**. Immediately to the south of this cluster of culture is the **Fort Worth Botanic Garden**, **Trinity Park**, and **Forest Park**, with its Log Cabin Village and the **Fort Worth Zoo**. This district annually attracts between five and six million visitors. Note: Plans are in progress to develop a Western Heritage Center in the Cultural District to include a new Cattle Raisers Museum tied in with the

National Cowgirl Museum and Hall of Fame, the Will Rogers Memorial Center, and a new Western-oriented wing in the Fort Worth Museum of Science and History.

SUNDANCE SQUARE DOWNTOWN ENTERTAINMENT DISTRICT

**Downtown, Throckmorton to Calhoun and Second to Fifth Streets •
Information: 817-339-7777 • www.sundancesquare.com**

Surrounded by modern skyscrapers, this 20-block historic district has red-brick-paved streets and courtyards that add to the early 1900s architecture that has been restored or replicated and now houses a collection of restaurants, live theaters and movie theaters, nightclubs, art galleries, and specialty shops. What was once a typical downtown, virtually dead after the workers left at the end of the business day, is now the city's most lively entertainment district. It's named after the Sundance Kid, who, with his partner Butch Cassidy, hid out in high fashion in the nearby Hell's Half Acre and became part of the legends of the Old West. Among the more fascinating attractions of Sundance Square are the extensive *trompe l'oeil* (fool the eye) paintings of Richard Haas, especially the three-story **Chisholm Trail Mural** on the south side of the building at 400 Main. Other Haas creations include the façade on the Civil Courts Building and a number of faux storefronts on Houston and Throckmorton Streets.

Although actually on the edge of the Square, the crown jewel and center of the many activities in Sundance is the **Nancy Lee and Perry R. Bass Performance Hall**, which occupies most of the block at Commerce and Fourth. The Bass family was the major force behind the revitalization of the decaying downtown that resulted in the development of Sundance Square, and this is the capstone of the successful master plan launched by Bass Brothers Enterprises in 1982 to create a vibrant marketplace for living, working, shopping, and entertainment.

The Convention and Visitors Bureau has a free downtown walking-tour map that gives details on many of the buildings in this area. (See SELF-GUIDED TOURS, p. 178) While popular in the day, the area livens up even more in the evenings. The sidewalks and street corners of Sundance are filled with strolling musicians, mimes, caricature artists, and other entertainers each Friday and Saturday evening throughout the year. One of the most visitor-friendly, and unusual, things about this entertainment district is that after 5:00 p.m. on weekdays and all day weekends and holidays, most of the Sundance parking lots are free (look for the Sundance logo on the lot). On a bustling Saturday night, you may have trouble finding a space in a lot close to where you want to go, but, at least, once you get parked, you won't have to pay, and just about everything is within walking distance.

Another point of interest is that, even at night, this may be one of the most crime-free downtowns in America. In addition to the city police, it's

heavily patrolled by specially trained private security police, all backed up by both outdoor and indoor surveillance cameras.

THE STOCKYARDS NATIONAL HISTORIC DISTRICT
North of downtown. North Main from 23rd to 28th streets

The Stockyards, once the second largest in the country, played a major role in the growth of Fort Worth. By 1873, the many rail lines, that extended like tarantula legs from downtown Fort Worth, included the

FORT WORTH HISTORIC STOCKYARDS

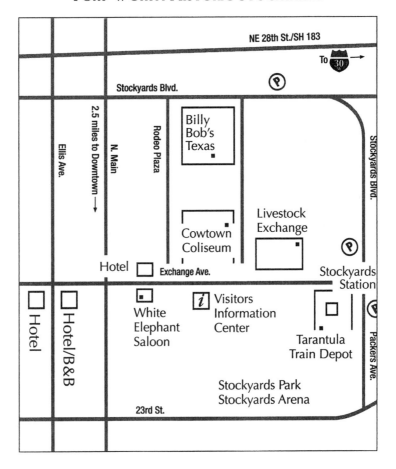

Fort Worth Stockyards Belt Railway, which specialized in moving livestock. Cattle pens extended for nearly a mile when the big meat packers established plants. In 1911, the area was incorporated as Niles City, a community composed almost entirely of the stockyards, set up as a defense by the meat packers to keep their tax haven from being annexed by Fort Worth. With a population of only 650 and property values of $25 million, its per capita wealth led to its being called the "Richest Little Town in the World." But the meat packers lost in court, and in 1922 Niles City was annexed and became part of Fort Worth. In its time, more than 160 million head of livestock were processed through here.

Just as the Sundance Square District was developed by the foresight and financial support of the Bass family, those in the know in Fort Worth agree that two people most responsible for the preservation and development of the Stockyards District are Sue McCafferty, who fought to preserve its history, and Holt Hickman, a local entrepreneur who put up much of the money. It is mostly because of their vision and efforts that the whole district is now on the National Register of Historic Places and still looks much as it did a hundred years ago, with its wooden sidewalks, red brick streets, and many of its buildings nearly a century old. But today, those old-timers exist side by side with a thriving entertainment complex that plays up their age to keep alive the spirit of the Old West. The Livestock Exchange Building, for example, built in 1904, is now the appropriate location for the **Stockyards Collection and Museum**. This building still lives up to its name as the site of livestock auctions in which entire herds of cattle are bought and sold. The cattle aren't here now, however, since the whole deal is done by closed-circuit nationwide satellite communications. The Thannisch Building, built in 1907, is now the **Stockyards Hotel**. And the **Cowtown Coliseum**, built in 1907, which made the history books as the home of the first indoor rodeo, still has Wild West shows during the summer and professional rodeo competitions most weekends. Among the other attractions in the Stockyards are the **Texas Cowboy Hall of Fame**, the **Stockyards Station**, which is both the depot for the Tarantula Excursion Train and a covered marketplace; and the **Texas Trail of Fame**, with about sixty bronze star markers scattered throughout the district honoring people who contributed to the history and grandeur of the Western Way, ranging from Charles Goodnight and Frederic Remington to Roy Rogers and John Wayne. And another not-to-miss sight is the country-and-western club, **Billy Bob's Texas**, which lays claim to be the "World's Largest Honky-Tonk." You can even get your photo taken on the back of a longhorn—a docile one, of course—from a street photographer.

There's one "sometimes free" parking lot at the northeast end of the Stockyards and street parking along East Exchange Avenue is also "free"—if you can find it. Otherwise, all the other lots in the area charge a fee, with the rates depending on whether there's a special event in the area or not.

FREE VISITOR SERVICES

FORT WORTH CONVENTION & VISITORS BUREAU

Downtown/Sundance Square. 415 Throckmorton (76102) • 817-336-8791 or 800-433-5747 • Monday–Friday, 8:30–5; Saturday, 10–4 • www.fortworth.com • W

The travel counselors here will help you find out everything you want to know about Fort Worth, with emphasis on the positive differences between Cowtown and other destinations. Visitor guides are available—in

English and a number of foreign languages—and maps of Fort Worth, the Metroplex, and Texas. They will also help you with accommodations and dining information, attraction and shopping guides, bus maps and schedules, calendar of events, and just generally good advice and suggestions. Parking on the street.

STOCKYARDS VISITORS INFORMATION CENTER

130 E. Exchange, near the Stockyards Station • 817-624-4741 • Monday–Friday, 10–6; Saturday, 10–7; Sunday, noon–6 • W+

Drop in here to pick up loads of free information before you start exploring the Stockyards. Note the mural on the wall. You can also sign up for a Stockyards Trails Walking Tour here. (See COMMERCIAL TOURS, p. 178)

The front porch is a good place to watch the daily parade of the Fort Worth Herd (See FAMILY FUN AND KID STUFF, p. 203). Information provided isn't restricted to the Stockyards. You can find out about attractions, lodging, dining, and whatever you want to know throughout the city.

CULTURAL DISTRICT VISITORS INFORMATION CENTER

3401 W. Lancaster near University Dr., by the ticket booth in front of the Will Rogers Memorial Complex • 817-882-8588 • Monday–Thursday, 9–5; Friday–Saturday, 9–6; Sunday, noon–4 • W+

To start, here you can pick up a Cultural District Self-Guided Walking Tour and a Visitors Guide to the Cultural District. In addition to details about all the museums, attractions, accommodations, and dining spots in the Cultural District, the counselors at this visitors center can provide information on just about anything in the city. And they say that if they don't know, they'll find out for you. Usually plenty of parking in front, except when there's a big event at the Will Rogers complex.

HELPFUL LOCAL PUBLICATIONS

Current information about events, activities, nightlife, theater, movies, and dining in Fort Worth and other Metroplex cities may be found in the *Fort Worth Weekly* and the *Fort Worth Star-Telegram*, especially in the *Star Time: Weekly Entertainment Guide* section published each Friday. Another source is the monthly *Fort Worth, Texas City Magazine*. Events and activities in the Stockyards are also highlighted in the monthly *Fort Worth Stockyards Gazette* which is available free throughout the city at restaurants and tourist attractions. A Convention and Visitors Bureau calendar of activities for each month is also available at hotels, restaurants, and many shops in Sundance Square and downtown, the Cultural District, and the

Stockyards. The most up-to-date information is at www.fortworth.com. Some coverage of Fort Worth is also included in the *Dallas Observer*, available free throughout the Fort Worth/Dallas area.

COMMERCIAL TOURS

CLASSIC CARRIAGES

817-336-0400 (Recorded message) • Stand at Second and Main by the Renaissance Worthington Hotel • www.classiccarriages.net

Quarter-hour public tours through Sundance Square in a horse-drawn carriage are available at the carriage stand on Friday and Saturday nights from 7:30 to midnight (weather permitting). Half-hour private tours are available seven days. Pick-ups at other hotels can be arranged.

STOCKYARDS TRAILS WALKING TOUR

130 E. Exchange in Visitors Information Center • 817-625-9715 • Monday–Saturday; 10-4; Sunday, noon–4 • Fee • www.stockyardsstation.com

These tours take you on a guided walk through the historic Stockyards district. They leave from the Stockyards Visitors Information Center and last a little over an hour. Special rates for groups, seniors, and children.

INDUSTRY TOURS

MRS. BAIRD'S BAKERY TOUR

7301 South Frwy. (76134) on west side of I-35W South Frwy. Exit Sycamore School Rd. • 817-293-6230 • Monday, Wednesday, Friday, 10–4 • Reservations required. Call at least two weeks in advance • Free • W

See how bread is made in huge mixing bowls and kneading machines the size of a small truck, while learning about this popular Texas bakery that traces its history back to 1908, when widow Ninnie L. Baird started selling her home-baked bread as a way to support her family. All visitors are given a sample of bread fresh from the oven. The tour lasts 30 to 45 minutes. Children must be at least six years old to take the tour.

SELF-GUIDED TOURS

SELF-GUIDED WALKING TOURS

The Convention & Visitors Bureau offers a free downtown walking tour map. If you follow it all, it covers about three miles and takes about

CULTURAL DISTRICT—PARKS AND ZOO

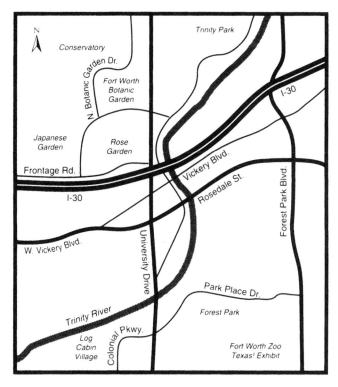

three hours to complete. However, it has sub-tours for art, architecture, and historic sites that cover one to two miles and take one to two hours to complete. Or you can use it to devise your own tour of just the places that most interest you.

GETTING AROUND

If you don't want the hassle of driving your car everywhere, you need to take a little time to learn the Fort Worth public transportation available to you.

The heart of the system is the **Intermodal Transportation Center** (ITC) located at Ninth and Jones downtown. (Look for the 70-foot clock tower.) The term "intermodal" refers to the many modes of transportation available at this center. Here you'll find city bus service for several routes—including the free downtown circular route—commuter rail service across the Metroplex to DFW Airport and Dallas on the Trinity Railway Express, and regional and national rail service on Amtrak.

The Convention and Visitors Bureau can give you schedule and fare details or contact any of the following: **The T** (City Bus Service), 817-215-8600, www.the-T.com; **Trinity Railway Express**, 877-657-0146 (toll-free), www.trinityrailwayexpress.org; or (for Dallas) **DART**, 214-979-1111, www.dart.org.

The **Yellow Checker Shuttle** (Airporter) makes daily runs between DFW Airport and the downtown hotels on a regular schedule. A one-way fare of about $15 (seniors get reduced price); 817-267-5150.

In addition to regular buses, The T operates some vintage-look trolleys to the Cultural District on the *University Route 7* and the Stockyards on *North Main Route 1*. Both these routes also serve the Intermodal Transportation Center and the Trinity Railway Express station in downtown Fort Worth. You can buy a one-day pass good for unlimited rides on both the trolley and all regular buses for about $5.

BIRD'S-EYE VIEW

It's not a high-level bird's-eye view, but a good low-level one of downtown can be seen from the front grounds of the **Amon Carter Museum**. You can thank Amon G. Carter Sr. for this. It was his wish that this museum be located on a hill commanding an excellent view. A panoramic view of the Trinity Valley looking out toward the Stockyards can be seen from **Heritage Park**, next to the Tarrant County Courthouse.

HISTORIC PLACES

BALL-EDDLEMAN-MCFARLAND HOUSE

1110 Penn (76102), south off West 7th • 817-332-5875 • Tours, Tuesdays and Thursdays at 10 a.m., 11 a.m., and 1 p.m., or by appointment • Adults, $2.50; children free (under 12 must be accompanied by an adult) • www.historicfortworth.org

Built in 1899 on a bluff overlooking the Trinity River, in an area once called "Quality Hill," this is one of the cattle barons' elegant Victorian homes. The home was occupied by only three families in its history, and its finely crafted woodwork and other architectural details remain largely unaltered from its original state. Listed on the National Register of Historic Places. Street parking only. Another Victorian home on the National Register is the **Pollock-Capps House**, at 1120 Penn. Built in 1899, it has been converted to offices.

ELIZABETH BOULEVARD HISTORICAL DISTRICT

Elizabeth between 8th and College, south of I-30, west of I-35

Elizabeth Boulevard is the central street in a neighborhood of the grand homes of cattlemen and oilmen built between 1910 and 1930. At that time it was known as "Silver Slipper Row." The construction of the mansions ended with the Depression, and smaller bungalows were built among the larger homes. The area is listed on the National Register of Historic Places and many of the houses have individual markers. All are private homes, not open to the public.

LOG CABIN VILLAGE

2100 Log Cabin Village Ln. (76109), take Colonial Pkwy. off S. University Dr. • 817-926-5881 • Tuesday–Friday, 9–5; Saturday, 10–5; Sunday, 1–5. Closed Monday • Adults, $2; seniors and children (4–17), $1.50; under age 4 free • W variable (one cabin accessible) • www.historicfortworth.org

This is a living-history museum containing seven pioneer cabins from the early and mid-1800s that were moved to this wooded 2½-acre site in Forest Park, restored, and furnished with period tools and furnishings. Interpreters dressed in period pioneer costumes demonstrate old crafts such as spinning and candle making. Milling equipment was installed into one of the cabins to convert it to a grist mill. There is also a staffed reproduction of a blacksmith shop from the period. The herb garden is planted with herbs that would have been used by settlers between the years 1850 and 1890. One of the cabins was the home of Isaac Parker, the uncle of Cynthia Ann Parker, who was captured by the Comanches as a young girl. She married Chief Nocona and was the mother of Quanah Parker, the last great Comanche war chief, who helped bring about peace between the settlers and the Indian tribes of North Texas. Gift shop. Free parking adjacent.

PIONEER REST CEMETERY

626 Samuels, northeast of downtown • Open seven days, 9 to dusk • W

This cemetery was started in 1850 to bury two children of Maj. Ripley Arnold, the officer who established Camp Worth. In 1853, Arnold, reputedly a strict disciplinarian of his troops, was killed by one of his men at Fort Graham, near Hillsboro, Texas, and his body brought back here to be buried with his children. Also buried here are Gen. Edward H. Tarrant, after whom the county is named, and eleven soldiers who served in the original fort. Among others buried here is Ephraim M. Daggett, who was sometimes called the Father of Fort Worth in recognition of his importance in the city's early days. Daggett was so influential that his likeness was engraved on the city seal for the first 50 years of its existence. The graves of the pioneers are in the rear of the cemetery. After this small cemetery was filled, starting around 1879, the latter-day Fort Worth giants and sinners were buried in Oakwood Cemetery, located across the Trinity River at 701

Grand between downtown and the Stockyards. These included prominent cattle and oil barons, like the little-known Fountain Goodlet Oxsheer, who once owned more than a million acres and 30,000 head of cattle, and oil-man/rancher W. T. Waggoner, who, in the early 1900s, gave each of his three children 90,000 acres of oil-rich land and 10,000 head of cattle.

TARRANT COUNTY COURTHOUSE

100 W. Weatherford at north end of Main • 817-884-1111 • Open to the public Monday–Friday during business hours • W

Built between 1893 and 1895 of Texas pink granite and marble, its Renaissance Revival style was designed to resemble the Texas Capitol building. At the time, it cost over $300,000 and this extravagance so incensed the taxpayers that in 1894, before the building was completed, they voted out the county commissioners who had voted for it. Displays in the hallways show photographs from the original construction, historical prints of the county, and the $12 million renovation in the 1980s that restored it to its original appearance. Listed on the National Register of Historic Places. Free tours are available. (This building might look familiar if you've seen the TV series, *Walker, Texas Ranger*, since it's Walker's home base.)

After you enter the Courthouse, a room to the left contains a model of the original Fort Worth, the fort that gave the city its name when it was built on the bluff over the Trinity River. On display here are authentic replicas of the uniforms of the soldiers who manned the fort, and many weapons, equipment, and tools that they might have used at that time. On occasion, docents in uniform are available here. Guided tours can be arranged in advance by calling 817-498-5150 or visiting www.cross-timbers.org.

On a flagpole on the east lawn of the courthouse, you can see a replica of the 28-star flag that flew here more than 150 years ago.

ST. PATRICK'S CATHEDRAL COMPLEX

1206 and 1208 Throckmorton • 817-332-4915 • W

Built of white Texas stone, the Gothic Revival cathedral was completed in 1892. The oldest ecclesiastical building in the city, it contains the original hand-painted stained- glass windows from Germany and a bell cast in Troy, New York, that has been in use since 1889. The church and St. Ignatius Academy next door, built in 1889, are on the National Register of Historic Places. The late William J. Marsh, organist at the cathedral for many years, was composer of the state song, "Texas Our Texas."

STOCKYARDS NATIONAL HISTORIC DISTRICT

(See NEIGHBORHOODS, p. 174–76)

THISTLE HILL

1509 Pennsylvania (76104), at south end of Summit. Parking and the entrance are in the rear on Pruitt • 817-336-1212 • Monday–Friday

11–2, Sunday, 1–3. Closed Saturday. Tours begin on the hour • Adults, $4; seniors and children (7–12), $2 • W downstairs only

This Georgian Revival mansion was built in 1903 as a wedding present from cattle baron W. T. Waggoner to his daughter Electra and her husband, Albert B. Wharton. In addition to being rich, Electra was considered a little eccentric. She set a record by being the first customer of Neiman Marcus to spend more than $20,000 in that store in one day, she never wore the same dress twice, came back from Europe with a butterfly tattoo, and spent three hours a day in a milk bath. The Whartons referred to their 18-room, 11,000-square-foot mansion as their "honeymoon cottage." Among the architectural highlights are a 14-foot-wide oak grand stairway, with Tiffany-style windows on the landing, and oak-paneled halls. Electra sold it in 1911 to Winfield Scott, who made several changes, the most prominent of which are the limestone columns on the front porch, which he had brought from Indiana on special railcars. Later the house was used as a girls' school, served as a dormitory for young women working in the nearby aircraft factories in World War II and as a home for delinquent teens, and finally fell into disrepair until it was saved in the 1970s by a group of concerned Fort Worth citizens and eventually restored to its 1912 condition. Tours last about 45 minutes to an hour. Listed on the National Register of Historic Places. A popular antiques fair is held here annually, usually the second weekend in September.

THE VAN ZANDT COTTAGE

2900 Crestline, in Trinity Park

Maj. Khleber Miller Van Zandt, of the Texas Seventh Regiment, Confederate Army, settled in Fort Worth after the Civil War and became a member of the Texas Legislature, banker, merchant, and cattleman. In the early 1870s, he acquired 600 acres, including this cottage, which had been used as collateral for a loan. The cottage is the only one in Fort Worth still standing in its original location. Although it is not open, the kitchen foundation is still visible behind it.

OTHER HISTORIC BUILDINGS

More than two dozen buildings in downtown Fort Worth are on the National Register of Historic Places. In addition to those described above, these include: **Knights of Pythias Hall** (1903), 313 Main; **Burk Burnett Building** (1914), 500 Main; **Ashton Hotel** (1915), 610 Main; **Blackstone Hotel** (1929), 601 Main (now the Courtyard by Marriott downtown); **Hotel Texas** (1921), 815 Main (now the Radisson Plaza Hotel) where President Kennedy spent his last night and delivered his final speech in November 1963; **First Christian Church** (1914), 612 Throckmorton; **Bryce Building** (1910), 909 Throckmorton; **Texas and Pacific Terminal Complex** (1931), 1600 Throckmorton; **Fort Worth Club Building** (1926), 306 W. 7th; **Neil P. Anderson Building** (1921), 411 W. 7th; **W. T. Waggoner Building** (1919), 810 Houston; **Flatiron Building** (1907), 1000

Houston; **U.S. Post Office Building** (1933), 251 W. Lancaster; and the **Union Passenger Station** (1900), 1501 Jones. The history of all these is included in the Downtown Fort Worth Walking Tour map available from the Convention & Visitors Bureau.

MUSEUMS AND PUBLIC ART GALLERIES

AMERICAN AIRLINES C. R. SMITH MUSEUM

4601 Hwy. 360 (76155) at FAA Rd., south of Hwy. 183. SW of DFW Airport • 817-967-1560 • Tuesday–Saturday, 10–6; Sunday, noon–5. Closed Monday and major holidays • Free • W+ • www.crsmithmuseum.org

Visitors are given a first-class boarding pass as they enter. Then, through large-screen films viewed from first-class airline seats, interactive displays, dioramas, hands-on exhibits, and videos, you can follow the history of commercial aviation and the worldwide operations of American Airlines from the 1930s to the present. Included is a close-up look at a jet engine, an airplane cockpit, a wind tunnel exhibit of the principles of aerodynamics, a restored 1940s DC-3, and how an airliner is flown and maintained. For a big extra, call ahead to find out if you can schedule a session in the flight simulator, which offers the opportunity to fly from one or more of 60 airfields in any one of six aircraft ranging from a P-51 Mustang to a twin-engine Beechcraft. Gift shop.

AMON CARTER MUSEUM

3501 Camp Bowie (76107) at Montgomery and W. Lancaster, in the Cultural District • 817-738-1933 • Tuesday–Saturday, 10–5 (Thursday, 10–8); Sunday, noon–5. Closed Monday and major holidays • Free • W+ ; use side entrance on Camp Bowie Blvd. • www.cartermuseum.org

Amon G. Carter Sr. worked his way from a one-room log cabin to riches as the publisher of the *Fort Worth Star-Telegram*. It was Carter who called Fort Worth the place "Where the West begins," a slogan he put on the masthead of his newspaper, where it remains today. Carter definitely was not into the arts—in an interview with *Time* he said that in all his life he had only read about a dozen books. But he knew that a great city needed art, and he wanted Fort Worth to be a great city. Will Rogers, his close friend, got him started collecting by introducing him to the art of Charles M. Russell. His collection soon expanded from Russell to the paintings and sculptures of Frederic Remington and other artists of the American West. When he died, in 1955, he left his collection and a foundation to establish this museum.

With Carter's early collection as its core, the museum now integrates its outstanding collection of Western art with works that trace the history of

American art. In keeping with this theme, architect Phillip Johnson designed the original museum building, built in 1961, to resemble an American Indian lodge. In 2001, a major expansion tripled the size of the galleries. This was also designed by Johnson, who was 95 years old when it opened.

Among the artists represented are Winslow Homer, William Michael Harnett, Grant Wood, Martin Johnson Heade, and Georgia O'Keeffe. The museum also has one of the world's premier collections of fine-art photographs, with more than 40,000 exhibition-quality prints. These range from the earliest daguerreotypes to contemporary photographs, including Southwest landscapes by Ansel Adams and the works of Dorothea Lange, Laura Gilpin, and Eliot Porter.

Videos on the collections are available for viewing in the museum theater. Free public tours are offered daily at 2:00 p.m. (For group tours, call 817-989-5037, preferably at least two weeks in advance.) Tape and player for an audio tour are available for $4 for adults, $2 for seniors/students and children under 12. The audio tours are designed so you can pick and chose what you want to see with over sixty audio "stops." Bookstore/gift shop. Free parking adjacent to museum off Camp Bowie Blvd. Additional free parking nearby at the Will Rogers Memorial off Lancaster Street.

THE CATTLE RAISERS MUSEUM

1301 W. 7th (76102) • 817-332-8551 • Monday–Saturday, 10–5; Sunday, 1–5. Closed major holidays • Adults $5; seniors and young adults (13–18), $2; children 4–12, $1 • W ; use rear parking lot entrance • www.cattleraisersmuseum.org

The fascinating story of the development of ranching and the cattle industry in Texas and the Southwest is told here on a self-guided tour through multimedia visuals and life-sized dioramas with talking mannequins, including a "Talking Longhorn." Added to this are displays of cowboy memorabilia and historic photos of legendary early Texas cattlemen like Charles Goodnight, who set up the Goodnight Trail, and Richard King, founder of the King Ranch. The museum's major collections include branding irons, saddles, spurs, 25,000 historic photographs, and a manuscript collection documenting ranch life. The 14 saddles in the collection date from the 1850s to the 1920s and feature a Miles City Montana saddle recognized as one of the finest in existence today. The collection of 52 pairs of spurs consists of works of both artistic distinction and historical interest. Among the 1,014 branding irons are historically significant irons like the Spanish brand that belonged to Stephen F. Austin, and modern brands registered by celebrity ranchers such as actor John Wayne and Texas Ranger pitcher Nolan Ryan. Call in advance for a docent-led tour. Gift shop. (Note: In progress are plans to build a new Cattle Raisers Museum in the Cultural District as part of a Western Heritage Center.)

FIRE STATION NO. 1: 150 YEARS OF FORT WORTH

203 Commerce (76102) at 2nd, downtown • 817-255-9300 (Fort Worth Museum of Science and History) • Seven days, 9–7 • Free • W

This historic building, which houses the history of Fort Worth, is ingeniously tucked into the contrasting, modern City Center Tower II. On this site the city's first fire station was built in 1876. It was also the site of Fort Worth's original city hall, with the city offices on the second floor and the volunteer firefighters on the first. Local legend has it that the firemen kept two panthers as mascots to tweak the nose of Dallas for saying Fort Worth was so quiet a panther could sleep in a downtown street without being disturbed. The present structure, which replaced the original building, was built in 1907 and served in continuous use as a fire station until 1980. Now it is filled with displays, videos, graphics, photographs, documents, and other historical artifacts from the city's history. A self-guided walk-through will acquaint you with Fort Worth's growth and development from its birth as a military outpost on the frontier through its rowdy youth period as a cowtown to its maturity as a modern city. Exhibits include a scale model of the original Camp Worth, established in 1849; an interactive bunkhouse model, and a bucking bronco that provides a photo opportunity for visitors. The museum is a project of the Fort Worth Museum of Science and History and the City Center Development Company. Street parking or pay parking in adjacent garage.

FORT WORTH MUSEUM OF SCIENCE AND HISTORY

1501 Montgomery (76107) at Crestline, in the Cultural District • 817-255-9300 • Exhibit gallery hours: Monday–Thursday, 9–5:30; Friday–Saturday, 9–8; Sunday, noon–5:30. Closed Thanksgiving and December 24–25 • Museum general admission: Adults, $7; seniors, $6; children 3–12, $5; under 3 free. Combination tickets available to museum galleries, Omni Theater, and Planetarium • W+ • www.fortworthmuseum.org

This is the largest museum of its type in the Southwest, attracting more than a million visitors a year. The six permanent galleries have exhibitions ranging from dinosaurs to local history. There are interactive exhibits for all ages, but special hands-on areas for kids include Kidspace®, a special discovery area for children under six (and their favorite adult), and the DinoDig®, where they dig for dinosaur bones in an outdoor area. The "Comin' Through Cowtown" exhibit gives you a chance to experience Fort Worth's colorful past. The museum also frequently offers world-class traveling exhibits.

There is also an admission fee to the two major permanent attractions: The Noble Planetarium ($3.50) and the Omni Theater (Adults, $7; seniors, $6; children 3–12, $5. Various combination tickets available at savings). Every afternoon, the Planetarium has frequent shows that explore the heavens and offers free telescope observations on the north lawn one night a month (call for date). The Omni is an IMAX® theater with an advanced super 70-mm projection and sound system that presents films on a huge tilted dome screen, so the film envelops the audience in sight and sound. Although the shows are presented frequently, they can be sold out at times. Good idea to call for show times and purchase advance tickets at the Museum box office or Ticketmaster locations throughout the Metroplex. (An Omni bargain is two tickets for $10, Monday–Friday evenings after 5.) Courtyard Café and Museum Store. Free parking.

KIMBELL ART MUSEUM

**3333 Camp Bowie (76107) at Arch Adams, in the Cultural District •
817-332-8451, Metro 817-654-1034 • Tuesday–Thursday and
Saturday, 10–5; Friday, 12–8; Sunday, 12–5. Closed Mondays, July
4, Thanksgiving, and Christmas • Free except for special exhibitions
• W+ • www.kimbellart.org**

Kay Kimbell, industrialist and entrepreneur, and his wife, Velma, started collecting art in the 1930s and shortly after, joined by his sister and her husband, Dr. and Mrs. Coleman Carter, formed the Kimbell Art Foundation. The Kimbells continued to add to their collection, and shortly before Mr. Kimbell's death in 1964, he bequeathed this art collection and his entire personal fortune to the Foundation to establish and maintain a first-rank public art museum in Fort Worth. His wishes have been well carried out by the Foundation, which today owns and operates this museum that has been called "America's Best Small Museum."

The permanent collection holdings range from antiquity to the twentieth century, including representative paintings by artists such as Caravaggio, Gainsborough, Holbein, El Greco, Velazquez, Rembrandt, Cézanne, Picasso, Rubens, Van Dyck, and Monet. Its strongest area of holdings is in European paintings and sculpture from the Renaissance to the mid-twentieth century, but it also has a substantial collection of Asian arts, Meso-American and African pieces, and Mediterranean antiquities. Even the building housing this museum is widely regarded as one of the most outstanding modern public art-gallery facilities in the world, especially acclaimed for its use of natural light.

An Introductory Walk tour featuring highlights of the permanent collection is offered Wednesdays at 2:00 p.m. and Sundays at 3:00 p.m. Interpreted tours for the hearing impaired are available by request. (For group and other special tours, call Tour Coordinator at extension 249.) Admission is charged for some special touring exhibitions, with tickets ranging from about $8–$10 for adults to $4 for children 6–11. Public programs include lectures and musical presentations. The Buffet Restaurant is open Tuesday–Sunday for lunch (see A SAMPLING OF FORT WORTH RESTAURANTS, p. 217) and dinner on Friday evening 5:30–7:30 (reservations recommended). Bookstore. Free parking nearby.

MODERN ART MUSEUM OF FORT WORTH

3200 Darnell at University (76107), in the Cultural District • 817-738-9215 • Tuesday–Friday, 10–5; Saturday, 11–5; Sunday, noon–5. Closed Mondays and major holidays • Free • W+ • www.themodern.org

Chartered in 1892 as the Fort Worth Public Library and Art Gallery, the Modern is the oldest art museum in Texas and one of the oldest in the Western United States. It had several homes in its century-plus history before the newest version opened on an 11-acre site across the street from the Kimbell in December 2002. Designed by Japanese architect Tadao Ando, the $60 million building is more than triple the size of the old Modern, increasing the gallery area from 10,000 to 53,000 square feet in gallery space dedicated to modern and contemporary works of art, making it second only to the New York's Museum of Modern Art. The outdoor sculpture garden also has been expanded.

The focus here is on post–World War II international art in all media. Represented in the permanent collection are more than 3,000 significant works including pieces by more than 100 artists such as Jackson Pollock, Andy Warhol, and Robert Motherwell. Contemporary sculpture is on view outdoors on the museum grounds. In addition to its permanent collection, it has an active program of outstanding traveling exhibitions. Tours can be arranged for groups by calling at least two weeks in advance. The Modern offers a series of free lectures and performances in its 250-seat auditorium on Tuesday evenings (call for times). Café Modern with outdoor dining terrace open for lunch. Museum store. Parking nearby.

NATIONAL COWBOYS OF COLOR MUSEUM AND HALL OF FAME

3400 Mount Vernon at Tandy • 817-922-9999 • Wednesday–Saturday, 11–6 • Adults, $6; seniors, $4; students, $3; 5 and under free • W+ • www.cowboysofcolor.org

The men and women who pioneered the development of the American West were as diverse as American society today. This small museum tells the story of the cowboys of color—blacks, Asians, Latinos—who contributed to that grand historical movement. The works of artists who documented the people and events of the time, journals, photographs, and other historical items are part of this collection of the lives of these long-overlooked pioneers, cowboys, and buffalo soldiers. The museum is partly supported by the annual tour of Cowboys of Color Rodeos, in which more than 300 cowboys and cowgirls compete in rodeos in a number of major Texas cities.

NATIONAL COWGIRL MUSEUM AND HALL OF FAME

1720 Gendy, off Montgomery, in the Cultural District • 817-336-4475 or 817-476-FAME (817-476-3263) • Tuesday, 10–8; Wednesday–Saturday, 10-5; Sunday, noon–5. Closed

Mondays and major holidays • Adults, $6; seniors, $5; children 6–18, $4; children 5 and under free. Wednesday admissions all half price • W+ • www.cowgirl.net

This is the only museum in the world dedicated to honoring the women who played such an important part in settling and taming the Old West and keeping the New West civilized. From its humble start in 1975, in the basement of the county library in the Panhandle town of Hereford, Texas, the museum has grown to this $21 million, 33,000-square-foot building, appropriately sited in the Cultural District of Cowtown.

The term "cowgirl"—reportedly coined by Will Rogers—is interpreted loosely here. It isn't restricted to women who rode the range, although many of them did, but includes women in all walks of life who had true grit, determination, and "cowgirl spirit" to make a difference in what most considered, and still consider, a "man's world." There are more than 150 women in the Hall of Fame, with new ones inducted every year. Honorees include legendary women ranging from Sacajawea, the principal guide to Lewis and Clark, to Supreme Court Justice Sandra Day O'-Connor, who was a real cowgirl in her youth on her family's Arizona ranch. Among the others are Tad Lucas, the world's greatest female rodeo rider; sharpshooter Annie Oakley; country singer Patsy Cline; Henrietta Chamberlain King, matriarch of the famed King Ranch; Dale Evans, who helped tame the Hollywood version of the West with Roy Rogers; and Alice Van-Springsteen who was not only the stunt riding double for Miss Evans, but also for other stars like Ginger Rogers and Ann Sheridan.

The focal point of the museum is the 45-foot-high domed rotunda housing the Hall of Fame honoree exhibits. Off this are a small theater and three gallery areas. One area is devoted to the arena performers in Wild West shows, rodeos and horse racing; another, to the pioneers and ranch workers, and the third, to Western-oriented pop-culture icons such as Hollywood heroines Barbara Stanwyck and Dale Evans and C&W singers.

Not to miss is the interactive bronc riding on a gently paced "bronc" modified from training bulls used by rodeo riders. Your ride is captured on video, sped up, and composited into rodeo footage.

Gift shop. Free parking.

SID RICHARDSON COLLECTION OF WESTERN ART

309 Main (76102) in Sundance Square • 817-332-6554 • Tuesday–Wednesday, 10–5; Thursday–Friday, 10–8; Saturday, 11–8; Sunday, 1–5. Closed Monday and major holidays • Free • W+ • www.sidrmuseum.org

On permanent display in this large one-room gallery, in a replica of an 1895 building, are 56 paintings and bronzes by premier Western artists Frederic Remington and Charles M. Russell. Reflecting both the art and reality of the American West, the works are the legacy of late oilman and philanthropist Sid W. Richardson, who collected them between 1942 and his death in 1959. Richardson had a preference for paintings depicting action or suspense, so, it's no wonder the major works on display include Remington's *Buffalo Runners, Big Horn Basin* (1909) and *The Puncher* (1895) and Russell's *The Bucker* (1904) and *Buffalo Bill's Duel with Yellowhand* (1917). Although his concentration was on Remington and Russell, he also collected works of other Western artists, and some of these, such as *The Hold Up* by William Robinson Leigh, are also on display here. Self-tour with a free gallery guidebook. Gift shop. Street or commercial lot parking during weekdays. Free parking in Sundance lots after 5:00 p.m. weekdays and all weekend.

STOCKYARDS COLLECTION AND MUSEUM

131 E. Exchange, in the Stockyard's Livestock Exchange Building, Suite 111–114 • 817-625-5087 • Monday–Saturday, 10-5. Closed Sunday • Free (donations accepted) • W

More a collection for browsing than a tidy museum, the rooms contain a widely diverse assortment of memorabilia and artifacts, most of which are related in some way to the history of the Stockyards, the railroads that served it, and the meat packing industry. These include saddles, antiques, and photographs. Also on display is a collection of more than 200 samples of barbed wire, gifts from every community visited by the 1986 Texas Sesquicentennial Wagon Train, and a Native American exhibit featuring artifacts from many tribes, with special emphasis on the last Comanche war chief, Quanah Parker. You might also want to check to see if the lightbulb that has been burning since 1908 is still lit. Gift shop.

TANDY ARCHAEOLOGICAL MUSEUM

2001 W. Seminary, in the library of the Southwestern Baptist Theological Seminary • 817-923-1921, ext. 2750 • Open library hours, call for times • Free • W

The items in the permanent collection date from about 1500 B.C. to 700 B.C. and consist of artifacts uncovered at digs in Tel-Batash (biblical Timnah), Israel. Visitor parking at the Memorial Building.

TEXAS COWBOY HALL OF FAME

128 E. Exchange, Suite 100 (76106) • 817-626-7131 • Monday–Thursday, 10–6; Friday–Saturday, 10–7; Sunday, noon–6 • Adults, $4; seniors, $3; children 3–12, $2 • W+ • www.texascowboyhalloffame.com

Texas cowboys and cowgirls who have excelled in the sports of rodeo and cutting are both honored in this Stockyards horse barn converted to a museum. These include Ty Murray, 7-time World Champion All Around Cowboy; Don Gay, 8-time World Champion Bull Rider; and Charmayne James, 10-time World Champion Barrel Racer. Each of the thirty-odd honorees has his or her own little Hall of Fame booth showing photos, memorabilia, and even videos of their careers. Another section features the Sterquell Wagon Collection of 60 restored antique wagons, carriages, and sleighs, billed as "the world's largest lifestyle wagon collection." Included in this exhibit is a dramatically painted Sicilian cart dating to the 1750s, a ranch chuck wagon, a Standard Oil fuel tank wagon, and a Welsh funeral hearse, complete with glass windows, gold leaf paint, and plumes. The third section is the John Justin Trail of Fame, paying tribute to the man who built the Justin Boot Company, with displays of a variety of boots that he made for famous customers.

If you want a personal souvenir, the Old Time Photo Parlor offers the chance to have your photo taken in old-time Western and Southern costumes (fee). Gift shop.

VINTAGE FLYING MUSEUM

505 NW 38th (76106), Hangar 33-S, adjacent to south end of Meacham Airport, just north of the Stockyards • 817-624-1935 • Saturday, 10–5; Sunday, noon–5 • Suggested donation $4 • W • www.vintageflyingmusuem.org

This is an antique aircraft restoration facility staffed almost entirely by volunteers who literally build "museums that fly." Tours cover displays of vintage aircraft, land vehicles, and support equipment in various stages of preservation. Prominent among these is "Chuckie," the last known B-17G *Pathfinder*. As the name states, this plane was one of those World War II B-17s especially equipped with an early form of secret target acquisition radar to lead waves of other B-17 Flying Fortresses when clouds hid the targets from the bombardier's sights. In contrast to this "advanced technology," one of the other planes on display here is a bi-wing Stearman that uses a hand crank as a starter. Inside are displays of Air Force and other military memorabilia. Call for weekday and group tours. Gift shop.

OUTDOOR PUBLIC ART

At times, driving around Fort Worth is like visiting an outdoor sculpture exhibition. Following are a few of the places to see this outdoor tribute to Fort Worth's Western heritage and art.

In the Stockyards: *Texas Gold*, at N. Main and Stockyards Blvd., depicts a herd of seven longhorn steers. Each steer represents one of the Texas families that, in the early 1900s, began efforts to preserve the longhorn breed. *The Bulldogger*, in front of the Cowtown Coliseum on E. Exchange is a statue of Bill Pickett, the rodeo cowboy who originated the bulldogging event and the first black cowboy inducted into the Cowboy Hall of Fame. Pickett, the star attraction at the first indoor rodeo, had a technique for downing the steer by sinking his teeth into its upper lip.

On the way to the Cultural District, outside the Cattle Raisers Museum on W. 7th, is *The Brand Inspector*, a life-sized statue of a mounted brand inspector, brand book in hand, as he checks out a longhorn in his job of tracking down cattle thieves. In the Cultural District, in addition to the sculpture gardens at the museums, there are important pieces in the Will Rogers Memorial Complex. *Midnight,* outside the Amon G. Carter Jr. Exhibits Hall, depicts the black stallion, "Midnight," tossing a bronc rider, in keeping with the legend that no one ever rode this rodeo bronc. And *Sweet Will Rogers Riding into the Sunset,* the statue in front of Will Rogers Coliseum, depicts the famed Western humorist on his favorite horse, "Soapsuds." Rogers considered Fort Worth his second home.

Downtown/Sundance Square art includes the famed *Chisholm Trail* mural, a three-story painting on the rear of the building in the 400 block of Main Street that shows a trail drive in trompe l'oeil; you'll think it's the real thing. This is one of the most photographed sights in Fort Worth. Then there are the 48-foot-tall trumpeting angels, weighing 250,000 pounds each, emerging from the Texas limestone façade of the Bass Performance Hall, and a 20-foot-high bronze replica of Frederic Remington's *Bronco Buster* at entrance to Barnes and Noble's store across the street. In Burnett Park, at 7th and Lamar, is the Jonathan Borosky sculpture *Man With a Briefcase,* and in the bank plaza at 500 W. 7th is *The Texas Sculpture.*

SPECIAL GARDENS

FORT WORTH BOTANIC GARDEN

3220 Botanic Garden Blvd. (76107) at University, just north of I-30, in the Cultural District • Information 817-871-7686 • Seven days. Usually opens at 8 a.m. Monday–Saturday, 1 p.m. Sunday. Closing depends on season and varies from 4 to 10 p.m. (call) • General admission: Adults, $1; seniors and children 4–12, $ .50; under 4 free. Extra admission for Conservatory and Japanese Garden • W variable • www.fwbg.org

An 18-foot floral clock graces the entrance to this botanic garden, the oldest in Texas, where, on 109 acres, you can see more 150,000 plants representing more than 2,500 native and exotic species in 21 specialty garden areas. Seasonal plantings provide color throughout the year. In late April and October, visitors can enjoy more than 2,000 roses reaching peaks of bloom in the Rose Gardens. The Fragrance Garden is designed for the visually impaired, but all can enjoy the fragrant leaves to touch and smell. Overall, the Botanic Garden lives up to its motto as a "Sanctuary for the Senses."

The two areas that have additional admission fees are the Japanese Garden and the Conservatory. The 7½-acre Japanese Garden (817-871-7685) features waterfalls and pools with koi (imperial carp) fish, a pagoda, a teahouse, and a meditation garden patterned after a temple garden in Kyoto. Open daily, but hours vary. Adults, $3 weekdays, $3.50 weekends and holidays; seniors, $.50 discount; children 4–12, $2. Ticket office, 817-871-7685. The 10,000-square-foot Conservatory, which displays lush tropical plants, is also open every day all year. Adult admission, $1; seniors and children 4–12, $.50. Hours vary. Information on tours and programs, 817-871-7682. Visitors number more than 700,000 annually. Also located here is The Texas Garden Club, Inc., headquarters of all affiliated state garden clubs.

Special events include the annual Fort Worth Garden Show and the Rose Society Show and Sale, both usually held in April, and the Fall Festival in the Japanese Garden in October. Concerts in the Garden are held several times in June and July (See ANNUAL EVENTS, p. 213). Gardens Restaurant open Tuesday–Sunday for lunch (817-731-2547). Gift shops in main gardens and Japanese Garden. Free parking.

OUTDOORS

FORT WORTH NATURE CENTER AND REFUGE

9601 Fossil Ridge Rd. (76135), exit Confederate Park Rd. off Hwy. 199 (Jacksboro Hwy.), 4 miles west of Loop I-820, on Lake Worth • 817-237-1111 • Visitor hours: Tuesday–Saturday, 9–4:30; Sunday, noon–4:30. Closed Monday and major holidays • Free • Hardwicke Interpretive Center W+

There are buffalo here, and if you're sharp-eyed you may also see white-tailed deer, armadillos, wild turkeys, egrets, and herons roaming the prairies, forest, and marshes amidst an abundance of wildflowers on this 3,500-acre sanctuary that remains much as it was 150 years ago. Nature programs, maps, and interpretive exhibits are available at the Hardwicke Interpretive Center. Hike the 25-mile trail system or canoe the Trinity River. Bird-watchers say it's a crossroads for both eastern and western species. Call for tour information and sign interpretive services. Call to check on guided tours, which are sometimes available on Saturdays for a small fee. Reportedly the largest city-owned nature center in the United States. Gift shop. Free parking.

FORT WORTH PARKS

Parks and Community Services Department • 4200 S. Frwy. (76115) • 817-871-8700

The Parks and Community Services Department has over 200 parks totaling more than 10,000 acres scattered throughout Fort Worth. They offer a wide variety of facilities, including recreation centers, three golf courses, swimming pools, and tennis courts. The parks provide all sorts of recreational opportunities, as well as quiet oases where one can get away from the hubbub of the city. The crown jewels of the Fort Worth parks are the two major parks along the Trinity River southwest of downtown: **Trinity Park**, which adjoins the Cultural District north of I-30, and **Forest Park**, which is south of I–30. Aside from the I–30 division, these parks are so closely linked it's hard to tell where one ends and the other begins. Trinity Park stretches for nearly two miles along the west bank of the Trinity River's Clear Fork. Built during the Depression, as part of the unemployment relief program, its present facilities include eight miles of jogging and cycling trails, an outdoor fitness course, the **Fort Worth Botanic Garden**, and a miniature train ride. Entrances are off W. Lancaster Dr. and University. Forest Park, farther to the south on the opposite bank of the Clear Fork, is most noted for two of its attractions: the **Fort Worth Zoo** and **Log Cabin Village**. Entrances are off Forest Park Blvd. and University. **Patricia Le Blanc Park**, 6300 Granbury Cut-off, is another highly popular park. In addition to hike and bike trails, sports fields, and a tennis court, the playground is designed to meet all ADA requirements so children have access to equipment equal to their abilities.

HERITAGE PARK

Bluff and Main, north of Tarrant County Courthouse • 817-871-8700 (Parks and Community Services Dept.) • Open at all times • Free • W variable

This restful park is located on the bluffs above the Trinity River at the approximate site of the original Camp Worth. You can walk among water walls and waterfalls and follow paths down to get a bird's-eye view of the Trinity River Valley to the north. Most of the 112-acre park is down the bluff. Hiking and biking trails.
Note: Although patrolled, this park is not the safest place to be after dark.

LAKE WORTH

Off Hwy. 199 (Jacksboro Hwy.) or Loop I-820 at northwest end of city • 817-871-8700 (Parks and Community Services Dept.) • Open at all times • Free • W variable

A 3,560-acre city-owned lake with both city parks and commercial facilities for fishing, boating, and other water sports and picnicking on the shoreline. Meandering Drive wanders almost all around it, offering many scenic vistas. Location of Fort Worth Nature Center and Refuge (see p. 193).

TRINITY RIVER TRAILS

These scenic trails currently extend more than 35 miles along the Trinity River and several feeding creeks. In addition to hiking, segments are available for biking and horseback trail riding, and some parts are paved for in-line skating. Future plans call for connecting the Fort Worth trails with the Arlington trail system.

COLLEGE CAMPUSES OF INTEREST TO VISITORS

TARRANT COUNTY COLLEGE

1500 Houston (76102), District Office • 817–515–7851 •
www.tccd.edu

The four campuses in this county's college system include two in Fort Worth: **South Campus** at 5301 Campus Drive, 76119 (817-515-4100), at Campus Drive exit off I-20; and the **Northwest Campus** at 4801 Marine Creek Drive, 76179 (817-515-7100), north of Loop 820. There are about 8,000 students at the South Campus and almost 4,000 at Northwest campus enrolled in both academic and technical programs. TCC ranks first in Texas and twenty-first in the nation in the number of associate degrees awarded annually. Visitors are welcome at the small art galleries on both campuses, and campus theaters that offer a spring and fall schedule of widely ranging entertainment that includes stage productions and musical concerts. Small admission price for most theater productions, while many other events are free. Call for schedule.

TEXAS CHRISTIAN UNIVERSITY

2800 S. University (TCU Box 297050, 76129) between W. Cantey
and W. Berry • 817–257–7000 or 817–257–7810 (Campus
Communications Office) • W variable • www.tcu.edu

In 1869, some Fort Worth citizens tried to get Addison and Randolph Clark to start a college in their city. Plans went forward, but then the notorious Hell's Half Acre grew up next to the planned building site, so, in 1873, the Clark's went to Thorp Springs, 40 miles away, and started AddRan Male and Female Academy, the forerunner of TCU. In 1889, the Clarks had money problems and turned the college over to the Brotherhood of the Christian Church, which changed the name to AddRan Christian University. From there, in 1896, the college moved to Waco, where its name was changed to Texas Christian University. And finally, in 1910, after a fire destroyed the main building, the college completed the circle back to Fort Worth when the trustees accepted an offer from that city. The name AddRan is still used in the title of TCU's AddRan College of Humanities and Social Sciences.

Today the university has an enrollment of more than 8,000 students studying in 82 undergraduate and graduate fields in 50 areas of study and 16 fields of doctoral study in the schools of business and education and the colleges of nursing, fine arts, and communication. TCU is an independent, self-governing university affiliated with the Christian Church (Disciples of Christ), a mainsteam Protestant denomination that emphasizes understanding among the world's religions.

Among the many interesting buildings on the 260–acre campus is the **Robert Carr Chapel**, which incorporates elements of several historic buildings in its delicate Williamsburg style and has a distinctive pulpit in

the shape of a wine chalice. **Jarvis Hall,** built in 1911, is the only original campus structure whose neo-Georgian exterior is largely preserved.
The Mills Glass Collection, with its more than 2,500 examples of early
American pressed glass, art glass, blown glass, cut glass, and porcelain
(some pieces dating as far back as 1608) is open to visitors. It is located
in the Faculty Center in Reed Hall (817-257-7808). Another collection
open to visitors is the Geology Department's **Oscar Monnig Meteorite
Museum** (817-257-7270) one of the finest private meteorite collections
in the Southwest, containing more than 400 different meteorites.

Student, faculty, and traveling art exhibitions in the **University Art
Gallery** in the Visual Arts and Communications Building (817–257–7601)
are open to visitors. Visitors may also attend public lectures by faculty and
eminent guest speakers. Among the performance venues on campus, the
1,200-seat **Ed Landreth Auditorium** is considered one of the finest
acoustical halls in the area and is the home of a world-class concert pipe organ. The **Mary D. and F. Howard Walsh Center for the Performing Arts**
is a 50,000-square-foot facility that wraps around the Ed Landreth Auditorium, providing a studio theatre and a recital hall.

Visitors are also welcome at intercollegiate sports events. The TCU
Horned Frogs compete in Conference USA in NCAA Division 1A athlet-
ics. Sports fans can enjoy family-oriented fun in Frog Alley outside **Amon
Carter Stadium** prior to every home football game. The carnival-like setting features live bands, street performers, and special activities for children
and adults. Men's and women's basketball is played in the **Daniel-Meyer
Coliseum,** baseball in the **Lupton Baseball Stadium,** soccer in the **Garvey-
Rosenthal Soccer Stadium,** and track and field events in the **Lowden Track
& Field Complex.** For sports schedules and ticket information call
817–257–FROG (257–3764). Tennis players are welcome to use the facilities of the **Friedman Tennis Center.** (See SPORTS—TENNIS, p. 209)

Visitors may pick up a campus map and parking instructions at **Dee J.
Kelly Alumni and Visitors Center.** Off-campus parking is also available
until midnight in the lots east and west of the University Christian
Church. Campus tours can be arranged through the Admissions Office,
817-257-7490.

TEXAS WESLEYAN UNIVERSITY
**1201 Wesleyan (76105), between E. Vickery and E. Rosedale •
817-531-4458 or Metro 817-429-8224 • W+ • www.twu.edu.**

Founded in 1890 by the Methodist Church, it was originally named
Polytechnic College, which has the literal meaning of "many arts and sciences." This concept has remained central to the mission of the University, which now has close to 3,000 students enrolled in programs leading
to undergraduate degrees in the arts, humanities, science, business, and
education, and graduate degrees in business, education, law, dentistry,
and nurse anesthesia.

The campus is located on approximately 75 acres just four miles southeast of downtown Fort Worth on Polytechnic Heights, one of the high-

est points in the city. Although most of the buildings are relatively new, the school's heritage is reflected in some of its historic structures, such as the **Boyd House** (1895), which is the oldest building on campus. Other buildings from the early days of the University include the **Oneal-Sells Administration Building** (1902), the **Ann Waggoner Fine Arts Building** (1908), **Mulkey Hall** (1909), the **Dillow House** (1912), and the **Firestation Theatre** (1914). However, most of these have gone through extensive remodeling over the years.

Visitors are welcome at a number of events, most of which are free. These include exhibits of art by students, faculty, and area artists, performances of the Wesleyan Singers, the Jazz Ensemble, and Wind Ensemble, the annual spring musical, and other voice and instrumental recitals. The location of theater performances varies but includes the intimate 57-seat Firestation Studio Theatre housed in the former firestation and city hall of Polytechnic Heights. Varsity sports events open to visitors include men's soccer, basketball, baseball, and tennis, and women's soccer, volleyball, basketball, softball, and tennis. Most games are free to spectators. Game locations vary. For schedule call 817–531–4210. Visitor parking is available at several locations on the campus.

MUSIC AND PERFORMING ARTS

NANCY LEE AND PERRY R. BASS PERFORMANCE HALL

330 E. 4th at Commerce (76102) in Sundance Square • 817-212-4200; information hotline (Tuesday–Friday), 817-212-4325 • Tickets: 817-212-4280 or toll-free 877-212-4280 • Admission varies by event • W+ • www.basshall.com

Many consider this hall the crown jewel of a city that already boasts the nation's third largest cultural district, and an important symbol of one of the most successful downtown revitalization efforts in the country. The $72.5 million facility, built entirely with private funds, is a 10–story showpiece as well as a showcase. The 2,056-seat multipurpose concert theater is patterned after the classic European opera house, with an 80-foot-diameter great dome topping the **Founders Concert Theater**, and 48-foot angels, sculpted from Texas limestone, gracing the grand façade. Every aspect of the Hall's design offers superb acoustics, exceptional sight lines, and an ambiance on a level with the great halls of Europe.

It is the permanent home of the Fort Worth Symphony Orchestra, Fort Worth Dallas Ballet, Fort Worth Opera, and the Van Cliburn International Piano Competition. In addition, it hosts a wide range of performances from major Casa Mañana musicals to the Performing Arts Fort Worth's "Hall Series" featuring an eclectic array of entertainers offering popular, jazz, and traditional music and dance performances. A thoughtful touch: The mirrors on all levels conceal TV screens for latecomers to watch performances until they can be seated.

Public tours Saturdays at 10:30 a.m., performance schedule permitting. Parking in Sundance Square lots and valet parking available ($10 cash only). Gift shop.

CASA MAÑANA THEATRE

3101 W. Lancaster (76107) at University, at east end of Cultural District • 817-332-CASA (332-2272) • Admission varies • W+ • www.casamanana.org

It started as Fort Worth's contribution to the 1936 Texas Centennial Celebration when Amon Carter built the largest revolving stage and café in the world, accommodating 4,000 diners and dancers, with a 600,000-gallon moat where gondolas with singing gondoliers floated until showtime. Then he hired famed showman Billy Rose at $1000 a day (a really tidy sum during the Depression) to produce the "Show of Shows." Rose shocked some citizens, and pleased others, by bringing in celebrated fan dancer Sally Rand as one of the headliners.

Expenses eventually killed that theater, but in 1958 the old theater was replaced by the present geodesic dome, one of the first commercial uses of Buckminster Fuller's architectural creation. The 1,800-seat dome theater gained fame as the home of the world's first permanent musical and for years the not-for-profit Casa Mañana concentrated on summer musicals. Musicals still make up most productions, but they are now produced all year long, with the major Broadway-style musicals performed in the Bass Performance Hall and the self-produced musicals here. This theater also occasionally features dramatic works, celebrity concerts, and smaller touring companies and is famed for its Children's Playhouse season (see FAMILY FUN AND KID STUFF, p. 203). The building recently went through a $3.2 million renovation and remodeling of everything from the lobby to the configuration of the stage and theater seating. Free parking in the garage behind the theater.

CIRCLE THEATRE

230 W. 4th (76102) • 817–877–3040 • Admission varies • W • www.circletheatre.com

Located downstairs in the Sanger Building, in the heart of Sundance Square, this intimate, nonprofit theater is arena style, with an open thrust stage and seating for 125. It derives its name from its original location on Bluebonnet Circle near Texas Christian University. Usually offers five or six contemporary plays with professional casts throughout the year, with the emphasis on comedy with a Southwestern connection. Free evening/weekend parking in Sundance Square parking lots.

CLIBURN CONCERTS

Bass Performance Hall (See p. 197) • Tickets: 817-335-9000 • Season usually September–February • W+

Begun in 1976, this annual concert series presents some of the world's finest artists in recital. This is just one of the activities sponsored by the Van Cliburn Foundation (817-738-6536). Another is sponsorship of concerts by past winners of the Van Cliburn International Piano Competition, which it holds every four years. (See ANNUAL EVENTS, p. 213)

COWTOWN OPRY

131 E. Exchange, Suite 100J, in the Livestock Exchange Bldg. in the Stockyards Historic District • 817-366-9675 or 817-281-4969 • Free • www.cowtownopry.org

The Opry musicians perform free shows at 2:00 p.m. most Sundays, on the steps of the Livestock Exchange Building. Programs range from Western swing, to old-time favorites, to singing movie-cowboy songs, all presented by professional musicians joined together to preserve, perform, and promote Texas heritage music.

FORT WORTH CONVENTION CENTER

1111 Houston (76102), just north of I-30 • 817–570–2222 • Admission varies by event • W+

Sure, this huge center hosts lots of conventions and trade shows (some of which are open to the public), but there's a lot more going on in the 13,500-seat arena, ranging from major concerts to the circus to ice hockey and auto shows. Do take a look at the Water Garden Plaza at the South Entrance. Part of the recent $75 million expansion and upgrades to the Center, its large terrazzo floor is designed as a giant rodeo belt buckle. The carpet around and nearby, fabricated in Ireland, when viewed from above, shows a stampede of cattle as a reminder that the Chisholm Trail once passed through the site where the Convention Center now stands.

FORT WORTH DALLAS BALLET

Bass Performance Hall (see p. 197) • 817-212-4280 • Season usually October–April • W+ • www.fwdballet.com

This is not a merger of the Fort Worth and Dallas ballet companies, as the name may imply, but rather an expansion of the performances of the professional Fort Worth Ballet to Dallas to fill in the void left when the Dallas Ballet was dissolved in 1988. This unique organization is a single professional company; however, each city maintains its own support entity to oversee its own season, so each city can claim this ballet as its own. Most Dallas performances are at the Music Hall in Fair Park. In addition to full production seasons locally, the company performs regularly throughout Texas and tours both nationally and internationally.

FORT WORTH OPERA ASSOCIATION

Bass Performance Hall (See p. 197) • 817-731-0200 • Season usually fall and winter • W+ • www.fwopera.org

The oldest continuing opera company in Texas, it presents three or four productions in its fall and winter season. Most company members are local professionals, but well-known artists are frequently brought in for lead roles. Placido Domingo starred in his first major operatic role in America with this company, and Lily Pons delivered her farewell operatic performance with it. In addition, *Travel & Leisure* magazine rated the Bass Performance Hall one of the ten top opera houses in the world. English translations are projected above the stage for foreign operas.

FORT WORTH SYMPHONY ORCHESTRA

Bass Performance Hall (See p. 197) • Tickets: 817-665-6000 • W+ • www.fwsymphony.org

This professional symphony orchestra, founded in 1925, presents more than 200 performances in the average year. Among these are Bass Performance Hall performances of more than 50 Symphonic and Pops Series subscription concerts, performances with the Fort Worth Opera and the Fort Worth Dallas Ballet, and more than a dozen outdoor performances at the Concerts in the Garden summer music festival at the Fort Worth Botanic Garden. It also gives a number of children's concerts. The core of the Symphony Orchestra is the Fort Worth Chamber Orchestra, composed of around three dozen full–time professional musicians recruited from across the United States. In addition to the symphony season, the chamber orchestra puts on concerts throughout the year. It was the first chamber orchestra to tour the People's Republic of China after the cultural revolution (1983). Both orchestras also travel extensively.

FORT WORTH THEATER

4401 Trail Lake (76109) • 817-921-5300 • Admission varies • W • www.fwtheatre.homestead.com

Founded in 1955, this is the city's oldest community theater company. It offers contemporary and classic theater, including a Hispanic series. It's a proving ground for developing and showcasing community talent.

HIP POCKET THEATRE

1620 Las Vegas Trail N. (76108); take exit 57B off Loop 820N and go west approximately 12 miles • 817-246-9775 • W • www.hippocket.org

Over a period of more than 25 years, this theater group has developed a reputation for innovative and original works. It performs a wide range of productions from musicals to science fiction, to comedy and spoofs. Performances are mainly in its theater under the stars in the **Oak Acres Amphitheatre** on Las Vegas Trail North. Adults, $10–$12; seniors, $8–$10; children 12 and under, $6–$8. Bring your own picnic basket and relax on the lawn before the show and stay after for live music.

JUBILEE THEATRE

506 Main (76102), in Sundance Square • 817-338-4411 • Admission varies • W+ • www.jubileetheatre.org

As the North Texas home of the African-American Musical Theatre, this is one of the few theaters in Texas that showcases professional black performers, directors, and choreographers. While most of the productions in the intimate 100-seat theater are musicals, with many composed in–house, it also presents a wide range of drama and comedy. The Jubilee usually puts on six shows during its year-round season, with most performances on weekends. Tickets up to $20. Free evening/weekend parking in Sundance Square parking lots.

WILLIAM EDRINGTON SCOTT THEATRE

3305 W. Lancaster (76107), in the Cultural District • 817-738-1938 • W+ • www.fwculture.com/scott.htm

There's no resident theater company here. This is essentially a public events facility theater for rent. Its tiered–theater seating for 480 has hosted a number of performance companies, including Contemporary Dance of Fort Worth, the Texas Boys Choir, and other production companies, as well as celebrity lecture series and readings. Call for schedule.

STAGE WEST

3055 S. University (76109) at Berry, next to TCU campus • 817-STG-WEST (817-784-9378) • W+ • www.stagewest.org

This professional regional company started in a downtown storefront in 1979. After several upgrading moves, in 1993 it bought and converted the old TCU movie house to its present 200-seat theater. Throughout the year, the company usually offers productions of eight or nine classic or contemporary plays. The theater's Shakespeare Pub serves desserts and beverages before the show and at intermission.

TEXAS BOYS CHOIR

3901 S. Hulen (76109) • 817-924-1482 • www.texasboyschoir.org

Igor Stravinsky once described this as the "best boys choir in the world." Founded in 1946, the Texas Boys Choir has built an international reputation, appeared on all major television networks, recorded 35 records, and won two Grammys. Their repertoire includes many different styles of music, ranging from show tunes to sacred and contemporary. In addition to performing both locally and on national stages, the touring choir has also performed in Europe, Japan, Australia, and Mexico. The boys range in age from 8 to18. Most are from Texas, but some are from other states. Their major at-home concert series is the Great Hall Series, performed at the Fort Worth Academy of Fine Arts (2925 Riverglen). These concerts feature not only the boys performing but also a variety of other musical talent accompanying them.

The boys attend the nearby Fort Worth Academy of Fine Arts. In 2001, that school added two new choirs: the Singing Girls of Texas and the Children's Choir of Texas. The Singing Girls of Texas performs a variety of music ranging from Renaissance to contemporary, sacred to folk. This choir will also tour. Call or check their website for information on local performances.

TEXAS GIRLS CHOIR

4449 Camp Bowie (76107) • 817-732-8161 • W+ • www.texasgirlschoir.org

Not to be outdone by the boys, this choir lays claim not only to being the only girls choir of its kind in the world, but also to being the most traveled choir in the United States. It is internationally known, having performed in more than 42 countries, on national and international television and before royalty, and recorded 90 CDs and tapes. Founded in 1962, with 16 girls, it has now grown to approximately 275 girls ranging in age from 8 to 16. It is divided into five choir levels, the top two being the concert choirs that annually give about 100 local performances. Some of these concerts are given at the choir's headquarters concert hall or recital hall, and others are free concerts at churches, malls, and hospitals; other local concerts are held in performance halls with admission. Call or check their website for information on local performances.

WILL ROGERS AUDITORIUM

Will Rogers Memorial Center, 3401 W. Lancaster (76107), at University in the Cultural District • 817-871-8150 • Admission varies with event • W+ • www.fwculture.com/wrogers.htm

This multipurpose auditorium, in the expansive Will Rogers Memorial Center, has 2,500 seats. In addition to the many equestrian and rodeo events, for which it is most famed, it also hosts plays, performing acts, car shows, and boxing matches. Each year, it is the major performance space for the approximately 800,000 people who attend the two week Southwestern Exposition and Livestock Show. (See ANNUAL EVENTS, p. 212)

FAMILY FUN AND KID STUFF

BURGERS LAKE

1200 Meandering Rd. (76114), off Hwy. 183 (River Oaks Blvd. and Roberts Cut-off Rd.) • 817-737-3414 • Admission • W

This one-acre spring-fed swimming pool resembles a large old-fashioned family swimming hole, with a sand bottom and two sand beaches set in a 27-acre park of giant trees and shady lawns. Open early May through Labor Day, 9:00 a.m. to dark. More than 300 picnic tables, many with grills. Lifeguards. Admission: Adults, $10; children 6 and under free.

CASA MAÑANA PLAYHOUSE

3101 W. Lancaster (76107), at University, at east end of Cultural District • 817-332-CASA (332-2272) • Admission varies • W+ • www.casamanana.org

The Playhouse is a professional children's theater troupe that has been performing children's plays for more than forty years. They usually put on a play a month from October through May, running two or three weekends. The troupe also has a theatrical training school for children from preschool to youths.

COWTOWN CATTLEPEN MAZE

145 E. Exchange (76106) in the Stockyards across from Stockyards Station • 817-624-6666 • Open daily, 10 to dusk • Adults, $4.25; children 5–12, $3.25; reruns, $2.25 • W • www.cowtowncattlepenmaze.com

Finding your way through this wooden maze, which resembles old cattle pens with high sides, is a challenge not only for kids but also for adults who are kids at heart. Prizes for fast times. The time record for getting to all the checkpoints in the labyrinth is about five minutes. (The longest time is well over an hour.) They change the pathways about once a month. You can watch the maze-goers, or preview the maze, for free from a second-story observation platform.

FORT WORTH HERD

E. Exchange, in the Stockyards • Daily, 11:30 a.m. and 4 p.m. (depending on weather), except major holidays • 817-336-HERD (336-4373) • Free • ww.fortworthherd.com

It's just a short cattle drive, but they are real longhorn cattle and real cowboys. Usually 10 to 15 longhorns participate, and the cowpunchers wear turn-of-the-century outfits and ride with historic period saddles and equipment. The longhorns are not pets or show animals, so the drive sometimes depends on their disposition. The animals are cleaned up but not tame, and they weigh up to a ton, with horn spans up to six feet. The drive starts at the cattle holding pens behind the Livestock Exchange Building, goes down Exchange Avenue, and winds up back at the holding pens. You can get a good view from anywhere between Stockyards Station and the Livestock Exchange Building. Between drives, you can view the longhorns from the catwalk above the holding pens. If seeing the drive is high on your list, best to call to make sure it's on.

FORT WORTH ZOO

1989 Colonial Pkwy. (76110), off University, one mile south of I-30, in the Cultural District • 817-759-7555 • Open every day, most days

10–5; weekend and holiday hours changed seasonally (call) • Adults, $9; seniors, $5.50; children 3–12, $6.50; under 3 free. Half-price admission on Wednesdays • Parking, $5 • W+ • www.fortworthzoo.com

Frequently listed among the top zoos in America, this is the home of one of the largest animal collections in the Western Hemisphere—nearly 5,000 native and exotic animals. The zoo is renowned for creating natural habitats for the animals as if they were in the wild. At many of the exhibits, visitors are separated from the animals only by a river or a waterfall and are often face-to-face with the animals through large viewing windows. The inhabitants include lowland gorillas, cheetahs, bears, Komodo dragons, colorful birds as well as birds of prey, a world-famous reptile collection, and an insect exhibit. The $40 million, 8-acre Texas Wild exhibit lets you walk through the state's six geographical areas and see just about everything that walks, creeps, flies, or swims in each area. It includes more than 200 native Texas animals plus a recreation of an 1890s pioneer Texas town. The oldest continuous zoo site in Texas (established in 1909), it draws well over a million visitors a year.

In late spring, the annual "Zoo Babies" event highlights all the newborn at the Zoo, which, considering the zoo's vast numbers of different species, may include everything from jaguar and lion cubs to baby rhinos, giraffes, and koalas.

One of its most popular special events for children is "Boo at the Zoo," which runs for a week before Halloween. There's also an overnight stay program available for ages six and older (about $30; call 817-871-7055).

Visitors can rent strollers and motorized carts and a limited number of complimentary wheelchairs are available. In addition to the food concessions, there are shaded outdoor picnic tables. What is reportedly the world's longest miniature train ride connects Trinity Park and Forest Park, where the Zoo is located (see below).

OLD WEST AMUSEMENT PARK

E. Exchange, in the Stockyards near Stockyards Visitors Information Center • W • 817-625-9715

Most of the rides here are Western-themed, like the smaller of two Ferris wheels in which the little kids ride in a replica of a cowboy boot, and a pony-cart ride. Admission for each ride.

PAWNEE BILL'S WILD WEST SHOW

Cowtown Coliseum, 121 E. Exchange, in the Stockyards • 817-625-1025 or 1-888-COWTOWN (269-8696) • Adults, $7.50; seniors, $6; children, $4 • W variable • www.cowtowncoliseum.com/pawneebillshow.asp

Back in the early 1900s, when Pawnee Bill toured the country with one of the largest Wild West shows in existence, one of his stops was the Cowtown Coliseum. Now, every Saturday and Sunday afternoon during the summer, this one-hour family show turns the Coliseum back in time for a historical reenactment of that famous show. Today's show is based on actual events and stunts from the original, with expert ropers and riders, trick shooters, a bull-whip artist, longhorns, buffalo, and old-time Western music. Performance usually also over Thanksgiving and New Year's weekends.

THE STOCKYARDS

East and West Exchange (See NEIGHBORHOODS, p. 174–76)

Items in the Stockyards of special interest to families are the Tarantula Train, Stockyards Station at the east end of Exchange, the small Old West Amusement Park near the Visitor Center, the Texas Cowboy Hall of Fame, the Cowtown Cattlepen Maze, the Fort Worth Herd, and the Rodeo and Pawnee Bill's Wild West Show in the Cowtown Coliseum. Even Billy Bob's Texas is open to families during the day. (See separate listing for each of these.) Check with the Stockyards Visitors Information Center for schedules and prices.

TRAIN RIDE IN THE PARKS

2100 Colonial Pkwy., in Forest Park (76110) • 817-475-1233 or 817-336-3328 • Tuesday–Sunday, late May to Labor Day; closed Monday • Children 12 and under and seniors, $2.50; adults and youths, $3; children 1 and under free

Billed as one the world's longest miniature train rides, the two ornate scaled-down trains carry passengers on a 5-mile round trip from the Forest Park Depot to Trinity Park Duck Pond and back. Weekdays, the train runs on the hour; Saturday, Sunday, and holidays, it runs every 45 minutes. Tuesday–Friday, 11:00 a.m–5:00 p.m.; Saturday–Sunday, 11:00 a.m.–6:00 p.m. Off-season, it operates 11:00 a.m.–5:00 p.m. Saturday–Sunday and holidays only.

TARANTULA STEAM TRAIN—FORT WORTH EXCURSION

Depot location: 140 E. Exchange, in the Stockyards • 817-625-Rail (625-7245) or 800-952-5717 • Fort Worth Roundtrip Excursion: Adults, $10; seniors, $9; children 3–12, $6 • W but call ahead • www.tarantulatrain.com

The main Tarantula schedule is for a round trip from the city of Grapevine to Stockyards Station in the Stockyards. (For this excursion, see GRAPEVINE, p. 259) But between the time it arrives in the Stockyards in the late morning and its departure for Grapevine in late afternoon, the train makes a one-hour round trip on what's called the Trinity River Run between the Stockyards and the old Eighth Avenue switching yards in Fort Worth. Even if you don't ride the train, it's fun for the kids to just to watch its arrival and departure, and the locomotive turning around on the turntable.

Depending on the day and maintenance requirements, the Tarantula's locomotive may be either a restored 1896 steam or a diesel. The passenger coaches are usually restored vintage cars equipped with ceiling fans, but not air-conditioned. The touring coaches are open-sided (with railings for passenger safety). Seating is on a first come, first served basis. Snacks, soft drinks, wine, and beer are available on board. The coaches are heated in winter.

Why "Tarantula"? The name goes back to a map published in 1870 that depicted a vision of Fort Worth newspaper editor B. B. Paddock, who saw Fort Worth at the center of nine radially extending rail lines. Some laughed at the map, saying the map lines resembled a hairy-legged tarantula and the railroad center just a dream. But by the 1890s the railroads had laid the nine legs centered on Fort Worth. So, when Fort Worth businessman William Davis came up with his modern vision of an excursion steam train, he named it after Paddock's vision.

SPORTS

AUTO RACING

TEXAS MOTOR SPEEDWAY

Approximately 20 miles north of downtown at Hwy. 114 exit off I-35W (P.O. Box 500, 76101-2500) • 817-215-8500 • Admission varies by event and seating • W+ • www.texasmotorspeedway.com

One of America's largest sports and entertainment facilities, it is also the only speedway in the country to host every form of American automobile racing. The 1.5-mile oval track is designed to accommodate stock car, truck, and open-wheel racing. Each year, for example, the speedway hosts the NASCAR Winston Cup, Busch Grand National and Craftsman Truck Series, and the Indy Racing League. There is also a dirt track that hosts sprint car and Monster Truck events, and the Lil' Texas Motor Speedway, a 1/5-mile banked asphalt oval for Legends Car and Bandolero Racing.

But it's not just racing. With a seating capacity of 154,861 and an infield area with a capacity of approximately 53,000, the Texas Motor Speedway can easily host over 200,000 guests for any kind of single event. As a result, it is used almost every day of the year for everything from racing to auto shows and celebrity concerts to TV and movie production.

There's more than 600 acres of parking, so finding a spot isn't a problem. But with more than 200,000 people and up to a 100,000 vehicles attending some events, getting to and getting out of the speedway can be a slow process, so give yourself plenty of time and make sure you have plenty of gas in your vehicle. Tram service is available from remote parking areas. And for RVs and other campers, there are 8,500 spaces for rent.

Speedway tours are available year round. They include a stop in race control on the luxury suite level, a high-level bird's-eye view of the whole complex, a visit to pit road, and laps of the speedway in a tour van. Adults, $6; seniors and youths, $4. (817-215-8565 or toll-free 1-888–816–TMS1 [888-816-8671])

You can purchase pit passes for selected events by calling the ticket office at 817-215-8500. Food concessions and gift shop.

RACE DRIVING SCHOOLS

Texas Motor Speedway • Information, 817-215-8500

There are several different types of driving programs you can choose from, ranging from one to four days. Some simply offer the basic training needed and the experience of driving at high speed on one or more of the tracks. The longer session Road Course schools teach you the fundamentals of becoming a competitive driver.

BASEBALL

FORT WORTH CATS

P.O. Box 4411 (76164) or LaGrave Field, 301 NE 6th (76106) • 817-266-2287 • W variable • www.fwcats.com

While fans are getting more and more irritated with major league baseball and its monster parks, the minor league game in small, fan-friendly parks is still fun. And that includes Fort Worth's minor-league club, the Cats, who play in LaGrave Field. The Cats are in the Central Independent Baseball League that includes teams from Texas, Louisiana, and Missouri. The ballpark is a modern rebirth of an older stadium that stood on this spot. With only 4,100 seats, it offers a close-to-the-action view for all fans. And to please the fans even more, the concessions include satellite kitchens of a couple of popular Fort Worth restaurants, and the top ticket price is only around $10.

COLLEGE SPORTS

(See COLLEGES AND UNIVERSITIES, p. 195–97)

EQUESTRIAN

BENBROOK STABLES

10001 US 377 South • 817-249-1001 • Tuesday–Sunday, 11–5

Hour-long trail rides and stable/arena rides are offered for about $20 per hour per horse. Children must be at least 9 years old for trail rides.

STOCKYARDS STATION LIVERY

130 E. Exchange in the Stockyards • 817-624-3446 • Daily, 9–4

Trail rides for one hour to half day, $22 for first hour, $15 for each additional hour. Children must be at least 8 years old for trail rides. Arena rides, $10/hour.

WILL ROGERS EQUESTRIAN CENTER

One Amon Carter Square (76107), in Will Rogers Memorial Center in the Cultural District • 817-871-8150 • Admission varies • W+ • ww.fwculture.com/equinectr.htm

This is one of the nation's premier equestrian centers. The site hosts dozens of horse shows each year, ranging from the annual Miniature Horse Show (there are 200 breeders and 4,000 miniature horses registered in Texas) to the National Cutting Horse Association Futurity with a $1 million purse and celebrity contestants. The Center includes a 1,900-seat arena and a 640-seat sale arena and 843 permanent stalls in one building and a 1,100-seat arena and space for 650 cattle or 260 horses in another building. The total number of stalls can be increased to 2,200 for a major event like the Southwestern Exposition and Livestock Show.

GOLF

PUBLIC COURSES

CARSWELL GOLF COURSE • 6520 White Settlement (76114) • 817-738-8402 • 18 holes.

CASINO BEACH ACADEMY • 7464 Jacksboro Hwy. (76135) • 817-237-3695 • 9 holes.

MEADOWBROOK MUNICIPAL GOLF COURSE • 1815 Jensen Road (76112) • 817-457-4616 • 18 holes.

PECAN VALLEY MUNICIPAL GOLF COURSE • 6400 Pecan Valley Dr. (P.O. Box 26632, 76126) • 817-249-1845 • 36 holes.

ROCKWOOD GOLF COURSE • 1851 Jacksboro Hwy. (76114) • 817-624-1771 • 27 holes.

ROCKWOOD PAR 3 GOLF COURSE • 1524 Rockwood Park (76114) • 817-824-8311 • 9-hole par 3.

SYCAMORE CREEK GOLF COURSE • 401 Martin Luther King Hwy. (76104) • 817-535-7241 • 9 holes.

TIMBER-VIEW GOLF CLUB • 4508 East Enon (76140) • 817-478-3601 • 18 holes.

Z. BOAZ GOLF COURSE • 3240 Lackland Road (76116) • 817-738-6287 • 18 holes.

ICE HOCKEY

FORT WORTH BRAHMAS

Office: 1314 Lake, Suite 200 (76102) • 817-336-4423 • www.brahmas.com

The Brahmas play in the 17-team Central Hockey League, which includes teams from Texas and six surrounding states, plus Indiana and Tennessee. Home games are normally played in the Fort Worth Convention Center, with occasional special events games at the Will Rogers Memorial Coliseum. Ticket prices range from about $10 to $25.

RODEO

STOCKYARDS CHAMPIONSHIP RODEO

Cowtown Coliseum, 121 E. Exchange (76106), in the Stockyards • 817-625-1025 • Tickets $9–$12 • W+ • www.cowtowncoliseum.com

This mission-style coliseum was built in just 88 days for the 1908 Fort Worth Feeders and Breeders Show. In 1918 it was the site of the first indoor rodeo. The modernized 2300-seat arena now features contestants from both the Professional Rodeo Cowboys Association and the Women's Professional Rodeo Association. The rodeos are held most weekends year-round. (Call or check website.) Events include bareback bronc riding, calf roping, breakaway roping, team roping, barrel racing, and bull riding. Plus a calf and mutton scramble for the kids.

SOUTHWESTERN EXPOSITION AND LIVESTOCK SHOW AND RODEO

(See ANNUAL EVENTS, p. 212)

TENNIS

FRIEDMAN TENNIS CENTER

3609 Bellaire N. (76109) on Texas Christian University Campus • 817-257-7960

All 22 lighted outdoor courts are recessed into the ground for better wind protection. It also has a five-court indoor tennis center. Covered courts, $22 for 1½ hours of play anytime. Outdoor courts $3–$3.50 per person for 1½ hours.

OTHER POINTS OF INTEREST

THE CLIBURN ORGAN

Broadway Baptist Church, 305 W. Broadway (76104) • 817-336-7464, ext. 8211 • W

The largest organ in the state of Texas, it is also the largest organ of French aesthetics in the world, reflecting the basic design concept of the eighteenth- and nineteenth-century French organ builders. The $2.5 million organ is officially named the Rildia Bee O'Bryan Cliburn Organ, in memory of the mother and principal teacher of famed pianist Van Cliburn, who is a member of the church. It was designed for use in both church and concert, which means it can produce a variety of sounds to fulfill a symphonic breadth of color and form. It has 10,615 pipes, the largest being 37 feet long with a diameter of 17-1/8 inches; the smallest pipe is eight inches long with a "speaking length" of 5/16 inch. If the pipes were stretched end to end they would extend approximately five miles. There is no set schedule for organ performances. Call for information.

FORT WORTH WATER GARDENS

1502 Commerce, between Houston and Commerce, downtown by the Convention Center • 817-871-8700 (Parks and Community Services Dept.) • Free • W

This $7 million, 4.3-acre park of terraced concrete and cascading water is spread over 4½ blocks of downtown adjoining the Convention Center. Completed in 1974, it was designed by the prominent architects John Burgee and Phillip Johnson, who also designed the Amon Carter Museum. The Gardens are a secluded oasis depicting a miniature mountain scene enhanced with rivers, waterfalls, and pools, except the mountains rise only a little above street level while the terraced pools stair-step down 40 feet. Each minute, 19,000 gallons of water flow, fall, sparkle, gurgle, spray and then are recirculated through ten miles of piping and the five major water features to do it all again. The biggest feature is the Active Water Pool, in which 10,500 gallons of water per minute cascade from the upper edge, down multiple tiers and into a pool surrounded by stepping stones. If you're a little adventurous, you can walk the table-sized stepping stones down into the center. And these are not barren mountains, they are set among 500 species of plants and trees, and the textured ground cover blends 32,000 plants of azaleas, junipers, Indian hawthorn, and English ivy. At night, the Water Gardens are illuminated with special lighting that simulates moonlight.

The Water Gardens are now connected to the Fort Worth Convention Center by a 55,000 square feet Events Plaza, which is designed to be a unique outdoor multi-use facility as well as the major ceremonial entrance to the Convention Center's Grand Ballroom. On-street or paid lot parking nearby.

MILLER MARKETPLACE AND BREW KETTLE MUSEUM

7001 S. Freeway (I-35W) on east side access road, take Sycamore School Rd. exit • 817-568-BEER (568-2337) • Memorial Day–Labor Day: Monday–Saturday, 10:30–5:30. Rest of year: Tuesday–Saturday, 11:30–5:30. Call for holiday hours • Free • W+

With an audiotape to guide you, this small museum will give you a condensed version of 5,000 years of brewing history as well as the more recent history of the growth of the Miller Brewing Company. One of the sights is a dome, made of an actual brew-kettle, that measures 22 feet in diameter and weighs two tons. Visitors of drinking age can end up the tour at the Pub and open-air courtyard for a free sample. The brewery next door produces about 8 million barrels of beer annually. Logo gift shop.

WILL ROGERS MEMORIAL CENTER

3401 W. Lancaster at University, in the Cultural District •
817-871-8150 • W+ but not all areas •
www.fwculture.com/wrogers.htm

This is an 85-acre multipurpose complex with 45 acres under roof. It consists of the Auditorium, Coliseum, Memorial Tower, the Equestrian Center, and large animal barns and stalls. The Center provides much of the Old West flavor to the Cultural District by hosting everything from the Southwestern Exposition and Livestock Show and equestrian events to trade shows and a regular Saturday and Sunday Flea Market. (For details, see listings in other appropriate sections.)

OFFBEAT

BOTANICAL RESEARCH INSTITUTE OF TEXAS

509 Pecan (In warehouse area; call for directions) • 817-332-4441 •
Monday–Friday, 9–5 (by appointment) • Free • W • www.brit.org

In a building tucked among several warehouses near downtown is a collection of hundreds of thousands of preserved samples of plants from around the world, collected over three centuries. While mainly for botanists, ecologists, and other scholars, the collection and the Institute's huge library of more than 70,000 volumes of botanical literature are open to the public by appointment and could be a gold mine for anyone interested in herbal medicine and the part plants play in our lives. The BRIT staff worked with the Fort Worth Herb Society on the living illustration of this at the Pioneer Herb Garden, which is part of the Fort Worth Log Cabin Village. Periodic lectures and workshops are also open to the public, some free, some for a small fee. And the BRIT usually offers a free noontime lecture on basic botany topics on the first Wednesday of each month.

BANK ONE TOWER—REMINDER OF A TORNADO'S POWER

500 Throckmorton

A 35-story eyesore in the heart of downtown, this gutted high-rise building is a grim reminder of the awesome power of nature versus man.

The skyscraper hulk is the result of a killer tornado that brought death and destruction as it cut a two-mile swath through Fort Worth on March 28, 2000. Fortunately, Fort Worth has recovered and continues to grow and prosper. Perhaps by the time you read this, the tower will have been demolished, but, if not, you can see what a tornado can do to even the proudest of man's structures.

ANNUAL EVENTS

JANUARY–FEBRUARY

SOUTHWESTERN EXPOSITION AND LIVESTOCK SHOW AND RODEO • 817-877-2400 • www.fwssr.com • Started in 1896, the nation's oldest livestock show moved to the Will Rogers Memorial Center in 1944, with Will Rogers as the first entertainer to appear at the rodeo. The biggest annual event in the city, it draws more than 800,000 visitors. Highlights include days and days of judging close to 20,000 head of livestock that range from pigeons and rabbits to bulls and horses from the industry's top herds, as well as livestock auctions, commercial exhibits, a six-acre carnival midway, and a petting zoo for the kids, plus the nation's top cowboys and cowgirls competing and name entertainers performing at the nightly rodeo.

APRIL

MAIN STREET FORT WORTH ART FESTIVAL • 817-336-2787 • www.festivalsandevents.org • For four days, nine blocks of brick-paved Main Street is blocked off to become the site of the Southwest's largest outdoor arts festival with more than 200 participating artists. Main Street is rated the top art show in Texas and among the top 20 in America by the Harris List, the art industry's standard ranking directory. Also lots of live entertainment and food.

APRIL–MAY

TEXAS FRONTIER FORTS MUSTER • 817-498-5150 • www.cross-timbers.org • Representatives come from many of the 15 forts in Texas to participate in the army camp setup for the weekend in the Stockyards; the camp is manned by soldier reenactors in historic costumes carrying century-old weapons. Visitors get to interact with both the soldiers and their wives at parades, musket and cannon drills, old-time cavalry training, singing, dancing, and other events that would take place at the forts in the past. Included in the event is a Comanche encampment and the annual Comanche Pow Wow.

MAY

MAYFEST • 817-332-1055 • At least 350,000 visitors come to Trinity Park for Fort Worth's own annual family festival rite of spring. It features sports, arts and crafts, fireworks, and a variety of entertainment that ranges from the Fort Worth Symphony Orchestra to popular local and regional bands. Children's area and activities. Proceeds go to local charities.

BANK OF AMERICA COLONIAL GOLF TOURNAMENT • 817-927-4280 • More than 100 of the nation's top golfers on the PGA tour compete in this nationally televised tournament for a piece of a several-million-dollar purse. One of four PGA tour invitation-only tournaments, it was first held at the Colonial Country Club in 1946, making it the oldest event on the PGA tour still held at the original site.

MAY–JUNE EVERY FOURTH YEAR

VAN CLIBURN INTERNATIONAL PIANO COMPETITION • 817-738-6536 • www.cliburn.org • Technically, since it takes place only every four years, this is not an Annual Event; however, it earns a listing here because it is now considered one of the most important music competitions in the world. The Van Cliburn Foundation organizes this competition, which started in 1962 and has been held every four years since, to seek out world-class concert pianists. Pianists from all over the world audition to earn the chance to be in the competition and earn the title of "one of the world's best." The next competition will be held in 2005.

JUNE–JULY

CONCERTS IN THE GARDEN • 817-665-6000 • www.fwsymphony .org • There's a little bit of everything on the menu of this annual summer music festival, which is held most weekends in the Fort Worth Botanic Gardens. Although most of the concerts are by the Fort Worth Symphony Orchestra, they also have special nights for country and western, rock, and other styles. Plus fireworks every night.

JULY

GRAN FIESTA de FORT WORTH • 214-855-1881 • www.mei festivals.com • Main Street is transformed for this weekend that celebrates the Hispanic influence on Texas music, art, food, and culture. Latin bands, singers, and dancers. Arts and crafts. Children activities, games, and cultural workshops. And, of course, plenty of gorditas, tacos, tamales, fajitas, and nachos.

OCTOBER

FORT WORTH INTERNATIONAL AIR SHOW • 817-870-1515 • www.allianceairshow.com • Fort Worth's place in aviation history is celebrated with heart-stopping displays of aerial aerobatics, stunt flying, wing-walking, and parachute team drops at the Alliance Airport. On the ground there are displays of all types of military and civilian aircraft, as well as exhibits recounting the history of aviation.

RED STEAGALL COWBOY GATHERING & WESTERN SWING FESTIVAL • 817-625-1025 • www.theredsteagallcowboygathering.com • This three-day gathering usually attracts about 35,000 to celebrate the cowboy way of life in its reality and its myth. Activities include ranch rodeos, in which real cowboys compete in everyday cowboy skills such as branding, bronc riding, sorting, and team roping. Also recitations of cowboy poetry (Red is the poet laureate of Texas, as well as a musician), events for kids, and musical entertainment that emphasizes Western swing at several locations throughout the Stockyards.

NOVEMBER–DECEMBER

NATIONAL CUTTING HORSE WORLD CHAMPIONSHIP FUTURITY • 817-244-6188 • www.nchacutting.com • Cutting is a traditional cowboy job in which horse and rider separate a particular cow from a herd. While still practiced on working ranches, cutting has also become a national sport, with riders no longer just cowboys but people from all walks of life, including a number of celebrities. The horse is the real star here, working against the clock to score points with controlled moves to cut two designated cows from a herd of about 45. This Futurity is considered the premier event of the National Cutting Horse Association's more than 1,400 NCHA-approved shows held nationwide annually. It's not unusual for well over a thousand entries to sign up for this event to compete for a piece of the $3 million purse.

SHOPPING

ANTIQUE SHOPS

The antique shops scattered throughout the city include several that gather together a number of dealers under one roof. Two of these collections of antique and collectible dealers are **Stockyards Antiques** and **The Antique Colony**. Stockyards Antiques is in a converted 1890s hotel at 1332 N. Main, at Northside (812-624-2311), where the 30,000 sq.-foot building houses 125 shops. There are 100 shops in The Antique Colony at 7200 Camp Bowie, at the intersection with Hwy. 183 and Southwest

Blvd. (817-731-7252). Another group of antique shops is the **Mont-gomery Street Antique Mall and Secret Café** at 200 Montgomery at I-30 (817-735-9685).

HULEN MALL

4800 S. Hulen (76132), at Loop 820 (I-20) • 817-294-1200 • W+ • www.hulenmall.com

Dillard's, Foley's, and Sears anchor more than 125 specialty shops, mostly national chain stores, in this two-level mall. Outside parking for more than 3,500 cars and garage parking for another 1,000. Cafeteria and a food court.

RIDGMAR MALL

2060 Green Oaks (76116), on I-30 and Hwy. 183 • 817-731-0856 • W variable

The major stores in this two-level mall are Dillard's, Foley's, Neiman Marcus, JCPenney, and Sears. They anchor more than 130 other spe-cialty stores (mostly representatives of national chains), a cafeteria, and fast-food outlets, plus the famed Zodiac restaurant at Neiman Marcus.

STOCKYARDS STATION

130 E. Exchange (76106) • 817-625-9715 or Metro 972-988-6877 • W variable • www.stockyardsstation.com

The Stockyards Station is truly a railway station, for the Tarantula Train, so the tracks run down the middle of the huge covered shed with the shops on both sides. As you might expect, many of the shops here are Western-oriented. You'll find a selection of everything from West-ern art to Western apparel, ranging from boots, jeans, and hats to custom belts and buckles. And for something a little bit different, there's the Stockyards Wedding Chapel at # 139 (817-624-1570), where you have the choice of a traditional wedding or one in historical costumes that you can choose at the Old Tyme Mercantile a few steps away at #132.

WESTERN WEAR

This is "Where the West Begins," and to be in the West you have to wear Western, or at least something that pays tribute to both the cowboy heritage and the cowboy's fine sense of utilitarian wear—like hats that keep off the sun and rain, long-wearing jeans, or heeled boots that help the rider keep his seat. Among the more popular of the many Western wear stores in the city are Maverick's (100 E. Exchange, 817-626-1129), Luskey's Western Wear, 101 N. Houston at Weatherford, downtown (817-335-5833); Leddy's Boot & Saddlery, 2455 N. Main (817-624-3149), and Ryon's Saddle and Ranch, 2601 N. Main (817-625-2391).

A SAMPLING OF FORT WORTH RESTAURANTS

Dinner for one, excluding drinks, tip, and tax: $ = up to $16, $$ = $16–$30, $$$ = $31–$50, $$$$ = over $50. It is strongly suggested that you make a reservation in those restaurants that take them, especially on weekends and holidays.

ANGELUNA ($$–$$$$)

214 E. 4th (76102) • 817-334-0080 • Lunch and dinner, seven days • Cr. • W+ • www.angelunabasshall.com

Angels watch over you at this restaurant. The painted angels that look down from the ceiling are backed up by the huge 48–foot angels across the street on the façade of the Bass Performance Hall. The One World Global fusion menu blends culinary influences from the South, Caribbean, Asia, and Europe into entrées such as sake pork tenderloin with *wasabi* mashed potatoes and tempura asparagus, and wood-grilled rib eye with truffle potato croquettes and balsamic reduction. Also designer pizzas such as prosciutto-asparagus and crushed olive–baby shrimp. Reservations recommended, especially when there's anything going on at the Bass Performance Hall. Valet parking.

ANGELO'S BAR–B–QUE ($)

2533 White Settlement Rd. (76107) • 817-332-0357 • Lunch and dinner, Monday–Saturday. Closed Sunday and major holidays • No cr. • W+

Angelo's started serving smoked brisket of beef and pork ribs in 1958 and since then has earned a reputation that not only keeps bringing in customers, but has virtually turned it into a shrine for barbecue lovers. And now you can get smoked chicken, too. Everything served with Angelo's traditional tangy sauce, with your choice of pinto beans, potato salad, or slaw, plus pickle, onion, and bread. If you can't decide among the choices on the simple list of plate dinners, try a combo plate of any two meats. Beer and wine.

BISTRO LOUISE ($$–$$$)

2900 S. Hulen, Suite 40, in Stonegate Commons (76109) • 817–922–9244 • Lunch and dinner, Monday–Saturday. Closed Sunday • Cr. • W+ • www.bistrolouisetexas.com

The Louise in the name is owner/executive chef Louise Lamensdorf, who brings to her restaurant years of apprenticeship and training under master chefs in France, England, Spain, Italy, and the Cordon Bleu in New York City. The result is a bistro that consistently gathers top ratings among Fort Worth restaurants. The sunny decor might be described as French comfortable, and the menu combines American cuisine with Old World traditions. In addition to entrées that include tea-smoked duck, potato crusted salmon, and medallions of fallow deer, she offers "Little Suppers" such as seafood paella Barcelona style and soft shell crab amandine. And to top it off you can order an assortment of the bistro's desserts on a tasting plate. Bar.

THE BUFFET AT THE KIMBELL ($)

3333 Camp Bowie, in the Kimbell Art Museum in the Cultural District • 817-332-8451 • Lunch, Tuesday–Sunday; light dinner buffet, Friday, 5:30–7:30. Closed Monday • Cr. • W+ • www.kimbellart.org

The cafeteria-style restaurant setting is pleasant, but the key point is that you are just steps away from the most elegant surroundings of the art treasures in this museum. The menu features light lunch fare with a variety of choices of inventive gourmet sandwiches, quiche, soups, salads, and simple but sweet desserts. Live jazz music at the Friday evening dinner. Beer and wine. And if you want to try the menu at home, *The Kimbell Cookbook* is available in the Museum Shop. Museum parking.

CAFÉ ASHTON ($$$–$$$$)

610 Main, in Ashton Hotel (76102), just south of Sundance Square • 817-332-0100 • Breakfast available; lunch and dinner seven days • Cr. • W+ • www.theashtonhotel.com

The 60-seat restaurant and bar, just off the hotel lobby, is as "boutique" as the 39-room hotel. The menu is basically New American with dishes like pan-seared fillet of Chilean sea bass with fresh crab, blackened fillet of pork, caramelized duck breast, roasted beef tenderloin, and seared loin of venison. Since it is a hotel restaurant, all three meals are available daily; however, note that the Sunday fare is normally lighter than the rest of the week. Dress is business casual. Valet parking.

CAFÉ ASPEN RESTAURANT AND BAR ($$)

6103 Camp Bowie, just west of Bryant Irvin Rd. (76116) • 817-738-0838 • Lunch, Monday–Friday; dinner, Monday–Saturday. Closed Sunday • Cr. • W+

The creative eclectic menu here is a major draw, with offerings that include imaginative salads, homemade soups, a club sandwich made with smoked salmon, and dinner selections like walnut-crusted chicken breast, pumpkin seed–crusted catfish, chef's giant grilled vegetable plate, and the signature dish of chicken fried lobster. Immensely popular homemade desserts include bread pudding and bourbon buttermilk fudge cake. Occasional live music. Bar.

CARSHON'S DELICATESSEN ($)

3133 Cleburne (76110) near W. Berry • 817-923-1907 • Breakfast and lunch, Monday–Saturday, 9–3. Closed Sunday and major holidays • No cr. • W+

More then three-quarters of a century after it was started as a kosher meat market in another location in 1928, Carshon's is now famed as kosher-style deli that offers everything you'd expect in a deli, from chicken soup to a huge selection of old-fashioned two-hander sandwiches piled high with pastrami, roast beef, corned beef, or turkey, and plate lunches. Beer and wine.

CATTLEMEN'S FORT WORTH STEAK HOUSE® ($–$$$)

2458 N. Main (76106), in the Stockyards, just north of Exchange • 817-624-3945 or Metro 214-429-8614 • Lunch and dinner, seven days • Cr. • W but call ahead • www.cattlemenssteakhouse.com

Founded in 1947, this restaurant has earned a place among the traditions of the Stockyards. As the name says, the big draw is the corn-fed, aged steaks, which are charcoal broiled and come in all sizes from an 8-oz. filet to a 24-oz. porterhouse. Other choices include seafood, chicken, lamb fries ("mountain oysters"), and barbecued ribs. Children's menu. Atmosphere is 1950s cowboy, including smoking in the dining room. Bar. Parking lot, but it fills quickly. Frozen steaks can be ordered by the box on the restaurant's website for home delivery.

DEL FRISCO'S DOUBLE EAGLE STEAK HOUSE ($$$–$$$$)

812 Main (76102) • 817-877-3999 • Dinner, Monday–Saturday. Closed Sunday • Cr. • W but call ahead

If you're an aficionado of full-size steaks you can almost cut with a fork, this luxurious and expensive downtown representative of a famed chain of steak houses will be the place you're looking for. The décor of dark woods, plush seating, mirrors, and chandeliers, a cigar lounge, and exemplary service all combine to provide a club-like setting. The menu features mostly fresh cuts of prime beef, with most cuts in the $25–$30 bracket. There is also a small selection of veal and seafood entrées. Vegetable sides are as well prepared as the meat, but all are added on at à la carte prices. Bar.

EDELWEISS RESTAURANT ($$–$$$)

3801-A Southwest Blvd. (76116), on the Old Weatherford traffic circle • 817-738-5934 • Dinner, Tuesday–Saturday. Closed Sunday–Monday • Cr. • W

The décor in this 350-seat restaurant is that of a German beer hall, and the atmosphere varies so you can choose between cozy corners with candlelight to being just a step or two short of an Oktoberfest party. An owner/chef from Germany means true German food with substantial portions of traditional dishes like sauerbraten, sausages, *rouladan*, and a variety of schnitzels. If it all looks too tempting to make a choice, try the combination plate. And if you want to be sure you can get up after the meal, try the "Smaller Portions" section on the menu. Also steaks and seafood. Band plays everything from polkas to waltzes to the chicken dance for dancing nightly. Children's menu. Bar. Same location for more than 35 years.

ESCARGOT ($$$–$$$$)

3427 W. 7th, just west of University, in the Cultural District • 817-336-3090 • Dinner, Tuesday–Saturday. Closed Sunday–Monday • Cr. • W+

Although most of his training was in other local French restaurants, it's still refreshing to know that owner/chef Frederic Angevin is actually from the Burgundy region in France. Naturally, his menu includes several namesake dishes as appetizers, like *escargot à la bourguignonne* and *escargot au persil*. Among the uncomplicated classic French entrées on the menu are duck breast medallions, river trout, and thyme-marinated lamb chops. If you want to sample, try the *prix fixe* tasting menu. The décor is cozy French country right down to the white lace curtains, and, of course, the wine list leans heavily toward French imports. Bar.

JOE T. GARCIA'S MEXICAN DISHES ($–$$)

2201 N. Commerce (76106), near the Stockyards • 817-626-4356 • Lunch and dinner, seven days. Closed some major holidays • No cr. • W+

In 1935 Joe T. Garcia opened part of his home as a Mexican restaurant with just 16 seats. Customers walked through the kitchen to get to the dining room and got beer from the family refrigerator. Now, the family still operates the restaurant, but over the years they've expanded the house until it fills about half a city block, making up what is probably the best known Tex-Mex restaurant in the city. It has seating for more than a thousand and serves around 3,000 dinners in the average night. If the weather's nice, the flower-laden garden patio is the best place to be. Enchiladas, tacos, fajitas, chiles rellenos—all the standard Tex-Mex dishes are on the menu. Dinners served family style with the usual accompaniments of rice, beans, chips, and hot sauce. Strolling mariachis enhance the atmosphere on weekends. Bar. No reservations. For what localites tout as the best place to get a Tex-Mex breakfast, there's Joe T. Garcia's **Esperanza's Mexican Bakery** around the corner from the restaurant at 2140 North Main and another bakery at 1109 Hemphill. Both serve breakfast and lunch and are open from about 6:30 or 7:00 a.m. to early evening.

HEDARY'S LEBANESE RESTAURANT ($$)

3308 Fairfield (76116), in the 6323 Shopping Center of Camp Bowie Blvd. • Dinner, Tuesday–Sunday and Sunday brunch. Closed Mondays • Cr. • W • www.hedarys.com

You've heard of tabbouleh and falafel and hummus, but you're not sure exactly what they are, to say nothing of the traditional Lebanese dishes called *sujak* or *shish tawuk*. Not to worry, Hedary's menu explains every dish in detail so you can order shish tawuk with competence, knowing it's lightly seasoned grilled chicken on skewers with bell peppers, tomatoes, and onions served with rice; and an order of sujak will be a generous portion of Antonine Hedary's own hot beef sausage brought to you with hot, fresh baked bread, lemon juice, and tomato slices. The lamb dishes are always a good choice, since Hedary's raises its own. Beer and wine. Lebanese music. Open since 1976. Parking lot.

JAPANESE PALACE ($$–$$$)

8445 Hwy. 80W (76116) • 817-244-0144 • Dinner, seven days • Cr. • W+ • www.japanesepalace.com

They've been serving authentic Japanese cuisine here for more than 25 years. You have two choices of eating style. If you want to be totally immersed in the traditional Japanese style, where you sit on pillows at a low table, then you'll want to dine in the Teri Yaki Room. The Teppan Yaki Room offers standard seating around a large cooking table where your dinner is prepared hibachi-style. The menus in both rooms overlap with sushi and sashimi appetizers and typical shrimp tempura and sukiyaki and teriyaki entrées, as well as beef and seafood dishes.

KINCAID'S HAMBURGERS ($)

4901 Camp Bowie (76116), • 817-732-2881 • Monday–Saturday, 11 a.m.–6 p.m. • No cr. • W

There are fast-food-chain burgers and other hamburger joints and then there's Kincaid's. The no-frills, lean ground chuck half-pound burgers here have consistently been voted among the best in the city—some say the best in the country. What began as a corner grocery store made its transition to a local institution when Charles Kincaid put in a grill in the early 1960s and started on the road to becoming a legend. You can stand up and savor your burger using the old grocery shelves as a table, or sit at one of the picnic tables. Plate lunches and desserts also available. Beer only.

LA PIAZZA ($$$–$$$$)

1600 S. University (76107) in University Park Village Shopping Center • 817-334-0000 • Lunch and dinner, seven days • Cr. • W+

It's in a strip mall, but a sign at the entrance requesting that you dress appropriately gives a clue that this is not your ordinary strip-mall jeans-and-t-shirt restaurant. La Piazza is definitely upscale Italian, with entrées that include grilled sea bass, Dover sole, and shrimp with Pernod sauce, as well as veal, beef, lamb, and basic and imaginative pasta dishes and other Italian favorites. Bar. Parking lot.

LONESOME DOVE WESTERN BISTRO ($$$–$$$$)

2406 N. Main (just south of Exchange) in the Stockyards • 817-740-8810 • Lunch and dinner, Tuesday–Saturday. Closed Sunday–Monday • AE, MC, V • W+ • www.lonesomedovebistro.com

Its rustic décor and the chef/owner wearing a cowboy hat fit in nicely with the Stockyards image, but, although beef is a major item on the menu, the white linens and pewter candlesticks show this is no mere beef-and-potatoes place. In fact, the beef entrée is more likely to be a beef tenderloin stuffed with roasted garlic and served with grilled asparagus and Western plaid hash (julienne potatoes, red and green cabbage, peppers, cooked in a wine sauce). Other entrées include sweet coffee-rubbed kangaroo, blackened Texas catfish with crawfish critters, and blue-corn-crusted Alaskan halibut. In other words, chef/owner Tim Love has brought sophistication without stuffiness to Western fare that ranges through all of Texas's diverse ethnic cuisines. Live music, Friday–Saturday. Bar. A small dining room, so reservations strongly recommended. Valet parking evenings ($3).

MICHAEL'S ($$–$$$)

3413 W. 7th (76107) in the Cultural District • 817-877-3413 • Lunch, Monday–Friday; dinner, Monday–Saturday. Closed Sunday • Cr. • W+ • www.michaelscuisine.com

Chef/proprietor Michael Thomson lists his menu as "Contemporary Ranch Cuisine." That includes steaks, of course, like pepper-crusted pan-seared beef tenderloin, but it also translates into entrées like charbroiled bone-in center-cut veal chops, pan-seared skin-on sea bass, and Michael's ranch-baked crab cakes with saffron orzo, grilled veggies, and *ancho chile* cream sauce. Décor includes the *Cowboys and Indians* series by Andy Warhol. If you have a party of four or more big eaters, check out Michael's Feed-Me Menu at $40 per person. Cigar-friendly bar.

PARIS COFFEE SHOP ($)

704 W. Magnolia at Hemphill (76104) • 817–335–2041 • Breakfast and lunch, Monday–Friday, 6 a.m.–2:30 p.m. Breakfast only, Saturday, 6–11 a.m. Closed Sunday • Cr. • W

When it opened in 1926, the counter was the only place to sit. Today this family-owned landmark seats 175. Devoted local patrons seeking a hearty and home-cooked breakfast or lunch go out of their way to eat here. Nothing fancy, just classic American breakfasts of eggs any style with bacon, ham, or sausage or a stack of fluffy pancakes. And for lunch you can choose home-cooking dishes like chicken and dumplings (hand-made the old-fashioned way), meat loaf, fried catfish, or turkey with cornbread dressing, all topped off with a slice of homemade pie or an egg custard, and still get change from a $10 bill. Parking.

PARTHENON ($–$$)

401 N. Henderson (76102) • 817-810-0800 • Lunch and dinner, Monday–Saturday. Closed Sunday • W

Authentic Greek and Mediterranean cuisine are on the menu at this inexpensive and cheery restaurant near downtown. That includes gyros, dolmas, moussaka, and spanakopita, and baklava for dessert. The wine list features retsina and other wines from Greece.

THE PEGASUS ($$–$$$)

2443 Forest Park at Park Hill (76110) • 817-922-0808 • Lunch, Monday–Friday; dinner, Monday–Saturday; Sunday brunch • AE, MC, V • W+ • www.thepegasus.net

Overall the eclectic menu is primarily Mediterranean-oriented, but Chef Denise Paul Shavandy and her co–owner and husband Majid Shavandy have combined world influences so they label it contemporary global cuisine. Each dish uses elements of one region but combines them to create a new version that's still true to the spirit of the original. For example, the Mixed Grill includes Za'atar, which is rubbed quail, double chop of lamb, and duck breast with sour-cherry devil-glacé and cilantro-scallion mashed potatoes. The pepper-crusted tuna mignon comes with papaya cream sauce, ginger mashed potatoes, and spinach. If you are a light eater or one who likes to sample, the Pegasus offers you two delightful choices. First is that many of the dinner entrées are available in half orders. The second is the Mezze Menu of small portions that can be appetizers or combined to make a meal. The setting includes a multilevel terrace and patio overlooking a creek. Bar. Live music, Friday and Saturday evenings. Parking.

RAILHEAD SMOKEHOUSE ($)

2900 Montgomery (76107) • 817-738-9808 • Lunch and dinner, Monday–Saturday. Closed Sunday • MC, V • W+

Barbecue is a way of life in Texas, and popular opinion says this chain consistently creates some of the best. Sandwiches and plate dinners of beef brisket, smoked pork ribs, chicken, turkey, and sausage are all on the menu, plus draft beer, longnecks, and wine. Cafeteria style. Just south of I–30 at the edge of the Cultural District.

REATA ($$–$$$)

310 Houston, in Sundance Square • 817-336-1009 • Lunch and dinner, seven days • Cr. • W+ • www.reata.net

It doesn't matter if you call the cuisine "cowboy-chic" or "fine western" or "upscale chuck wagon," it adds up to a dining experience. Most of the menu features creative reworkings of made-from-scratch Tex-Mex favorites like chicken-fried steak with cracked pepper cream gravy, BBQ shrimp enchiladas, or the Vaquero Sampler, consisting of a gourmet version of a tamale, an enchilada, and a chile relleno. Naturally, beef figures prominently on the menu, since one owner (a founder of the Reata, who named it after the ranch in the 1950s movie *Giant*) owns the CF Ranch in West Texas. The CF Ranch is one of the Southwest's largest family-owned commercial cattle operations and provides select cuts to the restaurant. Other choices include chicken, game, seafood, and even a vegetable plate.

You also have choices for your dining ambiance here. On the ground floor is the Western-decorated main dining room; the lower-level dining room offers enthralling floor–to–ceiling photographs of the panoramic view from the old Reata when it was the thirty-fifth-floor crown of the Bank One building (before a tornado turned that skyscraper into a ruin), and the third-floor rooftop has both indoor and outdoor seating with a 360-degree view of downtown. Bar. Valet parking or free parking evenings and weekend in Sundance Square designated lots.

RUFFINO'S RESTAURANTE ITALIANO ($$–$$$)

2455 Forest Park, north of Park Hill (76110) • 817-923-0522 • Lunch and dinner, Monday–Saturday. Closed Sunday • Cr. • W+

Classic Italian fare is well served in this cozy and romantic restaurant owned and operated by the Albanese brothers, Franco and Robert. Veal, chicken, beef, and seafood entrées, all enhanced with tasty sauces. If you're really hungry, try the family-style dinner for two, which runs from antipasto through pasta and entrée to dessert. Beer and wine.

SAINT–EMILION ($$$–$$$$)

3617 W. 7th, west of University (76107), near the Cultural District • 817-737-2781 • Dinner, Tuesday–Saturday. Closed Sunday–Monday • Cr. • W+

The décor of this brick home restaurant is so country French it could have been a chateau transplanted directly from a French village. And the menu follows through with well-crafted entrées that include such culinary delights as seafood in a puff pastry, veal medallions, duck, lamb, and seafood. Finish up sumptuously with a dessert like rum-laced creme brulée. Fixed priced dinner available (about $35). French-style leisurely dining is encouraged to give time to savor the pleasurable experience. Wine list includes selections from the Saint–Emilion region in France. Bar.

SPECIAL FOOD MARKETS FOR DO-IT-YOURSELF

If you don't want to brave the waiting lines, call to the restaurant that interests you and find out if it offers takeout. Surprisingly, some of the most upscale do. But if you want to prepare your own meals or make a picnic basket as a change from dining out, you might want to visit the Fort Worth Rail Market or the H-E-B Central Market, two markets where the emphasis is on fresh, high quality food.

The **Fort Worth Rail Market** is at 1401 Jones (817-335-6758). Also known locally as the Forth Worth Public Market, it is located in the historic Santa Fe Warehouse, next to the Intermodal Transportation Center and just two blocks east of the Convention Center. This 40,000-square-foot European-style market is open daily, selling everything from flowers to sandwiches, seafood to wine. On Saturdays, a farmers' market is open outside from early morning to mid-afternoon. Free parking. www.fortworthpublicmarket.com

H-E-B is one of the major grocery chains in Texas and the **H-E-B Central Market** is one of their several upscale groceries located in major cities in the state. This one is at 4651 West Freeway at the corner of I-30 and Hulen (817-989-4700). In addition to the routine grocery items, this 75,000-square-foot emporium also routinely stocks about 700 varieties of fresh produce, 600 varieties of cheese, 80 varieties fish, meats including bison and emu, and deli and bakery items. Its Café on the Run provides a wide variety of meals-to-go. www.heb.com

A SAMPLING OF FORT WORTH
CLUBS AND BARS

BILLY BOB'S TEXAS

2520 Rodeo Plaza (76106), in the Stockyards • 817-624-7117 or Metro 817-589-1711 • Admission • W+ • www.billybobstexas.com

Laying claim to being the "World's largest honky-tonk," Billy Bob's has room for 6,000, two dance floors (one with a rhinestone-studded saddle suspended like a disco ball over the dance floor), and several dozen bar stations. It's the only nightclub in the nation with an indoor arena where, every weekend, professional rodeo cowboys try to ride real bulls—not the mechanical kind—that don't want to be ridden. Live music most nights. Weekends, major country artists, and sometimes celebrity rock and popular groups, perform in concert. The Academy of Country Music and the Country Music Association have both awarded it the title of "Club of the Year" several times. Lessons in line-dancing and the Texas two-step are usually given for a small charge several times a week. (Call for schedule.) You can get barbecue here all day long, and children, with parents, are welcome in the video games arcade during the day. Sunday–Thursday, general admission $1 before 6:00 p.m., $3 after; Friday–Saturday, $1 before 5:00 p.m., $5.50–$8.50 after. Admission to concerts varies by artist but usually runs from $8 to $14. Gift shops, arcade games, restaurant. Free parking during the day, pay parking at night.

FLYING SAUCER DRAFT EMPORIUM

111 E. 4th (76102) in Sundance Square • 817-336-7470 • W+ • www.beerknurd.com

This is a beer enthusiast's heaven with around 70 different kinds of ales and lagers on tap and another hundred-plus of canned and bottled brands available from Britain and Ireland, Germany, the United States, and all around the world. To give you something to munch on while you savor the various brews, they offer sandwiches, wursts, and snacks. Live music nightly.

THE GRAPE ESCAPE WINE BAR

500 Commerce (76102) • 817-336-9463 • W+

The escape here is their offering of more than 80 kinds of wine served by the bottle, the glass, the half glass, or what they call a flight. A flight is a grouping of three to five 1½-ounce tasting glasses of a grape of your choice from several countries or brands—for example, a cabernet from Australia, California, Chile, and France. The food is mostly light and with tasting plates designed to complement the wine. Across from Bass Performance Hall.

WHITE ELEPHANT SALOON

106 E. Exchange (76106), in the Stockyards • 817-624-1887 •
Usually a cover upstairs on weekends • W

The 1887 in the phone number isn't just a coincidence. A permanent place in Fort Worth's history was ensured for the saloon, then located downtown, when its owner, gambler Luke Short, outdrew and killed former marshal "Long Hair" Jim Courtright in 1887. There have been changes since 1887, of course, but today's saloon still recalls the Old West with its long, wooden stand-up bar with a brass foot rail. Ceramic versions of the white elephants of its name line the walls, which also feature rubbings from the tombstones of Short and Courtright. The saloon has been listed in *Esquire* magazine's 100 best bars in America. Upstairs at the White Elephant has C&W music most nights (cover usually on weekends). Next door is the Beer Garden, open April through October with live music and dancing on weekend nights.

A SAMPLING OF FORT WORTH ACCOMMODATIONS

For a double room or suite: $ = up to $80, $$ = $80–$120, $$$ = $121–$180, $$$$ = $181–$280, $$$$$ = over $280. **Room tax 15%.**

Unless otherwise noted: Check in at 3:00 p.m., check out by noon. Unless otherwise noted, all these accommodations have handicapped rooms/facilities and no-smoking rooms. Check on visual alarms and other safety facilities for the hearing impaired with making reservations. Most accommodations permit children to stay free in room with parents. There may be a charge if this requires setting up an extra bed.

ASHTON HOTEL ($$$$–$$$$$ + 15%)

610 Main (76102) • 817-332-0100 or toll-free 866-327-4866 • All no-smoking rooms • www.theashtonhotel.com

There are just 29 rooms and 10 suites in this six-story boutique hotel, all impeccably and tastefully done in Art Deco décor. Small pets OK. Satellite TV with free premium channel. Complimentary coffee with wake-up call and in lobby in morning. Dataport in room. Electronic safe in room. Bell service. Small fitness room or $10 fee for use of nearby fitness center. One-day dry cleaning. Restaurant (see CAFÉ ASHTON, p. 217). Room service. Business services available. Concierge service. Bar with piano on weekends. Valet parking (fee). The hotel is in two buildings listed on the National Register of Historic Places. Member of Small Luxury Hotels of the World.

BEST WESTERN INN SUITES ($–$$$ + 15%)

2000 Beach (76103), two miles east of downtown at Beach Street exit off I-30 • 817-534-4801 or toll-free 800-989-3556 or 877-9FORTWORTH (936-7896) • www.innsuites.com

This two-story inn has 166 studio and two-room suites. Several buildings with outside access but inside access to rooms. Pets OK (fee). Free local calls. Cable TV with free premium channel and pay channels. Coffeemaker in room and free coffee in lobby at check-in. Dataport in room. Outdoor heated pool and whirlpool. Fitness facilities. Self-service laundry and one-day dry cleaning. Free breakfast buffet, seven days. Free evening social hour, seven days. Free Wednesday barbecue. Restaurant serving breakfast and dinner. Bar. Business services available. Free outdoor self-parking. Free transportation to DFW airport and some local shuttle services available. Small gift shop. Hilltop view of downtown from some suites. Small historic family cemetery in one corner of property.

COURTYARD BY MARRIOTT DOWNTOWN BLACKSTONE ($$–$$$ + 15%)

601 Main (76102) • 817-885-8700 or 800-321-2211 (reservations) • www.courtyard.com/dfwms

Aside from the fact that some of the upper suites feature open-air terraces, it's a little hard to fathom why Marriott put this hotel under its Courtyard logo, since the revitalized 20-story building was the first Fort Worth skyscraper when it was built in 1929 as the Blackstone Hotel. Although it looks different from the normal Courtyard, all the Marriott amenities are here in the 203 rooms and 14 suites. Satellite TV with free premium channel and pay channels. Coffeemaker in room and free coffee available in lobby. Dataport in room. Bell service. Outdoor heated pool and indoor whirlpool. Fitness facilities. Self-service laundry and one-day dry cleaning. Restaurant. Bar open evenings. Business services available. Valet parking (fee). Gift shop.

THE CREEKS AT BEECHWOOD HOTEL AND CONFERENCE CENTER ($$$–$$$$$ + 15%)

3300 Championship Pkwy. (76177), on Hwy 114, one block west of I-35W, across from Texas Motor Speedway • 817-961-0800 • www.westin.com

There are 273 rooms and 13 suites in this resort hotel, and you can choose if you'd prefer a view of the Greg Norman–designed golf course to the south or the Texas Motor Speedway to the north. Cable TV with free premium and pay channels. Coffeemaker in rooms. Dataport in room. Outdoor pool and whirlpool. Fitness center. Business services. One-day dry cleaning. Restaurants. Room service. Lounge. Business services available. Valet (fee) or free outdoor self-parking.

GREEN OAKS PARK HOTEL ($$ + 15%)

6901 W. Freeway (76116), off I-30 at Green Oaks exit • 817-738-7311 or 800-772-2341 • www.greenoakshotel.com

This two-story hotel has 282 units, including 55 suites. Small pets OK (deposit $20). Inside and outside access to rooms. Cable TV with free premium channel and pay channels. Two outdoor pools, sauna, exercise room. Two lighted tennis courts. Public golf course adjacent. Business services available. One-day dry cleaning. Restaurant. Room service. Lounge with entertainment and dancing. Business services available. Free outdoor self-parking. On 9.5 acres. Across from Ridgmar Mall. (See SHOPPING, p. 215)

HILTON GARDEN INN ($$–$$$ + 15%)

4400 N. Freeway (76137), exit 56A (Meacham Blvd.) off I-35W • 817-222-0222 or 800-HILTONS (445-8667) (reservations) • www.fortworthnorth.gardeninn.com

This three-story inn, about three miles north of the Stockyards in Mercantile Business Park, has 74 rooms and 24 suites. Cable TV with free premium channel and pay channels. Coffeemaker in room. Dataport in room. Heated outdoor/indoor pools with whirlpool. Fitness room. Self-service laundry and one-day dry cleaning. Restaurant. Room service. Lounge. Business services available. Free outdoor self-parking. Refrigerator, microwave in room.

RADISSON PLAZA ($$$–$$$$$ + 15%)

815 Main (76102) • 817-870-2100 or 800-333-3333 (reservations) • www.radisson.com

Opened in 1921 as the "Texas Hotel," it is listed on the National Register of Historic Places. President John F. Kennedy spent his last night here before his assassination. There are 502 rooms and 15 suites in this 15-story downtown hotel that is adjacent to the Fort Worth Convention Center. Concierge section offers extra amenities. Cable TV with free premium channel. Coffeemaker in room. Dataport in room. Heated outdoor rooftop pool and whirlpool. Sauna. Fitness room. One-day dry cleaning. Restaurant. Room service. Lounge. Business services available. 14,000-square-foot ballroom/exhibition room. Beauty/barber shop. Gift shop. Garage (fee) and valet parking (fee).

RENAISSANCE WORTHINGTON HOTEL
($$$$–$$$$$ +15%)

200 Main (76102), at Sundance Square • 817-870-1000 or 800-468-3571 (reservations) • www.renaissancehotels.com

This 12-story hotel has 504 units and 30 suites. Concierge section with extra amenities. Cable/satellite TV with free premium channel and pay channels. Coffeemaker in room. Dataport in room. Bell service. Indoor pool, sauna, exercise room. Concierge services available. One-day dry cleaning. Grill serving all meals and fine dining restaurant serving dinner only. Room service. Bar. Conference facilities. Business center. Garage (fee) and valet parking (fee). Gift shop. Hotel spans three city blocks. Excellent views of the city from upper floor rooms. Lobby mural depicts scenes from downtown Fort Worth. Rated 4-Diamonds by AAA.

RESIDENCE INN BY MARRIOTT ($$$ + 15%)

1701 S. University (76107), take University exit off I-30, go south 1/2 mile • 817-870-1011 or 800-331-3131 (reservations)

There are 120 one- and two-bedroom suites with kitchens in this two-story all-suites inn. Pets OK (daily fee). Outside access to rooms. Daily charge for local calls ($1 per day). Cable TV with free premium channel and pay channels. Coffeemaker in room and free coffee available in lobby. Dataport in room. Outdoor heated pool and whirlpool. Fitness facilities. Jogging trail. Self-service laundry and one-day dry cleaning. Free breakfast buffet daily. Free beverages, Monday–Thursday evenings. Free outdoor self-parking at door. Free transportation within 10-mile radius. Free grocery shopping service. Restaurants nearby. Fully equipped kitchen and refrigerator in all units, many with fireplaces. In the Cultural District.

STOCKYARDS HOTEL ($$$–$$$$$ + 15%)

109 E. Exchange at Main (76106), in the Stockyards • 817-625-6427

There are 48 rooms and 4 suites in this three-story hotel. Originally established in 1907, its guests included Bonnie and Clyde. Small pets OK ($50 fee). Satellite TV. Coffeemaker in room. Dataport in room. Bell service. Guest passes to downtown fitness center. Business services available. H-3 Ranch Live Hickory Wood Grill is attached, serving lunch and dinner daily and breakfast Saturday–Sunday (817-624-1246). Lounge with entertainment. Conference facilities. Valet parking (fee). Restored historical hotel with all sleeping rooms decorated in one of four periods: Victorian, Mountain Man, Cowboy, or Native American. Western décor even extends to saddle-topped stools in bar. Extensive gift shop.

BED AND BREAKFAST INNS

AZALEA PLANTATION ($$$ + 15%)

1400 Robinwood (76111) • 817-838-5882 or 800-68-RELAX
(687-3529) • www.azaleaplantation.com

A plantation-style home on two acres offering two rooms with private
baths and two private cottages with mini kitchens. Free local calls. Full
breakfast. Free lighted outdoor parking.

BED & BREAKFAST AT THE RANCH ($$–$$$ + 15%)

8275 Wagley Roberson (76131) • 817-232-5522 or toll-free
888-593-0352 • www.bandbattheranch.com

Built in the early 1900s as headquarters for a large cattle ranch, it is
now on 15 acres on the edge of a prairie. All four ranch-style rooms have
private bath; three have private patios. Breakfast buffet weekends, continental breakfast weekdays. Free outdoor self-parking.

ETTA'S PLACE ($$$ +15%)

200 W. 3rd at Houston, in Sundance Square (76102) • 817-654-
0267 • W+ elevator and some rooms • All no-smoking except for
outside terraces • www.ettas-place.com

According to the legend, Etta Place was the girlfriend of the Sundance
Kid. Now the place named after her is in the heart of Sundance Square,
on the second to fifth floors of the building around the corner from Reata
Restaurant. The 11 units include four suites, all with private bath. Children over 10 accepted. Cable TV. Local phone calls free. Dataport in
room. Some business services. Full breakfast. Room 206 (Laura's Lounge)
overlooks the Square. Street or lot parking.

MISS MOLLY'S HOTEL ($$–$$$$ +15%)

109 1/2 W. Exchange (76106), in Stockyards Historic District, just
west of Main • 817-626-1522 or 800-99MOLLY (996-6559) •
www.missmollys.com

A steep flight of stairs leads up to the eight rooms of this second-floor
B&B. One room has a private bath, and there are three bathrooms down
the hall for all the others. All rooms are no-smoking. No children. Breakfast buffet. Street parking. Don't expect B&B cute and cozy here. More
cowboy rough-and-ready old-style rooming house (once a bordello)
with just a few frills. In the heart of Stockyards, can be noisy until wee
hours, especially on weekends or during major events.

THE TEXAS WHITE HOUSE ($$$–$$$$ + 15%)

1417 8th (76104), near Texas Christian University • 817-923-3597
or 800-279-6491 • No smoking in house •
www.texaswhitehouse.com

The three rooms in this country-style house, built in 1910, are all on the second floor and all with private bath. There are also two suites in the Carriage House, one upstairs and one down. Children OK in one suite. Free local phone calls. TV in room on request. Some business services available. Full breakfast. Free off-street self-parking.

GARLAND

Dallas County • 220,000 • Area Code 972 (local calls require area code) • www.ci.garland.tx.us and www.garlandonline.com

Local history recounts that this is another city that was originally founded to settle a feud between the two rival towns. It started in 1886 when the Santa Fe Railroad laid its tracks about a mile to the east of the town of Duck Creek. Most, but not all, of the townspeople moved to the new area, called Embree, taking their post office with them. That same year, the Missouri, Kansas & Texas Railroad came through but declined to join the Santa Fe in a union station. Instead, the MK&T built its own depot a little farther north and called it Duck Creek. A feud developed between Embree and the new Duck Creek, which were barely a mile apart, over the location of the post office. To reinforce their claim, each town tried to lure the citizens from the old Duck Creek to their community. It's said that the feelings ran so high that a man from one town dared not go "courting" in the other without courting trouble.

Finally, in 1887, a local judge came to a Solomon-like decision and persuaded Congress to move the post office between the towns and order both railroads to deliver the mail there. The post office was named in honor of then Attorney General A. H. Garland. Surprisingly, the decision pleased everyone, and the citizens of the new and old Duck Creek and Embree soon dissolved their towns and combined to form the new city of Garland.

For many years, cotton was king here. But in the 1930s, during the Depression, farmers found the soil ideal for onions, making onion farming a major factor in the local economy. By the time World War II started, Garland had already begun to change from an agriculture-based economy to an industrial community, and the onion business yielded to the defense industry. After the war, the industrial base stayed and grew, and the city grew with it—and grew, and grew! As a result, Garland's 57 square miles, tucked into the northeast corner of Dallas County, is now a highly diversified industrial, high-tech center.

Garland is dry under the local options. Most restaurants and hotels/motels have private clubs that require you pay a small membership fee to buy alcoholic beverages by the drink.

GARLAND

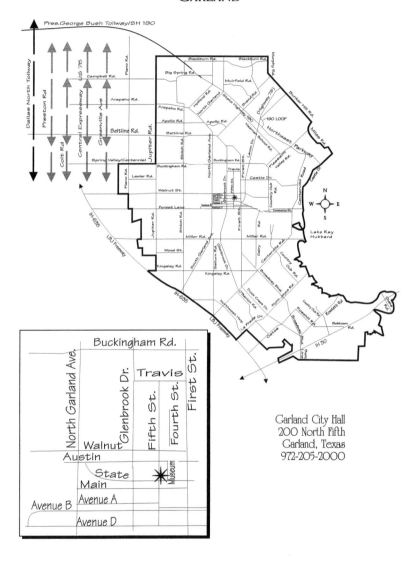

Garland City Hall
200 North Fifth
Garland, Texas
972-205-2000

FREE VISITOR SERVICES

GARLAND CONVENTION & VISITORS BUREAU

200 N. 5th (75040), at State, in City Hall • 972-205-2749 or toll-free 888-879-0264 • Monday–Friday, 8:30–4:30 • W+ • www.ci.garland.tx.us & www.garlandonline.com

You can pick up free brochures, maps, and specific information about Garland and the surrounding area here, as well as get help with hotel/motel accommodations.

HELPFUL LOCAL PUBLICATIONS

Current information about Garland events, activities, nightlife, theater, movies, and dining is sometimes listed in the *Garland Morning News*, the Garland section of the *Dallas Morning News* on Sunday and Thursday, and the *Friday Guide* in that newspaper. Other sources to check are the weekly *Dallas Observer*, which is available free at restaurants and tourist attractions throughout the Dallas area; and the monthly *D Magazine* and *Texas Monthly Magazine* available on newsstands.

HISTORIC PLACES

HERITAGE PARK

Museum Plaza Dr. and State, east of City Hall

The area east of City Hall is informally referred to as Garland's Heritage Park because it contains a historic home and the old Santa Fe Railroad Depot, with a railroad passenger car. The depot is now the home of the **Landmark Museum**, which features a small collection of memorabilia from Garland's early days. The Pullman car dates from the early 1900s. Next door is the **Pace House**, a one-story frame house built in 1895 that is considered an excellent example of a Texas Victorian farmhouse. Only the museum is open to the public (Monday–Friday, 8:30–4:30. Free).

OUTDOORS

GARLAND PARKS

Parks and Recreation Department, 634 Apollo (75040), in Coomer Park • 972-205-2750 • www.garlandonline.com

The dozens of large and small parks scattered around the city add up to over 2,500 acres offering a variety of outdoor facilities, including over 20 miles of jogging and bike trails, a 13-court tennis center, swimming pools, a wave pool, playgrounds, a marina, and picnic areas. Although not the biggest, the 144-acre **John J. Audubon Park** (342 Oates) is packed with outstanding facilities, including the city's Surf and Swim Wave-Action Pool, the Carter Softball Complex, the Duck Creek/Audubon Park Hike and Bike Trail, a recreation center with gym, 10 soccer fields, playgrounds, and picnic areas.

Spring Creek Greenbelt and Spring Creek Forest Preserve • The greenbelt stretches along 2½ miles of Spring Creek in northern Garland. The Harris section at 6006 N. Shiloh has parking, a playground, picnic tables, a half-mile paved trail, pond and fishing pier. The less developed Forest Preserve has trails starting at 1770 Holford and 4848 N. Garland. Access permit required from Garland Parks and Recreation.

Rowland Creek Preserve • 2525 Castle at Centerville. More than 12 miles of natural surface trails through woodlands and grasslands, a quarter-mile paved trail, parking, picnic shelter.

Woodland Basin Nature Area • 2332 East Miller Road at Lake Ray Hubbard. A quarter-mile wooden boardwalk jutting into the marshy area of Lake Ray Hubbard provides an ideal platform for observing the marsh inhabitants, from armadillos to waterfowl. Best viewing in early morning or late afternoon. Half-mile nature trail extends north and south of Miller Road. Canoe launch and bank fishing.

LAKE RAY HUBBARD

Take I-30 east to the lake • 214-670-0936 • Open at all times • Fee and non-fee areas • W

This 22,745-acre lake on the East Fork of the Trinity River is located between Garland and Rockwall. Owned by the City of Dallas, it is used for water supply and recreation. There are facilities for boating, fishing, picnicking, and camping (fee). No swimming. Several marinas on the lake rent boats. The *Texas Queen* excursion boat operates from Elgin B. Robinson Park on the lake. The double-decked paddle wheeler offers both daytime tours and dinner cruises. Call for 972-771-0039 for schedule, fares, and reservations.

MUSIC AND PERFORMING ARTS

GARLAND PERFORMING ARTS CENTER (PAC)

300 N. 5th at Austin (75046) (DART Light Rail Downtown Garland Station) • 972-205-2790 • W+

This center houses two complete theaters that can stage everything from touring Broadway shows to symphony concerts. The main theater, which seats 720, features a proscenium stage, hydraulic orchestra lift, and state-of-the-art sound and lighting systems. The smaller theater has a booth-controlled sound and lighting system and seats 200. A banquet hall seating 500 is connected to the center by a porte-cochère.

The following organizations are among those that call the PAC their performance home.

Garland Civic Theatre • Founded in 1968, this is the oldest community theater group in Dallas County. In a September–May season, this nonprofit Civic Theatre usually presents six shows in the small theater at the PAC. Productions include comedies, mysteries, drama, and classics. Performances are usually Thursday–Saturday at 8:00 p.m.; matinees Saturday–Sunday at 2:00 p.m. The group also produces the Children on Stage Program, which has its own season each year. (See FAMILY FUN AND KID STUFF, p. 235)

Garland Summer Musicals • As its name says, this group, which was founded in 1983, presents two musicals each summer.

Garland Symphony Orchestra • Founded in 1978, the 93-member professional orchestra offers six subscription concerts in its October–May season. Most concerts feature guest artists.

GARLAND COUNTRY MUSIC ASSOCIATION
605 W. State (75040) • 972-494-3835 • W

This group sponsors what's known locally as the "Big G Jamboree," a weekly Saturday-night performance of local and visiting Western, gospel, and bluegrass groups. Performances are in their own theater.

PLAZA THEATRE
521 W. State (75040), on the Square • 972-205-2780 (Performing Arts Center) • W+

The original Plaza building dates to 1918, and the theater was first opened as a movie theater in 1941. As with most small town theaters, TV spelled its eventual doom as a movie house. Donated to the city, it has been restored as a state-of-the-art 350-seat theater/auditorium used for plays, concerts, local and touring shows, and school theatrics. On-street parking on the Square.

FAMILY FUN AND KID STUFF

GARLAND CIVIC THEATRE/CHILDREN ON STAGE
Garland Center for the Performing Arts, 300 N. 5th (75046) • 972-205-2790 (PAC) • W+

This is theater for children by children. The actors and technicians who work the shows are primarily students aged 8 through 18. The majority of the productions are "school shows" held during the day as field trips for children bussed from schools; however, there are also several weekend productions during the summer, as well as one spring and one fall production, all with both matinee and evening performances.

SURF AND SWIM WAVE POOL

Audubon Park, 440 Oates (exit Oates Rd. off I-635, go east to park) • 972-686-1237 or 972-205-2757 • Open weekends in early May, daily late May–August, then weekends through Labor Day • W

The "surf" here is a wave-action pool that produces four-foot waves. This municipal pool has grass beaches, pecan groves, shaded picnic tables, bathhouses, and a snack bar. You can rent tubes. Special water play area for swimmers age six and under. Lifeguards. Admission by height: 60" and over, $5.50; under 60", $4.50. Children 2 and under free.

SPORTS

GOLF

PUBLIC COURSES

FIREWHEEL GOLF PARK

600 W. Campbell (75044) • 972-205-2795 • www.golffirewheel.com

The largest municipal golf facility in Texas and the third largest municipal golf facility in the United States, this golf park offers 63 holes on three courses: Old Course, Lakes Course, and The Bridges Course. Firewheel, which is named after a red wildflower, has hosted PGA Tour qualifying events. The original course, now called the Old Course, has been ranked number two among public courses in Texas. The **Branding Iron Restaurant** at the Bridges Course clubhouse is open to the public.

UP TO PAR DRIVING RANGE AND GOLF COURSE

3015 N. Shiloh (75045) • 972-530-0585 • 9-hole par 3 course

SOFTBALL

JERRY CARTER SOFTBALL COMPLEX

Audubon Park, 550 Oates (75043) • 972-613-7729 • W

This is not your ordinary park softball diamond. It's a dream setup for softball tournaments. The five softball fields are arranged in a "wagon wheel" configuration, all identical and all fenced at 300 feet. Players can warm up in either of two large fenced areas, and there are eight batting cages. Other facilities include high-pressure sodium lighting, shaded bleachers, and electric scoreboards and time clocks. Recognized as one of the best in the state, this complex hosts state and national tournaments.

WINTERS SOFTBALL COMPLEX

Winters Park, 1330 Spring Creek (75040) • 972-276-5483 • W

Another softball tournament facility with three identical back-to-back fields with 300-foot fences, glare-reducing lighting for night games, and an electric scoreboard. Adjacent to the softball complex is the 11-field Winters Soccer Complex.

TENNIS

GARLAND TENNIS CENTER

1010 W. Miller (75047) • 972-205-2778

The fee for using any of the 13 lighted courts is $2 per person for 1½ hours.

ANNUAL EVENTS

JULY

STAR SPANGLED 4TH

Three days including July 4th • Historic Downtown Square: State, Main, and 5th Streets (P.O. Box 469002, 75046) • 972-205-2632 • Admission free. Charge for some main stage performances • W • www.starspangledfourth.com

Just about every community in the country has a Fourth of July celebration, but Garland celebrates this historic event for up to five days with a lineup of shows and concerts featuring headline acts, other continuous entertainment, choreographed fireworks nightly, a midway, a children's area, arts-and-crafts booths, and a wide variety of special exhibits and demonstrations. There's also a Celebrity Golf Tournament at Firewheel Golf Park. Parking is free. Free shuttle service is available from Williams Stadium (510 Stadium Dr.) and Garland High School (310 S. Garland). Approximately 150,000 attend the festivities.

SHOPPING

ANTIQUE SHOPS

There are several antique shops in the downtown area along Main, and the streets around the Square.

A SAMPLING OF GARLAND RESTAURANTS

Since Garland is dry, check to see if the restaurant of your choice offers membership or permits you to Bring Your Own Bottle (BYOB).

ARC-EN-CIEL ($)

3555 W. Walnut (75042) • 972-272-2188 • Lunch and dinner, seven days • Cr. • W+

Of the more than 200 entrées on the menu, about half are American-ized versions of classic dishes from Szechuan and Hunan cuisine and the rest are traditional Chinese and Vietnamese dishes. Order off the menu or sit at your table and create a meal by selecting from the large variety of small portions of appetizers, entrées, and desserts on the many dim sum carts wheeled around by servers. Pointing is OK, since many of the servers speak limited English.

BABE'S CHICKEN DINNER HOUSE ($)

1456 Belt Line (75044) • 972-496-1041 • Dinner, Tuesday–Saturday; lunch and early dinner, Sunday. Closed Monday • Cr. • W

It's like home-style cooking, even to the limit on your choices. In keeping with this rustic restaurant's name, the small menu usually fea-tures only about five entrées that always include fried chicken and chicken-fried steak, and may also offer smoked chicken, pot roast, pork ribs, or fried catfish. Home-style carries over to the made-from-scratch biscuits and sides of mashed potatoes and a variety of vegetables served family style in extra-large bowls. And you don't have to worry that someone in your "family" will scoop it all up; the servers will just keep refilling the bowls.

DESPERADOS ($–$$)

3443 Campbell in shopping center • 972-530-8886 • Lunch and dinner, Monday–Saturday. Closed Sunday • Cr. • W

Both Tex-Mex and a little real-Mex are on the menu here. A Tex-Mex aficionado could make a meal of the appetizer Special Platter that includes

Desperado nachos, stuffed *jalapenos, empanadas,* and chicken *flauitas.* A specialty of the house is the Desperado Tacos, known as the "Juan and Only," consisting of two crispy flour tortillas, melted jack cheese, and your choice of beef or chicken. A variety of traditional Mexican steak, chicken, and seafood entrées round out the menu. Another location in Dallas.

LUNA DE NOCHE ($–$$)

7602 Jupiter (75044), in shopping center • 972-414-3616 • Lunch and dinner, seven days. Breakfast, Saturday and Sunday • Cr. • W+

This restaurant features upscale Tex-Mex. Part of a small chain of family-owned and -operated Metroplex restaurants, this one features a menu that includes all the familiar items from nachos and fajitas to chile relleno and spicy enchiladas. Among the number of Tex-Mex combo dishes available are the "Old Mexico," which includes two pork tamales served with chile con carne, one old-fashioned shredded beef taco, and rice and beans; and "El Cinco" with one cheese chalupa, one bean chalupa, and one guacamole chalupa. Other locations in Dallas.

A SAMPLING OF GARLAND ACCOMMODATIONS

*For a double room or suite: $ = up to $80, $$ = $81–$120, $$$ = $121–$180, $$$$ = $181–280, $$$$$ = over $280. **Room tax 13%.***

Unless otherwise noted, check in at 3:00 p.m., check out by noon. Unless otherwise noted, all the major accommodations have handicapped rooms/facilities and no-smoking rooms. The hearing impaired should check on visual alarms and other safety facilities when making reservations. Most accommodations permit children to stay free in room with parents. There may be a charge if this requires setting up an extra bed.

DAYS INN—DALLAS GARLAND ($–$$ + 13%)

3645 Leon (75041), off I-635 • 972-840-0020 or 800-DAYSINN (800-329-7466) • www.daysinn.com

The 45 units in this three-story inn include two jacuzzi suites. Local calls free. Cable TV with free premium channels. Coffeemaker available on request. Free coffee in lobby. Dataport in most room. Outdoor pool and hot tub. Guest memberships available in Fitness Center. Self-service laundry. Free continental breakfast. Free outdoor self-parking. Microwave and refrigerator in all rooms.

HOLIDAY INN SELECT—LBJ NORTHEAST ($–$$$ + 13%)

11350 LBJ Frwy. (75238), off Jupiter/Kingsley exit • 214-341-5400 • www.holiday-inn.com

There are 244 rooms and two suites in this five-story inn. Local calls free. Concierge section with extra amenities. Cable TV with free premium channel. Coffeemaker in room. Dataport in room. Bell service. Outdoor pool. Dry sauna. Fitness facilities. Gift shop. Self-service laundry and one-day dry cleaning. Restaurant. Room service. Lounge. Conference facilities. Business services available. Free outdoor self-parking.

GRAND PRAIRIE

Dallas and Tarrant Counties • 135,000 • Area Code 972 (local calls require area code) • www.gptexas.com and www.gptexas.org

In 1863, during the Civil War, A. M. Dechman, a trader who was in charge of the commissary at Fort Belknap, had his wagon break down near a prairie home. Ever the trader, Dechman swapped to the settler his disabled wagon, with the team of oxen and $200 in Confederate money, for about 240 acres of land. Dechman was not the first trader in the area. For years the Indians tribes from the north would meet here with the southern tribes to trade horses, cloth, grain, skins, and other items.

After the war, a town developed here that was named after Dechman. In the 1870s, the Texas and Pacific Railroad began closing the gap in its service between Dallas and Fort Worth. Dechman, still the trader, traded land in the Town of Dechman to get the Texas and Pacific Railroad to establish a depot in his town. The railroad did, and because the new depot sits on a vast expanse of grassland between two large bands of timber known as the Cross Timbers, the town was renamed Grand Prairie. When Grand Prairie was incorporated in 1909, it covered an area of only three square blocks and had a population of about fifty families.

The town grew slowly until the opening of several large defense plants in World War II spurred population growth. Today it is an 80-square-mile mostly residential city with some light industry and a growing number of attractions for visitors, including Lone Star Park race track, Traders Village, one of the largest permanent flea markets in the state, and the Palace of Wax and Ripley's Believe It or Not. Its newest attraction is Next Stage at Grand Prairie, a 6,350-seat state-of-the-art performance hall. The city borders two lakes: Joe Pool, with a number of public facilities, and Mountain View, which is not open to the public.

Under the local option laws the city is dry. Some restaurants have a special permit to sell liquor by the drink.

GRAND PRAIRIE

FREE VISITOR SERVICES

TERI JACKSON TOURIST INFORMATION CENTER

2170 Belt Line (75050), north of I-30 near Lone Star Park • Metro 972-263-9588 or 800-288-8FUN (800-288-8386) • Open seven days. Closed major holidays • W+ • www.gptexas.com

Travel counselors are available to assist with directions, lodging, information, and discount coupons for Grand Prairie and all the Metroplex. Brochures available for various cities and attractions throughout the state. Visitor information can also be obtained from the Grand Prairie Chamber of Commerce, 900 Conover, 75051 (972-264-1558) and Grand Prairie City Hall, 317 College, 75050 (972-237-8000).

HISTORIC PLACES

HISTORIC HOMES

Visitors are welcome to three historic homes in the city. The **Goodwin Cabin** (500 block S. Carrier at Jennifer McFalls Park) was built in 1846 of Tennessee notch construction, by which all the pieces stay in place with no pins, bolts, or fasteners. It was the home of Micajah Goodwin and his family, who came here from Alabama. According to local stories, this was once a hideout for Bonnie and Clyde. The **Jordan/Bowles Home** (700 block N.E. 28th and Bowles) was built in 1845. It is a typical double house of the period, with the two main rooms separated by an open hall, a room on the porch on the south end, and paired side rooms on the north. The large white clapboard home at 125 S.W. Dallas is known as the **Copeland Home.** Built in 1902, it was purchased by the Copeland family in 1908. It includes a six-room museum displaying furnishings and antiques from the Copeland family and donations from other leading Grand Prairie citizens. Visits to the homes may be arranged by calling the Grand Prairie Library (972-264-9523).

THE PENN FARM AGRICULTURAL HISTORY CENTER

(See JOE POOL LAKE, p. 244)

OUTDOORS

GRAND PRAIRIE PARKS

Grand Prairie Parks & Recreation Department, 326 W. Main (75050) • 972-237-8100 • www.gptx.org/parks

The 52 parks in the system total 4,911 acres. Among the facilities are several miles of hike and bike trails, including a 1.8-mile National Recreation Trail in Fish Creek Linear Park, a forest preserve, an equestrian arena, three outdoor swimming pools and one indoor pool, tennis and other sports courts and fields, fishing ponds, creative playgrounds, and two golf courses.

JOE POOL LAKE

817-467-2104 • From I-20 take Great Southwest exit south. This becomes Lake Ridge Pkwy. and leads to Lynn Creek Park, Loyd Park and Britton Park • W variable

Straddling the Dallas-Tarrant county line, the shoreline of this 7,500-surface-acre lake attracts more than a million visitors a year. Fishermen find the lake excellent for bass, catfish, and crappie. Boaters, water skiers, and sailors appreciate the lake's wide-open spaces. There are several local parks and one state park with facilities for boating, fishing, swimming, hiking, and camping and shaded picnic areas. The 791-acre **Loyd Park**, on the northwest side of the lake, includes a 3-mile hiking, equestrian, and off-road bike trail, RV and tent camping area, playground, boat ramp, beach, picnic areas. (Admission.) The 784-acre **Lynn Creek Park**, also on the northwest shore just north of the Lynn Creek Marina, offers boat ramps, a swimming beach, picnic areas, and an amphitheater. (Admission.)

The largest park on the lake is **Cedar Hill State Park** (972-291-3900). From I-20 take FM 1382 exit, go south four miles to state park on the lake. Fee for day use. Among the facilities at this 1,850-acre park are a marina with boats and jet skis for rent, two lighted fishing jetties, a fishing barge, five miles of hiking trails and 12 miles of mountain bike trails, a swim beach, playgrounds, and campsites. The **Penn Farm Agricultural History Center** is also located inside this park. The farm is architecturally significant as an example of rural farm buildings used by a single family for over a hundred years. It shows the evolution of structures constructed or adapted by the Penn family as needs changed and modern conveniences were added. The building complex is only the core of what at one time was a farm of over 1,100 acres. The farm is now frequently used as a setting for demonstrations and special events. For information call 972-291-3900. (Admission.)

MUSIC AND PERFORMING ARTS

GRAND PRAIRIE ARTS COUNCIL

P.O. Box 531613, 75053-1613 • 972-642-2787 (recording)

This Council encompasses all art forms, including juried art shows. On the music/theatrical front, it brings a variety of events to the city throughout the year. Call for schedule.

NEXT STAGE AT GRAND PRAIRIE

1001 NextStage Dr. (75050), north off I-30 at N. Belt Line, adjacent to Lone Star Park • 972-854-5050; Box Office, 972-854-1068 or 972-854-1067 • W+ • www.nextstage.com

This $62.9 million live performance hall seats 6,350 in a state-of-the-art theater that can be customized down to seat 2,200. It was designed to combine the best features of today's performing arts center, sports arena, and live event theater. This flexibility allows it to attract major touring shows and name entertainers while still retaining an intimacy with the audience. Admission depends on event. Free self-parking and valet parking (fee). For a big night out, some of the 16 luxury suites accommodating from 16 to 74 guests, with concierge amenities, are available for most events.

FAMILY FUN AND KID STUFF

GPX SKATE PARK AND ENTERTAINMENT CENTER
(See SPORTS, p. 247)

THE PALACE OF WAX AND RIPLEY'S BELIEVE IT OR NOT!

601 E. Safari Pkwy. (75050). From I-30 exit north at Belt Line; the museums can be seen from the highway • Metro 972-263-2391 • Open seven days. Closed Thanksgiving, Christmas, and New Year's Day • Call for times and prices. Single or discounted combined admission • W • www.palaceofwax.com

These two unusual museums share a large onion-domed building that looks like something from an Arabian fantasy. The Palace of Wax exhibits life-size and lifelike figures from real and reel Hollywood, history, fantasy, the United States presidents and world leaders, and an eight-scene journey through the life of Christ. There are also displays showing how the wax artist has created the figures—and you can be the judge of how lifelike the artist has made them. The galleries in Ripley's Believe It or Not! display about a hundred of the huge collection of bizarre oddities and fascinating facts that Robert Ripley collected during his travels to 198 countries in the 1930s. There are a number of hands-on exhibits and others that let visitors experience an earthquake and a Texas tornado. Some of these more active exhibits may be frightening to small children. Gift shop, game area, and snack bar.

SPLASH FACTORY

601 E. Grand Prairie Rd. (75050), adjacent to Charley Taylor Recreation Center • 972-264-6890 • W • www.gptx.org

Toddlers and little kids can splish and splash away in this water playground that includes a water wall, ground sprays, a Magic Touch water gun, a spraying cannon, and power geyser. Geared to smaller children, it features touch buttons that allow them to interact with many of the water features. Lifeguards. Park capacity is 75 in the play area and 25 nonparticipating adults. Admission: Children 12 and under, $1; 13 and older, $1.50.

SPORTS

BOATING AND FISHING

LYNN CREEK MARINA

5700 Lake Ridge Pkwy. (75052), at Joe Pool Lake • Metro 817-640-4200 • W • www.lynncreekmarina.com

This full-service marina features 514 wet slips, an all-weather fishing pier (fee), rentals for fishing boats, ski boats, personal watercraft, skis, and tubes; a ships' store, and the floating Oasis restaurant.

(See also Joe Pool Lake in OUTDOORS, p. 244)

GOLF

PUBLIC COURSES

GRAND PRAIRIE GOLF COURSE

3202 S.E. 14th (75051) • 972-263-0661 • Three 9-hole courses

TANGLE RIDGE GOLF CLUB

818 Tangle Ridge (75052), south of Joe Pool Lake • 972-299-6837 • www.tangleridge.com

Although this 18-hole championship course is owned and operated by the city, it resembles a country club course. Club house with dining room. Ranked one of the top courses in the state by *Golf Digest.*

HORSE RACING

LONE STAR PARK AT GRAND PRAIRIE

1000 Lone Star Pkwy. (75050), take Belt Line exit off I-30, then ½ mile north • 972-263-PONY (972-263-7669) or 800-795-RACE (800-795-7223) • Admission • W+ • www.lonestarpark.com

A Class 1 racecourse situated on 315 landscaped acres, Lone Star Park offers thoroughbred racing April–July and thoroughbred and

Quarter Horse racing October–November. The Park is in rotation for the Breeders Cup. Race days usually Wednesday–Sunday. The beautifully designed Southwestern-style, seven-story, air-conditioned grandstand seats 8,000. On race days: General admission, $3; Club House admission, $6; reserved seating, $6–$25. Suites for up to 25 people, with food and drink, rent for $2,500. Several dining facilities, bars, and gift shops. Self-parking, $2; preferred parking, $4; valet parking, $7. Barns can accommodate up to 1,250 horses. Simulcasting from tracks around the country in the Post Time Pavilion, which is open 363 days a year and has a capacity of 1,500 with 175 television monitors and restaurant. (Admission.) Family Fun Park with pony rides and a petting zoo adjacent to the Post Time Pavilion. Park also used for concerts, including after some of the races, and for many family activities and special events.

IN-LINE SKATING

GPX SKATE PARK AND ENTERTAINMENT CENTER

1000 Lone Star Pkwy. (75050), on grounds of Lone Star Park • 972-237-4370 • www.gpx8.com

This outdoor competitive skate park offers facilities for in-line skaters, bikers, and skateboarders to fly through the air in these aggressive action sports. They include an intermediate/advanced course, beginner's course, and a world-class vert ramp. There is also a roller hockey rink for in-line hockey players. You can watch free, but active skaters and others pay fees depending on sport and time. Helmets and protective gear can be rented. Call for hours and prices.

ANNUAL EVENTS

MARCH–APRIL

ANNUAL CRAPPIE MARATHON

Joe Pool Lake • 817-640-4200

There are daily, weekly, and monthly prizes ranging from $25 to $1000 if you catch any of the 600 tagged crappie released into the lake for this contest. Fish can be weighed at the Lynn Creek Marina. The $10 entry fee is good for the entire two months of this event.

The following annual events are all held at Traders Village, 2602 Mayfield Rd., off Hwy 360 • 972-647-2331. All are weekend events. Free admission. Parking, $2 • www.tradersvillage.com (See also SHOPPING—Traders Village, p. 249)

APRIL

PRAIRIE DOG CHILI COOKOFF AND WORLD CHAMPION-SHIP OF PICKLED QUAIL EGG EATING • Usually Saturday–Sunday early in month • If nothing else, the title ranks right up there with the longest titles of any Texas event. Fortunately, that's not all there is to this tongue-in-cheek tribute to "Texas Red," and some of the activities are as colorful as its title. The chili cookoff, which draws cooks from as far away as New York, is so popular they've had to limit the number of teams. Typical entries include such variations as Horny Toad Chili and Cow Pasture Disaster Chili. Other, noncooking contests include the Original Anvil Toss, the Cuzin Homer Page Invitational Eat-and-Run Stewed Prune Pit Spitting Contest, and the Chicken-flying contest. And, of course, there's the pickled quail egg eating contest, in which the winner eats the most in 60 seconds. On the more ordinary side, there's free, continuous entertainment. About 80,000 people usually attend over the two days.

MAY

CAJUN FEST • Usually Saturday–Sunday, mid-month • They move a little of the bayou here with authentic toe-tapping Cajun music performed by a Zydeco band and traditional South Louisiana dishes like spicy boiled crawfish, jambalaya, red beans and rice, and gumbo.

JUNE

ANTIQUE AUTO SWAP MEET • Usually Friday–Sunday, early in month • If it's on wheels, or ever was, there's a good chance you'll find it at this swap meet for car buffs. More than 1,100 spaces are filled by collectors and vendors from across the country to show off, horse trade, and sell cars, parts, accessories, and auto memorabilia.

SEPTEMBER

NATIONAL CHAMPIONSHIP INDIAN POW WOW • Usually Friday–Sunday, early in month • Representatives from dozens of Native American tribes from across the United States take part in this colorful celebration of culture and heritage that's open to the public. Tribal dance contests, arts and crafts, cultural heritage demonstrations, and Native American food are among the features of this powwow. Original Indian arts and crafts are exhibited and sold. Sponsorship by the Dallas/Fort Worth Inter-Tribal Association ensures authenticity of all aspects of the celebration, which has been held annually for more than 40 years.

OCTOBER

ANNUAL TRADERS VILLAGE BBQ COOKOFF • Usually Saturday and Sunday, mid-month • One of the largest BBQ events in Texas, it includes the International Barbeque Cookers Association Invitational (qualifiers by invitation only) and an open cookoff for anyone who wants to enter. Spectators can look and smell, and can also often taste, as most of the cookers offer samples. Entry fees (for charity) and prizes.

SHOPPING

MAIN STREET ANTIQUE MALL
110 W. Main (75050) • 972-237-1002 • W

In addition to the displays of American and European antiques, this shop offers a large selection of clocks of every description dating from the mid-1800s to the mid-1900s. Parking in rear.

TRADERS VILLAGE
2602 Mayfield (75052), take Mayfield exit off Hwy. 360, go east • Metro 972-647-2331 • Saturday–Sunday, year-round, 8 to dusk • Free (parking, $2) • W • www.tradersvillage.com

This is a Texas-sized 106-acre flea market on a 124-acre complex. First opened in 1973, it now attracts more than 2,000 dealers who set up in the bazaar that provides a variety of open lots, covered sheds, and enclosed buildings. Crowds of more than 60,000 bargain hunters come here each weekend to buy everything from antiques to garage sale items, imports to farm-fresh produce, and car parts and tires to hand-crafted gifts and jewelry. Country fair atmosphere where wheeling and dealing is expected. Some cheap flea-market junk, of course, but also some great buys if you know what you're looking for and have comparison-shopped the discount stores before coming here. There are children's rides, an arcade area, food vendors, and stroller and wheelchair rentals. Some vendors take credit cards, but best to bring cash, too. Over two dozen free special events are scheduled throughout the year (see ANNUAL EVENTS, p. 248). The RV Park and campground have 202 full hook-up sites.

A SAMPLING OF GRAND PRAIRIE RESTAURANTS

Dinner for one, excluding drinks, tax, and tip: $ = up to $16, $$ = $16–$30, $$$ = $31–$50, $$$$ = over $50. It is strongly suggested that you make a reservation in those restaurants that take them, especially on weekends and holidays.

DRAGONWOOD CHINESE RESTAURANT ($)

540 S. Carrier Pkwy. (75051) • 972-263-8882 • Lunch and dinner, seven days • Cr. • W+

This is a buffet restaurant with a wide variety of both familiar Chinese-American and traditional Chinese items, from appetizers to desserts available for both lunch and dinner. Parking.

MARSALA RESTAURANT ($$)

1618 N. Hwy. 360 (75050), at Avenue K • 972-988-1101 • Lunch, Monday–Friday; dinner, Monday–Saturday. Closed Sunday • Cr. • W+ • www.marsalarestaurant.com

The entrées on the French and Italian menu are divided into sections for pasta, poultry, veal, beef and lamb, and seafood. These include some vegetarian entrées. Examples of the many choices are pan-seared breast of chicken with shallots and French cognac and cream, and grilled medallions of veal tenderloin with grilled shrimp, mushrooms and rosemary. Also available are several dishes for two prepared table-side, including chateaubriand and rack of lamb. Classical guitarist enhances the romantic atmosphere during dinner, Wednesday–Saturday. Bar. Parking.

THE OASIS AT JOE POOL LAKE ($–$$)

5700 Lake Ridge Pkwy. (75052), at the Lynn Creek Marina • Metro 817-640-7676 • Lunch and dinner, seven days • Cr. • W+ • www.lynncreekmarina.com

One of the major attractions here is that this family-owned restaurant floats on Joe Pool Lake, with outside deck seating available. The menu emphasizes Southwestern cooking and includes seafood, steaks, pasta, and burgers. Among the specialties are the fried catfish and babyback ribs. Children's menu. Bar. Entertainment on Friday and Saturday evenings in the upstairs bar. Self-parking and free valet parking on weekends in summer.

A SAMPLING OF GRAND PRAIRIE ACCOMMODATIONS

*For a double room or suite: $ = up to $80, $$ = $81–$120, $$$ = $121–$180, $$$$ = $181–280, $$$$$ = over $280. **Room tax 13%.***

Unless otherwise noted, check in at 3:00 p.m., check out by noon. Unless otherwise noted, all the major accommodations have handicapped rooms/facilities and no-smoking rooms. The hearing impaired should check on visual alarms and other safety facilities when making reservations. Most accommodations permit children to stay free in room with parents. There may be a charge if this requires setting up an extra bed.

AMERISUITES GRAND PRAIRIE ($$ + 13%)

1542 N. Hwy. 360 (75050), from south take Brown Blvd./Ave. J–K exit, from north take Lamar exit • 972-988-6800 or 800-833-1516 (reservations) • www.amerisuites.com

The 135 units in this six-floor property are all suites. Pets OK (limited). Cable TV with free premium and pay channels. Coffeemaker in room, free coffee in lobby. Dataport in room. Outdoor heated pool. Fitness facilities. Self-service laundry and one-day dry cleaning. Free extended continental breakfast. Business services available. Free outdoor self-parking. Free airport transportation. Suites include refrigerator and microwave.

COMFORT SUITES DFW AIRPORT SOUTH ($$–$$$ + 13%)

2075 N. Hwy. 360 (75050), exit Green Oaks/Carrier • 817-633-6311, Metro 817-640-9607 or 800-472-6084 (reservations) • www.comfortsuites.com

There are 71 suites on the four floors of this property. Local calls free. Cable TV with free premium and pay channels. Coffeemaker in room. Dataport in room. Outdoor pool. Fitness facilities. Self-service laundry and one-day dry cleaning. Free extended continental breakfast. Free beverages Monday–Friday evenings. Business services available. Free outdoor self-parking. Free transportation to DFW Airport. Free transportation within 5-mile radius. Jacuzzi suites available. Microwave and refrigerator in all suites.

HAMPTON INN-DFW AIRPORT AREA ($–$$ + 13%)

2050 N. Hwy. 360 (75050), exit Green Oaks/Carrier • 972-988-8989 or 800-426-7866 (reservations) • www.hamptoninn.com

There are 138 rooms in this four-story inn. Cable TV with free premium channels. Coffeemaker in room. Dataport in room. Outdoor pools. Fitness facilities. Self-service laundry and one-day dry cleaning. Free extended continental breakfast. Business services available. Free outdoor self-parking. Free airport transportation. Restaurant nearby.

LAQUINTA INN ($-$$ + 13%)

1410 N.W. 19th (75050) at Hwy. 360 • 972-641-3021 or 800-NV-ROOMS (800-687-6667) (reservations) • www.laquinta.com

The 122 units in this two-story inn includes two suites. Outside access to rooms. Pets OK. Local calls free. Cable TV with free premium and pay channels available. Coffeemaker in room and free coffee in lobby. Dataport in room. Outdoor pool. Self-service laundry. Business services. Free continental breakfast. Free outdoor self-parking. Restaurant next door.

GRAPEVINE

Tarrant County • 42,000 • Area Codes 817 and 972 (local calls require area code) • www.grapevinetexasusa.com and www.ci.grapevine.tx.us

More than 150 years ago, wagon trains from Missouri, Tennessee, Alabama, Kentucky, and Ohio brought the first settlers to the Grape Vine Prairie. Today, many millions of people each year come to Grape Vine Prairie, but most don't know it because they don't realize that when they land at the huge DFW International Airport, they are landing in Grapevine. The major part of that airport lies almost entirely within the city limits of this historic town.

And it is historic, one of the oldest settlements in North Texas, settled in 1844, under the Republic of Texas, a year before Texas entered the Union. It was September of that year that Gen. Sam Houston of the Republic signed a treaty of "peace, friendship, and commerce" with leaders of the Comanche, Keechi, Waco, Delaware, and other tribes at nearby Bird's Fort. Grape Vine Springs and Grape Vine Prairie were named after the wild mustang grapes that grew profusely in the area. These names originated with the nomadic American Indian tribes that passed through the area and were continued by the settlers.

By 1854, the community leaders felt there were enough settlers to justify a town. Several names were suggested, mostly honoring the first settlers, but it was finally agreed to continue the name of Grapevine.

Today many of the outward signs of that history are preserved. Main Street, for example, with its famed Palace Theatre, historical museum, and 75 other restored historic sites, has earned a listing on the National Register of Historic Places. Community members initially worked together in 1973 to save the landmark 1901 Cotton Belt Railroad Depot, which was slated for destruction. The restored station eventually became the home for the historical museum and the depot for the Tarantula Steam Train excursions to Fort Worth. Their successful preservation efforts led to others and eventually to the formation of the present Grapevine Heritage Foundation and the Grapevine Historical Society. Working jointly, these two organizations have been able to

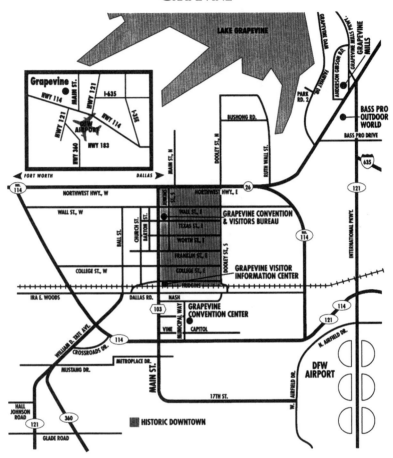

preserve much of Grapevine's past while the city moves rapidly into the future.

In keeping with the city's name, part of that future is the growing number of wineries that are settling here. There are already six wineries and tasting rooms in the city, and more on the way. If you're surprised to learn that Texas produces wines, you may be more surprised to learn that Texas was making wine before California did. In 1662, Spanish missionaries established the first North American vineyards in what is now Texas. And about half of the more that two dozen species of grapes in the world are native to Texas. So it's not surprising that Texas wines frequently win gold medals at many of the major international wine competitions. Since Grapevine is in a "wet" area, you can do a tasting of the local wines and also buy a bottle and drink it on the winery patio.

Another addition that is changing the face of the city is Grapevine

Mills Mall, a value mall that annually brings in over 16 million bargain shoppers.

For relaxation, just a mile north of downtown is the 7,380-acre Lake Grapevine with an extensive park system offering a variety of recreational facilities.

FREE VISITOR INFORMATION

GRAPEVINE CONVENTION & VISITORS BUREAU

One Liberty Park Plaza (Main at Texas) (76051) • Metro 817-410-3185 or 800-457-6338 • Monday–Friday, 8–5 • W+ (ramp in rear and elevator) • www.grapevinetexasusa.com

Brochures, maps, and other detailed information and assistance are available to help with your visit. Located in the re-creation of the 1891 Wallis Hotel. Some of the furnishings and statues are from the original hotel. The statue outside is known as *The Sidewalk Judge*. (See OUTDOOR PUBLIC ART, p. 257)

GRAPEVINE VISITOR INFORMATION CENTER

701 S. Main (76051), adjacent to the train depot • 817-410-8136 • Monday–Saturday, 9–5; Sunday, noon–5 • W+

In addition to the brochures, maps, and general information available on both the Grapevine area and other attractions in Texas, this center is the site of numerous other activities. For example, at 9:00 every Saturday morning, visitors are welcome to watch the gathering and work of the Grapevine Heritage Woodcarvers Club; the third Sunday at 3:00 p.m. the Southwest Bluegrass Club puts on a free bluegrass concert; and from mid-May through November, a farmers' market is held here on Saturday mornings and Wednesday afternoons.

HELPFUL LOCAL PUBLICATIONS

Since it is midway between Dallas and Fort Worth, current information about Grapevine events, activities, nightlife, theater, movies, and dining are often listed in both *The Dallas Morning News* and the *Fort Worth Star-Telegram*. Those two daily papers sponsor a combined website at www.dfw.com that includes entertainment guides. Other sources to check are the weekly *Dallas Observer*, which is available free at restaurants and tourist attractions throughout the Dallas area; and the monthly *D Magazine* and *Texas Monthly Magazine* available on newsstands.

INDUSTRY TOURS

DELANEY VINEYARDS AND WINERY

2000 Champagne Blvd. (76051) (Hwy. 121 at Glade Road) • 817-481-5668 • Free tours Saturday, 12–5 • W+ • www.delaneyvineyards.com

The architecture of the building and landscaping of the formal garden and 10-acre vineyard of this winery are designed to reflect a classic French-inspired style from the eighteenth century. You can wander on your own around the outdoor areas, the gift shop and sales room, but if you want a guided tour, they start on the hour from noon to 4:00 p.m. The tour takes about an hour to cover all the aspects of wine-making from the grapes to the bottle. If you want to taste the wines made here, with or without the tour, it costs $7 for five samples. (For additional tasting rooms, see OTHER POINTS OF INTEREST, p. 262.)

SELF-GUIDED TOURS

HERITAGE WALKING TOUR

A free *Historic Districts Map* is available at the Convention & Visitors Bureau and the Visitor Information Center. This can be used for a self-guided walking tour. For more detailed coverage of Grapevine historical sites and the downtown area, the Convention & Visitors Bureau offers two publications for a small fee: *A Guide For Conducting a Walking Tour of Historic Downtown Grapevine* and *A Quick-Reference Guide for Grapevine Historical Sites* (See HISTORIC PLACES, pp. 255–56)

HISTORIC PLACES

DOWNTOWN HISTORIC DISTRICT

Among the more than forty historic structures in the downtown area, the oldest is the **Torian Log Cabin** in Liberty Park at 201 S. Main. A "double-pen" style cabin, built of rough-hewn logs around 1845, it is also one of the oldest buildings in Tarrant County. Many of the downtown buildings were built in the late 1800s and early 1900s. The building at 330 S. Main, for example, was constructed in the 1890s as the lodge of the fraternal International Order of Odd Fellows. The IOOF Lodge is still upstairs, and the *Grapevine Sun* now occupies the ground floor The *Sun* newspaper was first published in 1895. Two interesting historic sidelights are the early 1900s horse-drawn hearse in a glass-enclosed outbuilding in front of the

Foust Funeral Home at 523 S. Main, and the Grapevine Calaboose on the corner of Main and Franklin. Now a favorite photo spot, this tiny calaboose was the town's first when it was built in 1909; it was used until the early 1950s to pen up overnight drunks and petty criminals.

OTHER HISTORIC PLACES

There are several nineteenth-century homes along College Street, east and west of Main. On the west side, these include the **Priest Lipscomb House** (1869) at 210, **Dr. William Lipscomb House** (1888) at 221, the **Lewis Buford House** (1895) at 314, and the **Bailey Payne House** (1865) at 504. On E. College is the **Dr. Thomas Benton Dorris House** (1896) at 224 and the **L. M. Chaffin House** (1893) at 319. The **J. E. Foust House** (1895) is at 211 W. Franklin, off Main. Most of these are private residences, not open to the public.

MUSEUMS AND PUBLIC ART GALLERIES

GRAPEVINE HERITAGE CENTER COMPLEX

701–707 S. Main (76051) • 817-424-0516 (Grapevine Heritage Foundation: Metro 817-481-0454 or 800-457-6338) • Depot Museum: Sunday–Friday, 1–5; Saturday, 10–5 • W

On this three-acre site are several restored buildings, including the 1901 **Cotton Belt Depot**, the 1888 Cotton Belt Railroad Grapevine **Section Foreman's House**, the replicated **Millican Blacksmith's Shop**, where the town smithy still works today (he'll make you a miniature lucky horseshoe, if you ask nicely); and the **Bragg House**, a tenant farmer's house built in 1907. The depot museum features exhibits and artifacts of city history that go back as far as dinosaur footprints. The depot now also serves as an information center and, in a revival of its original function, as the depot for the daily excursions of the **Tarantula Steam Train** (see FAMILY FUN AND KID STUFF, p. 259). Several skilled artisans here demonstrate craftsmanship techniques that were used more than 150 years ago, including saddle making and wood carving. Many of the items made here are for sale, and some of the artisans teach daily classes on their pioneer techniques. A small **Farmers Market** is usually set up here Wednesday afternoons and Saturday mornings from mid-May to mid-November.

OUTDOOR PUBLIC ART

The Grapevine Nightwatchman (Atop City Hall) • Keeping vigil over the city with his lantern, this statue honors the men who patrolled and protected the town from the early 1900s to the 1950s. The statue is 8 feet tall, weighs 640 pounds, and was designed and built by Jack Bryant of Springton.

The Homecoming (at the Depot) • A two-piece sculpture created by Michael Pavlovsky depicts a soldier coming home to a loving embrace. It's set in an arch that bears symbols of branches of military service and faiths.

New Season (in Botanical Gardens) • This sculpture, by Gary Price, celebrates Grapevine's location on the migration path of the monarch butterfly, between Canada and Mexico.

The Sidewalk Judge (in front of Convention & Visitors Bureau at Wallis Hotel) • A popular photo spot, the statue of the man on a park bench, by J. Seward Johnson, represents the early residents who sat on Main Street and "sized up" or "judged" the people passing by.

Walking to Texas (in Liberty Park) • This sculpture, by Michael Cunningham, is a tribute to the pioneer families who came to Grapevine. It depicts a couple with a baby by a fountain that has four horse heads pointing to the four directions, representing the spirit of the American Indians who lived on the prairie before the pioneers arrived.

OUTDOORS

GRAPEVINE LAKE

About one mile north of downtown Grapevine (From Main, go northeast on Hwy. 26 to Fairway Dr.) • Grapevine Lake Project, 110 Fairway (76051) • 817-481-3576 • Most areas open at all times • Fee and non-fee areas • W

This 7,380-acre U.S. Army Corps of Engineers lake is 19 miles long, stretching up into Denton County. Along its 146 miles of tree-lined shoreline are seven developed parks and five undeveloped ones. The Headquarters and Visitor Area is at the southeast end of the lake off Highway 26 near the dam and Silver Lake Park. Now one of the busiest lakes in Texas, it has facilities for power and sail boating (marinas and boat rentals), fishing, swimming, water-skiing, wind surfing, hiking, trail bike riding, picnicking, and camping (fee and non-fee).

GRAPEVINE PARKS

Parks and Recreation Department • 200 S. Main (P.O. Box 95104, 76099) • 817-410-3450 • www.ci.grapevine.tx.us

The more than three dozen parks in the system include facilities for a variety of team sports, tennis courts, swimming pools, picnic areas, trails, and a nature center. There are also playgrounds, including a 100-percent-wheelchair-accessible playground, and a botanical garden in Heritage Park (411 Ball St. at Wall).

MUSIC AND PERFORMING ARTS

GRAPEVINE CONCERT SERIES
Palace Theatre (300 S. Main) and other locations • Ticket prices vary

More than a dozen concerts and storytelling fests are presented during the year, both outdoors and inside the Palace Theatre. The mix is eclectic, ranging from bluegrass to opera, folk to the big band sounds, and harps to accordions. Ticket prices vary by event but are generally inexpensive.

THE GRAPEVINE OPRY
Palace Theatre (300 S. Main) (76051) • 817-481-8733 • W+

There's a foot-stompin'-hand-clappin' country and western music show here every Saturday night at 7:30. In the early years, The Opry featured rising stars like Willie Nelson, Ernest Tubb, and the Judds. There still are occasional specials with nationally known artists, but most of the family entertainment is a variety showcase for local and regional musicians and other performers, with most of the shows built around a theme. A Gospel Showcase is held the fourth Friday night of each month at 7:30. Adults, $12; children 12 and under, $8. Senior discounts available except for specials.

THE PALACE ARTS CENTER
300 S. Main (76051) • 817-410-3100 • W+ •
www.palace-theatre.com

Built in 1940 in Art Deco style as a movie theater, the Palace fell into disrepair after World War II and for a time was used as a hay barn. In 1975 it was rehabilitated enough to open as the home of the Grapevine Opry. The Grapevine Heritage Foundation acquired the building in 1991, to save it from demolition, and then, as now, the Opry remains its major tenant. In 2001, after a $5 million restoration, it reopened as the Palace Arts Center: A Theater for the Performing Arts. The Center consists of the 438-seat (including 11 love seats) Palace and the 175-seat "black box" Lancaster Theatre. Between them, they offer stage productions, live music shows (like the Opry), concerts, and motion pictures. And, since this is Grapevine, after all, they hold wine tasting here twice a month.

THE RUNWAY THEATRE
215 N. Dooley (76051) (just north of Northwest Hwy.) •
817-488-4842 • W • www.runwaytheatre.com

This community theater has been the home of the End of the Runway Players since 1983. The Players put on about eight productions a year, mainly comedies and musicals, in the September through July season.

Curtain times are at 8:00 on Friday and Saturday nights and 3:00 for the Sunday matinee. Each production runs two to four weekends.

FAMILY FUN AND KID STUFF

OLD-FASHIONED SODA FOUNTAIN

A Scoop In Time • 412 S. Main (76051) • 817-421-6393 • W

Ice cream cones, sodas, malts, shakes, banana splits are served to your order in this old-fashioned fountain shop in the heart of Main Street. And the lemonade comes from real lemons, not cans.

GAME WORKS

525 Grapevine Mills Mall, 3000 Grapevine Mills Pkwy. (76051) • 972-539-6757 • W • www.gameworks.com

Put together the combined playpower of Steven Spielberg's Dreamworks, Sega Games, and Universal Studio and what you get is this 32,000-square-foot complex where you can play more than 200 of the highest of high-tech games as well as the old classics, like PacMan. Buy Play Cards for $10 up. Parents can request a special V-card for their children that prevent access to the few games that have mature content. Full-service restaurant and bar. Located just inside mall Entry 5 (The Entertainment Entry).

TARANTULA STEAM TRAIN EXCURSIONS

Cotton Belt Depot (707 S. Main) • 817-625-RAIL (817-625-7245), Metro 817-654-0898 or 800-457-6338 (Convention & Visitors Bureau) • Round trip: Adults, about $20; children 3 to 12, about $10 • W but call ahead • www.tarantulatrain.com

Based in Grapevine, the Tarantula Steam Train runs daily round-trip excursions to the Fort Worth Stockyards. Weekdays the train departs Grapevine at 10:00 a.m., riding the 21 miles of track to arrive at the Fort Worth Stockyards at about 11:30. The return trip leaves at 2:30 p.m., arriving at its home base in Grapevine about 4 p.m. This schedule gives passengers a couple of hours to explore the Stockyard attractions (See FORT WORTH—STOCKYARDS, pp. 174–76). Sundays the excursions run from 1:00 to 6:30 p.m. The train also runs special excursions throughout the year.

Tarantula's primary steam locomotive, No. 2248, operates Friday through Sunday and the diesel engine runs the other days. Originally built in 1896 and fully restored, it pulls passenger cars and touring coaches dating from the 1920s. The passenger and touring cars have been restored with décor resembling day coaches from the early 1900s. Passenger cars are equipped with ceiling fans but are not air-conditioned. The touring coaches are open-sided (with railings for passenger safety). Seating is on a first-come basis. Snacks, soft drinks, wine, and beer are available on board.

The turntable, used to turn the steam locomotive around, weighs 300,000 pounds and was moved here from Saginaw, Texas, north of Fort Worth.

Why "Tarantula"? The name goes back to a map published in 1870 that depicted a vision of Fort Worth newspaper editor B. B. Paddock, who saw Fort Worth at the center of nine radially extending rail lines. Some laughed at the map, saying the map lines resembled a hairy-legged tarantula and that the railroad center was just a dream. But by the 1890s the railroads had laid the nine legs with the center in Fort Worth. So, when Fort Worth businessman William Davis came up with his vision of an excursion steam train, he named it after Paddock's vision.

SPORTS

GOLF

PUBLIC COURSE

GRAPEVINE MUNICIPAL GOLF COURSE

3800 Fairway Dr. (76051), off Hwy. 26 on north side of Grapevine Dam • Metro 817-410-3377

Eighteen-hole championship course designed by Byron Nelson and Joe Finger, rated among the top 20 municipal courses in Texas; has been listed in the top 50 municipal courses in the nation.

HORSEBACK RIDING

WAGON WHEEL RANCH

816 Ruth Wall Rd. (76051), a mile north of Grapevine Mills Mall on FM2499 • Metro 972-462-0894 or Metro 817-481-8284 • www.awagonwheelranch.com

Trail rides daily at about $20 hour. Children must be 7 years of age and 48 inches tall. Reservations required. English and Western riding lessons available.

ICE SKATING

POLAR ICE

613 Grapevine Mills Mall, 3000 Grapevine Mills Pkwy. (76051) • 972-874-1930

There are two National Hockey League–size ice rinks here for hockey league play, recreational skating, and figure skating. Pro shop and restaurant. Located just inside Entry 6 (the Wine Barrel Entry). Call for skating times and prices.

TENNIS

In addition to the tennis courts in several Grapevine parks (817-410-3450) there are courts available to visitors at the Hilton DFW Lakes Hotel and the Hyatt Regency DFW Hotel. (See A SAMPLING OF GRAPEVINE ACCOMMODATIONS, pp. 268–69)

OTHER POINTS OF INTEREST

DALLAS/FORT WORTH INTERNATIONAL AIRPORT (DFW)

P.O. Box 619428, DFW Airport (75261-9428) • 972-574-8888 • Open at all times • W+ • www.dfwairport.com

Like to watch planes? Even with heightened security restrictions, with a couple of thousand arrivals and departures each day, this is the place to be. At almost 30 square miles, DFW is the second largest in the United States in terms of land mass, and the third largest in the world. It is greater in area than Chicago's O'Hare, New York's JFK, and Atlanta's Hartsfield combined. In the average year, more than 60 million travelers pass through DFW. The airport is in the initial stage of a $2.6 billion expansion that includes consolidating all international flights in one terminal, an automated people mover system with an average terminal connect time of five minutes, runway extensions, increased parking, and other improvements.

If you're flying out, plan to arrive early enough to give yourself plenty of time to take a leisurely self-guided tour, during which you can see this monster airport in operation while you relax and watch everyone else bustling to catch a plane. Ride the Air Trans to get around. Air Trans is a small train system that runs between the terminals, the parking areas, and the Hyatt Regency DFW Hotel. (Kids will love the ride itself.) The Hyatt Hotel is also worth a visit, perhaps even for a hamburger and a shake lunch in its 50s style cafe—a little pricey, but excellent value for your money when compared to the prices in the terminal restaurants. If you didn't get to one of the wine tasting rooms in Grapevine, you can have the experience by going to Terminal A where, near Gate 15, you'll find the **La Bodega Winery,** the nation's first winery in an airport. Here you can see a miniature winery, with a grape press and fermentation vat that really produce. Try the reasonably priced tastings or buy from a selection of more than 50 varieties from more than a dozen Texas wineries.

You can do all this even if you're not flying out, but it'll cost you to park your car plus the toll fee to drive through the airport, and you may have problems with the heightened security measures.

GRAPEVINE MILLS MALL

(See SHOPPING, p. 265)

WINE TASTING ROOMS

Connoisseurs consider wine-tasting an art. But even if you know nothing about wine, as long as you like it, wine tastings can be fun. These tasting rooms offer a wide variety of Texas wines to taste. Depending on the winery, the wines, and whether you keep the souvenir glass, prices vary from $5 to $10 for about four wines. Wine is also for sale by the bottle or the case. (Warning! Don't try to do all these tasting rooms in one day.)

For more information about Texas wines, the Texas Wine and Grape Growers Association in Grapevine offers a free *Texas Wine Country Guide*. TWGGA, 701 S. Main (76051), 817-424-0570 • www.twgga.org. The Texas Department of Agriculture also offers information on Texas wines on its toll-free "Texas wine" number, 866-4TXWINE (866-489-9463).

Cap*Rock Winery • 409 S. Main • 817-329-9483 • www.caprock winery.com • This tasting room features a unique bar with a poured concrete top stained with Cap*Rock Cabernet Sauvignon. Gift shop.

Cross Timbers Winery • 805 N. Main • 817-488-6789 • Located in the Brock Farmhouse, one of Grapevine's Historic Homesteads. The tasting room serves both its own varietals and wines from other Texas vineyards.

Delaney Vineyards • 2000 Champagne Blvd. • 817-481-5668 • www.delaneyvineyards.com • (See INDUSTRY TOURS, p. 255)

Homestead Winery and Tasting Room • 211 E. Worth, off Main • 817-251-9463 • A converted cottage on a tree-lined side street downtown is the site of this tasting room and gift shop.

La Bodega Winery and Tasting Room • DFW Airport, Terminal A • 972-574-1440 • (See OTHER POINTS OF INTEREST—DFW Airport, p. 261)

La Buena Vida Vineyards • 416 E. College, off Main • 817-481-9463 • www.labuenavida.com • One of Texas's oldest producing wineries, this was the first to establish a winery and tasting room in Grapevine. The limestone building here contains an antique grape press and a fermentation tank. It also features a small winery museum and gift shop.

ANNUAL EVENTS

APRIL

NEW VINTAGE WINE EXPERIENCE

Usually Wednesday–Saturday, mid-month • Grapevine Convention Center (1209 South Main) and various locations • 817-410-3185 or 800-457-6338 (Grapevine Convention & Visitors Bureau) • Prices vary by event • W to W+ (depends on event location)

This is the occasion for more than two dozen Texas wineries to uncork their new vintages. At least one event each day is centered around a wine tasting. The festival begins with the Blessing of the Vines. There are also seminars for wine enthusiasts, tours of area vineyards and visits to local tasting rooms, and a sampling of area restaurant fare paired with compatible wines. This is an à la carte affair, with the various events priced from about $12 to $50. Unlike GrapeFest, which is a full-blown festival drawing many thousands of visitors, this festival is really geared to food and wine enthusiasts.

MAY

MAIN STREET DAYS

Usually Friday–Sunday, mid-month • Main Street Historic District • 817-410-3185 or 800-457-6338 (Grapevine Convention & Visitors Bureau) • Adults and teenagers, $6; seniors and children 6–12, $3. Weekend pass, $10 • W

Grapevine's celebration of its prairie and railroad heritage is geared to living history. Main Street is transformed for the event, and there are demonstrations of heritage arts and crafts, plus re-enactors and storytellers to make the past come to life. Even the competitors in the Beef Stew Contest must wear costumes approximating 1850s settlers, and their campsites must either be pre-1850s Pioneer or post-1850s Chuck Wagon. The roster of entertainment includes extra performances of the Grapevine Opry, continuous music ranging from C&W to rock on three stages, plus special entertainment Friday and Saturday nights and a street dance Saturday night. There's also a free carnival midway with a small children's midway. More than 100,000 people normally attend this three-day festival. All for a good cause: funding the projects of the Grapevine Heritage Foundation.

SEPTEMBER

GRAPEFEST

Usually second full weekend (Friday–Sunday) • Main Street Historic District • 817-410-3185 or 800-457-6338 (Grapevine Convention & Visitors Bureau) • General admission: Adults, $5; weekend pass, $7; seniors and children 6–12, $1 • W

One of the largest wine festivals in America and the oldest and largest in the Texas, GrapeFest attracts more than 150,000 visitors to the celebration. The Main Street festivities include nonstop entertainment by musicians, dancers, and other entertainers on three stages and a wine tasting and wine auction. Saturday and Sunday wine-tasting sessions each last about an hour and a half, and at the end you're asked to vote for the People's Choice awards for the best wines. In addition, there's a tennis tournament, a vintage and classic car display, vineyard tours, a carnival, and arts and crafts show. A premier event is a black-tie Texas Wine Tribute Gala, held on Saturday night, featuring a gourmet dinner paired with award-winning Texas wines ($95 per person). Among the other popular events are the barefoot Grape Stomp contest for the "Purple Foot" trophy, and a Champagne Brunch (Texas champagne, of course) on Sunday. This is another fund-raiser for the Grapevine Heritage Foundation.

SHOPPING

BASS PRO SHOPS OUTDOOR WORLD

2501 Bass Pro Dr. (Off intersection of I-635 and Hwy. 26, near Grapevine Mills Mall) (76051) • 972-724-2018 • W+ but not all areas • www.basspro.com

The use of the word "world" in the name of this store is most apt. Under a 190,000-square-foot roof you'll find just about everything you'll need for any outdoor activity and adventure, all in gear-packed departments surrounding a 30,000-gallon aquarium with waterfall and tied into a brewery and steak house. Camping, fishing, boating, hunting, golf—all the gear is here, plus the clothing and footwear to go along with your outdoor life. They even have RVs and boats to get you there. Hunters can try before they buy at an indoor handgun range, an archery range, and a rifle tube, while golfers can use an indoor driving range and putting green. And for those who just want fun, there's a state-of-the-art laser arcade/shooting gallery.

THE BRITISH EMPORIUM

140 N. Main (76051) • 817-421-2311 • W

A large selection of teas in tins and bulk are among the many imported foods found here. Although most items are from Britain, foods from other countries that were in the old British Empire, like India and South Africa, are also available.

GRAPEVINE ART GLASS

334 S. Barton (76051), one block west of Main • 817-251-5193 • W

One-of-a-kind glass *objets d'art* by over 80 different artists, including many Charles Lotton pieces, are on display in this art glass shop. Prices range from $10 to thousands. From September through May you can see the wonder of the glassblowing process next door at the **Vetro! Contemporary Glass Blowing Studio** (817-232-9436 • www.vetro-glass.com • Tuesday–Thursday, 6–10 p.m. and all day Saturday.) The colorful, unique custom-designed pieces of glass art hand-blown here are for sale.

GRAPEVINE DOLL AND GIFT SHOP

413 S. Main (76051) • 817-488-2226 • W

What was once the City Hall building, filled with politicians and civil servants, is now a 5,000-square-foot shop filled to overflowing with hundreds of dolls of every style and description. A childhood love of paper dolls evolved into serious doll collecting for owner Frances LaMerle Wiggins. Now she offers her customers a wide variety of choices, from play to collector dolls by world-renowned doll artists. These include a room devoted solely to Barbie and another to the popular Madame Alexander line. There are also many dolls from France and Germany that she brings back from her periodic trips to the Nuremberg Toy Fair, one of the largest such fairs in the world.

GRAPEVINE MILLS MALL

Hwy. 121 and International Pkwy. (FM2499), two miles north of DFW Airport • 972-742-4900 or toll-free 888-645-5748 • W+ • www.grapevinemills.com

One of the largest shopping centers in Texas, this is a mega-mall where you can literally shop till you drop. The 1.8 million square feet of roof is large enough to cover three ballparks the size of The Ballpark at Arlington. But, instead of ballparks, it covers more than 200 manufacturer and retail outlets, off-price retailers, specialty stores, restaurants, and entertainment facilities ranging from an ice rink to a 30-screen theater. The mall uses a one-level oval racetrack design, so all stores are directly on the racetrack. To make it easier to find your car among the 8,500 spaces, parking areas are coded, each of the six mall entrances is marked by 40-to-50-foot distinctive structural sign, an automated announcement reminds you, as you enter, of which entrance you used, and all the store numbers around that entrance have a three-digit address starting with that entrance number.

Among the many bargain stores in the mall are **Off 5th**—the Saks Fifth Avenue Outlet—and **Last Call** from Neiman Marcus. Last Call consolidates marked-down merchandise from that upscale retailer's 32 stores nationwide, as well as from Bergdorf Goodman. Themed restaurants include the **Rainforest Café**, where you dine among playful animated wildlife in a tropical rainforest, and Dick Clark's **American Bandstand Grill** which centers around music from the fifties to the nineties.

The mall is a destination in itself, annually attracting more than 16 million visitors, of which about 25 percent are tourists. Show an out-of-town ID or international passport at the customer service center and they'll give you a VIP package including discount coupons. (You can even get there on a long stopover at DFW airport. The Super Shuttle provides transport from DFW—just two miles away. Call 817-329-3846 for pickup information and rates.)

MAIN STREET HISTORIC DISTRICT SHOPS

(Call the Convention & Visitors Bureau, 817-410-3185, for map/brochure.)

Within an easy-walking four-block stretch of historic Main Street are a number of shops featuring everything from antiques to home décor, boutique and Western clothing to gift items.

OFF THE VINE

324 S. Main (76051) • 817-421-1091 • W • www.offthevine.com

This wine shop offers a selection of hundreds of wines, including all the wines presented at the annual New Vintage Wine Experience and GrapeFest, plus wine-related gift items.

A SAMPLING OF GRAPEVINE RESTAURANTS

Dinner for one, excluding drinks, tax, and tip: $ = up to $16, $$ = $16–$30, $$$ = $31–$50, $$$$ = over $50. It is strongly suggested that you make a reservation in those restaurants that take them, especially on weekends and holidays.

BIG BUCK BREWERY AND STEAK HOUSE ($$–$$$)

2501 Bass Pro Dr. #100 (76051), in Bass Pro Shops Outdoor World • 214-513-BEER (214-513-2337) • Lunch and dinner, seven days • Cr. • W+ • www.bigbuck.com

The size and décor of this restaurant are as impressive as the menu. More than 20,000 square feet, the 52-foot ceilings with Douglas fir beams, the 17-ton stone fireplace grill, and oak and hickory tables and chairs made by the Amish add up to an impressive hunting-lodge style. The Big Buck name theme carries over into the menu. In addition to a choice of steaks with hunter names, like Trophy Rack New York Strip, among the more standard items are buffalo burgers, venison sausage, venison Reuben, and several seafood selections cooked in ale and beer from the in-house brewery. The brewery produces about a dozen fresh draft brews ranging from a "light" to a stout, and you can sample them in 5-oz. glasses at 5 beers for $5. Children's menu.

CHARLIE'S CAFÉ ($–$$)

210 N. Main (76051), in Old Main Street Shopping Center • 817-421-6256 • Lunch and dinner, Tuesday–Saturday. Closed Sunday–Monday • MC, V • W+

Nothing fancy; the rule here is just solid home-style cooking with fresh ingredients. Standards and local favorites include chicken fried steak, Southern-style catfish fillets, marinated chicken breast, burgers, and home-made desserts. Daily plate specials. Vegetarian entrées available. Children's menu.

RAVIOLI RISTORANTE ($$)

120 E. Worth (76051), one block off Main • 817-488-1181 •
Lunch, Monday–Friday; dinner, seven days • Cr. • W ramp on west
side of building

Most entrées on the extensive menu are Northern Italian, a cuisine
that tends more toward cream sauces than the tomato sauces favored in
southern Italy. The extensive menu includes a wide selection of pasta entrées plus chicken, veal, and seafood. If you just want pasta, for around
$10 you have a choice of six types and six sauces. More imaginative en-
trées include grilled chicken breast topped with shrimp, mushrooms,
green onions, and a sherry cream sauce; and sautéed veal in a sherry
cream sauce with artichoke hearts and mushrooms. Bar. Parking.

SONNY BRYAN'S SMOKEHOUSE ($)

322 S. Park (76051) • 817-424-5978 or 800-5-SONNYS (576-6697)
• Lunch and dinner, seven days • Cr. • W

This is a branch of a Metroplex barbecue chain that's consistently
rated high by area residents. Texas-style barbecue items include brisket,
ribs, and smoked turkey. Also Tennessee-style pork barbecue. Children's
menu. Surprisingly, vegetarian plates are available. Beer and wine.

SOUTH PRAIRIE OYSTER BAR ($)

651 S. Main (76051) • 817-488-3909 • Lunch and dinner,
Tuesday–Saturday. Closed Sunday–Monday • No Cr. • W

A tiny seafood shack with fast servings of simple seafood, like Cajun-
fried oyster po'boys, baskets of fried seafood, and oysters on the half
shell. Its hush puppies are locally famed. Beer.

WILLHOITE'S RESTAURANT ($)

432 S. Main (76051) • Metro 817-481-7511 • Lunch and dinner,
seven days • Cr. • W+ • www.willhoites.com

In 1919, it was Grapevine's first gas station and garage. They've kept
some signs of its earlier garage life, like the Model T Ford that hangs over
the "all you can eat" buffet table, but now it's a popular restaurant and bar.
In addition to the inexpensive buffet, the menu includes steaks and
chicken entrees, burgers, and sandwiches. Children's menu. Popular bar
with live entertainment Tuesday–Saturday.

A SAMPLING OF GRAPEVINE
ACCOMMODATIONS

*For a double room or suite: $ = up to $80, $$ = $81–$120, $$$ = $121–$180, $$$$ =
$181–$280, $$$$$ = over $280. Room tax 12%.*

Unless otherwise noted, check in at 3:00 p.m., check out by noon. Unless otherwise noted, all these accommodations have handicapped rooms/facilities and no-smoking rooms. Check on visual alarms and other safety facilities for the hearing impaired when making reservation. Most accommodations permit children to stay free in room with parents. There may be a charge if this requires setting up an extra bed.

AMERISUITES DALLAS/DFW AIRPORT NORTH ($$–$$$ + 12%)

2220 Grapevine Mills Circle W. (76051), near Grapevine Mills Mall • 972-691-1199 or 800-833-1516 (reservations) • www.amerisuites.com

There are 126 suites in this six-story property. Pets OK (extra charge). Cable TV with free premium channels and pay channels. Coffeemaker in room. Dataport in room. Outdoor pool and hot tub. Fitness facilities. Self-service laundry and one-day dry cleaning. Free breakfast buffet. Free manager's reception, Wednesday evenings. Business services available. Free outdoor self-parking. Free DFW Airport transportation and area transportation within 5-mile radius. Suites have mini-kitchen with refrigerator and microwave.

EMBASSY SUITES HOTEL—OUTDOOR WORLD AT DFW AIRPORT ($$$–$$$$ + 12%)

2401 Bass Pro Dr. (76051), connected to Bass Pro Shops Outdoor World • 972-724-2600 or 800-EMBASSY (800-362-2778) (reservations) • www.embassysuitesoutdoorworld.com

There are 329 suites in this 12-story atrium hotel. Pets OK (extra charge). Cable TV with free premium and pay channels. Coffeemaker in room and free coffee in atrium. Dataport in room. Indoor heated pool. Hot tub and sauna. Fitness facilities. Guest memberships available for golf. Concierge services available. Gift shop. Self-service laundry and one-day dry cleaning. Free full cooked-to-order breakfast. Free cocktail hours. Restaurant. Room service. Lounge. Business services center. Conference facilities. Game room. Free outdoor self-parking or valet (fee). Free transportation to DFW Airport and scheduled shuttle to Grapevine and Grapevine Mills Mall. Refrigerator and microwave in all suites.

HILTON DFW LAKES ($$–$$$$$ + 12%)

1800 Hwy. 26E (76051), just south of junction with Hwy. 121 • 817-481-8844 or 800-HILTONS (800-445-86670) (reservations) • www.dfwlakes.hilton.com

The 395 units in this nine-story hotel include 12 suites. Concierge section with extra amenities. Cable TV with free premium and pay channels. Coffeemaker in room. Dataport in room. Bell service. Heated indoor and outdoor pools. Hot tub and sauna. Fitness facilities. Jogging trail, lighted outdoor and indoor tennis courts, racquetball, volleyball, and other resort-type sports facilities. Guest memberships available for golf. Concierge services available. Gift shop. One-day dry cleaning. Three restaurants, including one fine dining. Room service. Lounge. Convention facilities. Business services center. Free outdoor self-parking or valet parking (fee). Free transportation to DFW Airport and to Grapevine Mills Mall. The 40-acre grounds are on a lake. Western art throughout hotel, much depicting early Grapevine. Within walking distance of Grapevine Mills Mall. Welcome packet for children at check-in. Some supervised children's activities.

HYATT REGENCY DFW ($$$–$$$$$ + 12%

International Pkwy., DFW Airport (P.O. Box 619014, DFW Airport 75261) • 972-453-1234 or 800-233-1234 (reservations) • www.dallas.hyatt.com

The only hotel actually located within DFW Airport, this 12-story hotel has 811 units, including 11 suites. Cable TV with free premium and pay channels. Coffeemaker in room. Dataport in room. Bell service. Outdoor pool. Fitness facilities. Free transportation to Hyatt-operated Bear Creek Golf Club and tennis facilities at south entrance to airport. Gift shop and retail shops. One-day dry cleaning. Two restaurants. Room service. Lounge. Conference facilities. Business center. Free outdoor self-parking and valet parking (fee). Free transportation to DFW Airport terminals and to Grapevine Mills Mall.

SIDE TRIPS IN NORTH RICHLAND HILLS

The following are all in **North Richland Hills,** *southwest of Grapevine* • *www.nrhtx.com*

ADVENTURE WORLD PLAYGROUND

7451 Starnes (76180) • 817-581-5760

The largest handicapped-accessible park in Texas. Designed with ramps instead of stairs and other provisions that allow children in wheelchairs and with other handicaps to access the equipment. Located within the Cross Timbers Park (7680 Douglas).

BLUE LINE ICE COMPLEX

8851 Ice House Dr. (76180), next to Birdville High School on Mid Cities Blvd.) 817-788-5400 • www.bluelineice.com

This complex features two National Hockey League regulation-size rinks and one Olympic regulation-size rink. Public skating daily. Call for times and prices. Pro shop. Variety of local and other hockey leagues play here.

NRH2O FAMILY WATER PARK

9001 Grapevine Hwy. (Hwy 26)(76180) • 817-427-6500 or toll-free 888-WTR-PARK (888-987-7275) • Open mid-May to mid-

September. Open times vary by day and season. Call • Admission: 48″ tall and above, $13.45; under 48″, $11.45; age 2 and under free • www.nrh2o.com

Truly a family water park, with something for every age. For small fry it offers a children's area with its Tadpole Train Station, a variety of chutes, and the skill-testing balancing net and lily pad. Teens and adventurous adults can try their skill on the Black Falls, an enclosed slide that plummets riders through near-darkness to the water below. Other choices include the 7-story, 1,161-foot-long Green Extreme, said to be the world's largest uphill water coaster; the Purplepalooza, a totally enclosed double rider slide, and the Double Dipper, a double rider innertube slide. And for those who want relaxation rather than thrills, there's the gentle Endless River, where you can just float along. Free tubes available on a first come, first served basis. Life jackets available. No masks, fins, or snorkels. Lifeguards. Gift shop. Free parking. Friday nights you can watch a "dive-in" movie from the pool. **Mountasia Family Fun Center** with go carts, miniature golf, in-line skating, and other games and activities, is nearby at 8851 Grapevine Highway (817-788-0990).

RICHLAND TENNIS CENTER

7111 N.E. Loop 820 (76180) • 817-427-6680 • www.nrhtx.com

All 16 courts are lighted. One sunken court with tournament seating. Full-service center operated by city Recreation Department. Open seven days. Court fees $2.50 per person for 1½ hours. Lessons available.

IRVING

Dallas County • 190,000 • Area Code 972 (local calls require area code) • www.nrhtx.com and www.ci.irving.tx.us

The Republic of Texas settled its massive territory partly through agreements offering entrepreneurs huge tracts of land if they would bring in homesteaders—so much land for so many settlers. In 1841, such an agreement was signed with a group including William S. Peters, a musician and music publisher in Louisville, Kentucky. This group was given an enormous land grant covering several counties, including all of Tarrant County and all but a narrow band of eastern Dallas County—much of what is now the Metroplex. Because his name headed the list of group members, the area eventually became known as the Peters Colony. All of present-day Irving's more than 67 square miles lies entirely within the original Peters Colony.

But the city itself owes its origin to two young men, Julius O. Schulze, a railroad surveyor, and Otis Brown, his survey team rod man. These two recognized the values and opportunities that railroads bring to communities and, in 1902, while surveying a ten-mile route west of the Dallas County line for Chicago, Rock Island & Gulf Railway, they paid $2,169.30 for approximately 74 acres on which they planned to build a town. A year later, after they finished their stint with the Rock Island, they cleared the land, got married both within a week of each other, and drew their proposed town site on a tablecloth. With the help of a special excursion train out of Dallas, provided by the Rock Island, they held an auction at which they sold 20 lots at an average of $50 each.

They wanted a distinctive name that would set the town apart, so they named it after one of the most popular writers of the time, Washington Irving. It's said the name was suggested by Netta Brown, Otis's wife, because Irving was her favorite author. Coincidentally, while at the University of Iowa, Schulze had been a member of a literary/debating society that was also named after Irving.

LIVING IN THE SHADOW OF DALLAS

During the early years, Irving lived in the shadow of Dallas and grew slowly. The 1950 census listed the population as only 2,621. But in the

IRVING

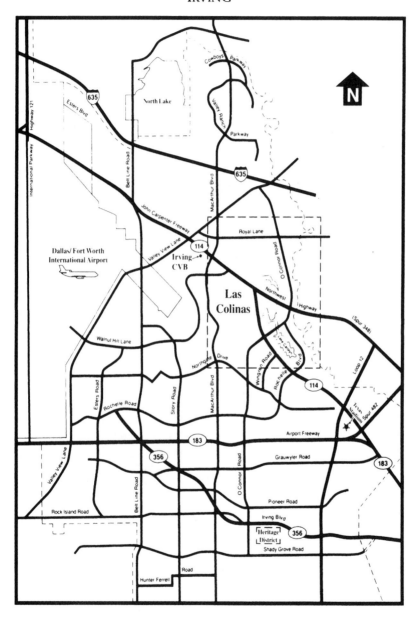

1970s several events contributed to a population jump to over 100,000. In 1971, the $30 million Texas Stadium was built as the home of the Dallas Cowboys, and in 1974 the Dallas/Fort Worth International Airport (DFW) opened, with its eastern border inside Irving's city limits and the major highways between the airport and Dallas passing through the city. This same decade saw the beginnings of what would become the 12,000-acre planned residential/commercial community called Las Colinas.

Although the city is a corporate center and the home of more than 400 multinational companies, its convenient location next to DFW Airport has led to the hotel/motel industry being its largest private employer, with more than 8,000 people employed in the 75 hotels/motels.

If you stay in Irving and want to go to Dallas for the day but don't want to drive all the way in, you can take the Trinity Railway Express, a diesel commuter train that makes the run from the South Irving Station (Rock Island and O'Connor) or the West Irving Station (Belt Line and Jackson) about fifteen times a day on weekdays, mostly during morning and evening rush hours. It makes it to the Medical Center/Market Station in around ten minutes and to the Dallas Union Station in around 16 minutes, with transfers available to either the Dallas Area Rapid Transit buses or the DART Light Rail System (see DALLAS, p. 70). (For information call DART at 214-979-1111 or www.DART.org.)

While it continues to move forward at a rapid pace, Irving has not neglected its past, emphasizing the preservation and revitalization of its historic downtown.

Under the local option laws, Irving is dry, but you can buy alcoholic beverages with food in restaurants and in hotels and motels.

FREE VISITOR SERVICES

IRVING CONVENTION & VISITORS BUREAU

1231 Greenway, Suite 1060 (75038), near intersection of Hwy. 114 and MacArthur • 972-252-7476 or 800-2-IRVING (247-8464) • Monday–Friday, 8–5 • W+ • www.irvingtexas.com

In addition to an array of maps, brochures, hotel and restaurant listings, and a calendar of events for visitors, this office sometimes has special discount coupons for area attractions. A little hard to find; call for directions.

HELPFUL LOCAL PUBLICATIONS

Current information about Irving events, activities, nightlife, theater, movies, and dining are often listed in the local edition of the *Dallas Morn-*

ing News, and the *Friday Guide* in that newspaper. The *Fort Worth Star-Telegram* is also a good source, and those two daily papers sponsor a combined website which includes entertainment guides at **www.dfw.com**. Other sources to check are the weekly *Dallas Observer*, which is available free at restaurants and tourist attractions throughout the Dallas area; and the monthly *D Magazine* and *Texas Monthly Magazine*, available on newsstands.

TOUR SERVICES

GONDOLA ADVENTURES

357 Westfork (75039), in Las Colinas • 972-506-8037 or toll-free 866-4-GONDOLA (466-3652)(Central reservations) • www.gondola.com

Gondolas in Texas? Yep! You can be serenaded by a gondolier and experience a little of Venice on the Mandalay Canals and Lake Carolyn in Las Colinas. The gondolas, which hold two to six, were built of mahogany in the traditional construction, with the exception that they are powered by silent motors rather than traditional oars. They usually operate from about 10:00 a.m to midnight, offering a variety of cruises that can be tailored to your wishes with prices depending on number of passengers and choice of cruise. Choices range from a simple half-hour ride along the canals (about $50 for up to six passengers) to a 1½-hour gourmet dinner cruise ($245–$345) or a romantic sunset or moonlight "Champagne and Chocolates" cruise ($125–$165). (Since Irving is "dry," it's nonalcoholic champagne, but you can BYOB.) Reservations required.

DR. PEPPER BOTTLING COMPANY TOUR

2304 Century Center Blvd. (75075), near Texas Stadium • 972-721-8394 • W

A free tour showing how Dr. Pepper is made and bottled is offered most Wednesday mornings, starting at 10:00 a.m. Of course, you'll get a free sample at the end. Call for reservations.

MOVIE STUDIOS AT LAS COLINAS TOUR

6301 N. O'Connor (75039), at Royal (Building One in Dallas Communications Complex. Follow signs to Tour) • 972-869-FILM (869-3456) • Adults, $12.95; seniors (over 65), $10.95; children 4–12, $8.95 • www.studioatlascolinas.com

Get a behind-the-scenes glimpse of TV and movie production techniques and how filmmakers create illusions, as well as actual film props and memorabilia, in this tour that takes about 1½ hours. The studios here in the vast Dallas Communications Complex have been used for films ranging from *Silkwood* to *JFK* and TV productions from *Barney and*

Friends to *Walker, Texas Ranger*. The tour has a number of audience-participation stops. Summer hours (May 1–August 31): Open daily, 10:00 a.m.–5:00 p.m., with tours scheduled beginning at 12:30. Saturday, Sunday, and holiday tours start at 10:30. Rest of year: Open Monday–Saturday, 10:00–5:00. Call for tour times. Gift shop.

TEXAS STADIUM TOUR

2401 E. Airport (75062), at junction of Hwys. 183 and 114 and Loop 12 • 972-785-4780 • Adults, $10; seniors and children 4–12, $6; under 4 free • www.dallascowboys.com

Tours are given Monday–Saturday, 10–4:00 and Sunday, 11–3:00. The tours usually start on the hour and last about an hour, beginning and ending at the Official Dallas Cowboys Pro Shop just outside Gate 8. Depending on what's going on in the stadium at the time, most tours will include a view from the stands that seat 65,812, a brief walk on the field, a view of the Dallas Cowboys' locker room, a walk-through of the Stadium Club, and a view of a private suite. (If you want to splurge, suites rent for about $3,500 a game, *plus* the cost of tickets.) Lots of walking and stairs. No tours on game days or during special events. Although best known as the home of the Dallas Cowboys, Texas Stadium is also frequently the site of concerts, festivals, and other major events. In fact, the first event in the stadium after it opened wasn't a football game but an appearance by the renowned evangelist Billy Graham, who drew a crown of 82,000. Gift shop.

TRINITY BROADCASTING NETWORK STUDIO TOUR

2900 W. Airport (75061) • 972-986-0037 • Free

The two buildings that make up this beautifully landscaped Christian broadcasting center are open for visitors Monday–Friday, 11:00 a.m.–3:00 p.m. One building houses the studios of Channel 58, the home of Trinity Broadcasting of Texas. The other, the International Production Center, as its name states, is where the Trinity Broadcasting Network produces programs for the rest of the world. The Virtual Reality Theater features an hour-long film and presentation on the life of Christ. Call for tour information. (Group tours, 972-313-1333)

SELF-GUIDED TOURS

WALKING TOURS

Brochures and maps for "A Walking Tour of Las Colinas," and "A Walking Tour of Irving" are available free from the Irving Convention and Visitors Bureau. (See FREE VISITOR SERVICES, p. 273)

HISTORIC PLACES

HERITAGE DISTRICT

Downtown. Bounded by Rock Island Rd. on north, 6th St. on south, O'Connor on west, and Britain on the east • W • www.ci.irving.tx.us

This downtown area is built on the original town site drawn up by Schulze and Brown in 1903. The heart of this old area is **Heritage Park** at Main and Second. This park is the site for one of Irving's oldest buildings, the **Caster Cabin**, built in 1887; Irving's original water tower; an old windmill; the Rock Island Depot, built in 1903; and the city's first library building. Today, the downtown area is mostly older homes and shops, including antique shops and the old-fashioned soda fountain in the **Big State Drugstore**, at Main and Irving, which has been serving sodas since 1948. A number of the historic buildings in this district are located on South O'Connor. These include the **Gilbert House** (1919) at 309, **Howard House** (1904) at 318, and **Mayors House** (1906), which was home to three mayors, at 321. The Irving Heritage Society conducts monthly tours of the period-furnished **Heritage House** at 303, which was built in 1912.

Also in this district, at Rock Island and O'Connor, is the South Irving station for the Trinity Railway Express, the commuter rail system linking Irving, Dallas, Fort Worth, and DFW Airport. At the western gateway to the Heritage District, at Irving and Sowers, is **Millennium Fountain**, with a central geyser that shoots up 30 feet from a 100-foot-diameter pool. The fountain is lighted at night. The site of the original auction of lots in Irving, in December 1903, is marked by the commemorative clock tower of Whistle Stop Plaza at Rock Island and Main.

MUSEUMS AND PUBLIC ART GALLERIES

IRVING ARTS CENTER

3333 MacArthur (75062) • 972-252-7558 or 972-252-ARTS (252-2787) • W+ • www.ci.irving.tx.us/arts

Home of more than a dozen Irving-based arts and cultural organizations, this arts complex includes four art gallery spaces featuring contemporary and traditional works by established and emerging artists. The galleries are open weekdays, 9:00 a.m.–5:00 p.m. (Thursday, 9–8); Saturday, 10–5; Sunday, 1–5. Closed holidays. All exhibitions are free. Always open is the two-acre outdoor Sculpture Garden. The permanent collection includes *Fountain Columns* by Jésus Bautista Moroles, composed of five monumental Dakota mahogany granite columns; recirculated water rises to the top of each 10-foot column, spilling down all four sides in clinging sheets. In addition to the permanent works, the Art Center features temporary installations of sculpture by various artists on a rotating basis. (See also MUSIC AND PERFORMING ARTS, p. 279)

NATIONAL SCOUTING MUSEUM

1329 W. Walnut Hill (75038) • 972-580-2100 or 800-303-3047 • Tuesday, Wednesday, Friday, 10–5; Thursday, Saturday, 10–7; Sunday, 1–5. Closed Monday, major holidays, and two weeks in January (call) • General admission, $10; seniors, $8; under 4 free. Scouts or Scouters, including den mothers, $5 • www.bsamuseum.org

The size of a football field, this facility is the official museum of the Boy Scouts of America. It is designed with state-of-the-art voice-activated displays that enhance a self-guided tour. In addition to films and displays telling the history of scouting from its beginning to the present, the museum offers visitors a wide variety of both static and interactive exhibits ranging from an art gallery on scouting, featuring a number of works by Norman Rockwell, to virtual reality adventures involving biking, kayaking, or climbing to the top of a mountain to rescue hikers. In the Cub Scout area, younger visitors can race miniature cars and compete with each other on a six-lane pinewood derby track. Scout Shop stocked with everything from merit badges to uniforms and gifts.

OUTDOOR PUBLIC ART

Mustangs of Las Colinas • (N. O'Connor, north of Hwy. 114 in Williams Square Plaza, Las Colinas • 972-869-9047) • The world's largest equestrian sculpture, this is a realistic bronze of nine mustangs wildly galloping through a granite stream. Created by African wildlife artist Robert Glen as a memorial to the heritage of Texas, it was seven years in the making. Each horse is one and a half times life-size and weighs between a ton and a ton and a half. Because the rose-colored granite Williams Square Plaza is the size of three football fields, even though the mustangs are boxed in on three sides by gleaming granite office towers, they appear to run free. In the lobby of West Tower of Williams Square is the Mustang Sculpture Exhibit, which includes a short film about the creation of this impressive work. The exhibit is open Tuesday–Saturday, 10:00 a.m.–6:00 p.m. Closed major holidays. Admission is free.

Marble Cows. The stampeding Mustangs of Las Colinas have gathered all the fame, but on Bluebonnet Hill, at Hwy.114 and Rochelle, is another group of Las Colinas's animals. Five marble cows, sculpted by Harold Clayton as a tribute to the ranches that once dominated the area, add a touch of serenity to the landscape.

OUTDOORS

IRVING PARKS

**Parks and Recreation Department, 825 W. Irving (75060) •
972-721-2501 • www.ci.irving.tx.us**

The more than 50 parks and recreation centers in the Irving system
range from the one-acre Heritage Park (see HISTORIC PLACES, p. 276)
in downtown to the 194-acre Sam Houston Trail Park. They offer a variety of outdoor facilities that include swimming pools, walking, jogging,
and bike trails, sports fields and courts, playgrounds, racquetball and tennis courts, an art center, a botanical garden, a golf course, picnic areas,
and even a petting farm.

Campión Trails is a major 10-year Parks and Recreation project calling for a series of parks and trails in a greenbelt on the city's 22 miles of
river frontage along the Elm and West Forks of the Trinity River. Several
miles of concrete primary trails, through hardwood forests and open
fields, and some smaller parks are already completed. The gateway
marker, at O'Connor and Northwest Highway, features two 10-foot
sandstone lions. (Parking lots at 1698 Rochelle and 5964 N. O'Connor)
The name comes from the flower used by ancient civilizations to crown
their champions.

Maps and details of the Irving parks and trails are available from the
Parks Department.

COLLEGE CAMPUSES OF INTEREST
TO VISITORS

NORTH LAKE COLLEGE

**5001 N. MacArthur (75038) • 972-273-3000 • W+ •
www.northlakecollege.edu**

North Lake, a two-year college that's one of seven campuses of the
Dallas County Community College District, sits on 276 mesquite-tree-
covered acres in the Las Colinas area. Its architecturally interesting
campus includes a 9-acre lake. The 12 college buildings are situated on
a series of terraces that follow the natural elevations of the site. The college offers both technical/vocational and academic programs to approximately 9,000 credit students and 5,000 continuing education students.
Daytime visitor parking is on Liberty Circle (look for the three tall flag-
poles). Visitors are welcome at sports events, including basketball and
men's and women's soccer, the Natatorium (972-273-3531), and the Art
Gallery in "J" Building. Student drama and music productions are also

open to visitors with most performances at the college's 450-seat Performance Hall.

UNIVERSITY OF DALLAS

**1845 E. Northgate (75062) at Tom Braniff • 972-721-5000 or
800-628-6999 • W+ • www.udallas.edu**

Founded in 1956, this Catholic University is located on a 225-acre campus just northwest of Texas Stadium on hills that overlook the Dallas skyline. The L. B. Houston Nature Preserve forms part of the eastern boundary of the campus. It has an enrollment of about 3,000 students in its undergraduate and graduate programs. Sophomore students are offered a semester at the school's campus in Rome, Italy. Daytime visitors should park in designated visitor parking areas. The university offers a series of free lectures by speakers of national repute in a variety of fields. Visitors are also welcome at student athletic events, including baseball and rugby, and the college swimming pool is open to visitors during the summer. Drama and music performances are also open to visitors. Most are held at the Margaret Jonsson Theater.

MUSIC AND PERFORMING ARTS

IRVING ARTS CENTER

**3333 MacArthur (75062) • 972-252-7558 or Arts Hotline,
972-252-ARTS (252-2787) • W+ • www.ci.irving.tx.us/arts**

This Center is the site for theater and concert programs in its two state-of-the-art performance theaters: the 706-seat Carpenter Performance Hall and the 259-seat Dupree Theater. It is also the home of a number of resident music and performing arts organizations, including the following:

Irving Ballet (972-252-7558) • The two-production season includes the *Nutcracker* in December and another ballet in the spring.

Irving Black Arts Council (214-993-8444 • www.dallasblack.com) • This organization strives to promote and develop local talent. It produces about a half dozen varied theatrical and musical programs between October and May.

Irving Chorale (972-416-3361) • A 70-plus mixed-voice choir whose repertoire extends from classics to stage hits. Usually gives four concerts annually in its October to June season.

Irving Community Concert Association (972-790-0705) • For more than four decades, this association has brought top music and dance entertainers to perform in Irving during its four-concert October-to-April season.

Irving Community Theatre Mainstage (ICT) (972-594-6104 • www. irvingtheatre.org) • North Texas talent is cast in the five-production season of comedies, dramas, mysteries, and musical productions in the November-to-July season. Most performances Thursday–Saturday evenings and Sunday matinee. Also ICT Children's Theatre—Youth Performing for Children (See FAMILY FUN AND KID STUFF, p. 281).

Irving Symphonic Band (972-252-7558 • www.irvingsymphonic band.com) • This volunteer band offers more than a half-dozen concerts in its October–June season, plus an annual children's concert and free summer concerts. The varied program feature marches, movie and show tunes, and traditional classical selections for band arrangement.

Irving Symphony Orchestra (972-831-8818 • www.irvingsymphony.com) • This professional orchestra has been performing each season for more than three decades. Concerts include an annual Christmas concert, free family and youth concerts, and a Fourth of July concert complete with fireworks at Williams Square in Las Colinas. Its season runs from October through April.

Las Colinas Symphony Orchestra (972-580-1566) • The largest arts group in Irving, since its founding in 1991 this professional orchestra has offered a fall/spring season of six concerts.

Lone Star Youth Orchestra (972-580-1566) • A component of the Las Colinas Symphony, this orchestra provides young instrumentalists free training in symphonic music. It annually presents a three-concert season between November and May.

Lyric Stage (972-594-1904 • www.lyricstage.com) • This locally produced, professional musical theater company is dedicated to the development and preservation of the American musical. In its September-through-April season, it offers evening performances of this uniquely American art form Thursday through Saturday and Sunday matinees.

New Philharmonic Orchestra of Irving (972-252-7558) • This 75-member community orchestra presents a five-concert classical season of evening performances from October through May. Each concert includes a preconcert recital.

FAMILY FUN AND KID STUFF

FRITZ PARK PETTING FARM

Fritz Park, 312 E. Vilbig (75060) • 972-721-2640, June and July; Parks and Recreation Department, 972-721-2501, rest of year •

Open June and July only, Tuesday–Saturday, 10–6; Sunday, 2–8 (weather permitting) • Free • W

Kids (and adults, too) can have as close an encounter as they want here with all types of domestic farm animals and birds in a clean, well-shaded environment. Animals include cows, horses, goats, sheep, deer, rabbits, chickens, turkeys, ducks, geese, and even peacocks.

IRVING CHILDREN'S THEATRE

Irving Arts Center, 3333 N. MacArthur (75062) • 972-594-6104 or 972-252-ARTS (252-2787) • www.irvingtheatre.org

Operating under the auspices of the Irving Community Theatre Mainstage, it is promoted as Youth Performing for Children. The group puts on about half a dozen productions in its October–June season. Tickets, $5–$8.

MOVIE STUDIOS AT LAS COLINAS TOUR (See TOUR SERVICES, pp. 274–75)

MUSTANGS OF LAS COLINAS (See MUSEUMS AND PUBLIC ART GALLERIES—OUTDOOR ART, p. 277)

NATIONAL SCOUTING MUSEUM (See MUSEUMS AND PUBLIC ART GALLERIES, p. 277)

TEXAS STADIUM TOUR (See TOUR SERVICES, p. 275)

SPORTS

EQUESTRIAN

LAS COLINAS EQUESTRIAN CENTER

600 W. Royal (75039) • 972-869-0600 • W • www.lascolinasequestrian.com

English riding and jumping are the major equestrian sports at this center that's often called a country club for horses. Site of numerous horse shows, including the prestigious Big D Charity Horse Show in May, which draws about 300 exhibitors and more than 2,000 guests and spectators. Permanent covered stabling accommodates 277 horses. Two covered arenas and three outdoor arenas. English and Western riding lessons at Las Colinas School of Horsemanship. Visitors welcome to watch training and most events. Trail rides along Elm Fork of Trinity River, Tuesday–Sunday ($28 an hour; reservations required). The Center also hosts other sports events, such as polo, including women's polo, weekends September–November (www.lascolinaspolo.com), and the United States Dog Agility competitions.

FOOTBALL

DALLAS COWBOYS

1 Cowboys Pkwy. (75063) (Headquarters) • 972-579-5000 •
www.dallascowboys.com

The name says Dallas, but Irving's Texas Stadium is the home field for
the Cowboys (2401 E. Airport at the junction of Hwys. 183 and 114 and
Loop 12). And when they play there, the stadium is usually packed solid
with fans because, although they've had their bad seasons, the Cowboys
have brought home such a long string of play-off and Super Bowl Championships that they've earned the title "America's Team." Evidence of that
fact is that, among all the teams that make up the National Football
League (NFL), almost a quarter of all the NFL team shirts, caps, and
other souvenirs sold bear the Cowboys logo.

GOLF

PUBLIC COURSE

Twin Wells Golf Course • 2000 E. Shady Grove (75060) • 972-438-
4340 • 18 holes.

ICE HOCKEY

DALLAS STARS

211 Cowboys Pkwy. (75063)(Headquarters) • 214-GO-STARS
(214-467-8277) • www.dallasstars.com

Texas's only National Hockey League team, the Stars play in the
league's Central Division. Their home games are played in the American
Airlines Center in Dallas, but they practice on the rink here, in the Dr.
Pepper StarCenter Ice Arena.

ICE SKATING

DR. PEPPER STARCENTER ICE ARENA

211 Cowboy Pkwy. (75063), in Valley Ranch off MacArthur •
972-831-2444 • www.drpepperstarcenter.com

This facility has two full-sized ice rinks. In addition to being the practice rink for the Dallas Stars, it also is home for the Dallas Junior Hockey
Association, a senior hockey league, a figure-skating club, and a speedskating club. Skating lessons are given here most days. Public skating is
also available when the rink is not otherwise booked (Adults, $5; stu-
dents, $4; 3 years and under skate free. Skate rental, $1). The Arena is
next door to the headquarters of the Dallas Cowboys. Skate Pro Shop.

TENNIS

Lighted public courses are at **Cimarron Park**, 201 Red River Trail; **Keeler Park**, 520 S. Rogers; **Nichols Park**, 2310 E. Newton; **Northwest Park**, 2800 Cheyenne; **Senter Park**, 901 S. Senter; **Sunrise Park**, 1809 E. Union Bower; and **Wyche Park**, 2850 W. Pioneer. For information, call Parks and Recreation, 972-721-2501. Also, after 5:00 p.m. on schools days and during the summer, the lighted courts at the following high schools are usually open: Irving (nine courts), 900 O'Connor; MacArthur (nine courts), 3700 N. MacArthur; and Nimitz (six courts), 100 W. Oakdale.

OTHER POINTS OF INTEREST

DALLAS/FORT WORTH INTERNATIONAL AIRPORT (DFW)

Part of the DFW Airport lies within the western boundary of Irving. You can watch airport activity and takeoffs and landings from the observation deck set up just off the airport grounds at Thirtieth and Carbon in Founder's Plaza. (For details on the airport, see GRAPEVINE—OTHER POINTS OF INTEREST, p. 261.)

LAS COLINAS URBAN CENTER

One of the world's best known urban developments, Las Colinas (Spanish for "the hills") is a 12,000-acre master-planned community in the northeast corner of Irving. In addition to a business center, with office towers housing corporate office of hundreds of multinational companies employing 70,000 during the business day, there are large single-family and apartment villages for 25,000 full-time residents. Almost half of the development is devoted to a greenbelt, parks, and public recreational space. The development is noted for its Mandalay Canal with Venetian-style gondolas, the world's largest equestrian statue, an equestrian center, a TV and motion picture production complex, several golf courses, a resort, and a number of hotels, restaurants, and shops.

The major places of visitor interest in Las Colinas are:

Dallas Communications Complex • 6301 N. O'Connor • This 125-acre development is a center for media, advertising, and communications and is the premiere film facility in the Southwest. The complex houses over a hundred communications-related companies servicing film, television, and other commercial projects. Except for the Las Colinas Movie Studio Tour, the buildings are not open to visitors.

Las Colinas Flower Clock • Hwy. 114 and O'Connor • Not just for show, this is a working clock, measuring 37 feet diagonally, with the metal hands set against the clock face of live flowers. Only miniature varieties of flowers and greenery can be planted since there are only 14 inches of clearance between the hands and the clock face. New flowers are planted at several times a year to make sure there are fresh colors year-round.

Las Colinas Equestrian Center. (See SPORTS, p. 281)

Mandalay Canal. This gently winding canal leading to the 125-acre Lake Carolyn was designed to resemble an old-world waterway with cobblestone walkways, a few dozen shops and restaurants, and Venetian-style gondolas on the water. One access to the canal is at O'Connor and Las Colinas Blvd. The canal, and the original hotel now called the Omni Mandalay, were named by Ben Carpenter, one of the developers of Las Colinas, to recall his World War II service in Burma (Myanmar).

ANNUAL EVENTS

MAY

EDS/BYRON NELSON GOLF CLASSIC

Thursday–Sunday in middle of month • Four Seasons Resort and Club, 4150 MacArthur (Tournament mailing address: Dallas Salesmanship Club, 400 S. Houston #350, Dallas 75202-4811 • 214-742-3896) • Admission • W • www.byronnelson.pgatour.com

Many of the top golf professionals in the world compete in this annual classic, the only PGA Tour event named after a professional golfer—a Texas golfer, of course. The four-day tournament has the largest attendance of any golf event in Texas, usually attracting more than 270,000 golf fans. It is the largest charity fund-raiser on the PGA tour, with all proceeds benefiting the Salesmanship Club Youth and Family Centers. Best place to see the pros come and go is around the nine-foot bronze statue of Byron Nelson at Nelson Plaza near the No. 1 tee. Some preliminary rounds played on Cottonwood Valley Course, and finals on Tournament Players Course. Public parking ($5) at Texas Stadium, Hwy. 183 at Hwy. 114 intersection, with shuttle buses running from 6:30 a.m. to 90 minutes after the conclusion of play.

SHOPPING

IRVING MALL

3800 Irving Mall (75062), at Hwy. 183 and Belt Line • 972-255-0571 • W+

There are more than 150 stores in this mall, anchored by Dillard's, Foley's, JCPenney, Mervyn's, and Sears. Other strip centers around this intersection augment this mall with almost as many shops, as well as fast-food and regular restaurants. Shuttle services available from some hotels/motels.

A SAMPLING OF IRVING RESTAURANTS

Dinner for one, excluding drinks, tax, and tip: $ = up to $16, $$ = $16–$30, $$$ = $31–$50, $$$$ = over $50. It is strongly suggested that you make a reservation in those restaurants that take them, especially on weekends and holidays.

CAFÉ CIPRIANI ($$–$$$)

220 E. Las Colinas (75039), across from the Omni Mandalay Hotel
• 972-869-0713 • Lunch, Monday–Friday; dinner,
Monday–Saturday. Closed Sunday • Cr. • W+ (elevator)

There is a bar and you'll find a few tables inside at the street entrance, but to reach the tasteful main dining room, take the 1920's Art Deco brass elevator down one level. The menu is gourmet Italian with dishes selected from several regions of that country. The emphasis, however, is on Northern Italian cuisine, with veal, chicken, seafood, and homemade pasta entrées dominating the choices. Specialties include lobster tail steamed with crabfingers and shrimp, veal scallopini with three different sauces, and breast of chicken stuffed with smoked ham and provolone cheese in a *poblano* sauce. Bar. Complimentary valet parking. Piano music at Friday and Saturday dinner.

CAFÉ ON THE GREEN ($$–$$$$)

Four Seasons Resort and Club, 4150 N. MacArthur (75038) •
972-717-0700 • Breakfast, lunch, and dinner, seven days; Sunday
brunch, 11:30–3 • Cr. • W+ • www.fourseasons.com

Note: Many of the luxury hotels in Irving have excellent restaurants. This is just a sample.

This restaurant specializes in New American Cuisine with Asian influences. The dinner menu includes such seafood entrées as herb-roasted grouper and cilantro-rubbed red snapper. Meat entrées include peanut-crusted lamb chops and herb-marinated baby chicken. A buffet is available at all meals. The dinner buffet offers a wide selection of hot and cold items from appetizer to desserts. Sunday brunch is also a buffet featuring a lavish selection of appetizers, cold seafoods, carved items, vegetable dishes, a pasta station, and a dessert station. Children's menu. Bar. The arched floor-to-ceiling windows of this restaurant overlook the resort's pool and landscaped grounds. Self-parking or valet parking available.

COOL RIVER CAFÉ ($$$–$$$$)

1045 Hidden Ridge (75038), at MacArthur • 972-871-8881 •
Lunch and dinner, seven days; Sunday brunch, 11–2 • Cr. • W+ •
www.coolrivercafe.com

Although it's huge (22,000 sq. ft.), this upscale steak house offers the warm and elegant ambiance of a private lodge. Part of a growing chain, it features steaks and chops and seafood with a Southwestern twist. Seafood entrées include pepper jack stuffed grilled shrimp wrapped in smoked bacon and grilled Atlantic salmon, while meat entrées range from Shiner Bock® rib eye to chicken-fried venison steak. Cigar and cognac lounge, billiard/bar room, large-screen TVs. Live dance music, weekend nights.

I FRATELLI ITALIAN RESTAURANT ($–$$)

7750 N. MacArthur, #195 (75063) • 972-501-9700 • Lunch and dinner, Sunday–Friday; dinner only, Saturday; Sunday brunch, 11–2 • Cr. • W+ • www.i-fratelli.com

The name is appropriate since it translates into "the brothers" and it is owned and operated by four brothers. Large selection of pasta dishes, of course, most with tomato, marinara, or alfredo sauce, but also thin-crust pizza, which is a local favorite and can be delivered. House dinner specialties include several veal and chicken entrées, a sausage and peppers dinner, and eggplant parmigiana. "Lasagna Tuesday" offers lasagna all day for around $5. Children's menu. Bar.

JINBEH ($–$$)

301 E. Las Colinas (75039), near the Omni Mandalay • 972-869-4011 • Lunch, Monday–Friday; dinner, Monday–Sunday. Closed Sunday • Cr. • W • www.jinbeh.com

Entrées in this Japanese restaurant include a wide selection of beef, chicken, and seafood prepared in tempura, teriyaki, or hibachi style. Also a variety of *sushi* and some lesser-known authentic Japanese specials like *shabu-shabu*, sliced beef, vegetable, and tofu cooked at your table; udon, a Japanese favorite made of thick white noodle soup with fish cake, Japanese mushrooms, and green onions; and *unaju*, broiled eel served on a bed of steamed rice with special sauce. Bar.

MUSTANG CAFÉ ($$–$$$$)

5205 N. O'Connor, #100 (75039), in the Towers of William Square • 972-869-9942 • Lunch, Monday–Friday; dinner, seven days; Sunday brunch, 11–2 • Cr. • W+ • www.mustangcafe.com

Teakwood floors and mahogany and leather walls are fitting for this upscale restaurant featuring New American cuisine with a Southwestern flair. In addition to the classic cuts of prime steaks, dinner entrée choices include a pepper-crusted filet with a sugarcane skewer of fire-roasted shrimp, twin grilled bone-in pork chops glazed with Marker Mark molasses sauce, and blackened red snapper seared with Cajun herbs and spices. There is also a selection of hand-tossed pasta entrées. Live music at Sunday brunch. Named for its atrium view of the Mustangs of Las Colinas in Williams Square. Bar. Self or free valet parking.

PASAND ($–$$)

2600 N. Belt Line (75062) • 972-594-0693 • Lunch and dinner, seven days • Cr. • W • www.pasand.net

The menu includes authentic classic dishes from both northern and southern India as well as a large variety of vegetarian and nonvegetarian curry entrées and tandoori dishes. If you are not familiar with Indian cuisine, try the First Timer Special that includes soup, a vegetable *pakora* appetizer, a choice of vegetarian or nonvegetarian curries, rice, bread baked in a tandoori oven, *riata* (fresh yogurt with spiced cucumber, onions, and tomatoes), and a dessert of either *kheer* (a traditional rice pudding) or *gulab jamun* (balls of milk and wheat flour soaked in a sweet syrup). Lunch buffet offers a little bit of everything. BYOB at dinner. Another location in Richardson (1377 W. Campbell).

TENAYA ($$–$$$)

525 Meadowcreek (75038), Hwy. 14 and Walnut Hill • 972-550-1122 • Lunch, Monday–Friday; dinner, Monday–Saturday. Closed Sunday • Cr. • W+ • www.tenayas.com

It is named after the last great chief of the Yosemite Indians, and the Native American theme is carried out in the décor of cypress timbers, earthy slate, granite, and tumbled river rock and Colorado ledge stone, accentuated with Native American arts and artifacts. That theme drives the menu. You'll find imaginative entrées of steaks, chicken, and seafood, but the strong emphasis is on wild game dishes that range from a buffalo burger to entrées of antelope, buffalo, venison, and elk. If you're unfamiliar with wild game dishes, try the Sampler on the Starter menu, which includes small portions of grilled elk, rabbit, and venison. Or, if already an aficionado, you might want to go for the Hunter's Feast entrée with elk, rabbit, venison, and quail. Bar. Another location in Plano (1900 N. Dallas Pkwy.).

TEXAS BAR & GRILL ($–$$)

220 E. Las Colinas, #260 (75039) • 972-869-2007 • Lunch and dinner, seven days • Cr. • W • www.theram.com

A typical Texas bar and grill offering an above-average menu of Tex-Mex, sandwiches, fried catfish and shrimp, beef and chicken burgers, and steak and chicken entrées. Daily weekday specials include all-you-can-eat chicken and chips on Monday, enchiladas on Wednesday, and fish and chips on Friday. Kid's menu. Band on Friday nights. Bar.

VIA REÁL ($$–$$$)

4020 N. MacArthur, #122 (75038) at Northgate, in Las Colinas Plaza shopping center • 972-650-9001 • Lunch, Monday–Friday and Sunday; dinner, seven days. Sunday brunch. • Cr. • W+ • www.viareal.com

Here Mexican cuisine comes with a flowing waterfall and cactus, Santa Fe style. Many of the Southwestern selections are seafood, including *camerones*, marinated Gulf shrimp topped with a cilantro cream sauce served on a bed of tortilla rice with fresh vegetables; and seafood tamales made with fresh market fish, scallops and shrimp stuffed in a corn husk and topped with tequila ancho sauce. Still, this is a Texas-Mexican restaurant, so all the favorite and classic Tex-Mex entrées are here, too, like enchiladas and flautas and fajitas, all prepared with a little more innovation by the chef that raises them to a gourmet/fine-dining class. Children's menu. Bar. Complimentary valet parking.

CLUBS AND BARS

Under the local option laws, Irving is dry. There are no liquor stores, and groceries do not sell beer or wine. The exceptions are that you can buy alcoholic beverages with food in restaurants, and they can have a bar to provide them.

A SAMPLING OF IRVING ACCOMMODATIONS

For a double room or suite: $ = up to $80, $$ = $81–$120, $$$ = $121–$180, $$$$ = $181–280, $$$$$ = over $280. **Room tax 11%.**

Unless otherwise noted, check in at 3:00 p.m., check out by noon. Unless otherwise noted, all the major accommodations have handicapped rooms/facilities and no-smoking rooms. The hearing impaired should check on visual alarms and other safety facilities when making reservations. Most accommodations permit children to stay free in room with parents. There may be a charge if this requires setting up an extra bed.

COMFORT INN—LAS COLINAS ($$–$$$ + 11%)

1223 Greenway (75038) • 972-518-0606 or 800-517-4000 (reservations) • www.comfortsuites.com

There are 54 suites on the three floors of this all-suites inn. Local calls free. Cable TV with pay channels. Coffeemaker in room. Dataport in room. Fitness facilities. Free continental breakfast. One-day dry cleaning. Business services available. Free outdoor self-parking. Microwave and refrigerator in suites.

DRURY INN & SUITES—DFW AIRPORT ($$ + 11%)

4210 W. Airport (75062) • 972-986-1200 or 800-378-7946 (reservations) • www.druryinn.com

The 129 units in this four-story inn include several suites. Pets OK (limited). Local calls free. Cable TV with free premium and pay channels.

Coffeemaker in room. Dataport in room. Outdoor pool. Fitness facilities. Guest membership available in health club. One-day dry cleaning. Free continental breakfast. Free beverages Monday–Thursday evenings. Restaurant nearby. Business services available. Free outdoor self-parking. Free airport transportation.

FOUR SEASONS RESORT AND CLUB ($$$$$ + 11%)

4150 N. MacArthur (75038) • 972-717-0700 or 800-332-3444 (reservations) • www.fourseasons.com

There are 301 rooms and six suites in the nine-story tower and 44 villa rooms and six suites located near the eighteenth green of the Tournament Players Course, on this 400-acre luxury resort. Pets OK (limited). Cable TV with free premium and pay channels. Coffeemakers in villa rooms. Dataport in room. Bell service. Heated indoor swimming pool, three outdoor pools, and a children's pool. Fitness center in adjacent 176,000-sq.-ft. Sports Club available to guests. Two championship golf courses and Bryon Nelson Golf School. Eight outdoor and four indoor tennis courts, racquetball, squash. Concierge services available. Beauty shop and full-service spa. Gift shop and golf/tennis pro shops. One-day dry cleaning. Three restaurants, including one fine dining (see CAFÉ ON THE GREEN, p. 285). Room service. Sports bar and lounge. Conference facilities. Business services center. Outdoor self-parking and valet parking (fee). Playground. Child Care Center. Free children's program for ages 5–13, daily from Memorial Day though Labor Day and Saturday–Sunday rest of year. Children's programs available for 5 and under (fee). *Condé Nast Traveler* magazine's readers poll rated it one of top 25 golf resorts in the Americas and top 25 American resorts. Rated 4-Diamond by AAA and 4-Star by Mobil.

HARVEY SUITES—DFW AIRPORT ($$$ + 11%)

4550 W. John Carpenter (75063), at Hwy. 114 and Esters • 972-929-4499 or 800-922-9222 (reservations) • www.bristolhotels.com

There are 164 studio and one-bedroom suites in this three-story property. Pets OK (fee and deposit). Cable TV with free premium channel and pay channels. Coffeemaker in room. Dataport in room. Outdoor heated pool, hot tub. Fitness facilities. Small gift shop. Self-service laundry and one-day dry cleaning. Free continental breakfast. Restaurant in nearby Harvey Hotel. Bar. Business services available. Free outdoor self-parking and valet parking (fee). Free airport transportation to DFW Airport. Gas barbecue grills and picnic tables in courtyard.

HOLIDAY INN SELECT—DFW AIRPORT SOUTH ($–$$$$$ +11%)

4440 W. Airport (75062) • 972-929-8181 or 800-465-4329 (reservations) • www.holiday-inn.com

There are 402 rooms and seven suites in this four-story inn. Concierge section with extra amenities. Cable TV with free premium and pay channels. Coffeemaker in room. Dataport in room. Bell service. Indoor heated and outdoor pool, hot tub, wading pool. Fitness facilities. Guest membership available in health club. Gift shop and retail shops. Self-service laundry and one-day dry cleaning. Restaurant. Room service. Conference facilities and business services center. Free outdoor self-parking. Free airport transportation. Refrigerator and microwave available.

LAQUINTA INN—DFW AIRPORT SOUTH ($$–$$$ + 11%)

4105 W. Airport (75062) • 972-252-6546 or 800-531-5900 (reservations) • www.laquinta.com

The 169 units in this two-story inn include several suites. Pets OK (fee). Local calls free. Cable TV with free premium and pay channels. Coffeemaker in room. Dataport in room. Outdoor pool and hot tub. Guest membership available in health club. Self-serve laundry and one-day dry cleaning. Free continental breakfast. Restaurant adjacent. Business services available. Free outdoor self-parking. Free airport transportation. Microwave and refrigerator available.

MARRIOTT—DFW AIRPORT ($$$–$$$$$ + 11%)

8440 Freeport (75063) • 972-929-8800 or 800-228-9290 (reservations) • www.marriott.com

There are 491 room and seven suites this 20-story hotel. Concierge section with extra amenities. Cable TV with free premium and pay channels. Coffeemaker in room. Dataport in room. Bell service. Indoor/outdoor pool, hot tub, sauna. Fitness facilities. Guest membership available for golf and tennis. Concierge services available. Gift shop. Self-service laundry and one-day dry cleaning. Two restaurants. Room service. Bar and lounge. Conference facilities. Business services center. Free outdoor self-parking or valet parking (fee). Free transportation to DFW Airport.

OMNI MANDALAY HOTEL AT LAS COLINAS ($$$$–$$$$$ + 11%)

221 E. Las Colinas (75039) • 972-566-0800 or 800-THE-OMNI (843-6664) • www.omnihotels.com

The 421 units in this 28-story hotel include 96 suites. Pets OK. Cable TV with free premium and pay channels. Coffeemaker in room. Dataport in room. Bell service. Outdoor heated pool, hot tub, sauna. Fitness facilities. Guest membership available for golf and tennis. Concierge services available. Retail stores, barber, gift shop, and full-service beauty salon and spa. One-day dry cleaning. Restaurant. Room service. Bar. Conference facilities. Business services center. Free outdoor self-parking or valet parking (fee). Free transportation within 5-mile radius. Located next to Lake Carolyn. Some private patios and balconies. "Get Fit" rooms available with motorized treadmill and other amenities (fee). Also fireplace rooms available. Rated 4-Diamond by AAA.

SHERATON GRAND HOTEL AT DFW AIRPORT ($$$–$$$$ + 11%)

4440 W. John Carpenter (75063) • 972-929-8400 or 800-345-5251 or 800-325-3535 (reservations) • www.sheratongranddfw.com

The 300 units in this 12-story hotel include four suites. Concierge section with extra amenities. Small pets OK (fee). Cable TV with free premium and pay channels. Coffeemaker in room. Dataport in room. Bell service. Indoor/outdoor heated pool, hot tub, sauna. Fitness facilities. Guest membership available for golf. Concierge services available. One-day dry cleaning. Restaurant. Room service. Sports Bar. Conference facilities. Business services center. Free outdoor self-parking. Free transportation to DFW Airport. Fine dining four-course dinners available for four to six in Ashley's Wine Cellar.

WYNDHAM GARDEN HOTEL—LAS COLINAS ($$–$$$$ +11%)

110 W. John Carpenter (75039) • 972-650-1600 or 800-996-3426 • www.wyndham.com

The 168 units in this three-story hotel include 45 suites. Local calls free. Cable TV with free premium and pay channels. Coffeemaker in room. Dataport in room. Heated indoor pool, hot tub. Fitness facilities. One-day dry cleaning. Restaurant. Room service (limited). Bar. Business services available. Free outdoor self-parking.

PLANO

Collin County • 236,500 • Area Codes 972 & 469 (local calls require area code) • www.planocvb.com & www.planotx.org

The birth of this city can be traced back to farmers from Tennessee and Kentucky who came and put down roots here in the 1840s. About 1846, William Forman started a sawmill and gristmill here and a settlement grew up around it. At first the town was called Fillmore, after President Millard Fillmore, but when the post office said that name was already used, the name was changed to Plano after its location on what was then open plains.

A spurt of growth came in 1872, when the railroad arrived. When major fires in 1881 and again in 1895 destroyed much of the city, the citizens rebuilt. Still, as late as the 1960 census, the population of this farming and ranching community was only 3,695 and there were still working farms and ranches within the city limits.

Then in the 1970s, several large firms moved in and other businesses and industry followed, causing the city's population to explode to what the 1980 census reported as 72,331 residents. Today, with a population over 236,000, it is the largest city in Collin County.

The city of roughly 69 square miles is cut by US 75 (N. Central Expressway). The eastern third contains the older commercial section, the revitalized and restored historic downtown area that has several of the buildings that survived the disastrous fires converted to specialty shops and restaurants, and the Plano Centre, a convention center which also houses the Convention & Visitors Bureau. The two-thirds of the city to the west of US 75 has many newer housing developments, shopping areas, and, in the far west, the Legacy Business Park, a 2,665-acre master-planned business development with the headquarters complexes of such companies as Electronic Data Systems Corp., JCPenney, and Frito-Lay.

The hot-air balloons that local enthusiasts frequently fly over the city mornings and evenings and the annual Balloon Festival held in the fall have inspired many to call Plano "The Balloon Capital of Texas."

In a *Money* Magazine survey, Plano ranked as one of the ten safest cities in the United States, and in a survey of 200 major U.S. cities, *Ladies Home Journal* ranked it in the top ten of the best cities for women to live in.

PLANO

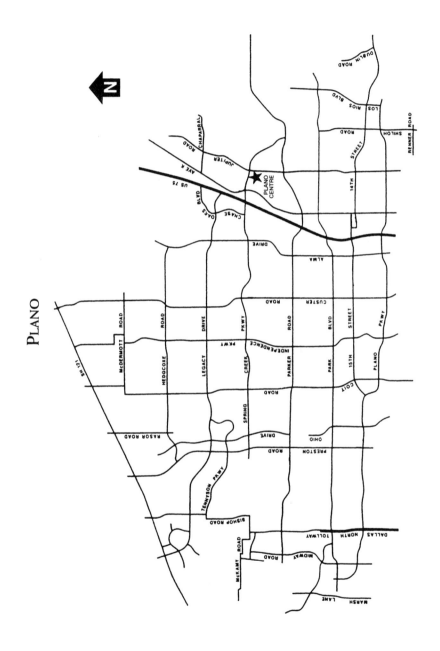

The commercially zoned areas of city are "wet" under the local options laws relating to alcoholic beverages.

It is easy to get to Dallas, Fort Worth, and many other Metroplex cities using the Dallas Area Rapid Transit (DART) Light Rail system. The two stations in Plano are the Downtown Station at Fifteenth and Avenue J and Park Blvd. Station at Park and Archerwood. (For details on the Light Rail system and the Trinity Railway Express to Fort Worth, see DART under GETTING AROUND in the Dallas section, pp. 71–72, or visit www.dart.org.)

FREE VISITOR SERVICES

PLANO CONVENTION & VISITORS BUREAU

2000 E. Spring Creek Pkwy. (P.O. Box 860358, 75086-0358), in the Plano Centre, take Spring Creek Pkwy. east off US 75 • 972-422-0296 or 800-81-PLANO (817-5266) • Monday–Friday, 8–5 • W+ • www.planocvb.com

Visitors can get detailed information on Plano, as well as most of the cities in the Metroplex, at the Convention & Visitors Bureau office located in Plano Centre.

HELPFUL LOCAL PUBLICATIONS

Current information about events, activities, nightlife, theater, movies, and dining in Plano is often published in the *Plano Star Courier, Dallas Morning News,* the *Dallas Observer, D Magazine,* and *Texas Monthly Magazine. Plano Profile,* a free monthly magazine, is available at most area hotels/motels, Plano Centre, a number of businesses, and other locations. Also scheduled activities are often on the city website, www.planotx.org; the Convention & Visitors Bureau website, www.planocvb.com; and the Plano Centre website, www.planocentre.com.

TOUR SERVICES

COMMERCIAL TOURS

DALLAS MORNING NEWS PLANO PRINTING PLANT TOUR

3900 W. Plano Pkwy. (75075) • 214-977-7668 (tour details) • www.dallasnews.com

There are eight presses in this plant, one of the largest printing facilities in the country. Tours include visits to the pressroom, paper warehouse, and distribution area. Reporters and editors at the downtown offices of the newspaper feed their stories to the plant through 22 miles of fiber-optic cables. Children have to be at least 10 years of age to take the tour.

SELF-GUIDED TOURS

WALKING TOUR OF HISTORIC DOWNTOWN PLANO

"Tour Historic Plano," a free brochure available from the Convention & Visitors Bureau, includes a map and detailed information about more than 20 properties, most of which are designated as local historic landmarks. Most of these are located within easy walking distance of the downtown area, starting from Fifteenth Street and Avenue J. (See HISTORIC PLACES, p. 295)

HISTORIC PLACES

HISTORIC DOWNTOWN PLANO

In 1979, recognizing that increasing development pressure would threaten historical sites in the community, the City Council adopted the Historic Landmark Preservation Ordinance. As a result, several blocks of the original downtown portion of Plano have not only been preserved but revitalized, with red common brick roadways and ornamental Victorian-style street lights to enhance the historic character. Of the seventeen historic landmark buildings in this area, the following are of special interest.

The **Interurban Building** at 901 E. Fifteenth was, from 1908 to 1948, a station on the Texas Electric Railroad's Interurban Line linking Denison and Dallas. (See MUSEUMS AND PUBLIC ART GALLERIES, p. 296) The **Carpenter-Edwards House**, 1211 E. Sixteenth, is a 16-room Queen Anne–style home built in 1898. It is now a bed & breakfast offering three upstairs bedrooms (972-424-1889). The **Matthews House**, 901 E. Seventeenth, was built between 1888 and 1890 by the family that operated the general store in Plano from 1895 to 1947. The **Olney Davis House**, 901 E. Eighteenth, is a two-story Victorian home built in 1890 by a prominent businessman and mayor. (For a complete listing of historic landmark buildings, see the free brochure "Tour Historic Plano." Most of these buildings are private residences, not open to the public.)

MUSEUMS AND PUBLIC ART GALLERIES

ARTCENTRE OF PLANO

1039 E. 15th at Avenue K (75074), downtown • 972-423-7809 •
Tuesday–Saturday, 10–6; closed Sunday–Monday • Free • W+ •
www.artcentreofplano.org

The three galleries in this corner building feature exhibits of the works
in all media by local, national, and international artists. Exhibits usually
run for 4 to 6 weeks. Visitor parking in nearby East Side Village parking
lot. The ArtCentre Theatre is co-located. (See MUSIC AND PER-
FORMING ARTS, p. 298)

HERITAGE FARMSTEAD MUSEUM

1900 W. 15th (75075), at Pitman • 972-424-7874 • All year:
Saturday–Sunday, 1–5. June 1–August 1: Tuesday–Friday, 10–1.
August 1–May 31: Thursday–Friday, 10–1 • Adults, $3.50; seniors
and children 3–12, $2.50 • W • www.heritagefarmstead.org

This is a four-acre museum of living agricultural history depicting a
sample of early Texas farm life on what was once a 365-acre farm that was
worked until 1972. Listed on the National Register of Historic Places, the
Farmstead features the Farrel-Wilson family house, an accurately restored
14-room Victorian home built in 1891, and 12 outbuildings, including the
smokehouse, a pole barn, the foreman's cottage, and a windmill. The
house is furnished with many original family pieces, and the outdoor
plants and flowers, including the heirloom roses in the Parlor Garden, are
authentic to the period. Chickens roam the grounds, and there is also a
livestock area with a variety of sheep, hogs, horses, mules, and cows.
Guides in period costumes give tours starting with an audiovisual presentation in the Orientation Center. Concerts and other special events on selected Saturday evenings in summer. Country Store gift shop.

INTERURBAN RAILWAY STATION MUSEUM

901 E. 15th (75075), downtown in Haggard Park • 972-461-7250 or
Plano Conservancy for Historic Preservation, 972-941-2117 •
Monday–Friday, 10–2; Saturday, 1–5 • Free (donations welcome) •
Reservations recommended for conducted individual or group tours • W

Between 1908 and 1948 the Texas Electric Railway ran between Denison and Waco. Called the Interurban, the railway had a dramatic impact
on rural life, as it ended the isolation of remote farm families. Not only did
the electric trains bring the mail, news, salesmen, and new products to
small towns and their stores, but they gave rural residents a means to
cheaply and safely explore the bright lights of the big city. This completely restored building is the only station remaining from the Sherman-
Dallas segment of the line. Its exhibits relate both Plano's transportation

and city history. Outside is an electric railway car that was used as a railway post office. The museum is located in Haggard Park, a pleasant park with a fountain, picnic tables, a gazebo, and restrooms, making it a good place to stop and relax when exploring the downtown area.

JCPENNEY MUSEUM

JCPenney Headquarters, 6501 Legacy (75024) • 972-431-1000 • Free • W+

This small museum might be worth a visit if you are interested in the history of retailing in general or the JCPenney stores in particular. It includes a short film of an Edward R. Morrow interview of J. C. Penney about the history of retailing and a small section of memorabilia from the original Golden Rule clothing store in Kemmerer, Wyoming, that Penney opened in 1902. Price lists from that store show that at that time men's suits cost $1.98 to $16.50, ladies shoes 49¢ to $2.98, and ladies' girdle corsets 15¢ to 98¢. For directions and parking instructions, tell the gate guard you're going to the museum.

OUTDOORS

PLANO PARKS

Parks and Recreation Department, Municipal Center South, 1409 Avenue K (P.O. Box 860358, 75086-0358) • 972-461-7250; Park Event Information Line, 972-941-PARK (972-941-7275) • W+ • www.planoparks.org

The city has a neighborhood park philosophy that brings at least one of its 65 public parks within blocks of most Plano homes. The 3,400 acres of park facilities include swimming pools, a tennis center, three golf courses, a playground for handicapped children, a park for dogs, and a network of over 35 miles of hike and bike trails that link parks, recreational facilities, schools, shopping centers, and neighborhoods. The 4½-mile Bluebonnet Trail and the 5-mile Chisholm Trail are designated as National Recreation Trails by the U.S. Department of the Interior. The Plano Bikeway Plan calls for expanding the current trail system to 127 miles.

COLLEGE CAMPUSES OF INTEREST TO VISITORS

COLLIN COUNTY COMMUNITY COLLEGE

2800 E. Spring Creek (75074) • 972-881-5790 • W+ • www.ccccd.edu

This Spring Creek campus is part of the Collin County Community College District. Each semester, about 9,000 students are enrolled in academic and technical/vocational programs at this 115-acre campus. Visitors are welcome to the **Art Gallery**, which has a changing program of fine art and photography that ranges from faculty and student works to occasional touring exhibits. Usually open weekdays, 9:00 a.m. to 8:00 p.m. (972-881-5873). Visitors are also welcome at the productions of the highly regarded **Quad-C Theatre**. A number of musical events are open to the public, including jazz concerts featuring the college's Jazz Lab Band and Expressions Vocal Jazz Ensemble. The highlight of the jazz year is the annual Jazz Festival in March. The largest jazz festival in North Texas, it is a showcase for a number of the best area jazz ensembles as well as special guest musicians. Other programs are presented by the college Chamber Singers, the CCCC Chorale, and the Dance Repertory. Most theater and music performances are at the John Anthony Theatre or Black Box Theatre on campus. The college participates in eight intercollegiate athletics programs, including baseball, softball, volleyball, and tennis. Most athletic events are also open to visitors.

MUSIC AND PERFORMING ARTS

ARTCENTRE THEATRE

1028 15th Place (75074), behind the ArtCentre • 972-423-7809 • W+ • www.planorep.org

The Plano Repertory Theatre is the resident professional company that puts on productions in both this theater and the Courtyard Theater (See below). Living up to its name, the Rep puts on about six plays in its year-round season, including classics, comedy, musicals, children's programs, and even popcorn-throwing melodramas.

COURTYARD THEATER

1517 Avenue H (75074), at 15th • 972-941-5600 • W+ • www.planotx.org

This is a city-owned theatrical roadhouse where production space is rented by a variety of both local and touring performing arts and musical groups. Originally a 1938 school gymnasium, it has been renovated into an acoustically excellent facility with a flexible stage that may be adapted to proscenium, thrust, or in-the round, and equally flexible seating for 100 to 325. Across the street from DART Light Rail Downtown Plano Station. Main parking on Avenue G.

PLANO CIVIC CHORUS AND THE YOUNGER GENERATION CHORUS

PMB 207, 7000 Independence Pkwy., Suite 160 (75025) • 972-964-SONG (964-7664) • www.planocivicchorus.org and www.youngergeneration.org

The 55 to 65 members of the Plano Civic Chorus are a combination of professional musicians and amateurs with a solid background in choral singing. Chartered since 1978, its season usually includes at least three or four major local concerts. It has also performed Mozart's Requiem at Carnegie Hall in New York City, given concerts at the Morton Meyerson Symphony Center in Dallas, and performed with the National Symphony Chamber Orchestra in Washington, D.C. **The Younger Generation Chorus**, a community children's choir, was formed in 1983 by the Plano Civic Chorus. This choir normally performs annual spring and winter concerts and at a number of other annual events, like the Plano Balloon Festival. In addition, it has sung at a number of places throughout Texas as well as a wide variety of out-of-state places ranging from the White House to Walt Disney World.

PLANO COMMUNITY BAND

P.O. Box 864441, 75086-4441 • www.planoband.com

A volunteer organization of 95 musicians, the band is best known for its five free summer concerts in Haggard Park. It also plays indoor concerts in fall and winter and performs at many city functions. See its website for schedule. (You can also listen to the band perform on its website.)

PLANO SYMPHONY ORCHESTRA

7317 Preston (office), Mailing address: 2701-C W. 15th, Suite 187 (75075) • 972-473-7262 • www.planosymphony.org

The 35-member professional orchestra was first established in 1983 as the Plano Chamber Orchestra. It usually performs around 20 concerts a year, including a regular winter/spring concert series, holiday pops concerts, two chamber ensemble concerts, and concerts in schools. The major concert series features guest artists or guest conductors. Most performances are in the theater of the Fellowship Bible Church, 850 Lexington.

QUAD-C THEATRE

(See Collin County Community College, p. 297)

FAMILY FUN AND KID STUFF

MAIN EVENT

3941 N. Central Expressway (75028) • 972-881-8181 • W+ • www.maineventusa.net

At 60,000 square feet, this is one of the larger indoor family recreation centers of its kind in the Metroplex. The Main Event offers bowling, a large laser tag arena, over 100 video, reality, and redemption games, billiards, shuffleboard, and darts. Snack bar. Bar with access denied to children. Another location in Grapevine.

PLANO CHILDREN'S THEATRE

1301 Custer, Suite 810 (75075), at 15th • 972-422-2575 • W • www.planochildrenstheatre.hypermart.net

This group produces children's theater shows performed by adults and also conducts theater classes for ages 3–18. Most shows are for ages 3 and above, last about one hour, and are performed early on Friday and Saturday evenings and Saturday and Sunday matinees. Tickets about $6. Call for schedule. A little hard to find; it's in the back corner of the shopping center.

WHIRLYBALL/LASER WHIRLD

3115 W. Parker (75203), at Independence • 972-398-7900 • Open daily, call for hours

There are video games and billiards available for individuals, but the major games here are the unusual team sports of Whirlyball and Laser Whirld. Whirlyball is a five-player sport played on a 50' x 80' enclosed court in Whirlybugs, highly maneuverable, specially equipped bumper cars. The players use a scoop device to pass and shoot goals in what is combination of jai alai and basketball, with a little hockey style contact in the bumper cars thrown in. Must be 10 years old and 4 feet tall to play. If you can't get a team together, it's still fun to watch. LaserWhirld is played in a 6,000-square-foot, two-story arena in which teams, or individuals, hunt, stalk, or snipe opponents using phasers and special vests.

SPORTS

BASEBALL AND SOFTBALL

FRITO LAY/PEPSI YOUTH BALLPARK

6000 Jupiter Rd. (75086), at Spring Creek Pkwy. • 972-941-7250 • www.planoparks.org/fritolay.stm

This facility is designed so youth-league baseball and softball games can be played in the atmosphere of a big-league stadium. Ballpark has shaded bleachers, fully lighted scoreboard, and public address system. Spectators are welcome at games.

HERITAGE YARDS

4525 Hedgcoxe (75093) • 972-712-3930

The nine softball diamonds all have lights, electronic scoreboards, and tournament administration offices, making this complex an ideal site for numerous tournaments as well as major events sponsored by the Softball Players Association, National Softball Association, and Amateur Softball Association. It also is the site for local adult softball league games. Spectators are welcome at games.

GOLF

PUBLIC COURSES

CHASE OAKS GOLF CLUB • 7201 Chase Oaks • 972-517-7777 • 18-hole and 9-hole courses.

PECAN HOLLOW GOLF COURSE • 4501 E. 14th • 972-941-7600 • 18 holes.

RIDGEVIEW RANCH GOLF CLUB • 2701 Ridgeview • 972-390-1039 • 18 holes.

ICE HOCKEY/ICE SKATING

DR. PEPPER STARCENTER

4020 W. Plano Pkwy. (75026) • 972-758-7528 • www.drpepperstarcenter.com/plano

This two-story entertainment center features two indoor ice rinks for public skating and ice hockey. It also has a video game room and food concessions. Fee for public skating: Adults, $5; students, $4; under 3 free. Skate rental, $1. Call for skating schedule. Admission charge for high school hockey games. Large pro shop.

IN-LINE SKATING/BMX BIKING

EISENBERG SKATEPARK

930 E. 15th (75074) • 972-509-7725 • www.eisenbergs.com

This indoor and outdoor skatepark offers ramps, walls, and other facilities for in-line skaters, skateboarders, and BMX bikers to do their stunts. Beginner and advanced courses. Open daily. Call for hours and fees. Lessons available. Equipment can be rented at pro shop.

TENNIS

HIGH POINT TENNIS CENTER

421 Spring Creek (75023), just west of N. Central Expressway •
972-941-7170

Twenty-one lighted outdoor courts. Courts can be reserved. Nonresi-
dent fees for one and a half hours are $3.50 for each adult and $2.50 for
each youth. Pro shop and lessons.

OTHER POINTS OF INTEREST

PLANO CENTRE

2000 E. Spring Creek (75074), east of US 75 off Spring Creek exit •
972-422-0296 • W+

Closed conventions and conferences, sure, but this 86,000-square-
foot facility also offers events open to visitors that range from kick boxing and frisbee championships to arts and crafts, antique, and home
shows. Call to see what's on the schedule. Also changing displays of local art in the corridors.

OFFBEAT

AIR-VENTURE BALLOON PORT

1791 Millard, Suite D (75074) • 972-422-0212 or 800-878-4212

If you want to get a slow-paced, floating bird's-eye view of Plano and an
adventure you can brag about, ballooning is the way to go. About a third
of the 90 or so professional balloon pilots in the Metroplex live in the
Plano area, but Air-Venture is the only *full-time* hot-air ballooning operation in North Texas, and the company has more than twenty years' experience with a perfect safety record. Since these flights do depend on the
winds, they are usually scheduled at sunrise and just before sunset when
the light winds are best. Flights last from about 45 minutes to an hour, depending on the winds, and they fly every day of the year, weather permitting. Passengers are picked up at the Harvey Hotel and taken to the
launch site selected for that day. Reservations are required. Most of the
balloons will carry four passengers plus a pilot. Private flights for two are
available. This adventure in the sky costs about $170 per passenger for a
regular flight and $200 per passenger for a private flight. All flights are
champagne flights ending with a traditional champagne toast. Children
must be at least 10 years old and tall enough to see out of the basket.

ANNUAL EVENTS

JANUARY

DALLAS AREA TRAIN SHOW

Usually Saturday–Sunday, mid-month • Plano Centre, 2000 E. Spring Creek • 972-422-0296 • Admission, $6; under 12 free • W+ • www.dfwtrainshows.com

The North Texas Council of Railroad Clubs, which sponsors this show, says there are 4 to 5 times as many layouts operating throughout this show than at any other train shows in the area. In addition there are large dealer displays, how-to clinics, and a flea market. Information and maps are also available for tours that visit many of the best home and club layouts in North Texas. (They also put on a similar train show in the Will Rodgers Memorial Center in Fort Worth every November.)

SEPTEMBER

PLANO BALLOON FESTIVAL

Three-day weekend, late in month. Oak Point Park, 2801 E. Spring Creek, east on Spring Creek Pkwy. exit off US 75 • 972-867-7566 • Admission, $3 • Parking, $5–$10, depending on location • W variable • www.planoballoonfest.org

It's an unforgettable sight: a dazzling kaleidoscopic array of hot-air balloons of all shapes, colors, and striking designs filling the sky during this consistently eye-filling festival. The most breathtaking view is when all the balloons, now up to around a hundred, take to the sky. From a small beginning of just a scattering of balloons and a few spectators more than 20 years ago, the festival now draws about 200,000 spectators to watch balloonists from all over the country flying the balloons.

It all starts on Friday afternoon with ground activities that include opening ceremonies, exhibits, demonstrations, and an arts and crafts show. Then come the balloon races. The races themselves are hard to follow from the park, but the events are usually arranged so some of the flying activities start in the park and others end there. One of the highlights for spectators is usually the Balloon Glow in which tethered balloons are brilliantly lit up by the burning gas from their gas generators. This glowing spectacle is so popular that it's usually repeated several times during the festival, both at dawn and evenings. Most of the flying events are also scheduled dawn and before sunset because this is when the winds are best for this silent flying. During all this, there's also continuous entertainment on two stages and, of course, food vendors.

SHOPPING

ANTIQUELAND MALL & INTERIOR MARKET

1300 Custer (75075), at 15th • 972-509-7878 • W •
www.antiquelandusa.com/plano

About 400 dealers have showrooms and booths in this 85,000-square-foot mall, selling just about every type of antique, collectible, decorative item, and furniture. Palm Court Restaurant & English Tea Garden offer a full menu of appetizers, entrées, and desserts. Formal afternoon tea by appointment.

COLLIN CREEK MALL

811 N. Central Expressway (75075), between Plano Pkwy. (exit 28) and FM 544 (exit 29) • 972-422-1070 • W+ •
www.collincreekmall.com

Dillard's, Foley's, Mervyn's, JCPenney, and Sears anchor about 160 specialty stores in this two-story mall, including a Dallas Cowboys Pro Shop. Stroller rental and wheelchairs are available at the Customer Service Center on the lower level.

DOWNTOWN SPECIALTY SHOPS

E. 15th between Avenues G and M • 972-423-7809

Along the brick streets of Historic Downtown Plano are over 40 specialty shops, including art galleries, craft, and antique shops. Free parking on Avenue J and Avenue K north and south of Fifteenth.

THE SHOPS AT WILLOW BEND

6121 W. Park (75093), at N. Dallas Tollway • 972-202-4900 • W+
• www.theshopsatwillowbend.com

This 1.4-million-square-foot two-level shopping center features Neiman Marcus, Lord & Taylor, Foley's, Dillard's, and approximately 190 specialty stores and dining facilities. More than 50 of the stores are unique to the Dallas area. Visitors from farther than 50 miles away can pick up a discount "Passport" at one of the concierge desks. Extensive shaded parking and valet parking available.

A SAMPLING OF PLANO RESTAURANTS

Dinner for one, excluding drinks, tax, and tip: $ = up to $16, $$ = $16–$30, $$$ = $31–$50, $$$$ = over $50. It is strongly suggested that you make a reservation in those restaurants that take them, especially on weekends and holidays.

BAVARIAN GRILL ($$–$$$)

221 W. Parker, Suite 527 (75023) • 972-881-0705 • Lunch and dinner, Tuesday–Saturday • Cr. • W+ • www.bavariangrill.com

In a Munich biergarten atmosphere this restaurant offers authentic German cuisine that includes several kinds of schnitzel, sauerbraten, and *tafelspits* (prime rib). Seasonal menus take advantage of what's best in the market. More than 50 types of German beers. Live entertainment nightly in both the dining room and the biergarten.

CHOW THAI PACIFIC RIM ($$–$$$)

3309 Dallas Pkwy. (75093), at Parker • 972-608-1883 • Lunch and dinner, seven days • Cr. • W+

As its name implies, the cuisine here is a fusion of Asian and American cuisine artistically presented in an equally attractive setting. A couple of the highlights on the extensive menu are the popular tea-smoked pork chops and the opportunity to create your own noodle soup. For the soup, you pick from a variety of noodles and meats and then the noodle vendor puts it together for you with a chef's broth. The pork chops are smoked over hickory wood and then sprinkled with Thai tea. Beef, pork, lamb, poultry, seafood, and vegetarian entrées, all prepared with a distinctive Asian twist.

FISHMONGERS SEAFOOD MARKET AND CAFÉ ($$)

1915 N. Central Expressway (75075), at Park in Chisholm Plaza Shopping Center • 972-423-3699 • Lunch and dinner, seven days • Cr. • W

The menu offers a variety of seafood fried, baked, mesquite grilled, or blackened Cajun style. All in large portions. A specialty is Fishmonger's Pontchartrain, which gives you a choice of tilapia or mahi mahi fillets topped with sautéed shrimp, crabmeat, and mushrooms. All-you-can-eat specials are available Monday–Thursday starting at 4:00 p.m. and Sunday starting at 11:00 a.m. Membership required for bar drinks. Regulars say "Save room" for the special bread pudding with whiskey sauce. Fresh seafood market.

GREEK ISLES GRILLE AND TAVERNA ($–$$)

3309 N. Central Expressway, Suite 370 (75023), at W. Parker in Ruisseau Village Shopping Center • Lunch, Monday–Friday; dinner, seven days • 972-423-7778 • Cr. • W+

The classic Greek dinner specialties here include *moussaka* (baked spiced ground beef and lamb layered with eggplant and cheese and topped with béchamel sauce); shrimp *Myconos* (baked in tomato, olive oil, garlic, and feta cheese); and *souvlaki* (marinated charbroiled meat on skewers). And the house specialty is rack of lamb oven roasted in Greek spices and charbroiled. In addition to the authentic Greek dishes, a range of American seafood, chicken, and steak entrées is offered. A belly dancer entertains every Thursday evening at 8:00. Bar.

LOVE AND WAR IN TEXAS ($–$$)

601 E. Plano Pkwy. (75074), at Hwy. 75 • 972-422-6201 • Lunch and dinner, seven days • Cr. • W+ • www.loveandwarintexas.com

The concept of this restaurant is to promote Texas, Texas food, and Texas heritage. In keeping with that, the décor promotes Texas heritage and the menu is divided into five sections, each promoting the cuisine of one region of the huge state to offer a taste tour of Texas. For example, the Border selections include fajitas, one of the most famous of Tex-Mex dishes. All the choices in the West Texas Plains are steaks. The Hill Country choices range from game entrées, like antelope filet and wild boar, to New Braunfels bratwurst. Caddo Lake catfish, BBQ, and baby-back ribs are the highlights from the East Texas Piney Woods. And, naturally, the Gulf Coast selections are all seafood, including swordfish, Texas blue crab, and Baytown oysters. Bar with lots of Texas wines and beers. All with live Texas music.

MARIO'S CHIQUITA ($–$$)

221 W. Parker (75023), in Ruisseau Village Shopping Center • 972-423-2977 • Lunch and dinner, Monday–Saturday. Closed Sunday • Cr. • W

The menu here offers you a choice of Tex-Mex or authentic dishes from interior Mexico. Most of the Tex-Mex entrées are combinations named after women. Order a "Rosita," for example, and your plate will be filled with a crispy meat taco, guacamole, chicken enchilada and a beef enchilada, with *ranchera* sauce and rice. The classic Mexican dishes include chile relleno (a stuffed *poblano* pepper), *carne asada* (charbroiled filet with onions and peppers), and red snapper Veracruz style. Children's plates. Bar.

THE MERCURY ($$–$$$$)

6121 W. Park (75093), in The Shops at Willowbend • 469-366-0107 • Lunch and dinner, Monday–Saturday. Closed Sunday • Cr. • W+

That this is an upscale fine-dining restaurant in an upscale shopping mall is evident not only from the stylish décor, but right from the choice of appetizers. How many mall restaurants offer starters of pan-seared scallops, roasted Maine lobster, *foie gras flan*, or sashimi of Yellowtail? Among the culinary creations in the entrée section is braised veal shank with mushrooms, tomato confit, braised romaine lettuce, Parma *prosciutto*, baby carrots, and fingerling potatoes. Other entrée choices include loin of venison, rack of lamb, pepper-crusted tuna *mignon*, pan-seared salmon, and crisp Cracklin' Chicken. Bar. Valet parking available.

MIGNON ($$–$$$$)

4005 Preston, #518 (75093), at Lorimar in Lakeside Market
Shopping Center • 972-943-3372 • Lunch and dinner, seven days;
Sunday brunch, 11–2 • Cr. • W+ • www.mignonplano.com

The management lists Mignon as a retro French steak house with décor invoking the spirit of Paris in the 1960s. In keeping with this, the menu offers a selection of French favorites starting with first-course selections of *escargot*, served with white wine cream sauce in a puff pastry cup; and skillet-roasted mussels. Classic French Onion heads the soup choices, while the authentic French entrées include steak *au poivre*, pork shank braised osso bucco style *cochon*, and macadamia-crusted rainbow trout *meunière*. Although a number of the other steak, chop, chicken, and seafood entrées are not strictly French, they all are prepared with a French flair. Patio dining available. Live jazz and blues with dinner. Bar.

NAKAMOTO JAPANESE CUISINE ($$–$$$$)

3309 N. Central Expressway #360 (75023), at Parker in Ruisseau
Village Shopping Center • 972-881-0328 • Lunch, Monday–Friday;
dinner, seven days • Cr. • W • www.nakamotos.com

Although many of the selections on the menu are Westernized versions of Japanese cuisine, overall this restaurant is traditional Japanese, even down to the no-shoes policy in the Tatami Room (shoes OK in rest of restaurant). Entrées offered include a variety of tempura and teriyaki selections, such as the ever popular shrimp tempura and chicken teriyaki. If you like both cooking styles, combination dinners are available for two or more patrons. The menu also includes less well known choices like salmon *batayaki* with the salmon sautéed in butter and served with Japanese vegetable. Sushi and sashimi, of course, with a sushi sampler on the list of appetizers. Bar.

ROY'S ($$–$$$$)

2840 Dallas Pkwy. (75093), at Park • 972-473-6263 • Dinner,
seven days • Cr. • W+ • www.roysrestaurants.com

"Hawaiian Fusion" is the way they describe this Pacific Rim cuisine that is fused with Japanese flavors and developed for American taste. This Plano location is part of a growing international chain. Started by Chef Roy Yamaguchi in Honolulu in 1988, it has since spread to more than 30 locations in Asia and the United States. Examples of this cross-cultural culinary mix can be seen in typical entrées such as Szechuan charred day boat scallops and sautéed shrimp, Korean style barbecued beef, crispy Thai stuffed chicken, Kahana style Hawaiian swordfish, and wood-roasted lemon grass shrimp with black rice risotto in truffled lobster sauce. However, note that menus change daily, guided by the chef's choice of the best of local ingredients. Six-course Tasting Menu available. Bar.

SPECIAL FOOD MARKETS FOR DO-IT-YOURSELF

If you don't want to brave the waiting lines, call to find out if the restaurant that interests you offers takeout. Or, if you want to prepare your own meals or make a picnic basket as a change to dining out, you might want to visit either the **Whole Foods Market** (2201 Preston, 972-612-6729 • www.wholefoodsmarket.com) or the **H-E-B Central Market** (7320 Coit at Hwy. 190, 469-241-8300 • www.centralmarket.com) where the emphasis is on fresh, high-quality food. Whole Foods carries what is probably the largest selection in the area of organically grown foods as well as seafood and meats without growth hormones or other additives. It also has some take-out meals. Central Market offers about 700 varieties of quality produce, 90 varieties of made-from-scratch breads, 650 varieties of cheese, 60 kinds of store-made sausage, 350 varieties of beer, deli items, and ready-to-eat meals, including dinners for two.

A SAMPLING OF PLANO ACCOMMODATIONS

For a double room or suite: $ = up to $80, $$ = $81–$120, $$$ = $121–$180, $$$$ = $181–280, $$$$$ = over $280. **Room tax 13%.**

Unless otherwise noted, check-in at 3:00 p.m., check-out by noon. Unless otherwise noted, all the major accommodations have handicapped rooms/facilities and no-smoking rooms. The hearing impaired should check on visual alarms and other safety facilities when making reservations. Most accommodations permit children to stay free in room with parents. There may be a charge if this requires setting up an extra bed.

BEST WESTERN PARK SUITES HOTEL ($–$$$ + 13%)
640 E. Park (75074) • 972-578-2243 • www.bestwestern.com

There are 84 one-bedroom suites in this three-story hotel. Small pets OK (fee). Cable TV with free premium and pay channels. Coffeemaker in room. Dataport in room. Outdoor heated pool and hot tub. Self-service laundry and one-day dry cleaning. Free continental breakfast. Business services available. Free outdoor self-parking. All suites have microwaves and refrigerators.

THE CARPENTER HOUSE BED & BREAKFAST ($$ + 13%)
1211 E. 16th St. (75074), at Avenue M • 972-424-1889 • www.thecarpenterhouse.com

This two-story historic home, built in 1898, has four upstairs bedrooms with bath nearby. Continental or South of the Border breakfast included. House has 14 original stained-glass windows.

COURTYARD DALLAS PLANO IN LEGACY PARK ($$–$$$$ + 13%)
6840 N. Dallas Pkwy. (75024) • 972-403-0802 • www.courtyard.com

There are 148 rooms and 5 suites in this three-story Courtyard. Cable TV with free premium and pay channels. Coffeemaker in room and free coffee in lobby. Dataport in room. Outdoor pool and whirlpool. Fitness facilities. Guest membership available in health club. Self-service laundry and one-day dry cleaning. Coffee shop. Lounge. Business services available. Free outdoor self-parking. Free transportation within 5-mile radius. Dinner delivery service from local restaurants.

DOUBLETREE HOTEL AND EXECUTIVE MEETING CENTER ($$$–$$$$$ + 13%)

7120 Dallas Pkwy. (75024), in Legacy Town Center • 972-473-6444 or 800-222-TREE (222-8733)(reservations) • www.doubletree.com

The 404 units in this six-story hotel include 40 suites. Concierge section with extra amenities. Cable TV with free premium and pay channels. Coffeemaker in room. Dataport in room. Outdoor heated pool and whirlpool. Fitness center with spa, dry and wet sauna. Concierge services available. Restaurant. Room service. Lounge. Conference center with business services available. Free self-parking, some covered. Free transportation within 3-mile radius. Overlooks park and lake and within walking distance of The Shops at Legacy.

HARVEY HOTEL—PLANO ($–$$$ + 13%)

1600 N. Central Expressway (75074) • 972-578-8555 • www.bristolhotels.com

The 279 units in this three-story hotel include 12 suites. Cable TV with free premium and pay channels. Coffeemaker in room and coffee in lobby. Dataport in room. Outdoor pool, hot tub. Fitness facilities. Gift shop. Restaurant. Room service. Bar. Conference facilities and business services available. Free outdoor self-parking. $1 daily charge for unlimited local calls.

HOLIDAY INN PLANO ($$–$$$ + 13%)

700 E. Central Pkwy. (75074) • 972-881-1881 • www.bristolhotels.com

There are 159 rooms and one suite in this six-story inn. Pets OK (deposit and fee). Cable TV with free premium and pay channels. Coffeemaker in room. Dataport in room. Outdoor pool and whirlpool. Limited fitness facilities. Gift shop. Self-service laundry and one-day dry cleaning. Two restaurants. Sports bar. Conference facilities and business services available. Free outdoor self-parking.

LAQUINTA INN & SUITES ($$–$$$$ + 13%)

4800 W. Plano Pkwy. (75093) • 972-599-0700 or 800-532-5900 (reservations) • www.laquinta.com

This four-story inn has 121 rooms and 8 suites. Local calls free. Cable TV with free premium and pay channels. Coffeemaker in room. Dataport in room. Outdoor heated pool and spa. Fitness facilities. Self-service laundry and one-day dry cleaning. Free continental breakfast. Business services available. Free outdoor self-parking. King rooms available with microwave and refrigerator.

RESIDENCE INN DALLAS PLANO ($$$–$$$$ + 13%)

5001 Whitestone (75024) • 972-473-6761 or 800-331-3131 (reservations) • www.residenceinn.com

The 126 suites in this three-story inn range from studio to two-bedroom. Pets OK (fee). Cable TV with free premium and pay channels. Coffeemaker in room. Dataport in room. Outdoor heated pool and whirlpool. Fitness facilities, volleyball and sports court. Self-service laundry and one-day dry cleaning. Free buffet breakfast and social hour in evening. Business services available. Free outdoor self-parking. Free transportation within a 5-mile radius. Fully equipped kitchen in all suites, fireplace in some. Outdoor barbecue grills. Free grocery shopping service. Dinner delivery available from local restaurants.

WELLESLEY SUITES PLANO ($$–$$$ + 13%)

2900 N. Dallas Pkwy. (75093) • 972-378-9978 • www.wellesleyinnandsuites.com

There are 64 rooms and 60 studio suites in this four-story inn. Small pets OK. Cable TV. Coffeemaker in room. Dataport in room. Outdoor heated pool. Fitness facilities. Self-service laundry and one-day dry cleaning. Free continental breakfast. Business services available. Free outdoor self-parking.

SIDE TRIPS

LAKE LAVON

Take Parker Rd. (FM 2514) east about 7 miles to St. Paul, then St. Paul Rd. to Collin Park on the lake • 972-442-3141 • Open at all times • Free • W variable

There are four large parks with hookups for campers and a number of day-use parks on this 21,400-acre Army Corps of Engineers lake. Boat ramps, marinas with boat rentals, swimming, fishing, water-skiing, picnicking, and motorcycle riding trails. Caddo Park is equipped for handicapped. For information write: Reservoir Manager, P.O. Box 429, Wylie, TX 75098.

SOUTHFORK RANCH

3700 Hogge Rd., Parker (75002), from US 75 (exit 30) take Parker Rd. east about 6 miles to Hogge Rd. (FM 2551) then south to entrance • 972-442-7800 • Open seven days, 9–5. • Adults, $8;

seniors, $7; children 4–12, $6; under 4 free • Free parking • W variable • www.southfork.com

The myths of the old TV show *Dallas* live on here. This ranch was the exterior setting for that TV series, which had a 13-season run from 1978 to 1990. Since the show was seen by millions in 83 countries (and is still shown in reruns in about 40 countries), this white, colonial-style plantation home is still recognized by almost as many people as is the White House. Tours of the mansion are available. Don't be surprised if the mansion rooms don't look familiar. All the show's interior shots were made on Hollywood sets. You can tour the small museum featuring show memorabilia and the grounds on your own. There's a tram, if you don't want to walk. The ranch's Western store is called "Lincolns and Longhorns." The Lincoln, on display in the store, is the one Jock Ewing drove in the show; the longhorns you can see in the fields as you wander around the grounds. The ranch annually attracts several hundred thousand visitors.

RICHARDSON

Dallas and Collin Counties • 92,000 • Area Codes 972, 469, 214 (local calls require area code) • www.telecomcorridor.com

In 1842, the Jackson family came from Tennessee and settled on land where Richland College is now located. As other settlers moved in from Tennessee and Kentucky, they clustered around the Jacksons and eventually formed a town they proudly named after John C. Breckenridge, the Kentuckian who served as vice president of the United States from 1857 to 1861.

After the Civil War, the railroads became the driving force in the development of the West. Unfortunately, Breckenridge was not in any railroad's plans. Then, in 1872, John Wheeler lured the Houston and Texas Railroad to the area by giving 100 acres of land northwest of Breckenridge for a right-of-way and a town site. Wheeler declined to have the new town named after him and, showing his political savvy, instead named it after E. H. Richardson, the railroad contractor who built the line from Dallas to Dennison. The railroad drew the settlers like a magnet and soon Richardson was the center of activity and Breckenridge disappeared.

It was during the early years of the town that local folklore says it was frequently visited by such notorious outlaws as Sam Bass, the Younger Brothers, and Belle Starr. And it's said that Jesse and Frank James often hid out in the area.

Not folklore but fact is that, after the town incorporated in 1924, Tom McKamy, its first mayor and a mortician, buried the infamous Bonnie Parker. Probably more important to the citizens, however, was that McKamy was also responsible for introducing indoor plumbing to the town.

Still, Richardson remained a farming community and, after Dallas started to grow, a bedroom suburb for that city. As late as 1950, its population was about thirteen hundred. Then, in 1951, Collins Radio opened a Richardson office and, with that, the door to the electronic age. Today, with more than 700 high-tech and telecommunications companies, the city encompasses one of the highest concentrations of leading-edge technology-based companies in the world in an area now called the Telecom

RICHARDSON

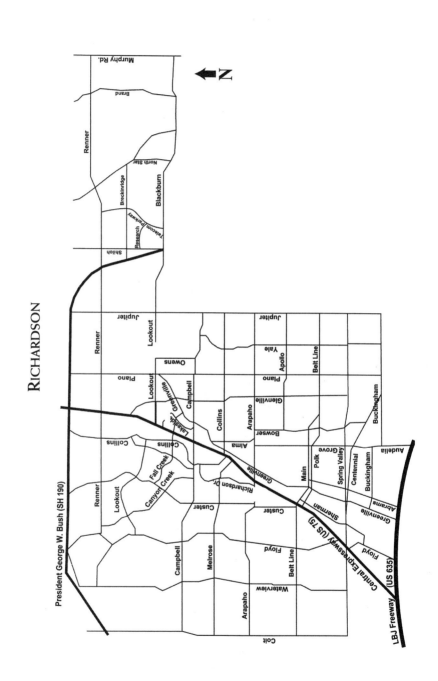

Corridor®. The industry concentrations along the Telecom Corridor are in the shape the letter "T" with the 5-mile long leg along both sides of North Central Expressway (US Hwy. 75) and the crossbar on the south side of TX Hwy. 190.

The county line splits the city so that there are 18.2 square miles in Dallas County and 9.2 square miles in Collin County.

Richardson is dry, and therefore on-premise consumption of alcoholic beverages is permitted only in certain designated areas that are zoned retail or commercial districts (e.g., restaurants, clubs, hotels). Private clubs are established in these facilities and membership (usually costing from $.50 to $2) is required to purchase a drink. Some hotels automatically give guests memberships in the hotel club.

The city has three DART Light Rail stations. Locations are at Spring Valley, Arapaho Center, and Galatyn Park. (For details on the Light Rail system and the Trinity Railway Express to Fort Worth, see DART under GETTING AROUND, p. 71–72, in the Dallas section or www.dart.org.)

FREE VISITOR SERVICES

RICHARDSON CONVENTION & VISITORS BUREAU

411 Belle Grove (75080), in Chamber of Commerce office • From I-75, exit Arapaho, take South access road to Belle Grove, first right • 972-234-4141 or 800-777-8001 • Monday–Friday, 8:30–5 • Free • W+ • www.telecomcorridor.com/cvb/

Brochures, maps, directions—everything you'd expect from a Convention & Visitors Bureau is available here, and more.

HELPFUL LOCAL PUBLICATIONS

Current information about events, activities, nightlife, theater, movies, and dining in Richardson is published in the Richardson insert of the Thursday and Sunday editions of the *Dallas Morning News*. Other sources include the *Dallas Observer, D Magazine,* and *Texas Monthly Magazine*.

OUTDOORS

RICHARDSON PARKS

Parks and Recreation Department • City Hall, 411 W. Arapaho Rd., Suite 208 (75080) • 972-744-4300 • www.cor.net

The facilities in the city's 29 parks include almost 29 miles of multi-use hike and bike trails, swimming pools, and recreation centers and a nature area containing a unique hardwood forest. The parks department also offers a 36-hole golf course and a tennis center. Among the major parks are Breckinridge (2600 N. Brand), a 379-acre nature area that includes sports fields, playgrounds, trails, fishing ponds, and a 10-acre lake, and Cottonwood Park (1321 Belt Line Rd.), a 25-acre park with swimming pool and kiddie pool (admission), athletic fields, tennis courts, and playground. The department also plants more than 100 acres of wildflowers annually.

COLLEGE CAMPUSES OF INTEREST TO VISITORS

RICHLAND COLLEGE

12800 Abrams (75243), just north of LBJ Frwy. (I-635) • 972-238-6106 • W+ • www.rlc.dcccd.edu

One of the seven campuses in the Dallas Community College District, Richland has an enrollment of more than 13,000 full- and part-time students in both academic and technical/vocational programs. The 243-acre campus features pedestrian bridges linking facilities along both sides of a spring-fed creek and two small lakes. Visitors are welcome at a number of activities on campus, including plays and dance and music concerts and recitals in the Performance Hall and exhibits in the art gallery in the Fannin Fine Arts Building. Free shows at the college planetarium in the Sabine Science Building are also open to the public. These tours of the heavens are given every second and third Saturday of the month at 2:00 and 3:00 p.m. (972-238-6013 or 972-238-6213). Visitors interested in gardening will not want to miss the award-winning demonstration garden at the Hondo Horticulture Building.

UNIVERSITY OF TEXAS AT DALLAS

2601 N. Floyd (75080), at Campbell (P.O. Box 830688, 75083-0688) • 972-883-2111 • W+ • www.utdallas.edu

Established in 1969 as a graduate school only, the university added freshman through senior levels over the years until it now also offers undergraduate degrees in a variety of fields of study to a total enrollment of over 12,000 students. Fittingly, for a university located in the Telecom Corridor®, the largest enrollment is in the Erik Jonsson School of Engineering and Computer Science.

Visitors are welcome at a number of cultural, intellectual, and leisure activities on the 500-acre campus. Each month concerts, plays, and films fill the performance spaces on campus (Arts Events line, 972-883-ARTS [883-2787]). Admission is usually charged at these events. Student and faculty art shows featured at the Students Visual Arts Gallery (972-883-2787) are normally free. The Special Collections Department of Eugene McDermott Library is the home of the archives of the History of Aviation collection, Wineburgh Philatelic Collection, the Belsterling Collection of Botanical Books, and an art history collection. (See OTHER POINTS OF INTEREST, p. 319–20)

Day visitors should check at the Information Center at the University Parkway entrance gate (off Campbell Road) for directions and the location of visitor parking.

MUSIC AND PERFORMING ARTS

CHAMBER MUSIC INTERNATIONAL
972-385-7267 • www.chambermusicinternational.com

This nonprofit arts organization, founded in 1986, sponsors a diversified program of concert and recording artists from all over the world performing classical chamber music. Concerts are normally at the Eisemann Center in Richardson and at Southern Methodist University in Dallas.

DALLAS REPERTOIRE BALLET
280 W. Renner, #1911 (75081) (Office) • 972-231-6883 • www.dallasrepballet.org

The official home of this preprofessional ballet company is at the Academy of Dance Arts in Allen, Texas; however, it performs a variety of works during the fall and winter seasons at the Eisemann Center, including its annual *Nutcracker,* which it has performed in Richardson since 1993. The company also performs at a number of annual events in Richardson and other Metroplex cities and has represented Texas and the USA at the Tanzsommer Dance Festival in Austria.

CHARLES W. EISEMANN CENTER FOR THE PERFORMING ARTS AND CORPORATE PRESENTATIONS
959 E. Lookout Dr. (75082) in Galatyn Park Urban Center; take Galatyn exit off Central Expressway (US 75) • 972-744-4600; ticket office, 972-744-4650 • W+ • www.eisemanncenter.com

Evidence of the careful planning that went into this $42 million center is that the main garage, which appears to be attached, is actually technically separated enough to keep traffic vibrations from affecting performances. The City of Richardson owns this attractive 116,900-square-foot multi-use facility, which is designed to meet the diverse needs of all of the performing arts and the corporate world. Its three main venues are the 1,550-seat Margaret and Al Hill Performance Hall, an adaptable theater that seats between 250 to 400, depending on its configuration, and a 3,150-square-foot multi-use room for meetings, receptions, and recitals.

The Center hosts a wide range of performing groups ranging from the symphony, ballet, and theater to the National Convention and Competition of the Sweet Adelines International.

The entrance plaza, featuring a fountain that can shoot up to 45 feet in the air, leads into the attractive three-level lobby and Grand Foyer. Three parking garages (fee) and a parking lot are all located close to the Center, and the Galatyn Park Station of the DART Light Rail Red Line is within easy walking distance.

RCT—A REPERTORY COMPANY THEATRE

2100 Promenade Center, #2176 (75050) • 972-690-5029 • www.rctheatre.com

This acting company, formerly known as the Richardson Children's Theatre, consists of a large professional troupe augmented with students who have successfully completed acting workshops. Five or six main stage productions of Broadway plays and musicals, designed for the entire family, are put on at the University of Texas at Dallas Theatre or the Eisemann Center. Additional smaller productions are given at its home in the RCT Studio Theatre.

RICHARDSON COMMUNITY BAND

Richardson Civic Center, 411 Arapaho Rd. (75080) (Office) • 972-851-9784 • www.richardsoncommunityband.org

First organized before World War I, the band was broken up during both world wars, but played in the many years between them. The present band was reorganized in 1970 and has been performing continuously since then. Composed of about 60 volunteer nonprofessional musicians, it performs free concerts year-round. Every summer it hosts a biweekly outdoor concert series Sunday evenings on the lawn of the Richardson Civic Center (411 W. Arapaho). Its schedule also includes performances at the Eisemann Center, city festivals, a fall concert, and a Children's Concert in spring.

RICHARDSON SYMPHONY ORCHESTRA

P.O. Box 831675 (75083) • 972-234-4195 • www.richardsonsymphony.com

Formed as a small community orchestra in 1961, now it is a well-received 70-member professional symphony orchestra. It usually performs six classical and pops concerts in its regular October-through-April subscription season at its home in the Eisemann Center. At least three of these concerts feature internationally acclaimed artists. The Symphony also performs other outdoor, family, and children's concerts during the year, usually in connection with city festivals or special events, and a spring concert in the Meyerson Symphony Center in Dallas.

RICHARDSON THEATRE CENTER

718 Canyon Creek Square (75080), at Custer and Lookout behind the supermarket • 972-699-1130 • W • www.rtc-inc.org

The resident company usually puts on five shows a year, either in this small 80-seat theater-in-the-round converted from retail space in a strip shopping center or at the Eisemann Center. Each production runs five or six weeks, with performances Thursday through Saturday at 8:00 p.m. and occasional Sunday matinees.

RICHLAND COLLEGE AND UNIVERSITY OF TEXAS AT DALLAS

(See COLLEGE CAMPUSES OF INTEREST TO VISITORS, p. 315–16)

FAMILY FUN AND KID STUFF

THE CLASSICS FAMILY THEATRE SERIES

3015 W. 15th, Plano (75075) (Office) • 972-596-0055 • www.classicsplano.org

Although the Classics' office is in Plano, the series of national and international touring productions for family audiences that the group sponsors is presented in Richardson's Eisemann Center (tickets, 972-744-4650). All shows are Sundays at 2:00 p.m. and 4:30 p.m. Tickets range from $6 to $15, depending on seating location.

OWENS SPRING CREEK FARM

1401 E. Lookout (75081), off Plano Road between Renner and Campbell • 972-235-0192 • Open daily, 9–4 • Free • W variable • www.owensinc.com

The main building on this 56-acre farm is a small museum with exhibits depicting life in the 1920s as well as how the Owens family started their sausage business, which has been well-known in Texas for more than 70 years. In the barn there are antique wagons and in the corrals outside are tiny Shetland ponies and, in contrast, a team of huge Belgian horses, each weighing an average of 2,300 pounds. There are also a number of farm animals, some of which can be petted. (Petting zoo open only weekdays, 9–4.) Guided tours are available Monday–Friday, 9–3. Also on the grounds, but not open to visitors, is Miss Belle's Place, a two-story house built around 1887 that was home to Miss Virginia Bell Robberson, who taught school in the town for almost 40 years.

RCT—A REPERTORY COMPANY THEATRE

(See MUSIC AND PERFORMING ARTS, p. 317)

RICHLAND COLLEGE PLANETARIUM
(See COLLEGE CAMPUSES OF INTEREST TO VISITORS, p. 315–16)

SPORTS

GOLF

PUBLIC COURSES • www.cor.net/golf

The Practice Tee • 2950 Waterview (75080), next to UT Dallas campus • 972-235-6540 • 9-hole par 3 course

Sherrill Park Municipal Golf Course • 2001 Lookout (75080) • 972-234-1416 • 36 holes. Has been ranked as one of the best municipal courses in the state by the *Dallas Morning News.*

TENNIS

HUFFHINES TENNIS CENTER
1601 Syracuse (75081) in Huffhines Park • 972-234-6697 • www.cor.net

Twenty-two courts, most of which are lighted. Open daily 8:00 a.m–10:00 p.m. Fees: $1.50 per person for an hour and a half. (In addition to the Tennis Center, lighted courts are available at a number of city parks. Call 972-744-4300 for information.)

OTHER POINTS OF INTEREST

UNIVERSITY OF TEXAS AT DALLAS SPECIAL COLLECTIONS
Third floor, Eugene McDermott Library, 2601 N. Floyd (75080) (P.O. Box 830643, 75083-0643) • 972-883-2570 • W+ • www.utdallas.edu/library/special

The Special Collections Department was originally established in the mid-1970s to house rare books acquired by the library. Since then this mission has been expanded to include several research collections. Although these collections are primarily archives for scholarly research, exhibits selected from them are in the Special Collections room that is open to visitors.

Among the four major collections here, the largest is the History of

Aviation Research Library, which contains more than 25,000 books, hundreds of thousands of periodicals, and over a thousand cubic feet of processed archives. Two small parts of this collection on display are from the Gen. James H. Doolittle Military Aviation History Library and the CAT/Air America Archive. The CAT display tells the story of the Civil Air Transport (CAT), an airline formed after World War II in China, whose civilian pilots flew in support of the Chinese Nationalists forces in the Chinese Civil War. After the Communists won that war, the CAT flew as both a scheduled airline out of Taiwan and on clandestine CIA missions in support of covert operations in Asia, including air-dropping supplies to the trapped French at Dien Bien Phu in Indochina. In 1959 CAT was renamed Air America and continued flying clandestine missions in South Vietnam and Laos as the CIA's airline until 1976.

The three other special collections are, The Wineburgh Philatelic Research Library, one of the country's top resources on stamps and stamp collecting; The Belsterling Collection of Botanical Books, which includes the oldest book in the library dating from 1499; and the collection of rare books on Art History. By special arrangement only, books may be checked out from all the collections except the Belsterling Collection.

ANNUAL EVENTS

Special Events Hotline, 972-744-4581

MAY

WILDFLOWER! ARTS & MUSIC FESTIVAL

Thursday–Sunday, early in month • Galatyn Park, US 75 and Galatyn Pkwy. • (Office: 2351 Performance Dr., 75082) • 972-680-7909 • Entrance free; admission to some events • W variable • www.wildflowerfestival.com

The festival itself is held in Galatyn Park, but its name celebrates the fact that the city will be in full bloom with over 100 acres of wildflowers in parks (50 acres in Breckenridge Park), along roadsides, in street medians, and along US 75.

What started as a small community event in 1993 is now one of the premier music events in the Metroplex, with more than 100,000 attending each year. The festival is designed to bring people together to celebrate both the wildflowers and the impact of music on our lives. Each year the event pays tribute to a specific genre of music; its history, its artists, and its lasting effects on the world. But the music is not restricted to that one genre. The six festival stages offer music in every shape and form, from concerts by national artists (admission), both on festival stages and in the Eisemann Center, to a Metroplex-wide Battle of the

Bands and the presentation of original works in the Singer/Songwriter Contest. In addition to the many musical events, there are clinics, street performers, more than 100 arts and crafts vendors, fireworks, food vendors, and award-winning kids' programs that include games, hands-on art projects, music experimentation, and other activities.

There are 10,000 parking spaces in garages and parking lots within the immediate area, and the DART Light Rail Galatyn Park Station is right at the site.

MAY AND OCTOBER

COTTONWOOD ART FESTIVAL

Saturday–Sunday • Cottonwood Park, 1321 West Belt Line, one block east of Coit • 972-638-9116 • Free • W variable • www.cor.net

More than 200 artists from across the country participate in this twice-a-year show of one of the oldest juried arts festivals in North Texas. Held for close to 30 years, it has built a reputation for the high quality of arts and crafts presented. There's a variety of live music, and food is available in the appropriately titled Culinary Arts area. Hands-on children's programs include the opportunity to create art and take it home. Free parking at the park and in the high school across from the park.

SHOPPING

THE ANTIQUE COTTAGE

107 E. Main (75080), at US 75 • 972-644-1558 • W

A small antiques mall with 22 dealers who specialize in antiques, collectibles, furniture, yard art, and vintage clothing. Parking in rear.

RICHARDSON SQUARE MALL

501 Plano (75081), at Belt Line • 972-783-0117 • W+ • www.shopsimon.com

Dillard's and Sears anchor more than 80 specialty stores in this 760,000-square-foot mall including a 174,000-square-foot SuperTarget.

A SAMPLING OF RICHARDSON RESTAURANTS

Dinner for one, excluding drinks, tax, and tip: $ = up to $16, $$ = $16–$30, $$$ = $31–$50, $$$$ = over $50. It is strongly suggested that you make a reservation in those restaurants that take them, especially on weekends and holidays.

Note: Most restaurants are located in "dry" areas, so membership is required to purchase alcohol. Most memberships are inexpensive.

THE BEANERY ($–$$)

525 W. Arapaho, #1 (75080), at Custer • 972-699-3408 •
Breakfast, lunch, and dinner, Tuesday–Friday; breakfast and lunch
only, Sunday–Monday. Closed Saturday • Cr. • W

While the menu in this simple restaurant favors Tex-Mex and Southwestern dishes, it also includes a long list of chicken dishes that range from chicken pot pie and chicken fried chicken to Chicken Tequila Fettuccini. Other entrées include chicken fried steak and a Cowboy rib eye served with pinto mushroom ragout, plus all the popular Tex-Mex choices. Pies and cakes baked in their kitchen are sold by the slice or whole.

DOS RIOS TEX-MEX GRILL ($–$$)

101 S. Coit (75080), at Belt Line in Dal-Rich Village
Shopping Center • 972-235-9250 • Lunch and dinner, seven days •
Cr. • W

If it's Tex-Mex, it's probably on the menu here. The Rios Appetizer Platter, besides resembling a tasting menu, is almost a meal in itself with beef fajita nachos, chicken quesadillas, chicken flautas, stuffed jalapenos, chile con queso guacamole, and pico de gallo. The long list of Tex-Mex dinners are all varying combinations of enchiladas, tacos, and tamales, but you can also order fajitas, seafood, grilled beef, and chicken entrées, and house specials like burritos, chalupas, and chile relleno. Bar.

GRAND CAFÉ AMERICAN AND MEDITERRANEAN GRILL ($)

1887 N. Plano (75081), near Campbell • 972-231-7400 • Lunch
and dinner, seven days • MC, V • W

It's just a small, strip-mall restaurant whose name is grander than the lunch counter setup, but it does serve good food made with heartfelt care. Named after a legendary restaurant in Beirut, it offers a menu mostly Lebanese, with some burgers and Philly-style sandwiches. Among the entrée choices are lamb kabobs, marinated grilled chicken, and several combination platters. If you are a smoker, for about $7 you can try a traditional hookah (water pipe) after dinner.

INO JAPANESE BISTRO ($$–$$$)

1920 N. Coit, #250 (75080), at Campbell • 972-889-3200 •
Lunch, Monday–Friday; dinner, Monday–Saturday. Closed Sunday •
Cr. • W

Japanese dining traditions are strong here, starting with a moist washcloth presented as soon as you are seated. And the menu is filled with authentic Japanese selections. Not just the ones familiar to most Americans, like sushi and sashimi or tempura and teriyaki entrées, but also the not-so-familiar, like a *Tara-Chari* Dinner of black cod with vegetables, tofu, mushrooms, and green onions cooked in fish stock at your table. For a variety of exotic tastes, try the *Shokado Bento*, a traditional Japanese sampler dinner (about $28), or go all the way and order Chef Ino's *Omakase* seven-course dinner (about $40 each for two or more). Bar.

KEBAB-N-KURRY INDIAN RESTAURANT ($–$$)

401 N. Central Expressway #300 (75080), at Arapaho • 972-231-5556 • Lunch and dinner, seven days • Cr. • W • www.kebabnkurry.com

In spite of the restaurant's name, the menu is not all kebabs and "kurries" (their spelling). They are there, of course, in many forms, but along with a wide variety of other authentic Indian dishes. There is *Noor Mahal Biryani*, for example, an entrée of lamb and beef cooked with herbs, garnished with nuts, and served with basmati rice. Or a vegetable entrée of *kadhai paneer*, made with homemade cheese, sautéed onions, fresh tomatoes, and hot green chilies cooked in an Indian wok (*kadhai*). Popular (extensive and inexpensive) lunch buffet. BYOB.

MAXIM'S RESTAURANT ($–$$)

310 Terrace (75081), at Greenville • 972-231-6371 • Lunch and dinner, seven days • Cr. • W+

If you order from the long menu here, you can select from all the entrées you'd expect to find in any good Chinese restaurant, from chow mein to shark's fin soup and sweet and sour pork to Peking duck. But the real fun is being here at lunch when they serve Hong Kong-style *dim sum*. Dim sum might be thought of as a moveable feast. You sit at your table and select from the little baskets of bite-sized and stir-fried and hearty soup and noodle offerings brought to you by dim-sum servers making rounds with trolleys loaded with tasty treats. English is not the main language of the servers, so be prepared to point. It's point and eat, point and eat—until you and everyone in your party are satisfied.

SWAN COURT RESTAURANT AND CLUB ($$–$$$$)

2435 N. Central Expressway (75080), near Campbell • 972-235-SWAN (235-7926) • Lunch, Monday–Friday; dinner, seven days; Sunday brunch, 10:30–2 • Cr. • W (Lounge) • www.swancourt.org

This restaurant and supper club, located on the first level of the U.S. Data Building, offers a menu featuring traditional continental cuisine, in a romantic setting. Chef specialties include entrées such as Steak Diane, sautéed with onions, mushrooms, and red wine and flamed with brandy; and Veal Swan Court, sautéed in lemon juice, shallots, mushrooms, capers, and Chardonnay. Other entrées of poultry and seafood, and combination dinners such as filet mignon and stuffed prawns, or prime rib and Alaskan king crab. Live music in the club Monday–Saturday. Bar.

VEGGIE GARDEN ($–$$)

510 W. Arapaho (75080) • 972-479-0888 • Lunch and dinner • MC, V • W+ • www.veggigarden.com

This restaurant not only delights vegetarians, but also those who prefer food without preservatives or food coloring. The menu is an interesting merging of vegetarian selections with Chinese cooking. Many of the entrées read like ones in a regular Chinese restaurant, but if you look carefully you'll see that the typical "beef with broccoli," for example, is actually "*soy* beef with broccoli." And all the other chicken, pork, and seafood entrées use skillfully made soy versions, instead of the animal products, that manage to fool the taste buds. There are also a number of strictly vegetable dishes. Buffet lunch Monday–Saturday.

SPECIAL FOOD MARKET FOR DO-IT-YOURSELF

If you don't want to brave the waiting lines, call to find out if the restaurant that interests you offers takeout. Or, if you want to prepare your own meals or make a picnic basket as a change to dining out, you might want to visit the **Whole Foods Market** (60 Dal-Rich Village at Coit and Belt Line • 972-699-8075 • www.wholefoodsmarket.com). This upscale grocery carries what is probably the largest selection in the area of organically grown foods as well as seafood and meats without growth hormones or other additives. It also has a deli and take-out meals.

A SAMPLING OF RICHARDSON ACCOMMODATIONS

For a double room or suite: $ = up to $80, $$ = $81–$120, $$$ = $121–$180, $$$$ = $181–280, $$$$$ = over $280. **Room tax 13%.**

Unless otherwise noted, check-in at 3:00 p.m., check-out by noon. Unless otherwise noted, all the major accommodations have handicapped rooms/facilities and no-smoking rooms. The hearing impaired should check on visual alarms and other safety facilities when making reservations. Most accommodations permit children to stay free in room with parents. There may be a charge if this requires setting up an extra bed.

COMFORT INN ($–$$ + 13%)

220 W. Spring Valley (75081) • 972-680-8884 • www.comfortinnrichardson.com

There are 56 rooms and one suite in this two-story inn. Exterior access to rooms. Local calls free. Cable TV with free premium and pay channels.

Dataport in room. Outdoor pool and hot tub. Sauna. Self-service laundry and one-day dry cleaning. Free continental breakfast. Business services available. Free outdoor self-parking. Refrigerator in room. Some jacuzzi rooms.

COURTYARD DALLAS RICHARDSON ($$–$$$ + 13%)

1000 S. Sherman (75081) • 972-235-5000 or 800-321-2211 • www.courtyard.com/dalne

There are 149 rooms and 12 suites in this three-story Courtyard. Cable TV with free premium and pay channels. Coffeemaker in room. Dataport in room. Outdoor heated pool and indoor whirlpool. Fitness facilities. Self-service laundry and one-day dry cleaning. Restaurant (breakfast only). Lounge. Business services available. Free outdoor self-parking. Dinner delivery available from local restaurants.

HOLIDAY INN SELECT ($$ + 13%)

1655 N. Central Expressway (75080) • 972-238-1900 or 800-HOLIDAY (465-4329)(reservations) • www.hiselect.com

This six-story inn has 220 units, including five suites. Concierge section with extra amenities. Free local calls. Cable TV with free premium and pay channels. Coffeemaker in room. Dataport in room. Indoor/outdoor heated pool. Sauna. Fitness facilities. Guest membership available in health club. Concierge services available. Self-service laundry and one-day dry cleaning. Restaurant. Room service. Lounge. Conference facilities and business center. Free outdoor self-parking.

OMNI RICHARDSON HOTEL ($$$–$$$$$ + 13%)

701 E. Campbell (75081) • 972-231-9600 or 1-800-THE OMNI (843-6664)(reservations) • www.omnihotels.com

There are 342 rooms and six suites in this 17-story hotel. Concierge section with extra amenities. Cable TV with free premium and pay channels. Coffeemaker in room. Dataport in room. Bell service. Outdoor heated pool. Hot tub/fitness facilities. Concierge services available. Gift shop. One-day dry cleaning. Two restaurants (one fine dining). Room service. Lounge. Convention facilities and business center. Free airport transportation.

RADISSON HOTEL DALLAS NORTH—RICHARDSON ($$–$$$ + 13%)

1981 N. Central Expressway (75080) • 972-644-4000 or 800-285-3434 (central reservations) • www.radisson.com/richardsontx

There are 294 rooms and two suites in this 12-story atrium-style hotel. Concierge section with extra amenities. Cable TV with free premium and pay channels. Coffeemaker in room. Dataport in room. Bell service. Outdoor pool. Sauna. Guest membership available in adjacent fitness club. Gift shop. Restaurant. Room service. Lounge. Conference facilities and business services available. Free outdoor self-parking. Free transportation within 5-mile radius.

RENAISSANCE DALLAS-RICHARDSON HOTEL ($$$–$$$$$ + 13%)

900 E. Lookout (75082), in Galatyn Urban Park • 972-367-2000 • www.renaissancehotels.com

This 12-story atrium-style hotel has 336 units, including 42 suites. Concierge section with extra amenities. Small pets OK (possible fee). Cable TV with free premium and pay channels. Coffeemaker in room. Dataport in room. Bell service. Indoor heated pool. Whirlpool and sauna. Fitness facilities. Concierge services available. Gift shop. Self-service laundry and one-day dry cleaning. Fine dining restaurant and café. Room service. Lounge. Conference facilities and business center. Valet parking (fee). Free transportation within an 8-mile radius. Whirlpool suites available. Biking and walking trail. Adjacent to the Eisemann Center and short walk to DART Light Rail Galatyn Station. AAA rates it 4-Diamond.

RESIDENCE INN RICHARDSON ($$$ + 13%)

1040 Waterwood (75082) • 972-669-5888 or 800-331-3131 (reservations) • www.residenceinn.com

This three-story inn has 36 rooms and 84 suites. Pets OK (fee). Cable TV with free premium and pay channels. Coffeemaker in room. Small outdoor pool. Sports court. Self-service laundry and one-day dry cleaning. Free breakfast buffet. Free evening beverages (Monday–Wednesday). Business services available. Free outdoor self-parking. Free transportation within 5-mile radius. Kitchens fully equipped. Fireplaces in some suites. Outdoor barbecue grills. Dinner delivery available from local restaurants.

INDEX